BARRON'S

FRENCH THE EASY WAY

Second Edition

By

CHRISTOPHER KENDRIS

B.S., M.S., Columbia University
in the City of New York
M.A., Ph.D., Northwestern University
in Evanston, Illinois
Diplomé, Faculté des Lettres, Université de Paris
(en Sorbonne)
et Institut de Phonétique, Paris

Formerly Assistant Professor
Department of Romance Languages
State University of New York
Albany, New York

BARRON'S EDUCATIONAL SERIES, INC.

All inquiries should be addressed to:
Barron's Educational Series, Inc.
250 Wireless Boulevard
Hauppauge, New York 11788

Library of Congress Catalog Card No. 88-37369
International Standard Book No. 0-8120-4205-0

Library of Congress Cataloging in Publication Data
Kendris, Christopher.
French the easy way/by Christopher Kendris.—New rev. ed.
   p. cm.
ISBN 0-8120-4205-0
1. French language—Textbooks for foreign speakers—English.
2. French language—Self-instruction.   3. French language—
—Grammer—1950-   I. Title.
PC2129.E5K43   1989   88-37369
448.2'421—dc19   CIP

PRINTED IN THE UNITED STATES OF AMERICA

 456   100   13 12

Table of Contents

About the Author

Christopher Kendris has worked as interpreter and translator for the U.S. State Department at the American Embassy in Paris.

Dr. Kendris earned his B.S. and M.S. degrees at Columbia University in the City of New York, where he held a New York State scholarship, and his M.A. and Ph.D. degrees at Northwestern University in Evanston, Illinois. He also earned two diplomas with *Mention très Honorable* at the Université de Paris (en Sorbonne), Faculté des Lettres, Ecole Supérieure de Préparation et de Perfectionnement des Professeurs de Français à l'Etranger, and at the Institut de Phonétique, Paris.

He has taught French at the College of The University of Chicago as visiting summer lecturer and at Northwestern University, where he held a Teaching Assistantship and Tutorial Fellowship for four years. He has also taught at Colby College, Duke University, Rutgers — The State University of New Jersey, and the State University of New York at Albany. He was Chairman of the Foreign Languages Department at Farmingdale High School, Farmingdale, New York, where he was also a teacher of French and Spanish.

He is the author of numerous school and college books, workbooks, dictionaries, and other language aids. Among his most popular works are *201, 301,* and *501 French Verbs Fully Conjugated in All the Tenses* (with special features), *201, 301,* and *501 Spanish Verbs Fully Conjugated in All the Tenses* (with special features), *French Now!* (a Level One textbook and workbook), *How to Prepare for the College Board Achievement Test in French, How to Prepare for the College Board Achievement Test in Spanish, Beginning to Write in French, Beginning to Write in Spanish;* he also wrote the English version of Grevisse's *Le français correct (Correct French),* first U.S. edition. All these popular books have been issued by this publisher.

In 1986 he was one of ninety-five American high school teachers of foreign languages across the United States who was honored with a Rockefeller Foundation Fellowship in a competition that included about 1,000 candidates. The Fellowship gave him the opportunity to study new teaching methods and techniques at the Pedagogical Institute at the International School of French Language and Civilization at the Alliance Française in Paris. He was one of only four winners in New York State.

Dr. Christopher Kendris is listed in *Contemporary Authors* and *Directory of American Scholars.*

A Guide to Pronunciation of French Sounds

PURE VOWEL SOUNDS

Phonetic Symbol	pronounced as in the French word	English word*
a	la	at
a	pas	father
e	été	ate
ɛ	ère	egg
i	ici	see
o	hôtel	over
ɔ	donne	bun
u	ou	too
œ	leur	urgent
ø	deux	pudding
y	tu	cute
ə	le	ago

NASAL VOWEL SOUNDS

œ̃	un	sung
ɔ̃	bon	song
ɛ̃	vin	sang
ã	blanc	dong

SEMI-CONSONANT SOUNDS

w	oui	west
ɥ	huit	you eat
j	fille	yes, see ya later

CONSONANT SOUNDS

Phonetic Symbol	pronounced as in the French word	English word*
b	bonne	bun
d	dans	dong
f	fou	first, pharmacy
g	gare	go
ʒ	je	measure
ʃ	chose	shake
k	café, qui	cap, key
l	le	let
m	mette	met
n	nette	net
ɲ	montagne	canyon, onion, union
p	père	pear
R	rose	rose
s	si, garçon	see, sit
t	te	lot
v	vous	vine
z	zèbre	zebra

*English words contain sounds that only approximate French sounds.

NOTE. The French letter **c** in front of a, o, or u is pronounced as **k**; in front of e, i, or y it is pronounced as **s**. The French letter **g** in front of a, o, or u is pronounced hard as in **go**; in front of e, i, or y it is pronounced as in **je** and the English word **measure**.

Abbreviations

adj.	adjective	*fam.*	familiar	*par.*	paragraph
adv.	adverb	*i.e.*	that is, that is to say	*part.*	participle
advl.	adverbial	*illus.*	illustration	*per.*	personal
art.	article	*indef.*	indefinite	*pers.*	person
conj.	conjunction	*indic.*	indicative	*pl.*	plural
def.	definite	*indir.*	indirect	*poss.*	possessive
dem.	demonstrative	*inf.*	infinitive	*prep.*	preposition
dir.	direct	*interj.*	interjection	*pres.*	present
disj.	disjunctive	*interrog.*	interrogative	*pron.*	pronoun
e.g.	for example	*m.* or *masc.*	masculine	*refl.*	reflexive
etc.	et cetera, and so on	*n.*	noun	*rel.*	relative
exclam.	exclamation	*no.*	number	*s.* or *sing.*	singular
expr.	expression	*obj.*	object	*subj.*	subject
f. or *fem.*	feminine	*p.*	page	*v.*	verb

Introduction

This second edition of *French the Easy Way* is for you if you are beginning to study French either in school, in college, at home on your own, or with a private tutor. It is also very suitable for review if you have already studied French and would like to refresh your memory of the basics of the language. I am certain that you will find the stories, dialogues, artwork and illustrations, as well as the exercises, word games and puzzles, very interesting, original and fun to do.

This new edition has been updated and designed to encourage you to continue your study of French. I wrote it specifically for adult students who want an all-inclusive self-help program. The book is strong in a commonsense approach to the study of French. It contains all essential elements of the language.

Two new features have been added for this second edition: a review test after every five work units and oral proficiency exercises for each work unit. In addition, an appendix has been added that includes important idioms and useful expressions, as well as a review of basic vocabulary by topics.

If I have inadvertently omitted any points in French grammar, vocabulary, and idiomatic expressions you think are important, please write to me, care of the publisher of this book, so that I may include them in the next edition.

Christopher Kendris
B.S., M.S., M.A., Ph.D.

How to Use This Book

1. First, become familiar with the entire book from cover to cover. Start with the table of contents, and read it to get an idea of what is in the book. Turn the pages, and look at the pictures, stories, and exercises. Take a close look at the vocabulary in the back of the book, and browse through the Answer Key.

2. The preliminary lessons on pages one to eighteen are very important because you are introduced to certain basic elements of the French language. Use the vocabulary at the back of the book.

3. Each unit contains a story or dialogue. First, study the vocabulary at the end of each story. Take a 3 × 5 card or an envelope, and try to cover the English. Read the French words on the vocabulary list aloud. Move the card down so you can see the English meaning. Then move the card up to cover the English. Try to recall the English for the French words. Do this as often as you need to, until you can associate the French word with the English word. In your mind try to see a picture of what the word represents. Then do the opposite. Try to recall the French for the English.

4. You can also use a stack of 3 × 5 blank cards. On one side of a card write the French word, and on the other side write the English equivalent. Then test yourself. Look at the French word, and try to remember the English meaning. Then flip the card to see the English meaning. You can also look at the English word on one side of the card and try to recall the French, flipping the card as often as you need to, until you know the word in both languages. Carry around with you about 10 cards of words, and when you have a few minutes, for example, while waiting for a bus or while on a bus, study the words on both sides of the cards.

5. Do all the exercises in order from the beginning to the end of the book. Use a pencil so you can erase mistakes. Do not skip around here and there, because the language progresses. Then check your answers in the Answer Key. If you have any wrong answers, draw a line through your answer, and write it correctly. Then, after you have studied your errors, erase all your answers on a page, and do the exercises again until your answers are correct. That is how you make progress.

Remember that you will get out of this book whatever you put into it. Work steadily, and follow the suggestions above.

Bonne chance! Good luck!

NOTE: Answers to all exercises are in the Answer Key at the back of the book.

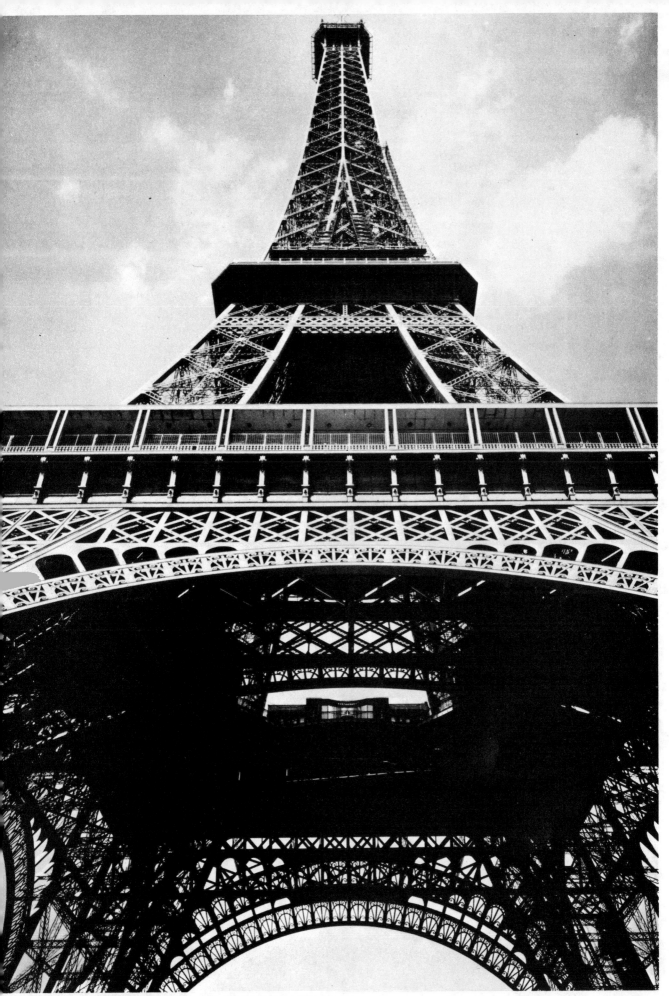

Eiffel Tower. Courtesy of Gakken Co., Ltd., Tokyo, Japan.

LEÇONS PRÉLIMINAIRES

I. La famille Paquet: Présentation

Nous sommes la famille Paquet.

Je suis Claire Paquet. Je suis la mère. J'ai un bon mari.

Je suis François Paquet. Je suis le père. J'ai une bonne épouse.

Je suis Janine. Je suis la fille. J'ai un bon frère.

Je suis Pierre. Je suis le fils. J'ai une bonne soeur.

Je suis Coco. Je suis le chien. J'ai une bonne famille.

Present Tense		Present Tense	
être *(to be)*		**avoir** *(to have)*	
je suis	I am	j'ai	I have
tu es	you are	tu as	you have
il est	he *or* it is	il a	he *or* it has
elle est	she *or* it is	elle a	she *or* it has
nous sommes	we are	nous avons	we have
vous êtes	you are	vous avez	you have
ils sont	they are	ils ont	they have
elles sont		elles ont	

1

NOTE: Look up the French words that you do not know in the Vocabulary in the back of this book.

Exercises

I. Fill in the missing French words on the blank lines. Refer to the preceding page if you have to.

1. Je suis François Paquet. Je suis ___le___ ___père___. J'ai ___une___ ___bonne___ ___épouse___.

2. Je suis Claire Paquet. Je ___suis___ la ___mère___. J'ai ___ai___ un ___bon___ mari.

3. Je suis Pierre. Je ___suis___ le fils. J'ai ___une___ bonne ___soeur___.

4. Je suis Janine. Je suis ___la fille___. J'ai un ___bon___ frère.

5. Je suis Coco. Je ___suis___ ___le___ chien. ___J'ai___ une bonne ___famille___.

II. Match the following.

1. I am the daughter

2. I am the father.

3. I am the son.

4. I am the mother.

5. I am the dog.

___3___ Je suis le fils.

___4___ Je suis la mère.

___1___ Je suis la fille.

___5___ Je suis le chien.

___2___ Je suis le père.

III. And match these.

1. the son

2. the father

3. the mother

4. the dog

5. the daughter

___3___ la mère

___5___ la fille

___2___ le père

___1___ le fils

___4___ le chien

IV.   And these.

1.   a good sister

2.   a good family

3.   a good husband

4.   a good brother

5.   a good wife

_____3_____ un bon mari

_____4_____ un bon frère

_____5_____ une bonne épouse

_____1_____ une bonne soeur

_____2_____ une bonne famille

V.   Qui est-ce? (Who is it?) On the blank line write in French the name of the person described. **C'est . . .** (It's . . .)

1.   Je suis la fille. J'ai un bon frère.
Qui est-ce? C'est _____Janine_____.

2.   Je suis la mère. J'ai un bon mari.
Qui est-ce? C'est _____Claire_____.

3.   Je suis le père. J'ai une bonne épouse.
Qui est-ce? C'est _____François_____.

4.   Je suis le chien. J'ai une bonne famille.
Qui est-ce? C'est _____Coco_____.

5.   Je suis le fils. J'ai une bonne soeur.
Qui est-ce? C'est _____Pierre_____.

VI.   Choose the correct answer and write the letter on the blank line.

1.   Janine est   (a) la mère.   (b) le père.   (c) la fille.   (d) le fils.   _____C_____

2.   Pierre est   (a) le père.   (b) la mère.   (c) la soeur.   (d) le frère.   _____D_____

3.   Claire Paquet est   (a) le père.   (b) la mère.   (c) la fille.   (d) le fils.   _____C_____

4.   Coco est   (a) le fils.   (b) la fille.   (c) la soeur.   (d) le chien.   _____D_____

5.   François Paquet est   (a) le frère.   (b) le fils.   (c) le père.
(d) la mère.   _____C_____

II. Choses (Things)   [Mon premier petit dictionnaire en images.]

The pictures are arranged alphabetically by word.

	L'arbre	Est-ce un arbre?	Oui, c'est un arbre. Il est grand.
	Le ballon	Est-ce un ballon?	Oui, c'est un ballon. Il est rond.
	La banane	Est-ce une orange? Est-ce une banane?	Non, ce n'est pas une orange. Oui, c'est une banane. Elle est bonne.
	La chaise	Est-ce une table? Est-ce une chaise?	Non, ce n'est pas une table. Oui, c'est une chaise. Elle est petite.

Exercises

I. Fill in the missing words (adjectives) in French. Refer to the statements above.

1. L'arbre est ___grand___ .   3. La banane est ___bonne___ .

2. Le ballon est ___rond___ .   4. La chaise est ___petite___ .

II. Choose the correct adjective. Refer to the statements above.

1. La chaise est   (a) petite.   (b) ronde.   (c) grande.   (d) bonne.   ___A___

2. La banane est   (a) ronde.   (b) grande.   (c) petite.   (d) bonne.   ___D___

3. Le ballon est   (a) rond.   (b) grand.   (c) bon.   (d) petit.   ___A___

4. L'arbre est   (a) grand.   (b) petit.   (c) rond.   (d) bon.   ___A___

III. Match the following.

1. the chair   ___4___ la banane

2. the ball   ___3___ l'arbre

3. the tree   ___1___ la chaise

4. the banana   ___2___ le ballon

4

	Le chapeau	Est-ce un chapeau?	Oui, c'est un chapeau. Il est joli. *pretty*
	La commode	Est-ce une chaise? Est-ce une commode?	Non, ce n'est pas une chaise. Oui, c'est une commode. Elle est belle. *beautiful*
	Le crayon	Est-ce un stylo? Est-ce un crayon?	Non, ce n'est pas un stylo. Oui, c'est un crayon. Il est long.
	La fleur	Est-ce une fleur?	Oui, c'est une fleur. Elle est jolie.

Exercises

I. Fill in the missing words (adjectives) in French. Refer to the statements above.

1. Le chapeau est _joli_.
2. La commode est _belle_.

3. Le crayon est _long_.
4. La fleur est _jolie_.

II. Match the following. Refer to the statements above.

1. the pencil
2. the hat
3. the flower
4. the dresser

_3_ la fleur
_1_ le crayon
_4_ la commode
_2_ le chapeau

III. Choose the correct adjective. Refer to the statements above.

1. Le chapeau est   (a) joli.   (b) long.   (c) bon.   (d) petit.   _A_
2. La commode est   (a) belle.   (b) ronde.   (c) longue.   (d) bonne.   _A_
3. Le crayon est   (a) joli.   (b) rond.   (c) bon.   (d) long.   _D_
4. La fleur est   (a) jolie.   (b) ronde.   (c) grande.   (d) longue.   _A_

	Le garage	Est-ce un garage?	Oui, c'est un garage. Il est grand.
	Le gâteau	Est-ce un chapeau?	Non, ce n'est pas un chapeau.
		Est-ce un gâteau?	Oui, c'est un gâteau. Il est délicieux.
	Le jambon	Est-ce un jambon?	Oui, c'est un jambon. Il est beau.
			beautiful
	Le journal	Est-ce un journal?	Oui, c'est un journal. Il est intéressant.

Exercises

I. Fill in the missing words (adjectives) in French. Refer to the statements above.

1. Le garage est ___*grand*___ .   3. Le jambon est ___*beau*___ .

2. Le gâteau est ___*délicieux*___ .   4. Le journal est ___*intéressant*___ .

II. Choose the correct adjective. Refer to the statements above.

1. Le garage est   (a) intéressant.   (b) délicieux.   (c) grand.   ___*C*___

2. Le gâteau est   (a) long.   (b) intéressant.   (c) délicieux.   ___*C*___

3. Le jambon est   (a) beau.   (b) grand.   (c) intéressant.   ___*A*___

4. Le journal est   (a) rond.   (b) intéressant.   (c) beau.   ___*B*___

III. Fill in the missing words in French. Refer to the statements next to the pictures.

1. Est-ce un garage? Oui, ___*c'est*___ ___*un*___ ___*garage*___ . Il ___*est*___ grand.

2. Est-ce un chapeau? Non, ce ___*n'est*___ ___*pas*___ un chapeau. C'est ___*un*___ gâteau.

3. Est-ce un jambon? Oui, ___*c'est*___ un jambon. Il est ___*beau*___ .

4. Est-ce un journal? Oui, ___*c'est*___ un journal. Il ___*est*___ intéressant.

	Une lampe	Est-ce une lampe?	Oui, c'est une lampe. Elle est splendide.
	Un lit	Est-ce une commode?	Non, ce n'est pas une commode.
		Est-ce un lit?	Oui, c'est un lit. Il est confortable.
	Une maison	Est-ce un garage?	Non, ce n'est pas un garage.
		Est-ce une maison?	Oui, c'est une maison. Elle est charmante.
	Un oeuf	Est-ce un ballon?	Non, ce n'est pas un ballon.
		Est-ce un oeuf?	Oui, c'est un oeuf. Il est blanc.

Exercises

I. Choose the correct adjective. Refer to the statements next to the pictures above.

1. Le lit est   (a) blanc.   (b) délicieux.   (c) intéressant.
   (d) confortable.   *D*

2. La lampe est   (a) confortable.   (b) splendide.   (c) bonne.
   (d) longue.   *B*

3. La maison est   (a) délicieuse.   (b) bonne.   (c) charmante.
   (d) ronde.   *C*

4. L'oeuf est   (a) blanc.   (b) charmant.   (c) confortable.   (d) beau.   *A*

II. Match the following.

1.	a house	*4*	un oeuf
2.	a lamp	*3*	un lit
3.	a bed	*1*	une maison
4.	an egg	*2*	une lampe

7

Un parapluie   Est-ce un parapluie?   Oui, c'est un parapluie. Il est ouvert.

open

Une pomme   Est-ce une banane?   Non, ce n'est pas une banane.

Est-ce une pomme?   Oui, c'est une pomme. Elle est magnifique.

Une robe   Est-ce un chapeau?   Non, ce n'est pas un chapeau.

Est-ce une robe?   Oui, c'est une robe. Elle est mignonne.

cute

Un sandwich   Est-ce un gâteau?   Non, ce n'est pas un gâteau.

Est-ce un sandwich?   Oui, c'est un sandwich. Il est délicieux.

Exercises

I. Fill in the missing words (adjectives) in French. Refer to the sentences next to the pictures.

1. Le parapluie est _ouvert_.

2. La pomme est _magnifique_.

3. La robe est _mignonne_.

4. Le sandwich est _délicieux_.

II. Fill in the missing words in French. Refer to the sentences next to the pictures.

1. Est-ce un parapluie? Oui, c'est _un_ _parapluie_. Il _est_ ouvert.

2. Est-ce une banane? Non, ce _n'est_ _pas_ une banane. C' _est_ une pomme.

3. Est-ce un chapeau? Non, _ce_ _n'est_ _pas_ un chapeau. C'est _une_ robe.

4. Est-ce un sandwich? Oui, c'est _un_ sandwich. Il est _délicieux_.

Un stylo Est-ce un crayon? Non, ce n'est pas un crayon.
Est-ce un stylo? Oui, c'est un stylo. Il est long.

Un téléphone Est-ce une radio? Non, ce n'est pas une radio.
Est-ce un téléphone? Oui, c'est un téléphone. Il est noir.

Un téléviseur Est-ce un téléviseur? Oui, c'est un téléviseur. Il est beau.

Exercises

I. Choose the correct adjective. Refer to the sentences next to the pictures.

1. Le stylo est (a) blanc. (b) délicieux. (c) ouvert. (d) long. _D_

2. Le téléphone est (a) confortable. (b) joli. (c) rond. (d) noir. _D_

3. Le téléviseur est (a) délicieux. (b) beau. (c) charmant.
(d) confortable. _B_

II. Match the following.

1. a television set

2. a chair

3. a flower

4. a pen

5. a telephone

6. an egg

_4_ un stylo

_5_ un téléphone

_1_ un téléviseur

_6_ un oeuf

_2_ une chaise

_3_ une fleur

III. Personnes (People)

Que fait-il?	Que fait-elle?	Que font-ils?
(What is he doing?)	(What is she doing?)	(What are they doing?)

Le garçon boit du lait.   Que fait-il?   Il boit du lait.

boy   milk

La jeune fille danse.   Que fait-elle?   Elle danse.

Le garçon lit un livre.   Que fait-il?   Il lit un livre.

La jeune fille et le garçon courent.   Que font-ils?   Ils courent.

Exercises

I. Fill in the missing words in French. Refer to the sentences next to the pictures above.

1. Le garçon boit du lait. Que fait-il? Il ___boit___ du ___lait___.

2. La jeune fille danse. Que fait-elle? Elle ___danse___.

3. Le garçon lit un livre. Que fait-il? Il lit ___un___ ___livre___.

4. La jeune fille et le garçon courent. Que font-ils? Ils ___courent___.

II. The following sentences are scrambled. Write them in the correct word order. Refer to the sentences next to the pictures above.

10   1. Le / lait / du / garçon / boit / ___Le garçon boit du lait___.

2. La / danse / jeune / fille / _La jeune fille danse._ .

3. Le / livre / un / garçon / lit / _Le garçon lit un livre._ .

4. La / fille / jeune / et / garçon / le / courent / _La jeune fille et le garçon courent._ .

La jeune femme chante. ~Sing~
C'est une chanteuse.   Que fait-elle?   Elle chante.
~Singer~

La femme écrit une lettre.   Que fait-elle?   Elle écrit une lettre.

L'agent de police arrête les autos.   Que fait-il?   Il arrête les autos.

I. Fill in the missing words in French. Refer to the sentences next to the pictures above.

1. La jeune femme chante. Que fait-elle? Elle _chante_ .

2. La femme écrit une lettre. Que fait-elle? Elle _écrit_ une lettre.

3. L'agent de police arrête les autos. Que fait-il? Il _arrête_ les _autos_ .

II. Choose the correct answer. Refer to the sentences next to the pictures above.

1. La jeune femme   (a) arrête les autos.   (b) chante.   (c) écrit une lettre.   _B_

2. La femme   (a) écrit une lettre.   (b) arrête les autos.   (c) danse.   _A_

3. L'agent de police   (a) boit du lait.   (b) lit un livre.   (c) arrête les autos.   _C_

11

IV. L'École: la salle de classe (The School: the classroom)

le tableau

l'horloge

le globe

la carte de France

la feuille de papier

le stylo

un élève

une élève

le livre
le crayon

le pupitre

le bureau

la chaise

la maîtresse de français

Bonjour, mes amis!

Exercises

I. Choose the sentence in Column A that corresponds to the picture and write it on the line next to the number of the picture in Column B. If you have to, look up the French words in the vocabulary at the end of the book.

Column A

Le garçon est debout.   *standing*

Le garçon lit un livre.

Il y a une carte de France sur le mur.   *wall*

Madame Duval est derrière le bureau.

La jeune fille lève la main.   *raise hand*

La jeune fille écrit une composition.

Il est une heure.   *hour*

Column B

1. Madame Duval est derrière le bureau.

2. Il est une heure.

3. Il y a carte de France sur le mur.

4. Le garçon lit un livre.

5. La jeune fille écrit une composition.

6. Le garçon est debout

7. La jeune fille leve la main

II. Answer each question following the example in the box.

Non, madame (mademoiselle, monsieur), ce n'est pas la table. C'est le bureau.

Est-ce la table?

1. Est-ce le stylo?   2. Est-ce la feuille de papier?   3. Est-ce le globe?

1. _Oui, c'est le stylo._
2. _Non, ce n'est pas la feuille de papier. C'est le livre._
3. _Non, ce n'est pas le globe. C'est l'horloge._

un banc

4. Est-ce un élève?   5. Est-ce la chaise?   6. Est-ce une élève?

4. _Non, ce n'est pas une élève. C'est la maîtresse._
5. _Non, ce n'est pas la chaise. C'est un banc._
6. _Oui, c'est une élève._

V. La Maison: la salle à manger
(The House: the dining room)

Exercises

I. Answer each question following the example in the box.

C'est une table.

C'est un vase.

Qu'est-ce que c'est?

Qu'est-ce que c'est?

1. Qu'est-ce que c'est?

assiette plate

2. Qu'est-ce que c'est?

tasse cup

3. Qu'est-ce que c'est?

cuiller

4. Qu'est-ce que c'est?

verre

5. Qu'est-ce que c'est?

couteau

6. Qu'est-ce que c'est?

1. *C'est un fleur.*
2. *C'est une assiette.*
3. *C'est une tasse.*
4. *C'est une cuiller.*
5. *C'est un verre.*
6. *C'est un couteau.*

II. Fill in the missing letters of these French words.

1. UNE CHA_I_SE
2. UNE AS_S_IET_T_E
3. UN TAPI_S_
4. UNE FO_U_RCHET_T_E
5. UN COUT_T_EAU

6. UNE NAP_P_E
7. UN VER_R_E
8. UN_E_ TAS_S_E
9. UNE CU_I_LLER
10. UN_E_ FL_E_U_R_

15

VI. La Ville: dans la rue (The City: in the street)

Exercises

I. Answer each question following the example in the box.

C'est une dame.

C'est un homme.

Qui est-ce?

Qui est-ce?

1. Qui est-ce?   2. Qui est-ce?   3. Qui est-ce?   4. Qui est-ce?   5. Qui est-ce?

1. _C'est une dame._
2. _C'est un homme._
3. _C'est une petite Fille._
4. _C'est un petit garçon._
5. _C'est un agent de police._

6. Qu'est-ce que c'est?   7. Qu'est-ce que c'est?   8. Qu'est-ce que c'est?

6. _C'est une voiture._
7. _C'est un immeuble._
8. _C'est un autobus._

II. Fill in the missing letters of these French words.

1. UNE VALISE
2. UN PETIT CHIEN

3. LE TROTTOIR
4. LE MÉTRO

VII. Summary of two very common irregular verbs: **avoir** and **être** in the present tense, affirmative and negative.

avoir (to have)

affirmative		negative	
j'ai	I have	je n'ai pas	I don't have
tu as	you have *(familiar)*	tu n'as pas	you don't have
il a	he *or* it has	il n'a pas	he *or* it doesn't have
elle a	she *or* it has	elle n'a pas	she *or* it doesn't have
nous avons	we have	nous n'avons pas	we don't have
vous avez	you have	vous n'avez pas	you don't have
ils ont }	they have	ils n'ont pas }	they don't have
elles ont }		elles n'ont pas }	

être (to be)

affirmative		negative	
je suis	I am	je ne suis pas	I am not
tu es	you are *(familiar)*	tu n'es pas	you are not
il est	he *or* it is	il n'est pas	he *or* it isn't
elle est	she *or* it is	elle n'est pas	she *or* it isn't
nous sommes	we are	nous ne sommes pas	we are not
vous êtes	you are	vous n'êtes pas	you are not
ils sont }	they are	ils ne sont pas }	they are not
elles sont }		elles ne sont pas }	

STRUCTURES AND VERBS

Concorde Takes Off. The world's first supersonic passenger aircraft cuts the flying time between New York and Paris to 3-1/2 hours. Reprinted with permission of Air France.

Madame Paquet cherche dans l'armoire, Janine cherche dans la commode, et Pierre cherche sous le lit.

The Noun and the Definite and Indefinite Articles (Singular)

*Have you ever looked high and low
for something you lost?*

Le chapeau échappé

Monsieur Paquet cherche son chapeau. Madame Paquet cherche le chapeau dans l'armoire, Janine cherche dans la commode, et Pierre cherche sous le lit. Le chien est sous la commode.

Monsieur Paquet:	Où est mon chapeau?
Janine:	Je cherche dans la commode, papa.
Pierre:	Nous cherchons partout, papa. Je cherche sous le lit maintenant.
Madame Paquet:	Je cherche aussi, François. Je cherche dans l'armoire. Oh! Je suis fatiguée de chercher le chapeau!
Monsieur Paquet:	Je cherche sous la chaise maintenant. Cherchons dans la cuisine, dans le salon, dans la salle de bains, dans la cave, sous le lit,. sous la commode, dans l'armoire, dans le garage. Partout dans la maison!
Janine:	Tiens! Papa! Coco mange le chapeau. Il est sous la commode!
Monsieur Paquet:	Ah, non! Quelle horreur!
	(Monsieur Paquet quitte la chambre vite.)
Madame Paquet:	Où vas-tu, François?
Monsieur Paquet:	Je vais en ville acheter un nouveau chapeau. Zut, alors!
Madame Paquet:	Attends, attends! Je vais avec toi. J'aimerais acheter une nouvelle robe.

Vocabulaire

acheter v., to buy
aimer v., to like, to love
l'armoire n. f., the closet
aussi adv., also, too
avec prep., with
la cave n., the cellar
la chaise n., the chair
la chambre n., the room
le chapeau n., the hat
chercher v., to look for, to search for
le chien m., **la chienne** f., n., the dog
la commode n., the dresser, the chest of drawers

la cuisine n., the kitchen
dans prep., in
de prep., of
échappé m., **échappée** f., adj., escaped
elle pron., she, it
en prep., in, into
et conj., and
être v., to be
la famille n., the family
fatigué m., **fatiguée** f., adj., tired
la fille n., the daughter

le fils n., the son
le garage n., the garage
l'horreur n. f., the horror
il pron., he, it
je pron., I
le m., **la** f., def. art., the
le lit n., the bed
madame n., Mrs., madam
maintenant adv., now
la maison n., the house
manger v., to eat
la mère n., the mother
mon m., **ma** f., poss. adj., my
monsieur n., Mr., sir

21

nous *pron.*, we, us
nouveau *m.*, **nouvelle** *f.*, *adj.*, new
où *adv.*, where
partout *adv.*, everywhere
le père *n.*, the father
petit *m.*, **petite** *f.*, *adj.*, small
quel *m.*, **quelle** *f.*, *adj.*, what
qui *pron.*, who
quitter *v.*, to leave
la robe *n.*, the dress
la salle de bains *n.*, the bathroom
le salon *n.*, the living room
son *m.*, **sa** *f.*, *poss. adj.*, his, her
sous *prep.*, under

tiens! *exclam.*, look!
toi *pron.*, you
un *m.*, **une** *f.*, *indef. art.*, a, an
la ville *n.*, the town, the city
vite *adv.*, quickly
le vocabulaire *n.*, the vocabulary
zut alors! *exclam.*, gosh darn it!

Verb forms used in this dialogue:

j'aimerais, I'd like, I'd love
attends, wait
je cherche, I look (for), I am looking (for)

il cherche, elle cherche, he is looking (for), she is looking (for)
qui cherche, who is looking (for)
nous cherchons, we are looking (for)
cherchons, let's look (for)
est, is
il est, he is, it is
il mange, he eats, he is eating
il quitte, he leaves, he is leaving
je suis, I am
je vais, I am going
vas-tu?, are you going?

Exercises

Review the dialogue and vocabulary before starting these exercises.

I. Choose the correct answer based on the dialogue in this unit.

1. Monsieur Paquet cherche (a) dans la commode. (b) sous le lit. (c) le chapeau. (d) dans l'armoire. ___C___

2. Janine cherche (a) sous le lit. (b) dans le salon. (c) sous la commode. (d) dans la commode. ___D___

3. Pierre cherche (a) sous la chaise (b) dans le garage. (c) dans la salle de bains. (d) sous le lit. ___D___

4. Le chapeau est (a) dans la commode. (b) sous la commode (c) sous le lit. (d) dans la cuisine. ___B___

5. Coco mange le chapeau sous (a) le lit. (b) la chaise. (c) l'armoire. (d) la commode. ___D___

II. Answer the following questions in French in complete sentences.

Model: Qui cherche sous le lit? (Who is searching under the bed?) **Answer: Pierre cherche sous le lit.** (Pierre is searching under the bed.)

1. Qui cherche dans la commode? _Janine cherche dans la commode._

2. Qui cherche dans l'armoire? _Claire cherche dans l'armoire_

3. Qui cherche sous la chaise? _François cherche sous la chaise._

22

III. Answer the following questions in French in complete sentences.

Model: Qui est Monsieur Paquet?   **Answer: Monsieur Paquet est le père.**
(Who is Mr. Paquet?)   (Mr. Paquet is the father.)

1. Qui est Madame Paquet? ___*P est la mère*___

2. Qui est Janine? ___*J est le Fille.*___

3. Qui est Pierre? ___*P est le Fils*___

4. Qui est Coco? ___*C est la chien*___

IV. Un acrostiche (an acrostic). Complete the French words in the squares across.

1. definite article, feminine singular   1. L | E

2. and   2. E | T

3. to search, to look for   3. C | H | E | R | C | H | E | R

4. horror   4. H | a | R | R | E | U | R

5. closet   5. A | R | M | a | I | R | E

6. father   6. P | E | R | E

7. she   7. E | L | L | E

8. to love, to like   8. A | I | M | E | R

9. indefinite article, masculine singular   9. U | N

Structures de la Langue

A. The definite articles

MASCULINE NOUNS			
le père	the father	**l'homme**	the man
le garcon	the boy	**l'ami**	the friend (boy)
le frère	the brother	**le fils**	the son

23

FEMININE NOUNS			
la mère	the mother	**la femme**	the woman, wife
la jeune fille	the girl	**l'amie**	the friend (girl)
la soeur	the sister	**la fille**	the daughter

Rules and observations:

1. Nouns are classified by gender, which means that they are either masculine or feminine. A noun is a word that refers to a person, thing, place, or quality; *e.g.*, **la mère, la chaise, le salon, la beauté** (beauty).

2. Nouns denoting persons of the male sex are naturally of the masculine gender.

3. Nouns denoting persons of the female sex are naturally of the feminine gender.

4. Animals that are male or female are naturally of the masculine or feminine gender; *e.g.*, **le chat, la chatte** (the cat).

5. Things are also either masculine or feminine, but there is no easy way to determine their gender. You must learn the gender of a noun when you learn the noun by putting **le** or **la** in front of it! **Le** is masculine, **la** is feminine.

6. Some nouns, whether masculine or feminine, take **l'** in front, if they begin with a vowel or a silent **h**. The **e** in **le** drops and the **a** in **la** drops. You're left with **l'**.

7. Some nouns are sometimes masculine, sometimes feminine, in which case the meaning changes; *e.g.*, **le livre** (the book), **la livre** (the pound).

8. To sum it up, French has three forms for the definite article in the singular: **le, la, l'** — they all mean **the**.

A FEW MORE COMMON MASCULINE NOUNS		
l'arbre the tree	**l'enfant** the child (boy)	
le beurre the butter	**le fils** the son	
le café the coffee, the café	**le garage** the garage	
le chapeau the hat	**le mari** the husband	
le chef the chief, the chef	**le nom** the name	

A FEW MORE COMMON FEMININE NOUNS	
la bouche the mouth	**l'heure** the hour
la campagne the countryside	**la maison** the house
la chaise the chair	**la montre** the watch
l'enfant the child (girl)	**la porte** the door
la famille the family	**la table** the table

Exercises

Review the preceding material before starting these exercises.

I. Use the appropriate definite article in the singular: le, la or l'.

1. _le_ garçon
2. _la_ mère
3. _le_ père
4. _la_ jeune fille
5. _l'_ ami

6. _le_ homme
7. _le_ café
8. _le_ chapeau
9. _l'_ enfant
10. _la_ commode

11. _le_ nom
12. _l'_ arbre
13. _le_ lit
14. _la_ porte
15. _l'_ amie

II. Word Hunt.   Can you find these 10 words in French in this puzzle?

1. the woman
2. the man
3. the boy
4. the girl
5. the sister
6. the tree
7. the child
8. the brother
9. the book
10. the mother

L	A	M	L	E	L	I	V	R	E	P	L
O	L	E	G	A	R	C	O	N	F	G	A
J	H	I	L	A	M	È	R	E	A	E	S
A	U	O	I	L	H	O	M	M	E	E	O
L	A	J	E	U	N	E	F	I	L	L	E
E	B	L	E	F	R	È	R	E	A	E	U
L	E	J	O	U	R	L	A	I	R	Ò	R
A	L	A	F	E	M	M	E	M	B	O	Y
L	E	L	E	N	F	A	N	T	R	U	E
Z	Y	L	E	L	A	M	O	I	E	N	A

25

III. Substitute the word in parentheses for the noun in italics. Use the appropriate definite article.
Then rewrite the sentence.

Model:	**Le livre est là-bas.**	**(femme)**	**La femme est là-bas.**
	(The book is over there.)		(The woman is over there.)

A. La *maison* est là-bas.   (The house is over there.)

1. (père) _____

2. (mère) _____

3. (garçon) _____

4. (jeune fille) _____

5. (ami) _____

Le chef parle beaucoup.

B. Le *chef* parle beaucoup.   (The boss talks a great deal.)

1. (femme) _____

2. (homme) _____

3. (frère) _____

4. (soeur) _____

5. (famille) _____

C.   La *porte* est ici.   (The door is here.)

1.   (table) _____

2.   (chapeau) _____

3.   (maison) _____

4.   (arbre) _____

5.   (café) _____

IV.   Write the answers to the question in complete French sentences. Use the noun in parentheses with the appropriate definite article: **le, la, l'**.

Question: **Où est le chapeau?**   **Model answer:**   **(salon)   Le chapeau est**
                 (Where is the hat?)   **dans le salon.**   (The hat
                                                                     is in the living room.)

1.   (cuisine) _____

2.   (armoire) _____

3.   (maison) _____

4.   (commode) _____

5.   (garage) _____

B.   The indefinite articles

MASCULINE NOUNS		FEMININE NOUNS	
un père	a father	**une mère**	a mother
un garçon	a boy	**une jeune fille**	a girl
un frère	a brother	**une soeur**	a sister
un homme	a man	**une femme**	a woman
un ami	a friend (boy)	**une amie**	a friend (girl)
un parapluie	an umbrella	**une orange**	an orange

27

Rules and observations:

1. The indefinite article has two forms: **un** and **une**. The first is masculine and the second is feminine. Each means **a** or **an**; *e.g.,* **un père**, **une mère**.

2. **Un** is used with a masculine noun whether it begins with a consonant, a vowel, or a silent **h**; *e.g.,* **un garçon, un ami, un homme**.

3. **Une** is used with a feminine noun whether it begins with a consonant, a vowel, or a silent **h**; *e.g.,* **une femme, une orange, une horreur**.

Exercises

Review the preceding material before starting these exercises.

I. Use the appropriate indefinite article in the singular: **un** or **une**.

1.	_____ garçon	6.	_____ homme	11.	_____ arbre
2.	_____ mère	7.	_____ café	12.	_____ orange
3.	_____ père	8.	_____ chat	13.	_____ porte
4.	_____ ami	9.	_____ chatte	14.	_____ famille
5.	_____ amie	10.	_____ nom	15.	_____ parapluie

II. Word Hunt.   Can you find these 5 words in French in this puzzle?

1. a tree

2. an orange

3. a boy

4. an umbrella

5. a girl

U	N	E	J	E	U	N	E	F	I	L	L	E	A
N	E	F	I	L	M	O	A	U	V	O	U	S	S
A	R	B	E	A	U	N	G	A	R	Ç	O	N	S
R	O	U	G	E	P	L	U	S	E	R	S	T	U
B	L	U	N	P	A	R	A	P	L	U	I	E	R
R	J	O	I	N	D	R	E	E	T	R	E	S	E
E	U	N	E	O	R	A	N	G	E	U	N	A	N

III. Substitute the word in parentheses for the noun in italics. Use the appropriate indefinite article. Then rewrite the sentence.

> **Model:** Une *femme* cherche dans l'armoire.
> (A woman is searching in the closet.)

Une femme cherche dans l'armoire.

A. Une *femme* cherche dans l'armoire. (A *woman* is searching in the closet.)

1. (homme) _____

2. (garçon) _____

3. (fils) _____

4. (mère) _____

5. (père) _____

B. Un *homme* mange dans la cuisine. (A *man* is eating in the kitchen.)

1. (femme) _____

2. (jeune fille) _____

3. (ami) _____

4. (chien) _____

5. (fille) _____

C. Une *femme* quitte la chambre.   (A *woman* is leaving the room.)

1. (homme) _____

2. (mère) _____

3. (père) _____

4. (garçon) _____

5. (jeune fille) _____

IV. Comment dit-on en français . . . ? (How do you say in French . . . ?)

Find the following statements in the dialogue at the beginning of this work unit and write them in French.

1. Mr. Paquet is looking for his hat. _____

2. The dog is under the dresser. _____

3. We are searching everywhere. _____

4. I'm going downtown to buy a new hat. _____

5. Coco is eating the hat. _____

V. Fill in the blanks with an appropriate singular definite or indefinite article.

Coco, _____ chien, est sous _____ commode. Madame Paquet, _____ mère, cherche
      1   2   3

dans _____ armoire. Janine cherche dans _____ commode, et Pierre cherche sous
         4   5

_____ lit. Madame Paquet est fatiguée de chercher _____ chapeau. Monsieur Paquet,
6   7

_____ père, va en ville acheter _____ nouveau chapeau et Madame Paquet va acheter
8   9

_____ nouvelle robe.
10

VI. Oral Proficiency. Respond orally in French to the situation described. (Later, you may write your responses for intensive practice.)

Situation: You have lost something. Your brother or sister asks you what you're looking for: *Qu'est-ce que tu cherches?* In three or four sentences, explain what you are looking for and where you are looking for it. You may use your own ideas or ideas suggested by the following: *chercher, mon livre, mon stylo, mon chapeau, sous la chaise, sous le lit, sur la table, partout.*

Centre Pompidou
Reprinted with permission of French Government Tourist Office, New York

Quel déjeuner!

The Noun and the Definite and Indefinite Articles (Plural)

*In this scene, Claire and François Paquet
are with their friends from Martinique,
Joséphine and Alphonse Banluc, who are
living in Paris. They are all with their
children at the Bois de Boulogne, a park
near Paris, to celebrate Bastille Day on
the 14th of July.*

Vive le quatorze juillet!

Claire Paquet:	Venez, tout le monde. Venez! Nous pouvons déjeuner sur l'herbe maintenant. Nous allons commencer avec les viandes. Janine, as-tu les sandwichs?
Janine:	Les sandwichs? Quels sandwichs? Je n'ai pas les sandwichs. J'ai seulement les gâteaux et les petits fours glacés. C'est pour le dessert.
Claire Paquet:	Tu n'as pas les sandwichs? Bon, bon. Pierre, tu as apporté les sandwichs, j'espère.
Pierre:	Mais non! J'ai seulement les éclairs.
Claire Paquet:	François, tu as sûrement apporté les viandes: le rosbif, le veau, le porc, le jambon, et le poulet.
François Paquet:	Mais non, ma chérie. J'ai apporté la glace.
Claire Paquet:	Joséphine, tu as sûrement apporté les viandes, j'espère.
Joséphine Banluc:	Mais non. J'ai apporté un gâteau!
Claire Paquet:	Alphonse, tu as les saucisses et les saucissons, j'espère.
Alphonse Banluc:	Mais non, Claire. J'ai apporté un grand gâteau et les petits fours glacés! C'est pour le dessert. J'ai apporté aussi une bouteille d'eau minérale pour la santé.
Claire Paquet:	Quel déjeuner!
Tous les enfants:	C'est merveilleux! Nous aimons mieux les desserts!
Claire Paquet:	Eh, bien! C' la Fêra te Nationale et, dans l'esprit de ce grand hour de fête, moi, je dis: mangeons les gâteaux!

Vocabulaire

l'an *n. m.*, the year
apporter *v.*, to bring
bien *adv.*, well
le bois *n.*, the woods
bon *m.*, **bonne** *f.*, *adj.*, good
la bouteille *n.*, the bottle
ce *dem. adj.*, this
chéri *m.*, **chérie** *f.*, *adj.*, darling
commencer *v.*, to begin
déjeuner *v.*, to have lunch
le déjeuner *n.*, the lunch
le dessert *n.*, the dessert
dire *v.*, to say
l'eau *n. f.*, the water; **l'eau minérale** *n.*, mineral water
l'éclair *n. m.*, the eclair
eh bien! *exclam.*, oh, well!
espérer *v.*, to hope
l'esprit *n. m.*, the spirit
la femme *n.*, the wife
la fête *n.*, the holiday
le gâteau *n.*, the cake
la glace *n.*, the ice cream
glacé *m.*, **glacée** *f.*, *adj.*, glazed, frosted
l'herbe *n. f.*, the grass
le jambon *n.*, the ham
le jour *n.*, the day
juillet *n. m.*, July
les *def. art., pl.*, the
mais non! *exclam.*, why no!
le mari *n.*, the husband
merveilleux *m.*, **merveilleuse** *f.*, *adj.*, marvelous, wonderful

mieux *adv.*, better
moi *pron.*, me
non *adv.*, no
ou *conj.*, or
oui *adv.*, yes
le parc *n.*, the park
la pâtisserie *n.*, the pastry
le petit four *n.*, the little cake
le porc *n.*, the pork
le poulet *n.*, the chicken
pour *prep.*, for
pouvoir *v.*, to be able
près (de) *adv.*, near (to)
quatorze *adj.*, fourteen
le quatorze juillet *n.*, the fourteenth of July, also known as Bastille Day, a French national holiday
quel *m.*, **quelle** *f.*, *adj.*, what; **quel déjeuner!** what a lunch!
le rosbif *n.*, the roast beef
le sandwich *n.*, the sandwich
la santé *n.*, health
la saucisse *n.*, the sausage
le saucisson *n.*, bologna
seulement *adv.*, only
sur *prep.*, on
sûrement *adv.*, surely
tous *m.*, **toutes** *f.*, *adj. pl.*, all, every
tous les enfants, all the children
tout *m.*, **toute** *f.*, *adj. sing.*, all, every

tout le monde, everybody
tu *per. pron.*, you
le veau *n.*, the veal
venir *v.*, to come
la viande *n.*, the meat
vivre *v.*, to live

Verb forms used in this dialogue:

j'ai, I have
je n'ai pas, I do not have
tu as, you have
tu n'as pas, you do not have
as-tu? have you?
nous aimons, we like, we love
nous allons, we are going
j'ai apporté, I brought
tu as apporté, you brought
il a apporté, elle a apporté, he brought, she brought
je dis, I say
j'espère, I hope
c'est, it is
mangeons! let us eat!
nous pouvons, we can, we are able
il va, elle va, he goes, she goes (is going)
venez! come!
ils viennent (de), they come (from)
vive —! long live —!

Exercises

Review the dialogue and vocabulary before starting these exercises.

I. Choose the correct answer based on the dialogue in this unit.

1. Le déjeuner dans le parc est sur   (a) les gâteaux: (b) le dessert.
   (c) les petits fours glacés.   (d) l'herbe.   _____

2. Joséphine et Alphonse Banluc viennent   (a) du Bois de Boulogne.
   (b) de la Bastille.   (c) de la Martinique.   (d) du parc.   _____

3. Le rosbif et le porc sont des   (a) viandes.   (b) gâteaux.   (c) desserts.
   (d) sandwichs.   _____

4. Tout le monde a apporté   (a) de la viande.   (b) des sandwichs.
   (c) de l'eau minérale.   (d) de la pâtisserie.   _____

5. Tout le monde mange   (a) du gâteau et de la glace.   (b) des
   saucisses.   (c) du veau.   (d) des sandwichs.   _____

II. Oui ou Non?

1. François est le mari de Claire Paquet.   _____

2. Joséphine est la femme de François.   _____

3. La Fête Nationale est le 14 juillet.   _____

4. Le Bois de Boulogne est un parc près de Paris.   _____

5. La pâtisserie est un dessert.   _____

III. Mots croisés (crossword puzzle).   Give the French words for the English clues.

Horizontalement

1. I
4. good, *masc. sing.*
6. also
8. the, *pl.*
9. definite article, *fem. sing.*
11. the sandwiches
13. with
16. definite article, *masc. sing.*
17. to bring
18. you, *fam. sing.*
19. at, to
20. my, *fem. sing.*
21. and

Verticalement

2. the ice cream
3. is
5. only
7. the cakes
10. year
12. on
14. she
15. for

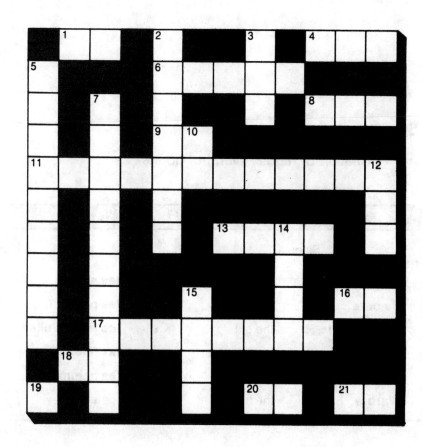

35

IV. Un acrostiche. Complete the French words in the squares across.

1.	the cakes
2.	and
3.	dessert
4.	eclair
5.	day
6.	to hope
7.	indefinite article, *fem. sing.*
8.	no
9.	spirit
10.	roast beef

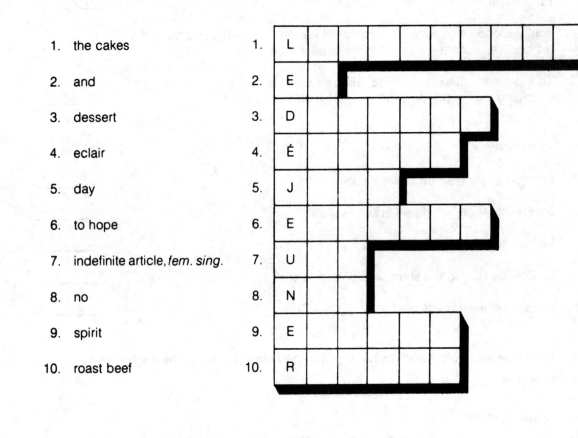

Structures de la Langue

A. Formation of regular plural of nouns

MASCULINE AND FEMININE NOUNS			
Singular		**Plural**	
la mère	the mother	**les mères**	the mothers
le père	the father	**les pères**	the fathers
la jeune fille	the girl	**les jeunes filles**	the girls
la fille	the daughter	**les filles**	the daughters
l'homme	the man	**les hommes**	the men
l'arbre	the tree	**les arbres**	the trees

Rules and observations:

1. To form the plural of a noun, whether masculine or feminine, ordinarily just add **s** to the singular form.

2. Change the definite article **the** from **le** to **les**, **la** to **les**, and **l'** to **les**.

3. In sum, French has only one form for the definite article in the plural: **les**.

B.   Formation of irregular plural of nouns

Rules and observations:

1. Nouns that end in **-s**, **-x**, **-z** in the singular, whether masculine or feminine, do not normally change in the plural. They remain the same. See examples in the box below. You can tell the noun is singular or plural from **le** or **la**, or **les**.

Singular		Plural	
le fils	the son	**les fils**	the sons
la voix	the voice	**les voix**	the voices
le nez	the nose	**les nez**	the noses

2. Nouns that end in **-au**, **-eu**, **-ou** in the singular, whether masculine or feminine, ordinarily add **-x** to form the plural. See examples in the box below.

Singular		Plural	
le gâteau	the cake	**les gâteaux**	the cakes
le jeu	the game	**les jeux**	the games
le genou	the knee	**les genoux**	the knees

3. Nouns that end in **-al** or **-ail** in the singular ordinarily drop that ending and add **-aux** to form the plural. See examples in the box below.

Singular		Plural	
le journal	the newspaper	**les journaux**	the newspapers
le travail	the work	**les travaux**	the works

4. There are other irregular plurals of nouns. Study the examples in the box below.

Singular		Plural	
le ciel	the sky, heaven	**les cieux**	the skies, heavens
l'oeil	the eye	**les yeux**	the eyes
madame	Mrs., madam	**mesdames**	ladies
mademoiselle	miss	**mesdemoiselles**	misses
monsieur	mister, sir, gentleman	**messieurs**	sirs, gentlemen

Exercises

Review the preceding material before starting these exercises.

I. Write the plural form in French for each noun.

1. le garçon _____
2. le fils _____
3. le chapeau _____
4. le journal _____
5. le ciel _____

6. l'oeil _____
7. le père _____
8. la voix _____
9. la mère _____
10. le chat _____

II. Write the singular form in French for each noun.

1. les tables _____
2. les nez _____
3. les genoux _____
4. les voix _____
5. les yeux _____

6. les messieurs _____
7. les hommes _____
8. les jeunes filles _____
9. les enfants _____
10. les arbres _____

III. Change to the singular or to the plural, depending on which is given.

1. les pères _____
2. les hommes _____
3. l'eau _____
4. le fils _____
5. la table _____

6. les journaux _____
7. le cheval _____
8. l'oiseau _____
9. les élèves _____
10. le pays _____

C. Contraction of the definite article with à and de

à + **le** *changes to* **au**	**de** + **le** *changes to* **du**
à + **les** *changes to* **aux**	**de** + **les** *changes to* **des**

Rules and observations:

1. When the preposition **à** (*at, to*) is in front of the definite article **le** or **les**, it changes to the forms given in the box above.

2. When the preposition **de** (*from, of*) is in front of the definite article **le** or **les**, it changes to the forms given in the box above.

3. There is no contraction of **à** followed by **l'** or **la**. It remains **à l'** or **à la**.

4. There is no contraction of **de** followed by **l'** or **la**. It remains **de l'** or **de la**.

Janine va au café.

Madame Paquet va aux grands magasins.

Janine va à la gare.

Madame Paquet donne un bonbon
à l'enfant.

Pierre vient du restaurant.

Madame Paquet vient des grands
magasins.

Pierre vient de l'école.

Janine vient de la bibliothèque.

Exercises

Review the preceding material before starting these exercises.

I. Match the following.

1. Janine is going to the station.
2. Pierre is coming from the restaurant.
3. Mr. Paquet is coming from the department stores.
4. Janine is coming from the library.
5. Pierre is coming from the school.
6. Mrs. Paquet is giving a candy to the child.
7. Janine is going to the café.
8. Mrs. Paquet is going to the department stores.

_____ Janine va au café.

_____ Madame Paquet va aux grands magasins.

_____ Pierre vient de l'école.

_____ Monsieur Paquet vient des grands magasins.

_____ Madame Paquet donne un bonbon à l'enfant.

_____ Pierre vient du restaurant.

_____ Janine va à la gare.

_____ Janine vient de la bibliothèque.

II. Fill in the missing words in French. Choose either **au, aux, à l'**, or **à la**.

1. Janine va _____ café.
2. Pierre va _____ gare.
3. Madame Paquet va _____ grands magasins.
4. Hélène va _____ école.

III. Fill in the missing words in French. Choose either **du, de l'**, **de la**, or **des**.

1. Pierre vient _____ restaurant.
2. Janine vient _____ école.
3. Monique vient _____ bibliothèque.
4. Marie vient _____ grands magasins.

D. Use of the definite article with **de** for possession

le livre **du** maître	the teacher's book
le livre **de la** maîtresse	the teacher's book
les livres **des** garçons	the boys' books
le livre **de** Janine	Janine's book
le livre **de l'**élève	the pupil's book

Rules and observations:

1. The preposition **de** is used to express possession, as shown in the examples in the above
   • box.

2. The preposition **de** changes to **du** or **des**, as shown in the examples in the above box.

Exercises

Review the preceding material before starting the exercises.

. I. Match the following.

1. le parapluie de Pierre	_____	the boy's hat
2. les robes des jeunes filles	_____	the boys' dogs
3. les cheveux de Janine	_____	the girl's skirt
4. le chapeau du garçon	_____	the girls' dresses
5. le journal de Pierre	_____	the pupil's pencil
6. les chiens des garçons	_____	the pupils' pens
7. la jupe de la jeune fille	_____	Janine's eyes
8. les yeux de Janine	_____	Janine's hair
9. les stylos des élèves	_____	Pierre's newspaper
10. le crayon de l'élève	_____	Pierre's umbrella

II. Fill in the missing words. Use either du, des, de, de l' or de la.

1. J'ai les crayons _____ jeunes filles.

2. J'ai le journal _____ femme.

3. J'ai les livres _____ Pierre.

4. J'ai les cahiers _____ garçon.

5. J'ai le stylo _____ élève.

6. J'ai le chapeau _____ homme.

7. J'ai le jeu _____ Janine.

8. J'ai les journaux _____ père.

9. J'ai les bonbons _____ enfant.

10. J'ai le parapluie _____ mère.

NICE GOING! NOW GO BACK AND REVIEW!

III. Oral Proficiency. Respond orally in French to the situations described. (Later, you may write your responses for intensive practice.) Review this Work Unit for ideas or words to use.

    A. Situation: You and your friends are planning a picnic in the park. You call your friend to discuss what you will each bring. In three sentences tell your friend what food you would like to have at the picnic. Then ask your friend which of these he would like to bring. You may use your own ideas or ideas suggested by the following: *avoir, apporter, les sandwichs, les desserts, les éclairs, la glace, le gâteau, le poulet, la viande, le veau, le jambon, la saucisse.*

    B. Situation: You are at a restaurant and your friend asks you why you like mineral water: *Pourquoi aimes-tu l'eau minérale?* Begin your response with: *Pour moi.* In three sentences tell why you like it. You may use your own ideas or ideas suggested by the following: *c'est bon, la santé, aimer mieux, le café.*

The Presidential office in the Élysée Palace, Paris, the official residence of the President of the French Republic. Reprinted with permission of French Cultural Services, New York.

Avez-vous de la viande? Avez-vous des saucisses? Avez-vous du café?

The Noun and the Definite and Indefinite Articles (Conclusion)

*Some people always know what to order
in a restaurant and some don't. Have you
ever done what Pierre does in this scene?*

La grande décision

Garçon: Bonjour. Vous désirez?

Pierre: Bonjour. Avez-vous de la viande?

Garçon: Oui. Nous avons de la viande.

Pierre: Avez-vous des saucisses?

Garçon: Oui. Nous avons de belles saucisses.

Pierre: Non, je ne veux pas de viande. Je ne veux pas de saucisses.

Garçon: Nous avons du poisson.

Pierre: Je ne veux pas de poisson . . . Avez-vous de l'eau minérale?

Garçon: Oui. Nous avons de l'eau minérale.

Pierre: Non, je ne veux pas d'eau minérale . . . Avez-vous du café?

Garçon: Oui. Nous avons du café.

Pierre: Non, je ne veux pas de café.

Garçon: Aimez-vous les éclairs et les tartes?

Pierre: Oui, oui. J'aime les éclairs et les tartes.

Garçon: Je regrette. Nous n'avons ni éclairs, ni tartes.

Vocabulaire

aimer *v.*, to like, to love;
  aimez-vous? do you like?
  j'aime, I like
avoir *v.*, to have;
  avez-vous? do you have?
  nous avons, we have;
  **nous n'avons ni éclairs,
  ni tartes,** we have neither
  eclairs nor tarts
beau *m.*, **belle** *f.*, *adj.*,
  beautiful

bonjour *salutation*, good day
la décision *n.*, decision
désirer *v.*, to wish, to desire;
  vous désirez? you wish?
l'école *n. f.*, the school
le garçon *n.*, the boy, the
  waiter (Note: Nowadays,
  there is a trend to address
  a waiter as "monsieur")
grand *m.*, **grande** *f.*, *adj.*,
  great, big
ni . . . ni *conj.*, neither . . . nor

parle *v., form of* **parler** (to
  talk, to speak); **Pierre
  parle,** Pierre is talking
le poisson *n.*, the fish
regretter *v.*, to regret, to be
  sorry; **je regrette,** I'm sorry
le restaurant *n.*, restaurant
veux *v. form of* **vouloir** (to
  want); **je ne veux pas,** I do
  not want; **Pierre veut,**
  Pierre wants
vous *pron.*, you

45

Exercises

Review the dialogue and vocabulary before starting these exercises.

I. Choose the correct answer based on the dialogue in this unit.

1. Pierre est dans   (a) une école.   (b) un parc.   (c) la maison. (d) un restaurant.   _____

2. Pierre parle avec   (a) un ami.   (b) une amie.   (c) une femme. (d) un garçon de restaurant.   _____

3. Pierre aime   (a) la viande.   (b) le poisson.   (c) les éclairs et les tartes.   (d) les saucisses.   _____

II. Oui ou Non?

1. Pierre est dans un restaurant.   _____

2. Pierre veut du café.   _____

3. Pierre aime les éclairs et les tartes.   _____

III. Word Hunt.   Can you find these words in French in this puzzle? Circle them.

1. I like

2. some fish

3. we have

4. the meat

5. some coffee

6. sir

7. some water

D	U	C	A	F	E	D	E	S
U	M	O	N	S	I	E	U	R
P	D	U	O	D	E	L	A	O
O	C	A	U	J	A	I	M	E
I	D	C	S	P	O	I	D	U
S	E	L	A	V	O	S	N	E
S	L	A	V	I	A	N	D	E
O	E	D	O	E	L	A	E	A
N	A	E	N	A	U	E	A	E
D	U	L	S	O	M	O	N	S

Structures de la Langue

A. The Partitive

Essentially, the plural of the indefinite articles **un** and **une** is **des**. The partitive denotes a part of a whole; or in other words, *some*. It can be plural or singular in form.

1. SIMPLE AFFIRMATIVE

J'ai **du** café.	I have *some* coffee.
J'ai **de la** viande.	I have *some* meat.
J'ai **de l'**eau.	I have *some* water.
J'ai **des** bonbons.	I have *some* candy.

2. SIMPLE NEGATIVE

Je n'ai pas **de** café.	I don't have *any* coffee.
Je n'ai pas **de** viande.	I don't have *any* meat.
Je n'ai pas **d'**eau.	I don't have *any* water.
Je n'ai pas **de** bonbons.	I don't have *any* candy.

3. WITH AN ADJECTIVE

J'ai **du** bon café.	I have *some* good coffee.
J'ai **de** jolis chapeaux.	I have *some* pretty hats.
J'ai **de** jolies jupes.	I have *some* pretty skirts.

Observations based on the examples given in the three boxes above:

1. Use either **du, de la, de l'**, or **des** in front of the noun, depending on whether the noun is masculine or feminine, singular or plural. Study the examples in the first box above.

2. The form **du** is used in front of a masculine singular noun beginning with a consonant, as in **j'ai du café**. See the first box above.

3. The form **de la** is used in front of a feminine singular noun beginning with a consonant, as in **j'ai de la viande.** See the first box above.

4. The form **de l'** is used in front of a feminine or masculine singular noun beginning with a vowel or a silent *h*, as in **j'ai de l'eau**. See the first box above.

5. The form **des** is used in front of all plural nouns.

6. To express *any* in front of a noun, when the verb is negative, use **de** in front of the noun. The noun can be feminine or masculine, singular or plural, but it *must* begin with a consonant, as in **je n'ai pas de café**. See the second box above.

7. To express *any* in front of a noun, when the verb is negative, use **d'** in front of the noun. The noun can be feminine or masculine, singular or plural, but it *must* begin with a vowel or silent *h*, as in **je n'ai pas d'eau**. See the second box above.

8. When the noun is preceded by an adjective, use **de**, as in **j'ai de jolis chapeaux**. See the third box above.

9. When the noun is preceded by an adverb or noun of quantity or measure, use **de**, as in **j'ai beaucoup de choses**.

10. When the noun is modified by another noun, use **de**, as in **une école de filles**.

11. The partitive is not used with **sans** or **ne . . . ni . . . ni**.

    Examples: Je quitte la maison **sans argent**.
    (I'm leaving the house *without any money*.)

    Je **n'**ai **ni** argent **ni** billets.
    (I have *neither* money *nor* tickets.)

Exercises

Review the preceding material before starting these exercises.

I. Answer the following questions in the affirmative.

Model: Avez-vous du café? **Answer: Oui, j'ai du café.**
(Do you have any coffee?) (Yes, I have some coffee.)

1. Avez-vous du pain? _____

2. Avez-vous de la viande? _____

3. Avez-vous de l'eau? _____

4. Avez-vous des bonbons? _____

5. Avez-vous du beurre? _____

48

Avez-vous des bonbons?

II. Answer the following questions in the negative.

> **Model: Avez-vous du café?**   **Answer: Non, je n'ai pas de café.**
> (Have you any coffee?)   (No, I haven't any coffee.)

1. Avez-vous du café? _____

2. Avez-vous de la viande? _____

3. Avez-vous de l'eau? _____

4. Avez-vous des bonbons? _____

5. Avez-vous du beurre? _____

III. Answer the following questions in the affirmative.

> **Model: Avez-vous du bon café?**   **Answer: Oui, j'ai du bon café.**
> (Do you have (any) good coffee?)   (Yes, I have (some) good coffee.)

1. Avez-vous du bon café? _____

2. Avez-vous de jolis chapeaux? _____

3. Avez-vous de jolies jupes? _____

4. Avez-vous du bon vin? _____

5. Avez-vous de jolies cravates? _____

49

IV. Answer the following questions in the negative.

> **Model: Avez-vous du bon café?**   **Answer: Non, je n'ai pas de bon café.**
> (Do you have (any) good coffee?)   (No, I don't have any good coffee.)

1. Avez-vous du bon café? _____

2. Avez-vous de jolis chapeaux? _____

3. Avez-vous de jolies jupes? _____

4. Avez-vous du bon vin? _____

5. Avez-vous de jolies cravates? _____

B. The definite article with parts of body and clothing

J'ai **les** mains sales.	My hands are dirty.
J'ai **les** yeux bruns.	My eyes are brown.
J'ai **les** cheveux noirs.	My hair is black.
J'ai **le** chapeau sur **la** tête.	I have my hat on my head.

Rule: Use the definite article instead of the possessive adjective when there is no doubt as to who the possessor is.

Exercises

I. Answer the following questions in the affirmative.

> **Model: Avez-vous les mains sales?**   **Answer: Oui, j'ai les mains sales.**
> (Are your hands dirty?)   (Yes, my hands are dirty.)

1. Avez-vous les mains sales? _____

2. Avez-vous le visage sale? _____

3. Avez-vous les pieds grands? _____

4. Avez-vous les yeux bruns? _____

5. Avez-vous les cheveux noirs? _____

II. Answer the following questions in the negative.

  Model: **Avez-vous les pieds grands?** **Answer:** **Non, je n'ai pas les pieds grands.**
     (Are your feet big?)   (No, my feet are not big.)

1. Avez-vous les pieds grands? _____

2. Avez-vous le visage sale? _____

3. Avez-vous les mains sales? _____

4. Avez-vous le chapeau sur la tête? _____

5. Avez-vous les cheveux noirs? _____

C. The definite article with parts of the day

Je vais à l'école **les** matins.	I go to school *in the* mornings.
Je joue **les** après-midi.	I play *in the* afternoons.
J'étudie **les** soirs.	I study *in the* evenings.

Rule: Use the definite article with parts of the day. It can also be used in the singular. In English it means *in the.*

Je vais à l'école les matins. **Je joue les après-midi.** **J'étudie les soirs.**

Exercises

I. Answer the following questions in the affirmative.

> **Model: Allez-vous à l'école les matins?** (Do you go to school in the mornings?)
>
> **Answer: Oui, je vais à l'école les matins.** (Yes, I go to school in the mornings.)

1. Allez-vous à l'école les matins? _____

2. Allez-vous à la bibliothèque les après-midi? _____

3. Allez-vous au restaurant les soirs? _____

4. Allez-vous au parc les après-midi? _____

5. Allez-vous au café les soirs? _____

II. Answer the following questions in the negative.

> **Model: Allez-vous au cinéma les soirs?** (Do you go to the movies in the evenings?)
>
> **Answer: Non, je ne vais pas au cinéma les soirs.** (No, I don't go to the movies in the evenings.)

1. Allez-vous au cinéma les soirs? _____

2. Allez-vous à l'école les matins? _____

3. Allez-vous à la bibliothèque les soirs? _____

D. Omission of the definite article with **parler**, **de**, and **en**

Janine vient **de** France.	Elle **parle** français.	Elle **prononce** bien **le français**.
Janine comes from France.	She speaks French.	She pronounces French well.
Julie répond **en** français dans la classe **de** français. Julie answers in French in the French class.			

Rules and observations:

1. Do not use the definite article in front of the name of a language if the verb **parler** directly precedes it.

2. Do not use the definite article in front of the name of a language if the preposition **de** or **en** directly precedes it.

3. **De** indicates *concerned with* in expressions such as the following: **la classe de français** (the French class), **la leçon de français** (the French lesson), **le professeur d'anglais** (the English teacher), **le maître de musique** (the music teacher).

4. Change **de** to **d'** if the word that follows starts with a vowel or a silent *h*.   Example: **le professeur d'anglais**.

E. Omission of the indefinite article with **cent** and **mille**

J'ai **cent dollars**.	I have *one hundred dollars*.
J'ai **mille dollars**.	I have *one thousand dollars*.

Rule: Do not use the indefinite article **un** or **une** in front of **cent** (100) or **mille** (1,000).

Exercises

Review the preceding material before starting these exercises.

I. Write two sentences using the word (language name) given in italics. Begin the first sentence with **il** (he) or **elle** (she) and use the verb **parle** (speaks). Begin the second sentence with the appropriate subject pronoun (**il** *or* **elle**) and use the verb **prononce** (pronounces) and the adverb **bien** (well).

Model: **Pierre vient de France.**	**You write:** **Il parle français.**
(Peter comes from France.)	(He speaks French.)
	Il prononce bien le français.
	(He pronounces French well.)

1. Louis vient de France.

   le français _____

2. María vient d'Espagne.

   l'espagnol _____

3. Madame Belini vient d'Italie.

   l'italien _____

4. Monsieur Armstrong vient d'Angleterre.

   l'anglais _____

5. Hilda vient d'Allemagne.

   l'allemand _____

II. **Answer the following questions in the affirmative.**

   Model: Avez-vous cent dollars?   **Answer: Oui, j'ai cent dollars.**
   (Have you 100 dollars?)   (Yes, I have 100 dollars.)

   1. Avez-vous cent dollars? _____

   2. Avez-vous mille francs? _____

   3. Avez-vous cent livres? _____

   4. Avez-vous mille amis? _____

III. **Complete with an appropriate selection: le, la, l', or les. Use a dash (—) if no definite article is required.**

   Le maître de _____ musique à _____ école est aussi professeur de _____ français. Il
                1   2   3

   parle _____ français dans _____ classe de français, et il prononce bien _____ français.
            4   5   6

   Il a _____ yeux bleus et _____ cheveux noirs.
      7   8

IV. **Change the words in italics to either the singular or plural, depending on which is given.**

   Model: J'ai le gâteau.   **Answer: J'ai les gâteaux.**
   (I have the cake.)   (I have the cakes.)

   1. J'ai *le sandwich.* _____   5. J'ai *des jupes.* _____

   2. J'ai *l'éclair.* _____   6. J'ai *le chapeau.* _____

   3. J'ai *les saucisses.* _____   7. J'ai *les desserts.* _____

   4. J'ai *un dollar.* _____   8. J'ai *des gâteaux.* _____

54

V. Jeu de mots (Word game.) **Translate these 14 words into French to fill in the squares.**

1. the news-papers
2. water
3. health
4. dress
5. children
6. on
7. works (noun)
8. afternoon
9. indefinite article, *fem. sing.*
10. roast beef
11. tree
12. nose
13. head
14. evening

1	2	3	4	5	6	7	8	9	10	11	12	13	14
L	E	S	R	E	S	T	A	U	R	A	N	T	S

VI. Oral Proficiency. Respond orally in French to the situations described. (Later, you may write your responses for intensive practice.) Review this unit for ideas or words to use. You may use your own ideas or the vocabulary suggested in each situation.

A. Situation: You are in a restaurant. The waiter asks you what you want: *Vous désirez?* Respond to the question using words of your own or any of the following: *du poisson, de la viande, des tartes.* Begin your response with: *Je voudrais* (I would like). In two sentences, tell what you would like to have.

B. Situation: You are in a bakery. You approach the clerk who asks you what you want to buy: *Vous désirez acheter?* In three sentences, explain that you need a birthday cake and tell him you need a large cake for all your friends. You may use your own ideas or ideas suggested by the following: *grand, le gâteau, pouvoir, avez-vous, beau, désirer.*

Maman, papa, le téléviseur ne marche pas!

Present Indicative Tense of Regular Verbs Ending in — er

*Can Janine and Pierre live without
violence on television for one evening?*

La beauté ou la violence?

Janine et Pierre allument le téléviseur mais il ne marche pas. Tous les deux sont inquiets parce que l'émission ce soir est "La violence triomphe!" La mère et le père entrent dans le salon et Pierre et Janine s'exclament:

— Maman, papa, le téléviseur ne marche pas!

— Bon! Vous regardez trop de violence à la télévision, vous deux, dit la mère.

— Mais l'émission ce soir est très importante! C'est "La violence triomphe!" s'exclament Janine et Pierre.

— La violence ne triomphe pas dans cette maison. Je regrette, dit le père.

— Est-ce que nous allons faire réparer le téléviseur? demandent Janine et Pierre.

— Allons-nous faire réparer le téléviseur?! répètent la mère et le père. Oh! s'exclament-ils. Oh, non! Aujourd'hui, non!

Pierre et Janine regardent dans les journaux. L'émission "Les oeuvres d'art dans le Louvre" est à la télévision ce soir avant l'émission "La violence triomphe!" Alors, ils s'exclament:

— Papa, maman, c'est l'émission "Les oeuvres d'art dans le Louvre" à la télévision ce soir!

— Quoi?! Vite! Au téléphone. Nous allons faire réparer le téléviseur tout de suite!

Vocabulaire

aller *v.*, to go; **nous allons**, we are going

allumer *v.*, to turn on (an apparatus)

alors *adv.*, then

après *prep.*, after

aujourd'hui *adv.*, today

avant *prep.*, before

la beauté *n.*, beauty

cet *m.*, **cette** *f.*, *adj.*, this

demander *v.*, *to ask*

deux *adj.*, two; **tous les deux**, both

dire *v.*, to say, to tell; **dit la mère**, says the mother

l'émission *n. f.*, the show, the television program

entrer *v.*, to enter

s'exclamer *v.*, *refl.*, to exclaim

faire *v.*, to do, to make

inquiet *m.*, **inquiète** *f.*, *adj.*, upset

mais *conj.*, but

marcher *v.*, to walk; to run, to work (a machine or apparatus)

l'oeuvre *n. f.*, **d'art** *n. m.*, the work of art

parce que *conj.*, because

quoi *interr. pron.*, what

regarder *v.*, to look (at), to watch

réparer *v.*, to repair; **faire réparer**, to have (something) repaired

répéter *v.*, to repeat

le soir *n.*, the evening

le téléphone *n.*, the telephone; **au téléphone**, to the telephone

le téléviseur *n.*, the television set

la télévision *n.*, television

tout de suite *adv.*, right away, immediately, at once

très *adv.*, very

triompher *v.*, to triumph

trop (de) *adv.*, too much (of)

la violence *n.*, violence

Exercises

Review the story and vocabulary before starting these exercises.

I. Answer the following questions in French in complete sentences. They are based on the story, "La beauté ou la violence?"

1. Qui allume le téléviseur? _____

2. Qui entre dans le salon? _____

3. Qui regarde dans les journaux? _____

II. Oui ou Non?

1. Janine et Pierre allument le téléviseur. _____

2. Le téléviseur marche très bien. _____

3. L'émission ce soir est "La violence triomphe!" _____

4. L'émission "Les oeuvres d'art dans le Louvre" est à la télévision ce soir
   après "La violence triomphe!" _____

5. Le téléviseur va être réparé. _____

III. Choose the correct answer based on the story in this unit.

1. Janine et Pierre allument   (a) la radio.   (b) le téléviseur.
   (c) l'émission. _____

2. Janine et Pierre regardent dans   (a) le téléviseur.   (b) le téléphone.
   (c) les journaux. _____

3. Madame et Monsieur Paquet entrent dans   (a) la cuisine.   (b) le
   salon.   (c) le garage. _____

IV. Complete by writing the missing French words. Find them in the story in this unit.

Janine et Pierre _____ le téléviseur mais il ne _____ pas. La mère et le

père _____ dans le salon et Pierre et Janine s'_____.

— Maman, papa, le téléviseur ne _____ pas!

La mère dit: Bon! Vous _____ trop de violence à la télévision, vous deux.

— Est-ce que nous allons faire réparer le téléviseur? _____ Janine et Pierre.

— Oh! Oh, non! Aujourd'hui, non! s'exclament la _____ et le _____.

Structures de la Langue

A. Introduction

A verb is a word that expresses an action *(to dance)* or a state of being *(to think)*. Tense means time. French and English verb tenses are divided into three main groups of time: past, present, and future. A verb tense shows if an action took place (past), is taking place (present), or will take place (future). Here, we will study the present tense.

French verbs are divided into three main conjugations (types) according to the infinitive ending, which can be either **-er**, **-ir**, **-re**. You might say that these endings mean *to* in English; for example, **danser** means "*to* dance." In this unit, we will concentrate on the first conjugation (**-er** ending).

You must memorize the personal endings for the **-er** verbs because they indicate the subject. You must also memorize the personal subject pronouns in French because each one is used with its own personal ending on the verb. These are all given in dark letters in the following chart:

FIRST CONJUGATION

	-er
Infinitive →	**danser** *to dance*

Required subject pronouns
 	
 SINGULAR
 	
 1. **je**   I
 2. **tu**   you *(familiar only)*
 3. **Il**   he *or* it
     elle   she *or* it
 	
 PLURAL
 	
 1. **nous**   we
 2. **vous**   you
 3. **Ils**
     elles   they
	I dance, *or*
	 I do dance, *or*
	 I am dancing;
	 you dance, *etc.*
	
	 dans**e**
	 dans**es**
	
	 dans**e**
	
	 dans**ons**
	 dans**ez**
	
	 dans**ent**

Rules and observations:

1. To form the present tense of a regular verb ending in **-er**, drop the **-er**. What remains is called the *stem*. Add to the stem the correct personal ending; **-e**, **-es**, **-e**, **-ons**, **-ez**, or **-ent**.

2. Note that *do, am, are, does, is* (which are used in English in the present tense) are *not translated* into French. Therefore, **je danse** can mean *I dance,* or *I do dance,* or *I am dancing.* The same applies to the rest of the conjugation, for example, *you dance,* or *you do dance,* or *you are dancing, etc.*

SINGULAR	
With noun	With pronoun
Janine danse tous les soirs.	**Elle danse tous les soirs.**
(Janine dances every night.)	(She dances every night.)
L'ours danse.	**Il danse.**
(The bear is dancing.)	(It (or he) is dancing.)
PLURAL	
Janine et Marie dansent souvent.	**Elles dansent souvent.**
(Janine and Mary dance often.)	(They dance often.)
Janine et Pierre dansent beaucoup.	**Ils dansent beaucoup.**
(Janine and Pierre dance a lot.)	(They dance a lot.)
Les ours dansent.	**Ils dansent.**
(The bears are dancing.)	(They are dancing.)

B. The subject pronouns

1. Study the subject pronouns in the chart on page 59.

2. The subject pronoun is placed in front of the verb in an affirmative statement: **Je danse tous les soirs**. I dance every night.

3. The subject pronoun is always used with the verb.

4. In French there are two subject pronouns that mean *you:*

   (a) **tu** is used when you are speaking to a member of your family, a close friend, a classmate, or someone younger than you.

   (b) **vous** is the polite form of *you* and is used at all other times.

   (c) **vous** is also the plural of **tu**; when you are speaking to two or more members of your family at the same time, or two or more close friends at the same time, use **vous**.

5. If the first letter of a verb is a vowel, drop **e** in **je** and add an apostrophe: **j'aime la glace**. *I like ice cream.*

6. The subject pronouns **il, elle, ils, elles** are used to take the place of a noun, whether it is a person, place, thing, or animal.

7. The subject pronoun **il** is used to take the place of a masculine singular noun.

8. The subject pronoun **elle** is used to take the place of a feminine singular noun.

9. The subject pronoun **ils** is used to take the place of two or more masculine nouns. It is also used to take the place of one masculine and one feminine noun. There could be any number of feminine nouns as subjects, but as long as there is at least one masculine noun mixed in with the subjects, the pronoun must be **ils**.

10. The subject pronoun **elles** is used to take the place of two or more feminine nouns *only*.

C. Some common regular verbs of the first conjugation

aimer to love, to like; **apporter** to bring; **chanter** to sing; **chercher** to look for; **demander** to ask (for); **désirer** to desire, to wish; **donner** to give; **écouter** to listen (to); **étudier** to study; **fermer** to close; **jouer** to play; **montrer** to show; **oublier** to forget; **parler** to talk, to speak; **porter** to carry, to wear; **regarder** to look (at); **réparer** to fix, to repair; **trouver** to find

D. The uses of the present tense

This tense is used much of the time in both French and English. It indicates:

(a) An action or a state of being at the present time.

Examples:
1. **Je vais** à l'école maintenant. *I am going* to school now.
2. **Je pense**; donc, **je suis**. *I think;* therefore, *I am*.

(b) Habitual action.

Example:
1. **Je vais** à la bibliothèque tous les jours. *I go* to the library every day.

(c) A general truth, something which is permanently true.

Example:
1. Deux et deux **font** quatre. Two and two *are* four.

(d) Vividness when talking or writing about past events. This is called the *historical present*.

Example:
1. Marie-Antoinette **est** condamnée à mort. Elle **entre** dans la charrette et **est** en route pour la guillotine. Marie-Antoinette *is* condemned to die. She *goes* into the cart and *is* on her way to the guillotine.

(e) The near future.

Example:
1. Il **arrive** demain. He *arrives* tomorrow.

(f) An action or state of being that occurred in the past and *continues up to the present*. In English, this tense is the *present perfect*.

Examples:
1. Je **suis** ici depuis dix minutes. I *have been* here for ten minutes. (meaning: I am still here at present.)
2. Elle **est** malade depuis trois jours. She *has been* sick for three days. (meaning: She is still sick at present.)

61

E. The verb in the negative

1. To use a verb in the negative, place **ne** in front of the verb and **pas** after it:

Je **ne** danse **pas**.   I do not dance (or, I am not dancing).

---

2. If the first letter of a verb is a vowel, drop **e** in **ne** and add an apostrophe:

Je **n'**aime **pas** le café.   I do not like coffee.

F. The verb in the interrogative

1. To use a verb in a question, put **est-ce que** in front of the subject:

Est-ce que vous dansez?   Do you dance?

Est-ce que Janine danse?   Is Janine dancing?

---

2. If the first letter of the subject is a *vowel* or *silent h*, drop **e** in **que** and add an apostrophe:

Est-ce qu'Albert danse?   **Est-ce qu'**il danse?

Is Albert dancing?   Is he dancing?

Est-ce qu'Hélène danse?   **Est-ce qu'**elle danse?

Is Helen dancing?   Is she dancing?

---

3. To use a verb in a question, there is something else you can do instead of using the **est-ce que** form. You can use the *inverted form*. Move the subject pronoun and put it after the verb, joining it with a hyphen:

Dansez-vous?   Do you dance?

---

4. If the subject pronoun is **je**, do not use the inverted form. Use the **est-ce que** form. The inverted form with **je** is used only with certain verbs.

5. In the inverted form, when the last letter of the verb is a vowel in the third person singular, insert **-t-** in front of **il** or **elle**:

Danse-t-il?	Does he dance? Is he dancing?
Danse-t-elle?	Does she dance? Is she dancing?

6. In the inverted form, if the subject is a noun, mention the noun first and use the pronoun of of the noun:

Pierre danse-t-il?	Does Pierre dance?
Janine danse-t-elle?	Does Janine dance?
Le garçon danse-t-il?	Is the boy dancing?
La jeune fille danse-t-elle?	Is the girl dancing?

G. The verb in the negative-interrogative

1. To use a verb in a question that is negative, first use the interrogative form you learned above (par. F).

2. Put **ne** in front of the verb.

3. Put **pas** after the verb if you use the **est-ce que** form.

4. Or, if you use the inverted form, put **pas** after the subject pronoun:

Est-ce que vous ne dansez pas?	Don't you dance?
Est-ce qu'Albert ne danse pas?	Doesn't Albert dance?
Est-ce qu'elle ne danse pas?	Doesn't she dance?
Ne dansez-vous pas?	Don't you dance?
Ne danse-t-il pas?	Doesn't he dance?
Janine ne danse-t-elle pas?	Doesn't Janine dance?
Le garçon ne danse-t-il pas?	Doesn't the boy dance?

Exercises

I. Match the following, keeping in mind that you are supposed to choose one subject pronoun to take the place of the noun or nouns as given.

(a)

1. il _____ Janine
2. elles _____ Pierre et moi
3. nous _____ le garçon
4. ils _____ Alice et elle
5. elle _____ Paul et Robert

(b)

1. elles _____ Roger et moi
2. elle _____ le chien
3. ils _____ Marie et sa mère
4. nous _____ la télévision
5. il _____ Alice et Pierre

II. Substitute only one appropriate subject pronoun for the word or words in italics and rewrite the entire sentence in French.

> **Model:** **Janine allume le téléviseur.**   **You write:** **Elle allume le téléviseur.**
> (Janine turns on the   (She turns on the television set.)
> television set.)

1. *Madame Paquet* entre dans le salon. _____

2. *Pierre* cherche le journal. _____

3. *Marie et Alice* chantent bien. _____

4. *Robert et Georges* jouent à la balle. _____

5. *Janine et Pierre* regardent trop de violence à la télévision. _____

_____

Janine et Pierre regardent trop de violence à la télévision.

III. Use the subject pronoun in parentheses to take the place of the subject in italics. Rewrite each sentence in French, making the required changes in the verb forms.

> **Model:** **Nous regardons la télévision.** **(Je)** **You write:** **Je regarde la télévision.**
> (We watch television.) (I watch television.)

Nous dansons beaucoup.

1. (Tu) _____

2. (Il) _____

3. (Elle) _____

4. (Vous) _____

5. (Ils) _____

6. (Elles) _____

IV. Use the subject pronoun in parentheses to take the place of the subject in italics. Rewrite each sentence in French, making the required changes in the verb forms. Keep them all in the negative.

> **Model:** **Tu ne danses pas.** **(Je)** **You write:** **Je ne danse pas.**
> (You don't dance.) (I don't dance.)

Nous ne dansons pas.

1. (Je) _____

2. (Tu) _____

3. (Il) _____

4. (Vous) _____

5. (Ils) _____

6. (Elles) _____

V. Answer the following questions in the affirmative in complete French sentences. In answer (a) use **oui**. In answer (b) use **aussi** (also). Study the models. Use subject pronouns in your answers.

> **Models:** **(a) Chantez-vous les matins?** (Do you sing in the mornings?)
> **You write:** **(a) Oui, je chante les matins.** (Yes, I sing in the mornings.)
>
> **(b) Et Simone?** (And Simone?)
> **You write:** **(b) Elle chante aussi.** (She sings also.)

1. (a) Dansez-vous les matins? _____

   (b) Et François? _____

2. (a) Pierre cherche-t-il le chapeau? _____

   (b) Et Janine? _____

3. (a) Hélène étudie-t-elle la leçon? _____

   (b) Et vous? _____

65

VI. Answer the following questions in the negative in complete French sentences. In answer (a) use **non**. In answer (b) use **non plus** (either). Study the models carefully. Use subject pronouns in your answers.

> **Models:** **(a) Est-ce que vous dansez?** You write: **(a) Non, je ne danse pas.**
> (Do you dance?) (No, I don't dance.)
>
> **(b) Et Charles?** You write: **(b) Il ne danse pas non plus.**
> (And Charles?) (He doesn't dance either.)

1. (a) Est-ce que vous dansez? _____

   (b) Et Paul? _____

2. (a) Est-ce qu'il étudie? _____

   (b) Et Monique? _____

3. (a) Est-ce que Paul cherche la balle? _____

   (b) Et les enfants? _____

4. (a) Est-ce que la femme écoute la musique? _____

   (b) Et vous? _____

5. (a) Est-ce que tu fermes la fenêtre? _____

   (b) Et nous? _____

VII. Choose the correct verb form and write it with its subject on the blank line.

1. Je (fermes, ferme, fermons) la porte. *Je ferme*

2. Tu (apportes, apportez, apportent) le gâteau. _____

3. Il (étudient, étudions, étudie) les devoirs. _____

4. Elle (parlent, parle, parlez) bien. _____

5. Nous (marche, marchez, marchons) lentement. _____

6. Vous (donner, donnez, donnons) des fleurs à la maîtresse. _____

7. Ils (joue, jouent, jouons) dans la rue. _____

8. Elles (chante, chantent, chantes) doucement. _____

9. Vous (cherchez, cherches, cherchent) le chapeau. _____

10. J' (aimes, aime, aimons) la glace. _____

VIII. **Word Search.** Can you find these verb forms with their subject pronouns *in French* in this puzzle? Circle them.

1. I dance.

2. You (familiar) study.

3. She plays.

4. We love.

5. They (m.) are singing.

6. I love.

7. He arrives.

8. He talks.

9. He forgets.

J	E	D	A	N	S	E	N	T	C	O
A	J	A	I	M	E	J	I	U	N	I
I	L	P	A	R	L	E	O	É	O	E
I	L	O	U	B	L	I	E	T	U	A
E	L	L	E	J	O	U	E	U	S	U
J	E	J	O	U	E	A	L	D	A	O
I	L	A	R	R	I	V	E	I	I	I
E	L	L	E	A	R	R	I	E	M	E
N	O	U	S	J	O	U	O	S	O	A
I	L	S	C	H	A	N	T	E	N	T
A	E	I	O	U	I	L	S	P	S	L

IX. Change the following affirmative statements to negative sentences.

Model: **Je danse.** (I dance.)   **You write:** **Je ne danse pas.** (I don't dance.)

1. Je parle. _____

2. Tu chantes. _____

3. Il écoute. _____

4. Elle oublie. _____

5. Nous jouons. _____

6. Vous désirez. _____

X. **Oral Proficiency.** Respond orally in French to the situations described. (Later, you may write your responses for intensive practice.) Review this unit for ideas or words to use. You may use your own ideas or the vocabulary suggested in each situation.

A. **Situation:** You are at home. Your mother and father want to watch a TV show about French art. You and your brother (or sister) want to watch *Le Tour de France* on TV. In three short sentences tell your mother and father why you prefer to watch the sports program. You may use your own words, those in this lesson, or any or all of the following: *allumer le téléviseur, regarder mon programme favori, je préfère, nous préférons, j'aime, nous aimons, les sports, les cyclistes, la télé, la télévision.*

B. **Situation:** You and your girlfriend (or boyfriend) cannot decide on what to do this Saturday night. You want to go dancing but your friend wants to go to a concert. In four sentences tell what you want to do and why. You may use your own words, those in this unit, or the following: *préférer, aimer mieux, danser, aller, écouter la musique, au concert.*

67

Au revoir, Monsieur!

Present Indicative Tense of Regular Verbs Ending in — *ir*

*Have you ever received a note from a boy
or girl in a class at school? In this scene,
Pierre is reading a note that was just
passed to him.*

Tout est bien qui finit bien

Pierre est en classe de mathématiques. Il lit un petit mot caché dans les pages de son livre.
Voici le mot:

Pierre, mon chéri:
   Je déteste ce cours et je déteste le professeur. Il est très mauvais. Il choisit des
leçons difficiles et il punit les élèves quand ils ne finissent pas leurs devoirs.
   Je t'aime et je t'adore.
                                 Anne-Marie

Le professeur dit à Pierre:

— Tu ne finis pas tes devoirs! Tu as un mot caché dans les pages de ton livre! De qui est ce
mot? Donne-moi le mot!

Pierre rougit. Il regarde la belle Anne-Marie et elle lui dit tendrement de ses beaux yeux bleus
de ne pas révéler leur amour secret et de ne pas donner le petit mot au professeur.
   A ce moment-là, le signal retentit. Le cours est fini! Tous les élèves quittent la salle de classe
immédiatement et Pierre aussi, avec le petit mot caché dans les pages de son livre.

Quand il est à la porte, Pierre s'exclame:

— Au revoir, monsieur!

Dans le couloir, Anne-Marie dit à Pierre:

— Chéri, tu es formidable! Un vrai homme! Merci!

Pierre dit:

— Ouf! Je l'ai échappé belle! Tout est bien qui finit bien!

Vocabulaire

à *prep.*, to, at
aimer *v.*, to love, to like; **je t'aime** I love you
au revoir *salutation*, good-bye

cacher *v.*, to hide; **caché** hidden
choisir *v.*, to choose; **il choisit** he chooses
le cours *n.*, the course

détester *v.*, to detest
les devoirs *n. m. pl.*, the homework, the assignments

69

dit v. form of **dire** (to say, to tell); **le professeur dit** the teacher says

donner v., to give; **donne-moi** give me

'**échapper** v., to escape; **je l'ai échappé belle!** I had a narrow escape!

'**l'élève** n. m. f., the student, the pupil; **tous les élèves** all the students

fini, finis, finit, finissent v forms of **finir** (to finish); **fini** finished; **tu ne finis pas** you are not finishing; **ils ne finissent pas** they do not finish; **tout est bien qui finit bien!** all's well that ends well!

ils subject pron. m., **elles** subject pron. f., they

immédiatement adv., immediately

la leçon n., the lesson

leur, leurs poss. adj., their

lit v. form of **lire** (to read); **il lit** he is reading

le livre n., the book

lui indir. obj. pron., to him, to her; **elle lui dit** she says to him

mauvais adj. m. s., bad

le moment n., moment; **à ce moment-là** at that moment

le mot n., the word, the note; **un petit mot** a note

ne pas révéler not to reveal; **ne pas donner** not to give

ouf! interj., whew!

la porte n., the door

le professeur n., the teacher

punit v. form of **punir** (to punish); **il punit** he punishes

quand adv., when

qui pron., who, whom, which; **de qui** from whom

quittent v. form of **quitter** (to leave); **tous les élèves quittent la salle de classe** all the students leave the classroom

retentit v. form of **retentir** (to resound, to ring); **le signal retentit** the signal sounds, the bell rings

rougit v. form of **rougir** (to blush); **Pierre rougit** Pierre blushes

la salle n., the room; **la salle de classe** the classroom

son poss. adj. m. sing., his

ton poss. adj. m. sing., your

voici here is

Exercises

Review the story and vocabulary before starting these exercises.

I. Choose the correct answer based on the story in this unit.

1. Pierre est dans (a) le restaurant. (b) le garage. (c) l'école. (d) la bibliothèque. _____

2. Pierre lit (a) un journal. (b) un livre. (c) un menu. (d) un petit mot. _____

3. Le petit mot est caché dans les pages du livre (a) du professeur. (b) de son ami. (c) de Pierre. (d) de son amie. _____

II. Oui ou Non?

1. Le professeur choisit des leçons faciles. _____

2. Pierre ne finit pas les devoirs. _____

3. Anne-Marie déteste le cours de mathématiques. _____

4. Pierre ne rougit pas. _____

5. Le professeur punit les élèves quand ils ne finissent pas les devoirs. _____

6. Anne-Marie aime Pierre. _____

III. Choose the appropriate French word and write it on the blank line. Base your choice only on the content of the story in this unit.

rougit   **finit**   **retentit**   **choisit**   **finissent**

1. Le professeur _____ des leçons difficiles.

2. Pierre _____.

3. Tout est bien qui _____ bien.

4. Les élèves ne _____ pas les devoirs.

5. Le signal _____.

Structures de la Langue

A. Introduction

Go back to the preceding unit (work unit four) and read again the material presented on page 59. Here are the personal endings for verbs of the second conjugation (**-ir**).

SECOND CONJUGATION

	-ir
Infinitive →	**finir** *to finish*

Required subject pronouns
 	
SINGULAR
 	
1. **je**   I
2. **tu**   you *(familiar only)*
3. **il**   he *or* it
   elle   she *or* it
 	
PLURAL
 	
1. **nous**   we
2. **vous**   you
3. **ils**
   elles   they
	I finish, *or*
	I do finish, *or*
	I am finishing;
	you finish, *etc.*
	
	fin**is**
	fin**is**
	
	fin**it**
	
	fin**issons**
	fin**issez**
	
	fin**issent**

Rules and observations:

1. To form the present tense of a regular verb ending in **-ir**, drop the **-ir**. What remains is called the *stem*. Add to the stem the personal endings shown in the above chart. They are: **-is**, **-is**, **-it**, **-issons**, **-issez**, **-issent**.

2. Note that *do, am, are, does, is* (which are used in English in the present tense) are *not translated* into French. Therefore, **je finis** can mean *I finish*, or *I do finish*, or *I am finishing*. The same applies to the rest of the conjugation, for example, *you finish*, or *you do finish*, or *you are finishing, etc.*

B. The subject pronouns

Go back to the preceding unit (work unit four) and read again the material presented on page 60.

C. Some common regular verbs of the second conjugation

accomplir to accomplish; **bâtir** to build; **bénir** to bless; **choisir** to choose; **désobéir (à)** to disobey; **obéir (à)** to obey; **punir** to punish; **remplir** to fill; **réussir (à)** to succeed (in); **rougir** to blush; **saisir** to seize; **salir** to soil, to dirty

Exercises

Review the preceding material before starting these exercises.

   I. Match the following, keeping in mind that you are supposed to choose one subject pronoun to take the place of the noun or nouns as given.

(a)

1. il _____ Anne-Marie
2. elles _____ Joseph
3. ils _____ Hélène et Janine
4. elle _____ Pierre et Anne

(b)

1. ils _____ le chien
2. elle _____ les maisons
3. il _____ la France
4. elles _____ les chiens

   II. Substitute only one appropriate subject pronoun for the word or words in italics and rewrite the entire sentence in French.

     Model: **Le signal retentit.**
           (The signal sounds.)

     You write: **Il retentit.**
           (It sounds.)

1. *Le professeur* choisit des leçons difficiles. _____

2. *La jeune fille* saisit la balle. _____

3. *Madame Berty* punit les élèves. _____

4. *Madame et Monsieur Banluc* choisissent une nouvelle automobile. _____

   _____

5. *Les élèves* finissent toujours les devoirs. _____

6. *Anne et Monique* rougissent facilement. _____

Madame Berty punit les élèves.

III. Use the subject pronoun in parentheses to take the place of the subject pronoun in italics. Rewrite each sentence in French, making the required changes in the verb forms.

Model: *Nous* **finissons la leçon.**   **(Je)** **You write:** **Je finis la leçon.**
(We are finishing the lesson.)   (I am finishing the lesson.)

1. (Ils) _____   4. (Elle) _____

2. (Tu) _____   5. (Vous) _____

3. (Il), _____   6. (Elles) _____

73

IV. Use the subject pronoun in parentheses to take the place of the subject pronoun in italics. Rewrite each sentence in French, making the required changes in the verb forms. Keep them all in the negative.

Model: *Elle* **ne finit pas le dîner.**
(She is not finishing the dinner.)

(Je) You write: **Je ne finis pas le dîner.**
(I am not finishing the dinner.)

1. (Vous) _____

2. (Il) _____

3. (Tu) _____

4. (Elles) _____

5. (Ils) _____

6. (Nous) _____

V. Answer the following questions in the affirmative in complete French sentences, using subject pronouns in your answers. In answer (a) use **Oui.** In answer (b) use **aussi.**

Models: (a) **Henri finit-il la leçon?**
(Is Henry finishing the lesson?)

You write: (a) **Oui, il finit la leçon.**
(Yes, he is finishing the lesson.)

(b) **Et vous?**
(And you?)

You write: (b) **Je finis la leçon aussi.**
(I am finishing the lesson also.)

1. (a) Henri finit-il le livre? _____

(b) Et vous? _____

2. (a) Les professeurs punissent-ils les mauvais élèves? _____

_____

(b) Et Monsieur Fouchy? _____

3. (a) Monsieur Banluc choisit-il une nouvelle automobile? _____

_____

(b) Et Madame et Monsieur Paquet? _____

_____

4. (a) Le chien obéit-il au garçon? _____

(b) Et les chats? _____

5. (a) Finissez-vous la leçon aujourd'hui? _____

(b) Et Janine? _____

VI. Answer the following questions in the negative in complete sentences in French, using subject pronouns in your answers. In answer (a) use **Non**. In answer (b) use **non plus** (either).

Models: **(a) Est-ce que vous finissez la leçon?** (Are you finishing the lesson?)

You write: **(a) Non, je ne finis pas la leçon.** (No, I am not finishing the lesson.)

(b) Et Charles? (And Charles?)

You write: **(b) Il ne finit pas la leçon non plus.** (He isn't finishing the lesson either.)

1. (a) Est-ce qu'Henri désobéit? _____

   (b) Et vous? _____

2. (a) Est-ce que tu finis la leçon? _____

   (b) Et Pierre? _____

3. (a) Est-ce que Monsieur Paquet choisit une auto? _____

   (b) Et Madame Paquet? _____

4. (a) Est-ce que nous bâtissons une maison? _____

   (b) Et Monsieur et Madame Banluc? _____

5. (a) Est-ce que vous rougissez? _____

   (b) Et les jeunes filles? _____

VII. Choose the correct verb form and write it with its subject on the blank line.

1. Je (finissons, finis, finissez) la leçon. _____

2. Tu (saisis, saisit, saisissons) la balle. _____

3. Il (accomplis, accomplit, accomplissez) les devoirs. _____

4. Elle (bâtit, bâtissons, bâtissent) une maison. _____

5. Nous (choisissons, choisissez, choisissent) un dessert. _____

6. Vous (punis, punit, punissez) le chien. _____

7. Ils (rougit, rougissez, rougissent) facilement. _____

8. Elles (désobéissent, désobéit, désobéissez) à leurs parents. _____

9. Je (remplis, remplit, remplissons) le vase. _____

10. Vous (finis, finissons, finissez) les devoirs. _____

VIII. Word Search. Can you find these verb forms with their subject pronouns *in French* in this puzzle? Circle them.

1. We finish.
2. You *(polite)* succeed.
3. I choose.
4. You *(familiar)* obey.
5. He seizes.
6. I finish.
7. She punishes.
8. He blesses.
9. I build.

A	E	I	O	J	E	C	H	O	I	S	I	S	J
E	A	E	L	L	E	P	U	N	I	T	A	E	O
I	L	B	É	N	I	T	A	E	O	U	I	F	B
V	O	U	S	R	É	U	S	S	I	S	S	E	Z
F	O	T	N	Z	Z	S	S	I	L	F	I	N	I
N	O	U	S	F	I	N	I	S	S	O	N	S	E
J	E	O	E	L	J	E	L	L	A	N	O	U	S
E	L	B	S	J	E	B	Â	T	I	S	F	I	N
I	S	É	S	S	F	O	N	S	S	I	T	S	T
V	O	I	U	R	I	U	E	S	I	S	E	Z	S
J	E	S	F	O	N	L	M	O	T	N	L	L	E
I	L	C	H	O	I	M	N	A	E	I	U	A	N
B	N	E	I	T	S	N	O	U	S	P	A	L	R

IX. Oral Proficiency. Respond orally in French to the situations described. (Later, you may write your responses for intensive practice.)

A. Situation: You are in French class. All the students have finished an exercise in writing except you. The teacher approaches and asks you why you have not finished the assignment: *Pourquoi ne finis-tu pas le devoir?* In two sentences tell your teacher why. You may use your own words, those in this lesson, or the following: *finir, accomplir, choisir, la leçon, l'exercice, parce que, difficile.*

B. Situation: You and a friend are in the school cafeteria talking about homework. In three sentences tell your friend about an assignment one of your teachers gave your class. Explain why the assignment was given. You may use your own words, those in this lesson, or the following: *punir, choisir, les exercices, faciles, difficiles, parce que.*

Review Test: Work Units 1–5

I. Write the appropriate definite article in front of each noun.

1. _____ jeune fille

2. _____ garçon

3. _____ arbre

4. _____ livres

5. _____ homme

6. _____ parapluies

II. Write the appropriate indefinite article in front of each noun.

1. _____ soeur

2. _____ frère

3. _____ amie

4. _____ porte

5. _____ café

6. _____ orange

III. Change the following nouns in the singular to the plural.
Example: le garçon   <u>les garçons</u>

1. la mère _____

2. le journal _____

3. la voix _____

4. le monsieur _____

5. l'oeil _____

6. le fils _____

IV. Change the following nouns to the singular or to the plural, depending on which is given.

1. les tables _____

2. l'eau _____

3. les nez _____

4. le genou _____

5. les journaux _____

6. le pays _____

V. Fill in the missing words in French. Choose either au, aux, à l', or à la.

1. _____ restaurant

2. _____ hôtel

3. _____ bibliothèque

4. _____ magasins

5. _____ école

6. _____ maison

VI. Match the following.

1. les stylos des élèves   _____ the girl's dresses

2. la jupe de la jeune fille   _____ the pupils' pens

3. les chiens des garçons   _____ the pupil's pencil

4. les robes de la jeune fille   _____ the boys' dogs

5. le crayon de l'élève   _____ the girl's skirt

VII. Write the French for the following sentences.

1. I have some coffee. _____   3. I don't have any coffee. _____

2. I have some meat. _____   4. I don't have any candies. _____

VIII. Write the missing letters in the following words.

1. J_____ V A I_____ A L'E_____O_____E L_____S MAT_____N_____.

2. JANINE V_____ENT D_____ FRA_____C_____.

3. M_____N_____IEU_____ ARMSTRONG P_____RLE A_____GLA_____S.

IX. Change the following statements into questions using **Est-ce que.**
Example: Janine danse. <u>Est-ce que Janine danse?</u>_____

1. Vous parlez français. _____

2. Jacqueline regarde la télévision. _____

3. Ils étudient la leçon. _____

X. Change the following statements into questions using the inverted form.
Example: Pierre danse. <u>Pierre danse-t-il?</u>_____

1. Odette et Yvette chantent bien. _____

2. Robert et Pierre jouent à la balle. _____

3. Vous regardez trop de télévision. _____

XI. Choose the correct verb form and write it with its subject.
Example: Elle (parlent, parle, parlez) français. <u>Elle parle français.</u>

1. J' (aimes, aimons, aime) la glace au chocolat. _____

2. Vous (donner, donnez, donne) des fleurs à la dame. _____

3. Je (fermons, fermez, ferme) la porte. _____

4. Michelle (choisis, choisit, choisissez) une jolie robe. _____

5. Vous (finissez, finis, finissent) les devoirs. _____

6. Nous (bâtis, bâtissons, bâtissent) une maison. _____

Pour combien vendez-vous ce vase, madame?

Present Indicative Tense of Regular Verbs Ending in — *re*

*Have you ever bought anything at a
flea market? Sometimes you can pick up
something interesting.*

Le vase extraordinaire

Aujourd'hui Janine est au marché aux puces avec son amie Monique. Elles passent la journée au marché parce que c'est un endroit très intéressant.

— Oh, Monique! Regarde! Un joli vase. Il est superbe! s'exclame Janine.

— Pour combien vendez-vous ce vase, madame? demande Monique.

— Je vends ce vase pour dix francs, mademoiselle, répond la marchande. Il est vraiment très joli.

— Oui, il a une beauté très rare! dit Janine. Mais je n'ai pas dix francs sur moi. J'ai deux francs. Monique, as-tu huit francs?

— Non, Janine, je n'ai pas huit francs, répond Monique.

— Je vais retourner à la maison pour demander à ma mère les huit francs. Je veux avoir ce vase. Il est extraordinaire, dit Janine à la femme. Viens, Monique!

Après une heure, Janine et Monique reviennent avec l'argent. Quand elles arrivent à la boutique où la femme vend le vase, Janine s'exclame:

— Oh! Le vase n'est pas ici! Où est le vase extraordinaire, madame? Le vase rare! Le joli vase!

— Je regrette, mademoiselle, mais il est vendu, répond la femme.

Janine et Monique vont partir et après un moment, la femme ajoute:

— Attendez! Attendez! Attendez, mesdemoiselles! J'ai beaucoup de vases exactement comme l'autre.

La marchande ouvre une grande boîte et elle met sur la table quinze vases exactement comme l'autre.

— Choisissez, mademoiselle! dit la femme.

Vocabulaire

ai, as *v. forms of* **avoir** (to have); **j'ai** I have; **je n'ai pas** I don't have; **as-tu?** do you have?

ajoute *v. form of* **ajouter** (to add); **la femme ajoute** the woman adds

l'argent *n. m.,* money

arrivent *v. form of* **arriver** (to arrive); **elles arrivent** they arrive

attendez v. form of **attendre** (to wait); **attendez!** wait!

aujourd'hui adv., today

autre adj., pron. other; **l'autre** the other one

la boîte n., the box

la boutique n., the shop

c'est it's, it is

choisissez v. form of **choisir** (to choose); **choisissez!** choose!

combien adv., how much

comme adv., like, as

dix adj., ten

l'endroit n. m., the place

exactement adv., exactly

extraordinaire adj., extraordinary, unusual

huit adj., eight

ici adv., here

intéressant adj., interesting

joli m., **jolie** f., adj., pretty

la journée n., the day

le marchand n., **la**

marchande n., the merchant, shopkeeper

le marché n., the market; **au marché aux puces** at the flea market

met v. form of **mettre** (to put); **elle met** she puts

ouvre v. form of **ouvrir** (to open); **elle ouvre** she opens

partir v., to leave

passent v. form of **passer** (to spend time); **elles passent** they are spending

la puce n., the flea

quinze adj., fifteen

rare adj., rare

regarde v. form of **regarder** (to look, to look at); **regarde!** look!

répond v. form of **répondre** (to reply, to answer); **répond la marchande** answers the shopkeeper

retourner v., to return, to go back

reviennent v. form of **revenir** (to return, to come back); **elles reviennent** they return

vais v. form of **aller** (to go); **je vais** I'm going

le vase n., the vase

vend, vendez, vends, vendu v. forms of **vendre** (to sell); **la femme vend** the woman is selling; **vendez-vous?** are you selling?; **je vends** I am selling; **vendu** sold

veux v. form of **vouloir** (to want); **je veux** I want

viens v. form of **venir** (to come); **viens!** come!

vont v. form of **aller** (to go); **elles vont** they are going

vraiment adv., really

Exercises

Review the story and vocabulary before starting these exercises.

I. Oui ou Non?

1. Aujourd'hui Janine est au marché aux puces. _____

2. La marchande vend le vase pour quinze francs. _____

3. Monique n'a pas huit francs. _____

4. Janine et Monique retournent à la maison. _____

5. Quand elles retournent à la boutique avec l'argent, le vase est vendu. _____

II. In French, complete the dialogue between Janine and the merchant. Refer to the dialogue in this unit if you have to.

1. Janine: Pour combien _____-vous ce vase, madame?

2. La Marchande: Je _____ ce vase pour _____ francs, mademoiselle.

3. Janine: Oh! Il est _____ très rare!

4. La Marchande: Oui, et il est très _____ aussi.

III. The words in the following boxes are scrambled. Unscramble them to find a meaningful sentence. Write the sentences on the lines provided.

Model:

combien	pour	madame?
vase	ce	vendez-vous

You write: *Pour combien vendez-vous ce vase, madame?*

1.

vends	vase	pour
dix francs	ce	je

You write: _____

2.

marchande	de	la
vend	beaucoup	vases

You write: _____

3.

moment	un	après
ajoute	femme	la

You write: _____

Structures de la Langue

A. Introduction

Go back to work unit four and read again the material presented on page 61. Here are the personal endings for verbs of the third conjugation (**-re**).

THIRD CONJUGATION

	-re
Infinitive →	**vendre** *to sell*
	I sell, *or* I do sell, *or* I am selling; you sell, *etc.*
Required subject pronouns SINGULAR 1. **je** I	ven**ds**
2. **tu** you *(familiar only)*	ven**ds**
3. **il** he *or* it **elle** she *or* it	vend
PLURAL 1. **nous** we	vend**ons**
2. **vous** you	vend**ez**
3. **ils** **elles** they	vend**ent**

Rules and observations:

1. To form the present tense of a regular verb ending in **-re**, drop the **-re**. What remains is called the *stem*. Add to the stem the personal endings shown in the above chart. They are: **-s, -s, -, -ons, -ez, -ent**.

2. Note that for an **-re** verb there is normally no ending to add in the third person singular. The last letter of the stem is often **d**, so the verb form remains the same as the stem, for example, **il** or **elle vend**. However, there are some **-re** verbs whose last letter in the stem is not **d**. In that case, you have to add **t**:

interrompre *to interrupt*	**rompre** *to break*
il, elle interromp**t**	il, elle romp**t**

3.   Note that, in the plural, the personal endings for an **-re** verb are the same as those for an **-er** verb. Go back to work unit four (page 59) and compare those endings with these in the plural.

4.   Finally, note also that *do, am, are, does, is* (which are used in English in the present tense) *are not translated* into French. Therefore, **je vends** can mean *I sell*, or *I do sell*, or *I am selling*. The same applies to the rest of the persons, for example, *you sell*, or *you do sell*, or *you are selling, etc.*

B.   The subject pronouns

Go back to work unit four and read again the material presented on page 60.

C.   Some common regular verbs of the third conjugation

attendre to wait (for); **défendre** to defend, to forbid; **descendre** to go (come) down, to descend; **entendre** to hear; **interrompre** to interrupt; **perdre** to lose; **rendre** to give back, to return; **répondre (à)** to answer, to reply; **rompre** to break.

Exercises

Review the preceding material before starting these exercises.

I.   Substitute only one appropriate subject pronoun for the word or words in italics and rewrite the entire sentence in French.

Model: *La dame* répond au téléphone.   You write: Elle répond au téléphone.
(The lady is answering the phone.)

1.   *Le soldat* défend sa patrie. _____

2.   *La marchande* vend des vases. _____

3.   *Anne et Georges* entendent la musique. _____

4.   *L'homme et la femme* vendent leur maison. _____

5.   *Le grand chien* rompt la petite barrière. _____

85

II. Use the subject pronoun in parentheses to take the place of the subject pronoun in italics. Rewrite each sentence in French, making the required changes in the verb forms.

      Model: *Nous* **vendons des livres.**   **(Je)** You write: **Je vends des livres.**
               (We are selling books.)

1. (Elle) _____   4. (Ils) _____

2. (Tu) _____   5. (Vous) _____

3. (Vous et moi) _____   6. (Elles) _____

III. Use the subject pronoun in parentheses to take the place of the subject pronoun in italics. Rewrite each sentence in French, making the required changes in the verb forms. Keep them all in the negative.

      Model: *Vous* **ne vendez pas la**   **(Elle)** You write: **Elle ne vend pas la**
                 voiture. (You are not   **voiture.**
                 selling the car.)

1. (Nous) _____   4. (Il) _____

2. (Je) _____   5. (Elles) _____

3. (Tu) _____   6. (Ils) _____

IV. Answer the following questions in the affirmative in complete French sentences, using subject pronouns in your answers. In answer (a) use **oui**. In answer (b) use **aussi** (also). Make the required changes in the verb forms.

      Models: **(a) La dame répond-elle**   You write: **(a) Oui, elle répond au**
                   au téléphone?   **téléphone.**
                   (Is the lady answering
                   the phone?)

                   (b) Et les dames?   You write: **(b) Elles répondent au**
                   (And the ladies?)   **téléphone aussi.**

1. (a) Pierre répond-il à la lettre? _____

   (b) Et vous? _____

2. (a) Monsieur Coty vend-il la maison? _____

   (b) Et Monsieur Dupont? _____

3. (a) Le soldat défend-il la patrie? _____

   (b) Et vous? _____

4. (a) Le vase est-il joli? _____

(b) Et le parapluie? _____

5. (a) Janine est-elle au marché aux puces? _____

    (b) Et Monique? _____

V. Change the following affirmative statements to interrogative sentences. Use the inverted form only.

    Model: Pierre danse tous les soirs.   **You write: Pierre danse-t-il tous les**
    (Pierre dances every evening.)   **soirs?**

1. Janine étudie dans la bibliothèque. _____

2. Elle cherche le chapeau. _____

3. Il finit la leçon. _____

4. Elle choisit une jolie robe. _____

5. Nous répondons à la lettre. _____

6. Ils vendent la maison. _____

VI. Change to the plural or singular, according to what is given.

    Models: Il vend.   **You write: Ils vendent.**

        Elles chantent.   **Elle chante.**

1. Elle attend. _____   4. Il écoute. _____

2. Je vends. _____   5. Tu finis. _____

3. Nous dansons. _____   6. Ils répondent. _____

VII. Change the following affirmative statements to interrogative sentences. Use the **est-ce que** form only.

    Model: Pierre étudie.   **You write: Est-ce que Pierre étudie?**

1. Elle finit le livre. _____

2. Monsieur Berty vend la voiture. _____

3. Elle choisit un joli chapeau. _____

4. Il défend la patrie. _____

5. Hélène ouvre la boîte. _____

VIII. Write the French word opposite each picture. Use the definite article with the word. Write one letter in each box.

IX. Complete each verb form in the present indicative by writing the correct letter or letters on the blank lines.

1. J'aim_____ le français.

2. Vous chant_____ bien.

3. Janine étudi_____ beaucoup.

4. Je chois_____ un chapeau.

5. Ils attend_____ l'autobus.

6. Je vend_____ l'automobile.

7. Vous chois_____ une leçon facile.

8. Nous fin_____ les devoirs.

X. Give the three English translations for each of the following French verb forms in the present indicative.

1. Je danse. _____ _____ _____

2. Vous finissez. _____ _____ _____

3. Nous vendons. _____ _____ _____

XI.   Word Search.   Can you find these verb forms with their subject pronouns *in French* in this puzzle? Circle them.

1.   He sells.

2.   She waits.

3.   We answer.

4.   They *(m.)* lose.

5.   You *(familiar)* forbid.

6.   They *(f.)* lose.

7.   I give back.

8.   You answer.

N	N	O	I	L	V	E	N	D	O	U	I	N
I	L	S	P	E	R	D	E	N	T	I	C	I
E	L	L	E	S	I	M	P	O	R	T	A	N
L	U	I	E	L	L	E	A	T	T	E	N	D
E	L	L	E	S	P	E	R	D	E	N	T	O
E	J	E	R	E	N	D	S	A	L	O	R	S
V	O	S	S	E	T	M	O	I	S	O	N	T
N	O	U	S	R	É	P	O	N	D	O	N	S
U	E	A	I	P	N	A	C	E	G	L	I	L
A	E	I	T	U	D	É	F	E	N	D	S	T
V	O	U	S	R	E	P	O	N	D	E	Z	U

XII.   Oral Proficiency. Respond orally in French to the situation described. (Later, you may write your responses for intensive practice.)

Situation: There is a county fair in the suburbs of the city where you live. You want to go there but your parents don't like the idea. In four sentences, persuade them to let you go. You may use your own words, those in this lesson, or the following: *aller, vendre, attendre, acheter, beaucoup de choses* (many things), *entendre, perdre; j'aimerais aller à la foire* (I would like to go to the fair).

Pierre aime les sports. Son sport favori est le football.

Formation and Use of Reflexive Verbs in the Present Indicative

*Are you as eager as Pierre to play in a
soccer game?*

Surprise!   Surprise!

Pierre aime les sports. Son sport favori est le football. Il veut être toujours en forme parce qu'il est gardien de but dans son équipe à l'école. Il veut être toujours prêt à bien jouer. Il est au régime. Il mange seulement des aliments qui sont bons pour la santé. Pendant la saison de football, il évite les glaces, les pommes frites, et toute la pâtisserie. C'est un brave garçon.

Il se couche de bonne heure, il se lève avec le soleil, il se lave soigneusement, il s'habille vite, et il prend le petit déjeuner.

Il annonce à ses parents:

— C'est le grand match de football aujourd'hui! C'est après les classes.

Pierre dit à Janine:

— Janine, tu vas jouer dans l'équipe avec les garçons et les jeunes filles aussi, n'est-ce pas?

— Oui, répond Janine. Les jeunes filles aiment les sports aussi. Je vais être au stade pour jouer avec les garçons et les jeunes filles cet après-midi.

Pierre se dépêche pour arriver tôt dans la grande cour de l'école. Il court un kilomètre sur la piste avant d'entrer dans l'école.

Pour Pierre, le football est tout. Il se rappelle les bons conseils de son entraîneur de football:

— Attention au filet, Pierre! Attention au filet! Garde le but! Le but!

Pierre joue extrêmement bien. C'est un très bon garçon, bon étudiant, bon joueur. Ses camarades aiment beaucoup Pierre.

Après la dernière classe, Pierre va au gymnase. Il se prépare pour le grand match. Il met sa tenue d'exercice. Il fait de la gymnastique avant de commencer le match.

Pierre fait de la gymnastique pendant quelques heures. Maintenant il est prêt pour le grand match!

Pierre court à toute vitesse au stade. Quand il arrive au stade, il voit que tout le monde part.

— Pierre! Pourquoi es-tu en retard? demande l'entraîneur.

Pierre ne répond pas. Il est stupéfié.

— Le match est terminé, dit l'entraîneur.

— Le match est terminé?! s'exclame Pierre.

— Oui, terminé, fini. Surprise! Surprise!

STRUCTURES AND VERBS

Vocabulaire

l'aliment *n. m.*, food
annoncer *v.*, to announce
l'après-midi *n.m.*, the afternoon
attention à watch out for
brave *adj., m. f.*, good, fine, honest (when **brave** follows a noun, it means *brave;* **une femme brave, un homme brave** a brave woman, a brave man)
le but *n.*, the goal; **gardien de but** goalie
c'est . . . it's (*sometimes* he's . . . (*or*) she's . . .)
le conseil *n.*, advice
se coucher *refl. v.*, to go to bed
la cour *n.*, the yard
court *v. form of* **courir** (to run); **Pierre court** Pierre runs
se dépêcher *refl. v.*, to hurry
dernier *m.*, **dernière** *f., adj.*, last
l'entraîneur *n. m.*, the coach, sports instructor
l'équipe *n. f.*, the team
éviter *v.*, to avoid
fais, fait *v. forms of* **faire** (to do, to make); **il fait de la gymnastique** he does gymnastics

le filet *n.*, the net
le football *n.*, soccer (in the U.S.A.)
la forme *n.*, the shape, the form; **en forme** in good shape
garder *v.*, to guard; **gardien de but** goalie
le gymnase *n.*, the gymnasium; **la gymnastique** *n.*, gymnastics
s'habiller *refl. v.*, to get dressed
jouer *v.*, to play; **le joueur** *m.*, **la joueuse** *f., n.*, the player
le kilomètre *n.*, kilometer (about 0.62 miles)
se laver *refl. v.*, to wash oneself
se lever *refl. v.*, to get up
le match *n.*, the game, the match (sport)
mettre *v.*, to put, to put on (wear); **il met** he puts on
n'est-ce pas? isn't it so? aren't you?
le petit déjeuner *n.*, breakfast
la piste *n.*, the track
les pommes frites *n. f.*, fried potatoes, French fries
prendre *v.*, to take; **prendre**

le petit déjeuner to have breakfast
se préparer *refl. v.*, to prepare oneself, to get ready
prêt *m.*, **prête** *f., adj.*, ready, prepared
que *interrog. pron.*, what; *as a conj.*, that
quel *adj. m. s.*, what (which); **quel sport?** what (which) sport?
se rappeler *refl. v.*, to remember, to recall
le régime *n.*, diet; **au régime** on a diet
se *refl. pron.*, himself, herself, oneself, itself, themselves
soigneusement *adv.*, carefully
le soleil *n.*, the sun
son *poss. adj., m. sing.*, **ses** *pl.*, his
le stade *n.*, the stadium
tard *adv.*, late
la tenue d'exercice gym suit
tôt *adv.*, early
toujours *adv.*, always
veut *v. form of* **vouloir** (to want); **il veut** he wants
la vitesse *n.*, speed; **à toute vitesse** very fast
voit *v. form of* **voir** (to see); **il voit** he sees

Exercises

Review the story and vocabulary before starting these exercises.

I. Answer the following questions in French in complete sentences. They are based on the story, "Surprise! Surprise!"

1. Quel est le sport favori de Pierre? _____

2. Pourquoi veut-il être toujours en forme? _____

3. Quels aliments mange-t-il? _____

4. Se lève-t-il tôt ou tard? _____

92   5. Est-ce que Janine va jouer dans le match aussi? _____

II.   Answer the following questions in French in complete sentences. They are personal questions and require answers of your own.

1.   Aimez-vous les sports? _____

2.   Est-ce que vous vous couchez tôt ou tard? _____

3.   Vous dépêchez-vous pour arriver à l'école? _____

4.   Est-ce que vous vous lavez soigneusement? _____

5.   Vous habillez-vous vite? _____

III.   Oui ou Non?

1.   Le sport favori de Pierre est le tennis.   _____

2.   Pierre est gardien de but.   _____

3.   Janine aime les sports aussi.   _____

4.   Pierre se lève tard.   _____

5.   Janine va au stade pour jouer avec les garçons et les jeunes filles.   _____

IV.   Un acrostiche.   Complete the French words in the squares across.

1.   slowly
2.   to avoid
3.   to go to bed
4.   to get up
5.   for
6.   or
7.   to answer
8.   late
9.   to wash oneself

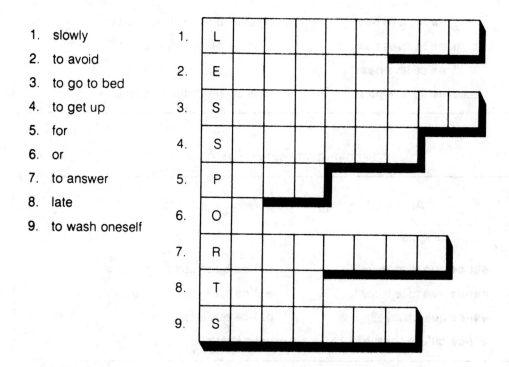

93

Structures de la Langue

A. Formation and use of reflexive verbs in the present indicative; all four forms: Affirmative, Negative, Interrogative, Negative-Interrogative

se laver   *to wash oneself*

AFFIRMATIVE

I wash myself, I am washing myself, I do wash myself, *etc.*

Singular	Plural
je **me lave**	nous **nous lavons**
tu **te laves**	vous **vous lavez**
il **se lave**	ils **se lavent**
elle **se lave**	elles **se lavent**

NEGATIVE

I am not washing myself, I do not wash myself, *etc.*

Singular	Plural
je **ne** me lave **pas**	nous **ne** nous lavons **pas**
tu **ne** te laves **pas**	vous **ne** vous lavez **pas**
il **ne** se lave **pas**	ils **ne** se lavent **pas**
elle **ne** se lave **pas**	elles **ne** se lavent **pas**

INTERROGATIVE WITH **est-ce que** FORM

Am I washing myself? Do I wash myself? *etc.*

Singular	Plural
est-ce que je me lave?	**est-ce que** nous nous lavons?
est-ce que tu te laves?	**est-ce que** vous vous lavez?
est-ce qu'il se lave?	**est-ce qu'**ils se lavent?
est-ce qu'elle se lave?	**est-ce qu'**elles se lavent?

INTERROGATIVE WITH *INVERTED FORM*

Am I washing myself? Do I wash myself? *etc.*

Singular	Plural
***est-ce que** je me lave?*	**nous** lavons-nous?
te laves-tu?	**vous** lavez-vous?
se lave-t-il?	**se** lavent-ils?
se lave-t-elle?	**se** lavent-elles?

*The inverted form is ordinarily used in the first person singular *only* with certain verbs.

Observe that the subject pronoun shifts in the interrogative when using the inverted form; it is joined to the verb with a hyphen:

Affirmative:	Tu te laves.	Nous nous lavons.
Interrogative:	Te laves-tu?	Nous lavons-nous?

Est-ce que je ne me lave pas?

NEGATIVE-INTERROGATIVE WITH **est-ce que** FORM

Am I not washing myself? Don't I wash myself? *etc.*

Singular	Plural
est-ce que je **ne** me lave **pas**?	**est-ce que** nous **ne** nous lavons **pas**?
est-ce que tu **ne** te laves **pas**?	**est-ce que** vous **ne** vous lavez **pas**?
est-ce qu'il **ne** se lave **pas**?	**est-ce qu'**ils **ne** se lavent **pas**?
est-ce qu'elle **ne** se lave **pas**?	**est-ce qu'**elles **ne** se lavent **pas**?

NEGATIVE INTERROGATIVE WITH *INVERTED FORM*

Am I not washing myself? Don't I wash myself? *etc.*

Singular	Plural
*****est-ce que** je **ne** me lave **pas**?	**ne** nous lavons-nous **pas**?
ne te laves-tu **pas**?	**ne** vous lavez-vous **pas**?
ne se lave-t-il **pas**?	**ne** se lavent-ils **pas**?
ne se lave-t-elle **pas**?	**ne** se lavent-elles **pas**?

*****The inverted form is ordinarily used in the first person singular *only* with certain verbs.

Observe that the subject pronoun shifts in the negative-interrogative when using the inverted form; it is joined to the verb with a hyphen:

Negative:	Tu ne te laves pas.	Nous ne nous lavons pas.
Negative-Interrogative:	Ne te laves-tu pas?	Ne nous lavons-nous pas?

Rules and observations:

1. To form the present tense of a reflexive verb in a simple affirmative sentence, put the reflexive pronoun in front of the verb. Study the first box (Affirmative).

2. A reflexive verb expresses an action that is turned back upon the subject; for example, I wash *myself* (je **me** lave). The reflexive pronoun in the English sentence is *myself*; in the French sentence it is **me**.

3. The reflexive pronouns in French are: **me, te, se, nous**, and **vous**.

4. The reflexive pronouns in English are: **myself, yourself, herself, himself, itself, ourselves, yourselves**, and **themselves**.

REFLEXIVE PRONOUNS

	Singular		Plural
me	myself	**nous**	ourselves
te	yourself	**vous**	yourselves (yourself)
se	himself, herself, itself	**se**	themselves

5. You must be careful to use the appropriate reflexive pronoun, the one that matches the subject pronoun. You already know the subject pronouns, but here they are again, beside the reflexive pronouns.

	Singular		Plural
1.	**je me ...**	1.	**nous nous ...**
2.	**tu te ...**	2.	**vous vous ...**
3.	**il se ...**	3.	**ils se ...**
	elle se ...		**elles se ...**

6. Note that in the third person singular and third person plural the reflexive pronoun is the same: **se** (himself, herself, itself, themselves).

7. Note that in the first person plural, the reflexive pronoun is the same as the subject pronoun: **nous** (ourselves).

8. Note that in the second person plural, the reflexive pronoun is the same as the subject pronoun: **vous** (yourself, yourselves).

9. Most of the time, a verb that is reflexive in French is also reflexive in English. One example of a verb that is not reflexive in English but is in French:

se dépêcher   to hurry

je me dépêche   I hurry, *or* I do hurry, *or* I am hurrying

10. Note the position of the reflexive pronouns and the **ne** and **pas** in the boxes above.

11. The reflexive pronouns **me**, **te**, and **se** become **m'**, **t'**, and **s'** when they are in front of a verb beginning with a vowel or silent *h*, as in the following example:

s'appeler   to be called, named

je **m'**appelle Marie.	My name is Mary.
tu **t'**appelles Hélène.	Your name is Helen.
il **s'**appelle Henri.	His name is Henry.
elle **s'**appelle Jeanne.	Her name is Jeanne.

97

B. Formation of some irregular reflexive verbs

s'asseoir *to sit down*	
je **m'assieds**	nous **nous asseyons**
tu **t'assieds**	vous **vous asseyez**
il **s'assied**	ils **s'asseyent**
elle **s'assied**	elles **s'asseyent**

s'endormir *to fall asleep*	
je **m'endors**	nous **nous endormons**
tu **t'endors**	vous **vous endormez**
il **s'endort**	ils **s'endorment**
elle **s'endort**	elles **s'endorment**

se servir *to use*	
je **me sers**	nous **nous servons**
tu **te sers**	vous **vous servez**
il **se sert**	ils **se servent**
elle **se sert**	elles **se servent**

se souvenir *to remember*	
je **me souviens**	nous **nous souvenons**
tu **te souviens**	vous **vous souvenez**
il **se souvient**	ils **se souviennent**
elle **se souvient**	elles **se souviennent**

C. Some other reflexive verbs

s'amuser to enjoy oneself, to have a good time; **se coucher** to go to bed, to lie down; **s'habiller** to get dressed, to dress oneself; **se lever** to get up; **se rappeler** to remember, to recall; **se regarder** to look at oneself; **se reposer** to rest; **se trouver** to be situated, to be located

Exercises

Review the preceding material before starting these exercises.

I. Fill in the missing reflexive pronouns in French.

1. Je _____ lave.

2. Je ne _____ dépêche pas.

3. Tu _____ amuses.

4. Il _____ couche.

5. Elle _____ habille.

6. Nous _____ levons.

7. Vous _____ rappelez.

8. Ils _____ amusent.

9. Elles _____ reposent.

10. Il _____ regarde.

II. Match the following.

1. Je me dépêche.   _____ She is falling asleep.
2. Je m'appelle Yves.   _____ You are having a good time here.
3. Vous vous couchez de bonne heure.   _____ Are you washing yourself?
4. Tu t'amuses ici.   _____ Aren't I washing myself?
5. Il s'habille.   _____ My name is Yves.
6. Est-ce que je ne me lave pas?   _____ I sit down.
7. Je m'assieds.   _____ I hurry.
8. Elle s'endort.   _____ You go to bed early.
9. Te laves-tu?   _____ He is getting dressed.
10. Vous ne vous lavez pas.   _____ You don't wash yourself.

III. Word Search. Can you find the following five verb forms in French with their subject pronouns in this puzzle?

1. I am getting dressed.
2. You are washing yourself.
3. He is hurrying.
4. They (m.) are enjoying themselves.
5. I am resting.

D	E	I	P	T	E	C	H	E	J
J	E	L	A	U	L	A	V	R	E
D	I	S	D	T	E	J	A	U	M
I	L	S	U	E	L	O	I	N	E
A	S	A	I	L	M	A	N	G	R
J	E	M	H	A	B	I	L	L	E
I	D	U	O	V	E	E	O	A	P
I	É	S	S	E	M	E	T	S	O
O	P	E	I	S	S	E	L	V	S
J	Ê	N	A	P	P	E	L	E	E
U	C	T	I	L	S	E	M	E	L
A	H	J	E	I	U	O	I	L	T
J	E	M	E	R	E	G	A	R	E

IV. Fill in the missing subject pronouns in French.

1. _____ m'amuse.

2. _____ t'habilles.

3. _____ vous regardez.

4. _____ (or) _____ se servent.

5. _____ (or) _____ se souvient.

6. _____ nous couchons.

7. _____ vous levez.

8. _____ (or) _____ s'assied.

9. _____ (or) _____ se reposent.

10. _____ m'endors.

V. Answer the following questions in the affirmative in French.

Model: **Vous lavez-vous?**
(Do you wash yourself?)

You write: **Oui, je me lave.**
(Yes, I wash myself.)

1. Vous amusez-vous? _____

2. Vous couchez-vous? _____

3. Vous reposez-vous? _____

4. Vous habillez-vous? _____

5. Vous asseyez-vous? _____

VI. Answer the following questions in the negative in French.

Model: **Vous lavez-vous tous les jours?**
(Do you wash yourself every day?)

You write: **Non, je ne me lave pas tous les jours.**

1. Vous amusez-vous ici? _____

2. Vous couchez-vous de bonne heure tous les soirs? _____

_____

3. Vous habillez-vous vite tous les matins? _____

_____

4. Vous appelez-vous Jean-Jacques? _____

5. Vous asseyez-vous ici? _____ _____

VII. Change each sentence by replacing the verb in italics with the proper form of the verb in parentheses. Keep the same subject. Rewrite the entire sentence in French.

> **Model:**   **Se dépêche-t-il tous les**   **You write:**   **S'habille-t-il tous les matins?**
> **matins?   (s'habiller)**

1. *Se lave*-t-il tous les soirs? (se dépêcher) _____

2. Je *m'assieds* sur cette chaise. (s'endormir) _____

3. Nous *nous couchons* de bonne heure. (se lever) _____

4. Il *s'habille* vite. (se laver) _____

5. Je *me lave* tous les jours. (s'amuser) _____

VIII. The words in the following boxes are scrambled. Unscramble them to find a meaningful sentence. Write the complete sentences on the lines provided on the next page.

Model:

nous	café	maintenant
servons	du	nous

You write: ___ **Nous nous servons du café maintenant.** ___

1.
m'	ma	habille
dans	je	chambre

4.
me	heure	bonne
couche	je	de

2.
ils	samedis	théâtre
au	tous les	s'amusent

5.
dépêchons	pour	à l'école
nous	aller	nous

3.
tu	reposes	te
dîner	après	le

6.
je	tous	matins
les	lave	me

1. _____

2. _____

3. _____

101

4. _____

5. _____

6. _____

IX. Change the following statements into questions. Use the **est-ce que** form only.

Model: **Elle s'appelle Hélène.**   You write: **Est-ce qu'elle s'appelle Hélène?**
(Her name is Helen.)

1. Robert s'amuse. _____

2. Vous vous endormez vite. _____

3. Ils se couchent tard. _____

4. Henri est absent aujourd'hui. _____

5. Alice se dépêche pour aller à l'école. _____

X. Change the following statements into questions. Use the inverted form only.

Model: **Il se lave avant de manger.**   You write: **Se lave-t-il avant de manger?**
(He washes himself before   (Does he wash himself before
eating.)   eating?)

1. Elle se repose après dîner. _____

2. Vous vous levez très tard le matin. _____

3. Elle s'assied devant la porte. _____

4. Nous nous dépêchons. _____

5. Ils se couchent tard. _____

XI. Change the following statements into negative-interrogative sentences. Use the **est-ce que** form or the inverted form.

Model: **Pierre se lève avec le**   You write: **Pierre ne se lève-t-il pas avec**
soleil. (Pierre gets up   **le soleil?**
with the sun.)   Or: **Est-ce que Pierre ne se lève pas**
                                                         avec le soleil?

1. Pierre se couche de bonne heure. _____

2. Il se lave soigneusement. _____

3. Il s'habille vite. _____

4. Il se dépêche. _____

5. Il se prépare à jouer au football. _____

XII. **Choose the correct form and write it on the blank line. Write the verb form with the subject.**

1. Je (me lave, vous lavez, se lavent) tous les matins. _____

2. Vous (vous amusez, s'amusent, nous amusons) tout le temps. _____

3. Il (s'endorment, s'endort, vous endormez) vite. _____

4. Elle (s'habille, s'habillent, nous habillons) dans la chambre. _____

5. Nous (me couche, vous couchez, nous couchons) de bonne heure. _____

6. Tu (t'amuses, s'amuse, s'amusent) tous les jours! _____

7. Ils (se sert, se servent, nous servons) du café noir. _____

8. Elles (s'endort, vous endormez, s'endorment) tranquillement. _____

9. Je (s'amuse, m'amuse, nous amusons) tous les soirs au café. _____

10. Madame Paquet (se dépêche, nous dépêchons, vous dépêchez) pour sortir. _____

XIII. **Oral Proficiency.** You have just arrived in Paris by airplane and a representative of the airline is asking you questions. Imagine a conversation between yourself and him.

Le représentant: Bonjour. Est-ce que vous connaissez déjà la France?

1. Vous: _____

Le représentant: Le voyage est agréable?

2. Vous: _____

Le représentant: Pourquoi faites-vous ce voyage en France?

3. Vous: _____

Le représentant: Est-ce que vous voyagez seul?

4. Vous: _____

Le représentant: Est-ce que vous avez des suggestions pour le service?

5. Vous: _____

– Ch! Ch! Filez! Filez! Oh, ces mouches! s'exclame Madame Paquet.

Cardinal and Ordinal Numbers

Have you ever been at a public auction?
Let's see what happens to
Madame Paquet.

Ch! Ch! Filez! Filez!

Madame et Monsieur Paquet quittent la maison pour aller à une vente aux enchères. Madame Paquet aime beaucoup les ventes aux enchères. Elle veut acheter une petite table ronde pour le foyer dans la maison.

Ils arrivent et ils entrent dans la salle des ventes. Ils entendent le commissaire-priseur qui parle à un groupe de personnes:

Le Commissaire-priseur: Mesdames, Messieurs, attention! S'il vous plaît!

(Monsieur et Madame Paquet prennent deux places au cinquième rang près de la porte.)

Le Commissaire-priseur: J'ai ici, mesdames et messieurs, un très, très beau fauteuil. Qui offre cinquante francs?

(Monsieur Paquet parle à sa femme à voix basse: – Tout est si élégant ici. Très élégant.)

(Madame Paquet répond à voix basse: – Oui, mais je n'aime pas les mouches! Et le fauteuil est très laid!

Le Commissaire-priseur: Merci, monsieur! J'ai cinquante francs pour ce beau fauteuil. Qui offre soixante francs? . . . Soixante francs, ce n'est pas beaucoup pour ce beau fauteuil! Qui offre soixante francs?

(Madame Paquet dit à son mari à voix basse: – Les mouches dans cette salle sont terribles!)

Le Commissaire-priseur: Merci, madame! Merci! J'ai soixante francs de la dame au premier rang. Qui offre soixante-dix francs?

(Madame Paquet demande à son mari à voix basse: – François, qui est la dame au premier rang qui offre soixante francs pour ce fauteuil monstrueux? Elle doit être folle!)

(Monsieur Paquet répond: – Je ne sais pas, ma chérie.)

Le Commissaire-priseur: Merci encore, madame! J'ai une offre de soixante-dix francs! Qui offre quatre-vingts? . . . Merci, monsieur! J'ai une offre de quatre-vingts francs. Qui offre quatre-vingt-dix francs? . . . Merci, madame! J'ai quatre-vingt-dix francs de la dame là-bas au troisième rang. Qui offre cent francs? Cent francs? Qui offre cent francs?

(Madame Paquet lève la main pour chasser les mouches de son nez. — Ch! Ch! Filez! Filez! Oh, ces mouches!)

Le Commissaire-priseur: Merci, madame! J'ai cent francs de la dame au cinquième rang près de la porte! J'ai cent francs! C'est la dernière mise! Une fois, deux fois, trois fois. C'est fini! Vendu à la charmante dame avec son mari au cinquième rang près de la porte! Vous pouvez payer à la caisse, s'il vous plaît, madame.

(Tout le monde regarde Madame Paquet.)

Madame Paquet: Qui? Moi?

Vocabulaire

ai *v. form of* **avoir** (to have); **j'ai** I have

assister à *v.*, to be present at, to attend

beau *m.*, **belle** *f.*, *adj.*, beautiful, handsome

la caisse *n.*, the cash box; **à la caisse** at the cashier

Ch! Ch! *interj.*, Shoo! Shoo!

charmant *m.*, **charmante** *f.*, *adj.*, charming

chasser *v.*, to chase away

le commissaire-priseur *n.*, the auctioneer

doit *v. form of* **devoir** (to owe, ought to, must); **elle doit être folle** she must be crazy

l'enchère *n. f.*, the bid, the bidding

le fauteuil *n.*, the armchair

filez! *exclam.*, go away!

fois *n. f.*, time; **une fois** one time, once; **deux fois** two times, twice

folle *f.*, **fou, fol** *m.*, *adj.*, crazy

le franc *n.*, the franc, the French unit of money

là-bas *adv.*, over there

laid *m.*, **laide** *f.*, *adj.*, ugly

lève *v. form of* **lever** (to raise, to lift); **elle lève la main** she raises her hand

la mise *n.*, the bid; **la dernière mise** the last bid

moi *pron.*, me

monstrueux *m.*, **monstrueuse** *f.*, *adj.*, monstrous

la mouche *n.*, the fly

le nez *n.*, the nose

offre *v. form of* **offrir** (to offer); **une offre** an offer; **qui offre?** who offers?

payer *v.*, to pay

la place *n.*, the seat, the place

pouvez *v. form of* **pouvoir** (to be able, can, may); **vous pouvez** you can, you may

prennent *v. form of* **prendre** (to take); **ils prennent** they take

le rang *n.*, the row

rond *m.*, **ronde** *f.*, *adj.*, round

sais *v. form of* **savoir** (to know); **je sais** I know; **je ne sais pas** I don't know

la salle *n.*, the (large) room; **la salle des ventes** the auction sales room

si *adv.*, so; *conj.*, if

s'il vous plaît please

tout *pron.*, everything, all; **tout le monde** everybody

vendu *v. form of* **vendre** (to sell) sold

la vente *n.*, the sale; **la vente aux enchères** the auction

la voix *n.*, the voice; **à voix basse** in a low voice

Exercises

Review the story and vocabulary before starting these exercises.

I. Answer the following questions in complete sentences in French. They are based on the story in this unit.

1. Qui aime beaucoup les ventes aux enchères? _____

2. Qui entre dans la salle des ventes? _____

3. Pourquoi Madame Paquet lève-t-elle la main? _____

4. Qui offre cent francs pour le fauteuil? _____

5. Qui regarde Madame Paquet? _____

II. Answer the following questions in complete sentences in French. They are personal questions and require answers of your own.

1. Aimez-vous les ventes aux enchères? _____

2. Avez-vous un foyer dans votre maison? _____

3. Avez-vous une jolie petite table ronde dans votre maison? _____

   _____

III. **Comment dit-on en français . . .?** (How do you say in French . . .?) Find these statements in the story and write them in French.

1. Mr. Paquet talks to his wife in a low voice. _____

   _____

2. Mrs. Paquet raises her hand to chase away the flies from her nose. _____

   _____

3. I have one hundred francs. _____

IV. The words in the following boxes are scrambled. Unscramble them to find a meaningful sentence. Write the sentence in French on the line provided.

Model:

de	ils	maison
la	bonne heure	quittent

You write: ____**Ils quittent la maison de bonne heure.**____

They leave the house early.

1.

salle	ils	la
dans	des ventes	entrent

3.

est	élégant	dans
cette salle	si	tout

2.

n'aime	je	ce
fauteuil	pas	monstrueux

4.

veux	une	je
ronde	table	jolie petite

1. _____

2. _____

3. _____

4. _____

Structures de la Langue

A. Cardinal Numbers: 1 to 1,000

0 zéro	**50 cinquante**	502 cinq cent deux, *etc.*
1 un, une	51 cinquante et un	**600 six cents**
2 deux	52 cinquante-deux, *etc.*	601 six cent un
3 trois	**60 soixante**	602 six cent deux, *etc.*
4 quatre	61 soixante et un	**700 sept cents**
5 cinq	62 soixante-deux, *etc.*	701 sept cent un
6 six	**70 soixante-dix**	702 sept cent deux, *etc.*
7 sept	71 soixante et **onze**	**800 huit cents**
8 huit	72 soixante-douze, *etc.*	801 huit cent un
9 neuf	**80 quatre-vingts**	802 huit cent deux, *etc.*
10 dix	81 quatre-vingt-un	**900 neuf cents**
11 onze	82 quatre-vingt-deux, *etc.*	901 neuf cent un
12 douze	**90 quatre-vingt-dix**	902 neuf cent deux, *etc.*
13 treize	91 quatre-vingt-onze	**1,000 mille**
14 quatorze	92 quatre-vingt-douze, *etc.*	
15 quinze	**100 cent**	
16 seize	101 cent un	
17 dix-sept	102 cent deux, *etc.*	
18 dix-huit	**200 deux cents**	
19 dix-neuf	201 deux cent un	
20 vingt	202 deux cent deux, *etc.*	
21 vingt et un	**300 trois cents**	
22 vingt-deux, *etc.*	301 trois cent un	
30 trente	302 trois cent deux, *etc.*	
31 trente et un	**400 quatre cents**	
32 trente-deux, *etc.*	401 quatre cent un	
40 quarante	402 quatre cent deux, *etc.*	
41 quarante et un	**500 cinq cents**	
42 quarante-deux, *etc.*	501 cinq cent un	

Rules and observations:

1. Learning numbers in French is easy. It's very much like the way we form numbers in English.

2. From 0 through 16 it's a matter of learning new vocabulary because there is, naturally, a word for each number. Study the simple words in French from 0 to 16 in the above table.

3. Next, notice that numbers 17, 18, 19 are based on 10 plus 7, 8, 9. The word for 10 (**dix**) is joined with a hyphen to the word for 7 (**sept**), 8 (**huit**), and 9 (**neuf**). Examine these three numbers in the above table.

4. The compound numbers actually start with 20. From 20 to 29, just state the word for 20 (**vingt**) and add to that word the cardinal numbers from 1 to 9. This is how we form the numbers in English, also. There is one exception: You are supposed to use the word **et** (*and*) with **un** (*one*). The **et** is omitted after one: vingt-deux, vingt-trois, *etc.* Don't forget to join the added word with a hyphen.

5. Next, it's a matter of learning new vocabulary after 20: **vingt** (20), **trente** (30), **quarante** (40), and so on. To each whole number add **un** through **neuf**. Don't forget to use **et** (*and*) with **un** only and drop it from **deux** to **neuf**. Study these numbers in the table above.

6. The word 100 is also new vocabulary for you: **cent**, with no **un** in front of it for one hundred. It's just plain **cent**.

7. From 200 to 900, it's only a matter of using words you have already learned: 200 is **deux cents**, 300 is **trois cents**, just as in English. Notice the **s** on **cents**. The **s** drops with compound numbers in the hundreds: **deux cent un** (201), **trois cent un** (301), and so on. In brief, there is an **s** on **cents** only in the round whole number in the hundreds: 200 (**deux cents**), 300 (**trois cents**), 400 (**quatre cents**), and so on. In the hundreds, never use **et** (*and*). Any multiple, any other number added to the round whole number drops the **s** on **cents**: **cent un** (101), **cent deux** (102), and so on.

B. Simple arithmetical expressions

deux **et** deux **font** quatre	$2 + 2 = 4$
trois **fois** cinq **font** quinze	$3 \times 5 = 15$
douze **moins** dix **font** deux	$12 - 10 = 2$
dix **divisés par** deux **font** cinq	$10 \div 2 = 5$

Rules and observations:

1. In French you need to state **et** (*and*) as we do in English when adding. Besides saying two *and* two are four, we can say two *plus* two are four. In French, we say **et** (*and*).

2. The symbol **x** (meaning *times*) is expressed by **fois** in French.

3. In French, we use the word **moins** to express *minus* or *less*.

4. In French, we say **divisés par** to express *divided by*.

5. In French, we use the word **font** (meaning *make*) to express *are* or *make*.

C. Fractions

$^1/_2$	**un demi**	a (one) half
$^1/_3$	**un tiers**	a (one) third
$^1/_4$	**un quart**	a (one) fourth
$^1/_5$	**un cinquième**	a (one) fifth

D. Approximate amounts

une dizaine	about ten
une quinzaine	about fifteen
une vingtaine	about twenty
une trentaine	about thirty
une quarantaine	about forty
une cinquantaine	about fifty
une soixantaine	about sixty
une centaine	about a hundred
un millier	about a thousand

Observations:

1. Notice that each of the above approximate amounts is based on a cardinal number.

2. Did you notice that **une quarantaine** (*about forty*) is related to the English word *quarantine,* which means a period of *forty* days?

E. Ordinal numbers: first to twentieth

first	**premier, première**	1st	**1er, 1re**
second	**deuxième (second, seconde)**	2d	**2e**
third	**troisième**	3d	**3e**
fourth	**quatrième**	4th	**4e**
fifth	**cinquième**	5th	**5e**
sixth	**sixième**	6th	**6e**
seventh	**septième**	7th	**7e**
eighth	**huitième**	8th	**8e**
ninth	**neuvième**	9th	**9e**
tenth	**dixième**	10th	**10e**
eleventh	**onzième**	11th	**11e**
twelfth	**douzième**	12th	**12e**
thirteenth	**treizième**	13th	**13e**
fourteenth	**quatorzième**	14th	**14e**
fifteenth	**quinzième**	15th	**15e**
sixteenth	**seizième**	16th	**16e**
seventeenth	**dix-septième**	17th	**17e**
eighteenth	**dix-huitième**	18th	**18e**
nineteenth	**dix-neuvième**	19th	**19e**
twentieth	**vingtième**	20th	**20e**

Rules and observations:

1. You must learn the difference between a **cardinal** number and an **ordinal** number. If you have trouble distinguishing between the two, just remember that we use the cardinal numbers most of the time: un, deux, trois (one, two, three), and so on.

2. Use the *ordinal* numbers to express a certain *order:* premier (première, if the noun following is feminine), deuxième, troisième (first, second, third), and so on.

3. **Premier** is the masculine singular form and **première** is the feminine singular form. Examples: **le premier homme** (*the first man*), **la première femme** (*the first woman*).

4. The masculine singular form **second**, or the feminine singular form **seconde**, is used to mean *second* when there are only two. When there are more than two, **deuxième** is used. Examples: **le Second Empire**, because there were only two empires in France; however, **la Deuxième République**, because there have been more than two Republics in France.

5. The raised letters in **1ᵉʳ** are the last two letters in the word **premier**; it is equivalent to our *st* in *1st*. The raised letters in **1ʳᵉ** are the last two letters in the word **première**, which is the *feminine* singular form of *first*.

6. The raised letter **e** after an ordinal number (for example, **2ᵉ**) stands for the **ième** ending of a French ordinal number.

7. When referring to sovereigns or rulers, the only ordinal number used is **Premier**. For all other designations, the cardinal numbers are used. The definite article (*the*) is used in English but not in French. Examples:

	François 1ᵉʳ	François Premier	Francis the First
but:			
	Louis XIV	Louis Quatorze	Louis the Fourteenth

F. Weights, Measures, Values* (Poids, mesures, valeurs)

un gramme = 0.035274 ounce (1 gram)

28.3 grammes = 1 ounce

100 grammes = 3.52 ounces

453.6 grammes = 1 pound

500 grammes = 17.63 ounces
(about 1.1 pounds)

1000 grammes = 1 kilogram

un kilogramme = 2.2 pounds
(1 kilogram)

une livre = 17.63 ounces
(about 1.1 pounds)

un litre = 1.0567 quarts
(0.26417 gallon)

---

un franc = 20 cents
(There are **100 centimes** in one franc.)

5 francs = $1.00

25 francs = $5.00

50 francs = $10.00

---

un kilomètre = 0.62137 mile
(about ⅝ mile or 1000 meters)

1.61 kilomètres = 1 mile

10 kilomètres = 6.21 miles

---

un centimètre = 0.39 inch
(1 centimeter)

2.54 centimètres = 1 inch

30.5 centimètres = 1 foot

91.4 centimètres = 1 yard

un mètre = 39.37 inches
(100 centimeters)

0.9144 mètre = 1 yard

---

1. To convert Fahrenheit degrees into Celsius (Centigrade): subtract 32, multiply by 5, and divide by 9.

2. To convert Celsius (Centigrade) into Fahrenheit: multiply by 9, divide by 5, and add 32.

3. A Fahrenheit degree is smaller than a Celsius degree. One F degree is ⁵/₉ of a C degree.

4. France uses the Celsius scale.

---

* All the equivalents given are approximate. To obtain the current rate of exchange of American dollars for French francs, inquire at a commercial bank.

Exercises

A. Cardinal numbers

I. Complete the following by writing in the French word or words.

1. Deux et deux font _____
2. Trois et quatre font _____
3. Cinq et sept font _____
4. Six et quatre font _____
5. Huit et neuf font _____
6. Neuf et trois font _____

II. Write the French word or words for the following cardinal numbers.

1. 2 _____
2. 4 _____
3. 6 _____
4. 8 _____
5. 10 _____
6. 20 _____
7. 21 _____
8. 22 _____
9. 30 _____
10. 37 _____
11. 61 _____
12. 69 _____
13. 70 _____
14. 80 _____
15. 100 _____

III. Match the following.

1. seize _____ seventeen
2. dix-sept _____ twenty
3. dix-neuf _____ eighteen
4. vingt _____ nineteen
5. dix-huit _____ sixteen
6. quatre-vingts _____ one hundred
7. soixante _____ ninety
8. cent _____ eighty
9. quatre-vingt-dix _____ seventy
10. soixante-dix _____ sixty

IV. Choose the correct answer and write the word on the line.

1. Deux et cinq font (a) quatre (b) six (c) sept (d) neuf. _____
2. Trois fois cinq font (a) quinze (b) vingt (c) dix-sept (d) huit. _____
3. Douze moins dix font (a) vingt-deux (b) cent vingt (c) deux (d) vingt. _____
4. Dix divisés par deux font (a) douze (b) cinquante (c) six (d) cinq. _____
5. Douze divisés par six font (a) douze (b) dix-huit (c) deux (d) dix. _____

B. Ordinal numbers

I. Match the following.

1. troisième	_____ first	6. vingtième	_____ fifteenth
2. cinquième	_____ second	7. quinzième	_____ seventeenth
3. premier	_____ third	8. dix-neuvième	_____ twentieth
4. deuxième	_____ fourth	9. seizième	_____ nineteenth
5. quatrième	_____ fifth	10. dix-septième	_____ sixteenth

II. Write the French word or words for the following ordinal numbers.

1. first (feminine) _____

2. first (masculine) _____

3. second (of only 2, masculine) _____

4. second (of only 2, feminine) _____

5. second (of more than 2) _____

6. fourth _____

7. fifth _____

8. ninth _____

9. tenth _____

10. third _____

III. Match the following.

1. Henri Quatre	_____ Francis I
2. Louis Seize	_____ Louis XIV
3. François Premier	_____ Henry V
4. Henri Cinq	_____ Louis XVI
5. Louis Quatorze	_____ Henry IV

C. Cardinals, fractions approximate amounts, ordinals, simple arithmetical expressions, weights and measures

I. Complete the following by writing in the French word or words.

1. Six moins quatre font _____

2. Vingt et quarante font _____

3. Cinquante divisés par deux font _____

4. Trois cents moins cent font _____

5. Mille moins deux cents font _____

115

II. Word Search. Find these seven words in French in this puzzle and circle them.

1. one hundred
2. thirty
3. third
4. one thousand
5. fifty
6. five
7. twelve

U	N	M	I	C	T	R	E	N	T	E	X
N	D	E	C	I	N	Q	U	A	N	T	E
M	T	R	C	C	E	N	T	A	I	N	E
T	R	O	I	S	I	È	M	E	U	N	E
O	M	I	N	L	D	O	U	Z	E	L	L
Q	C	I	Q	N	T	R	M	I	L	L	E

III. Match the following.

1. four   _____ un quart

2. about a thousand   _____ une centaine

3. eighty   _____ quatorze

4. one half   _____ quatre

5. fourteenth   _____ soixante-neuf

6. about a hundred   _____ quatre-vingts

7. one fourth   _____ quatorzième

8. fourteen   _____ un demi

9. ninety   _____ quatre-vingt-dix

10. sixty-nine   _____ un millier

IV. Transcribe the following into French words.

Model: 2 × 5 = 10   **You write: Deux fois cinq font dix.**

1. $3 \times 9 = 27$ _____

2. $8 - 6 = 2$ _____

3. $20 \div 5 = 4$ _____

4. $7 \times 100 = 700$ _____

5. 80 et 10 = 90   _____

V. Transcribe the following French words into simple arithmetical expressions using symbols and figures.

> **Model: Deux fois dix font vingt.**   **You write: $2 \times 10 = 20$.**

1. Trois fois cinq font quinze. _____

2. Douze moins dix font deux. _____

3. Dix divisés par deux font cinq. _____

4. Deux et deux font quatre. _____

5. Neuf fois dix font quatre-vingt-dix. _____

VI. Match the following.

1. un kilogramme	___ 0.62137 mile
2. une livre	___ 39.37 inches
3. un centimètre	___ 100 centimes
4. un kilomètre	___ 1.0567 quarts
5. un mètre	___ 1.1 pounds
6. un litre	___ 6.21 miles
7. un franc français	___ 0.39 inch
8. 10 kilomètres	___ 2.2 pounds
9. 1,000 grammes	___ 1 yard
10. 0.9144 mètre	___ 1 kilogram

VII.   Oral Proficiency. Respond orally in French to the situation described. (Later, you may write your responses for intensive practice.)

Situation: You are at an auction with a friend. You are not making any bids and you want to leave the place immediately. Your friend asks why you want to leave: *Pourquoi veux-tu partir?* In five sentences give your reasons for wanting to leave. You may use your own words, those in this unit or any of the following: *aller, partir, être, les choses, laid, monstrueux, le fauteuil, les meubles* (furniture), and any of the numbers given in this lesson.

Deux fois cinq font dix.

117

Monsieur Paquet dit: Quel embarras! Je n'ai pas de revolver! L'avion va partir sans nous! Il est dix heures moins deux!

Time Expressions, Telling Time, Dates, Age, Months, Days, Seasons

In this scene Monsieur and Madame Paquet, Janine, and Pierre are going through customs at Charles de Gaulle Airport. What an experience!

Bon voyage! Bon retour!

La famille Paquet fait des préparations pour un voyage par avion aux Etats-Unis. Madame Paquet a une soeur qui habite à La Nouvelle-Orléans avec son mari et ses trois enfants. Maintenant, ils font les valises et dans quelques minutes ils vont quitter la maison pour aller à l'aéroport Charles de Gaulle.

— Quelle heure est-il? demande Monsieur Paquet.

— Il est huit heures, répond sa femme.

— Il faut se dépêcher, dit Pierre. L'avion va partir dans deux heures.

Madame Paquet est très heureuse parce qu'elle va revoir sa soeur. Janine et Pierre sont heureux aussi parce qu'ils vont voir leurs cousins pour la première fois. Monsieur Paquet est heureux parce qu'il va voir la Louisiane.

Ils montent dans le taxi et dans quelques minutes ils arrivent à l'aéroport. Ils cherchent les billets, qui sont déjà payés.

— Votre nom, s'il vous plaît, demande la jeune dame au guichet.

— Paquet. Vous avez les billets pour la famille Paquet. Nous allons aux Etats-Unis pour quelques semaines, à La Nouvelle-Orléans, en Louisiane.

— Vous êtes sûr que c'est pour aujourd'hui, monsieur? demande la jeune dame.

— Oui, oui. Quelle est la date aujourd'hui? C'est le premier juillet, n'est-ce pas? demande Monsieur Paquet.

— Oui, c'est bien ça, répond-elle. Quel âge ont les deux enfants?

— Janine, dis à la dame ton âge, dit la mère.

— J'ai quinze ans, répond Janine.

— Pierre, dis ton âge à la dame.

— J'ai dix ans, répond Pierre.

— Parfait. C'est parfait, répond la dame au guichet. Voici les billets. L'avion va partir dans quelques minutes. Bon voyage et bon retour!

119

— Merci, merci, merci, merci, répondent-ils.

Ils passent à la douane où il y a une machine automatique qui détecte des objets en métal. Quand Monsieur Paquet passe par la machine avec une valise, ils entendent un signal d'alarme assourdissant. Un agent de police arrive vite.

— Halte! crie-t-il. Avez-vous un revolver dans votre valise? Il faut chercher dans la valise, dit l'agent.

— Quel embarras! C'est très ennuyant, dit Monsieur Paquet. Je n'ai pas de revolver! L'avion va partir sans nous. Il est dix heures moins deux!

— Je regrette, monsieur, mais les règles sont les règles.

L'agent de police cherche dans la valise de Monsieur Paquet.

— Ah! Ha! Un pistolet! Vous êtes arrêté! Terroriste! s'exclame l'agent.

— Mais ce n'est pas une arme! C'est un pistolet d'enfant. C'est le jouet de Pierre, mon fils.

— Mon jouet! Donnez-moi mon pistolet! s'exclame Pierre.

— Mille pardons, dit l'agent. Vous pouvez passer.

— Mille pardons?! Mille pardons?! Oh! C'est une honte!

— Vite! crie Madame Paquet. L'avion va partir sans nous!

Vocabulaire

l'aéroport n. m., the airport
l'arme n. f., the weapon
arrêter v., to stop; **l'arrêt** n. m., the stop, the arrest; **vous êtes arrêté** you are under arrest
assourdir v., to deafen; **assourdissant** adj., deafening
avez v. form of **avoir** (to have); **vous avez** you have
l'avion n. m., the airplane
le billet n., the ticket
bon retour! exclam., have a good return (trip)!
bon voyage! exclam., have a good trip!
cela dem. pron., that (**ça** is short for **cela**); **c'est ça** that's it; **c'est bien ça**

that's quite right
crie v. form of **crier** (to shout, to cry out); **crie-t-il** he shouts
déjà adv., already
dis v. form of **dire** (to tell, to say); **dis à la dame . . .** tell the lady . . .
la douane n., customs
ennuyer v., to annoy; **ennuyant** annoying
les Etats-Unis n. m., the United States; **aux Etats-Unis** to (in) the United States
fait, font v. forms of **faire** (to do, to make); **faire un voyage** to take a trip
falloir v., to be necessary; **il faut** it is necessary

le guichet n., the ticket window
habiter v., to live, to reside
l'heure n. f., the hour (used in telling time); **quelle heure est-il?** what time is it?
heureux m., **heureuse** f., adj., happy
il est dix heures moins deux it's two minutes to ten
il y a there is, there are
j'ai quinze ans I'm fifteen years old; **j'ai dix ans** I'm ten years old
leurs poss. adj. pl., their
la Louisiane n., Louisiana
merci thank you
monter v., to climb up or into, to ascend, to get into; **ils montent dans le taxi** they

get into the taxi
le nom *n.*, the name
La Nouvelle-Orléans *n.*, New Orleans
l'objet *n. m.*, the object
par *prep.*, by
parfait *adj.*, perfect
passent *v. form of* **passer** (to pass, to go by); **ils passent à la douane** they

go to customs
quel âge ont les deux enfants? how old are the two children? **quelle est la date aujourd'hui?** what's the date today? **quelle heure est-il?** what time is it?
quelque *adj.*, some, any; **quelque chose** something

le signal *n.*, the signal; **le signal d'alarme** the alarm
sûr *adj.*, sure, certain; **bien sûr** of course, certainly
ton *poss. adj. m. s.*, your
va, vont *v. forms of* **aller** (to go); **elle va** she is going; **ils vont** they are going
voir *v.*, to see
le voyage *n.*, the trip

Exercises

Review the story and vocabulary before starting these exercises.

I. Choose the correct answer based on the story.

1. La famille Paquet va faire un voyage à   (a) Paris.   (b) Chicago.
   (c) La Nouvelle-Orléans.   (d) New York.   _____

2. Madame Paquet est heureuse parce qu'elle va revoir   (a) son frère.
   (b) sa mère.   (c) ses cousins.   (d) sa soeur.   _____

3. Janine et Pierre sont heureux parce qu'ils vont voir   (a) leur chien.
   (b) leurs amis.   (c) leurs cousins.   (d) l'aéroport.   _____

4. Janine a   (a) douze ans.   (b) treize ans.   (c) quatorze
   ans.   (d) quinze ans.   _____

5. Pierre a   (a) treize ans.   (b) douze ans.   (c) onze ans.
   (d) dix ans.   _____

II. Oui ou Non?

1. Monsieur Paquet est heureux parce qu'il va voir la Louisiane.   _____

2. L'avion va partir à dix heures.   _____

3. Monsieur Paquet a un revolver dans sa poche.   _____

4. L'agent de police trouve une clef dans la poche de Monsieur Paquet.   _____

5. La famille Paquet va faire un voyage par avion aux Etats-Unis.   _____

III. Scrambled sentences. Unscramble each sentence so that it is meaningful. Write them in proper word order. Look for them in the story.

1. Quinze ans j'ai. _____

2. Heure est quelle il? _____

3. Aujourd'hui date la est quelle? _____

4. Huit heures est il. _____

5. Un revolver vous avez? _____

IV. Answer the following questions in French in complete sentences. They are personal questions and require answers of your own.

1. Aimez-vous faire des voyages? _____

2. Aimez-vous les avions ou les trains? _____

3. Aimez-vous regarder un avion dans le ciel? _____

Structures de la Langue

A. Telling time

TIME EXPRESSIONS

Quelle heure est-il?	What time is it?
Il est une heure.	It is one o'clock.
Il est une heure dix.	It is ten minutes after one.
Il est une heure et quart.	It is a quarter after one.
Il est deux heures et demie.	It is half past two; it is two thirty.
Il est trois heures moins vingt.	It is twenty minutes to three.
Il est trois heures moins un quart.	It is a quarter to three.
Il est midi.	It is noon.
Il est minuit.	It is midnight.
à quelle heure?	at what time?
à une heure	at one o'clock
à une heure précise	at exactly one o'clock
à trois heures précises	at exactly three o'clock
à neuf heures du matin	at nine in the morning
à trois heures de l'après-midi	at three in the afternoon
à dix heures du soir	at ten in the evening
à l'heure	on time
à temps	in time
vers trois heures	around three o'clock
un quart d'heure	a quarter of an hour
une demi-heure	a half hour
Il est midi et demi.	It is twelve thirty.

Il est une heure.

**Il est une heure
dix.**

**Il est une heure
et quart.**

**Il est deux heures
et demie.**

**Il est trois heures
moins vingt.**

**Il est trois heures
moins un quart.**

Rules and observations:

1. In telling time, **Il est** is used plus the hour, whether it is one or more than one, *e.g.,* **Il est une heure, Il est deux heures**.

2. If the time is *after* the hour, state the hour, then the minutes, *e.g.,* **Il est une heure dix**.

3. The conjunction **et** is used with **quart** after the hour and with **demi** or **demie**, *e ~.,* **Il est une heure et quart, Il est une heure et demie, Il est midi et demi**.

4. The masculine form **demi** is used after a masculine noun, *e.g.,* **Il est midi et demi**. The feminine form **demie** is used after a feminine noun, *e.g.,* **Il est deux heures et demie**.

5. **Demi** remains **demi** when *before* a feminine or masculine noun and it is joined to the noun with a hyphen, *e.g.,* **une demi-heure**.

6. If the time expressed is *before* the hour, **moins** is used, *e.g.,* **Il est trois heures moins vingt**.

7. A quarter *after* the hour is **et quart**; a quarter *to* the hour is **moins un quart**.

8. To express A.M. use **du matin**; to express P.M. use **de l'après-midi** if it is the afternoon or **du soir** if it is the evening.

9. The 24-hour system of telling time is used by the French government on radio and TV, in railroad and bus stations, and at airports. In this system, **quart** and **demi** or **demie** are not used. **Moins** and **et** are not used. When you hear or see the stated time, subtract 12 from the number that you hear or see. If the number is less than 12 it is A.M. time, except for **24 heures,** which is midnight (**zéro heure** is also midnight).

    Examples: **Il est treize heures.** / It is 1:00 P.M.
                        Il est quinze heures. / It is 3:00 P.M.

123

Il est vingt heures trente. / It is 8:30 P.M.
Il est vingt-quatre heures. / It is midnight.
Il est zéro heure. / It is midnight.
Il est seize heures trente. / It is 4:30 P.M.
Il est dix-huit heures quinze. / It is 6:15 P.M.
Il est vingt heures quarante-cinq. / It is 8:45 P.M.
Il est vingt-deux heures cinquante. / It is 10:50 P.M.

The abbreviation for **heure** or **heures** is **h**.

Examples: **Il est 20 h. 20.** / It is 8:20 P.M.
Il est 15 h. 50. / It is 3:50 P.M.
Il est 23 h. 30. / It is 11:30 P.M.

B.   Asking the date, giving the date

Quelle est la date aujourd'hui?	
Quel jour du mois est-ce aujourd'hui?	What's the date today?
Quel jour du mois sommes-nous aujourd'hui?	
C'est aujourd'hui le premier mai.	Today is May first.
C'est aujourd'hui le deux mai.	Today is May second.

Rule:

In giving the date, use the cardinal numbers, except for the first of the month which is always **le premier**.

C.   Asking your age, giving your age

Quel âge avez-vous?	How old are you?
J'ai quinze ans.	I am fifteen (years old).

Rules:

1. In giving your age, use the cardinal numbers.

2. The verb **avoir** is used in French; the verb *to be* is used in English.

D.   Months of the year

Les mois de l'année sont: **janvier**, **février**, **mars**, **avril**, **mai**, **juin**, **juillet**, **août**, ˙
septembre, **octobre**, **novembre**, **décembre**.

The months of the year are: January, February, March, April, May, June, July, August,
September, October, November, December.

Rules:

1.   The months are not ordinarily capitalized.

2.   They are all masculine in gender.

E.   Days of the week

Les jours de la semaine sont: **dimanche**, **lundi**, **mardi**, **mercredi**, **jeudi**, **vendredi**,
samedi.

The days of the week are: Sunday, Monday, Tuesday, Wednesday, Thursday, Friday,
Saturday.

Quel jour est-ce aujourd'hui?   **C'est aujourd'hui lundi.**

(What day is it today?)   (Today is Monday.)

Rules:

1.   The days are not capitalized.

2.   They are also all masculine in gender.

F.   Seasons of the year

Les saisons de l'année sont: **le printemps**, **l'été**, **l'automne**, **l'hiver**.

The seasons of the year are: spring, summer, fall, winter.

Rules:

1.   Tne seasons are not capitalized.

2.   They are masculine in gender.

125

Exercises

Review the preceding material before starting these exercises.

I. Match the following.

1. Quelle heure est-il?   _____ It is 9 o'clock.

2. Est-il deux heures?   _____ It is noon.

3. Il est neuf heures.   _____ Is it 2 o'clock?

4. Il est midi.   _____ What time is it?

5. Il est minuit.   _____ It is midnight.

6. Il est une heure.   _____ It is 1 o'clock.

II. Quelle heure est-il? Write the answer in a complete sentence (in French) on the line provided under each clock.

Model:

You write: Il est dix heures moins deux.

1.

_____

2.

_____

3.

_____

4.

_____

III. Quelle est la date aujourd'hui? Write the answer in a complete sentence (in French) on the line provided under each calendar.

Model:

SEPTEMBRE						
D	L	M	M	J	V	S
	1	2	3	4	5	6
7	8	9	10	11	12	13
14	15	16	17	18	19	20
21	22	23	24	25	26	27
28	29	30				

You write: **C'est aujourd'hui le seize septembre.**

1.

OCTOBRE						
D	L	M	M	J	V	S
		1	2	3	4	
5	6	7	8	9	10	11
12	13	14	15	16	17	18
19	20	21	22	23	24	25
26	27	28	29	30	31	

_____

2.

NOVEMBRE						
D	L	M	M	J	V	S
						1
2	3	4	5	6	7	8
9	10	11	12	13	14	15
16	17	18	19	20	21	22
23	24	25	26	27	28	29
30						

_____

IV. A quelle heure? (At what time?) Answer the following questions in complete sentences (in French) using the time given in parentheses. Be sure to use one of the following with each time stated: **du matin, de l'après-midi, du soir.**

Model: **A quelle heure étudiez-vous? (8:00 PM)** (At what time do you study?)   You write: **J'étudie à huit heures du soir.** (I study at 8 o'clock in the evening.)

1. A quelle heure vous levez-vous? (6:30 AM) _____

2. A quelle heure allez-vous à l'école? (8:00 AM) _____

3. A quelle heure regardez-vous la télévision? (4:00 PM) _____

4. A quelle heure dînez-vous? (6:00 PM) _____

5. A quelle heure vous couchez-vous? (10:30 PM) _____

V. Answer the following questions in complete sentences (in French).

1. Quels sont les mois de l'année? _____

_____

2. Quels sont les jours de la semaine? _____

_____

3. Quelles sont les saisons de l'année? _____

_____

VI. Answer the following questions in complete sentences (in French). You will write two sentences. In your first sentence (a) answer the question in the negative. In your second sentence (b) give the day that **precedes** the day asked in the question.

Model: Est-ce dimanche aujourd'hui?   (Is today Sunday?)

You write: **(a) Non, ce n'est pas dimanche.**   **No, it's not Sunday.**
                 (b) C'est aujourd'hui samedi.   **Today is Saturday.**

1. Est-ce lundi aujourd'hui?

   (a) _____   (b) _____

2. Est-ce mardi aujourd'hui?

   (a) _____   (b) _____

3. Est-ce mercredi aujourd'hui?

   (a) _____   (b) _____

4. Est-ce vendredi aujourd'hui?

   (a) _____   (b) _____

5. Est-ce jeudi aujourd'hui?

   (a) _____   (b) _____

6. Est-ce samedi aujourd'hui?

   (a) _____   (b) _____

7. Est-ce dimanche aujourd'hui?

   (a) _____   (b) _____

VII. Write in French the questions that would have been asked.

> **Model: Elle a vingt-huit ans.** (She is twenty-eight years old.)
>
> You write the question that would have been asked: **Quel âge a-t-elle?**

1. Il a cinquante ans. _____

2. Il est trois heures. _____

3. Elle a trente ans. _____

4. C'est aujourd'hui le premier mai. _____

5. Il est minuit. _____

6. C'est aujourd'hui le cinq avril. _____

7. Elles ont quinze ans. _____

8. Il est midi. _____

9. J'ai vingt ans. _____

10. C'est aujourd'hui lundi. _____

VIII. **Oral Proficiency.** Respond orally in French to the situation described. (Later, you may write your responses for intensive practice.)

Situation: You and your friend have saved enough money to go on a vacation by plane. Your friend isn't sure about going. You telephone to persuade your friend to go. Begin with *Salut! C'est moi* and end with *à bientôt!* (See you soon!) In six statements or questions persuade your friend to travel with you. You may use your own ideas or ideas suggested by the following: a good season or month to travel, where you want to go, what you two are to see there, what you are going to do in the evening and in the daytime, does he or she want to spend the vacation there.

Tout d'un coup, Coco arrive en courant dans la grande salle. Sur la tête, il a le chapeau haut de forme, dans la gueule le bâton et la cape, et sur le dos le lapin!

Formation and Use of the Imperative (Command)

*Who do you suppose wins the big talent
show prize?*

Le concours de talents à l'école

C'est aujourd'hui vendredi. C'est le grand jour du concours de talents dans la grande salle de l'école. Il y a des étudiants qui vont chanter, danser, faire des tours de force et des tours de main, jouer d'un instrument de musique, et raconter des contes drôles. Janine et Pierre sont dans le concours de talents, aussi. Pierre est le magicien et Janine l'assistante. Ils préparent leur représentation.

— Donne-moi mon chapeau haut de forme, dit Pierre à Janine.

— Je n'ai pas ton chapeau haut de forme, répond Janine.

— Apporte-moi mon bâton, dit Pierre à Janine.

— Je n'ai pas ton bâton, répond Janine.

— Donne-moi ma cape, dit Pierre.

— Je n'ai pas ta cape, répond Janine.

— Apporte-moi le lapin, dit Pierre.

— Je n'ai pas le lapin, répond Janine.

En ce moment, quelques spectateurs dans la grande salle crient:

— Dansez! Chantez! Faites quelque chose!

Ce sont les étudiants, les maîtres, et les maîtresses qui crient.

— Zut, alors! Ne finissons pas, Janine. Nous n'avons pas le chapeau haut de forme, le bâton, la cape, le lapin.

— Ne choisis pas cette alternative, dit Janine à Pierre.

— Alors, restons-nous ou partons-nous? demande Pierre. Il faut faire quelque chose!

— Allez-vous faire quelque chose, enfin?! demandent tous les spectateurs.

— Ne réponds pas, Janine, dit Pierre.

Tout d'un coup, Coco arrive en courant dans la grande salle. Sur la tête il a le chapeau haut de forme, dans la gueule le bâton et la cape, et sur le dos le lapin!

— Viens ici, Coco! s'exclame Pierre.

— Assieds-toi, Coco! s'exclame Janine.

— C'est merveilleux! dit Pierre. Maintenant, finissons la représentation.

Janine et Pierre finissent leur représentation. Les autres étudiants finissent leurs représentations, aussi. Et qui gagne le grand prix? Coco, naturellement! Parce qu'il a beaucoup de talent!

Vocabulaire

apporte! bring!;
  apporte-moi bring me
assieds-toi! sit down!
le bâton n., the wand, stick, baton
ce sont . . . they are . . ., it's . . .
le chapeau haut de forme n., the black silk top hat
la chose n., thing; **quelque chose** something
le concours de talents the talent show
le conte n., the story, tale
courant pres. part. of **courir**; **en courant** (while) running
donne-moi give me
le dos n., the back
drôle adj., funny, droll, odd
faites v. form of **faire** (to do,

to make); **faites quelque chose!** do something!
finissons! let's finish!; **ne finissons pas!** let's not finish!
gagner v., to win
la grande salle n., the auditorium
la gueule n., the mouth of an animal
le lapin n., the rabbit
le magicien, la magicienne n., the magician
le maître, la maîtresse n., the teacher
naturellement adv., naturally
partons-nous? are we leaving?
le prix n., the price, the prize;

le grand prix the grand prize
raconter v., to tell, to relate
la représentation n., the presentation, performance, show
restons-nous? are we staying?
le spectateur, la spectatrice n., the spectator
la tête n., the head
tour de force feat of strength; **tour de main** sleight of hand, hand trick
tous adj. m. pl., all
tout d'un coup all of a sudden
viens ici! come here!
zut, alors! gosh darn it!

Exercises

Review the story and vocabulary before starting these exercises.

I. Answer the following questions in complete sentences (in French). They are based on the story.

132 1. Quel jour est-ce aujourd'hui? _____ _____

2.   Dans le concours de talents, qui va jouer le magicien? _____

_____

3.   Qui est l'assistante de Pierre? _____

4.   Est-ce que Pierre et Janine ont le chapeau haut de forme, le bâton, la cape, et le lapin?

_____

5.   Qui arrive dans la grande salle avec le chapeau, le bâton, la cape et le lapin? _____

_____

6.   Qui gagne le grand prix de talent? _____

II.   Answer the following questions in complete sentences (in French). They are personal questions that require answers of your own.

1.   Avez-vous du talent? Dansez-vous? Chantez-vous? _____

_____

2.   Est-ce que vous jouez d'un instrument de musique? _____

3.   Aimez-vous le français? _____

4.   Quel jour de la semaine allez-vous au cinéma? _____

III.   Comment dit-on en français . . .?

Find these statements in the story and write them in French.

1.   Today is Friday. _____

2.   It's the big day of the talent show. _____

3.   Bring me my wand, bring me the rabbit. _____

4.   I don't have your cape. _____

5.   And who wins the grand prize? Coco, naturally! Because he has much talent! _____

_____

Structures de la Langue

A. Formation and use of the imperative (command) in the three regular conjugations (**–er, –ir, –re**)

AFFIRMATIVE

	2d person singular **(tu)**	2d person plural **(vous)**	1st person plural **(nous)**
DANSER	**danse!** *dance!*	**dansez!** *dance!*	**dansons!** *let's dance!*
FINIR	**finis!** *finish!*	**finissez!** *finish!*	**finissons!** *let's finish!*
VENDRE	**vends!** *sell!*	**vendez!** *sell!*	**vendons!** *let's sell!*

NEGATIVE

DANSER	**ne** danse **pas!** *don't dance!*	**ne** dansez **pas!** *don't dance!*	**ne** dansons **pas!** *let's not dance!*
FINIR	**ne** finis **pas!** *don't finish!*	**ne** finissez **pas!** *don't finish!*	**ne** finissons **pas!** *let's not finish!*
VENDRE	**ne** vends **pas!** *don't sell!*	**ne** vendez **pas!** *don't sell!*	**ne** vendons **pas!** *let's not sell!*

Rules and observations:

1. In the two boxes above, the 2d person singular and the 2d person plural are right next to each other so that you can compare the forms. The 1st person plural stands alone at the right.

2. To form the *imperative* in the affirmative, use the same verb form as in the present indicative, which you have already learned. Drop the subject pronouns, **tu**, **vous**, or **nous**.

3.   There is one exception. You must drop the final **s** in the 2d person singular of an **–er** verb. This is done in the affirmative and negative, as shown above, as in **danse!** For more about this, see work unit eleven, page 152.

4.   To form the negative of the imperative, place **ne** in front of the verb and **pas** after it, as you learned to do when forming the negative of the present indicative.

Exercises

Review the preceding material before starting these exercises.

I.   Write, in French, the three forms of the imperative in the affirmative.

   Model: danser   **You write:**   **danse**   **dansez**   **dansons**

A.   –ER verbs

   1.   **donner**   _____   _____   _____

   2.   **apporter**   _____   _____   _____

   3.   **chercher**   _____   _____   _____

   4.   **aider**   _____   _____   _____

   5.   **chanter**   _____   _____   _____

B.   –IR verbs

   1.   **finir**   _____   _____   _____

   2.   **choisir**   _____   _____   _____

   3.   **bâtir**   _____   _____   _____

   4.   **punir**   _____   _____   _____

   5.   **obéir**   _____   _____   _____

C.   –RE verbs

   1.   **vendre**   _____   _____   _____

   2.   **attendre**   _____   _____   _____

   3.   **descendre**   _____   _____   _____

   4.   **répondre**   _____   _____   _____

   5.   **rendre**   _____   _____   _____

135

II. Change the following imperative sentences to the negative.

   Model: Danse, mon enfant!   You write: Ne danse pas, mon enfant!
   (Dance, my child!)

1. Chantez, Janine! _____

2. Finissons le travail maintenant! _____

3. Vendez la maison, Monsieur Paquet! _____

4. Ecoute la musique, Pierre! _____

5. Attendez l'autobus! _____

B.   Formation and use of reflexive verbs in the imperative

AFFIRMATIVE

	2d person singular **(tu)**	2d person plural **(vous)**	1st person plural **(nous)**
S'ASSEOIR *to sit down*	**assieds-toi!** *sit down!*	**asseyez-vous!** *sit down!*	**asseyons-nous!** *let's sit down!*
SE LEVER *to get up*	**lève-toi!** *get up!*	**levez-vous!** *get up!*	**levons-nous!** *let's get up!*
SE LAVER *to wash oneself*	**lave-toi!** *wash yourself!*	**lavez-vous!** *wash yourself! or wash yourselves!*	**lavons-nous!** *let's wash ourselves!*

NEGATIVE

	2nd person singular **(tu)**	2nd person plural **(vous)**	1st person plural **(nous)**
S'ASSEOIR	**ne** t'assieds **pas!** *don't sit down!*	**ne** vous asseyez **pas!** *don't sit down!*	**ne** nous asseyons **pas!** *let's not sit down!*
SE LEVER	**ne** te lève **pas!** *don't get up!*	**ne** vous levez **pas!** *don't get up!*	**ne** nous levons **pas!** *let's not get up!*
SE LAVER	**ne** te lave **pas!** *don't wash yourself!*	**ne** vous lavez **pas!** *don't wash yourself! or don't wash yourselves!*	**ne** nous lavons **pas!** *let's not wash ourselves!*

Rules and observations:

1. To form the imperative of a reflexive verb in the affirmative use the same verb form as in the present indicative, unless the form is irregular in the imperative.

2. Drop the subject pronouns **tu**, **vous**, and **nous**.

3. You must drop the **s** in the 2d person singular of an **–ER** verb. This is done in the affirmative and negative, as shown above. See **se lever** and **se laver** in the 2d person singular.

4. Keep the reflexive pronouns **te**, **vous**, and **nous**. They serve as direct object pronouns. **Vous** and **nous** are reflexive pronouns as well as subject pronouns.

5. The reflexive pronoun is placed *after* the verb in the affirmative of the imperative. The verb and pronoun are joined with a hyphen. **Te** becomes **toi** when it is placed *after* the verb with a hyphen. This happens only in the affirmative.

6. To form the imperative of a reflexive verb in the negative, keep the reflexive pronoun *in front of* the verb form. **Te** becomes **t'** in the negative imperative when the verb right after it starts with a vowel or a silent *h*, as in **ne t'assieds pas**.

7. To form the negative imperative, place **ne** before the reflexive pronoun and **pas** after the verb.

Exercises

Review the preceding material before starting these exercises.

I. Choose the correct verb form and write it on the line.

1. Wash yourself! (lavez-vous, lavons-nous, vous vous lavez) _____

2. Sit down! (asseyons-nous, assieds-toi, vous vous asseyez) _____

3. Get up! (levons-nous, noun nous levons, levez-vous) _____ _____

4. Sit down! (asseyez-vous, asseyons-nous, levez-vous) _____

5. Let's wash ourselves! (lavez-vous, vous vous lavez, lavons-nous) _____

6. Get up! (lève-toi, levons-nous, lave-toi) _____

7. Don't wash yourself! (ne te lave pas, ne te lève pas, lave-toi) _____

8. Let's not get up! (ne nous levons pas, ne vous levez pas, levez-vous) _____

II. Change the following affirmative imperatives to the negative imperative.

Model: **Levez-vous!**   You write: **Ne vous levez pas!**

1. Lavons-nous! _____   4. Assieds-toi! _____

2. Asseyez-vous! _____   5. Lavez-vous! _____

3. Lave-toi! _____   6. Lève-toi! _____

137

III. Match the following.

1. Ne vous lavez pas.

2. Assieds-toi.

3. Ne te lève pas.

4. Levez-vous.

5. Asseyons-nous.

____ Sit down.

____ Get up.

____ Let's sit down.

____ Don't wash yourself!

____ Don't get up.

IV. Fill in the missing letters to form the imperative.

Model: Dance!   **Answer: DANSE _Z_ !**

1. Listen!   ÉCOUTE ___ !
2. Give!   DONN ___ ___ !
3. Sing!   CHANTE ___ !
4. Finish!   FIN ___ ___ ___ EZ!
5. Choose!   CHOISISS ___ ___ !
6. Let's not sell!   NE VEND ___ ___ ___ PAS!
7. Don't wait!   N'ATTEN ___ ___ ___ PAS!
8. Answer!   RÉ ___ ___ N ___ ___ Z!
9. Wait!   ATT ___ ___ D ___ ___ !
10. Sit down!   A ___ ___ EY ___ ___ -VOUS!
11. Get up!   LEV ___ ___ -VOUS!
12. Wash yourself!   L ___ VE ___ -VOUS!

V. **Oral Proficiency.** You are in a florist shop because you want to buy a plant for a friend. You are talking with the salesclerk. Complete the conversation.

Le fleuriste: Bonjour! Vous désirez?

1. Vous: _____

Le fleuriste: C'est pour vous? Ou c'est pour offrir comme cadeau?

2. Vous: _____

Le fleuriste: Ah, bon! C'est pour une occasion spéciale?

3. Vous: _____

Le fleuriste: Aimez-vous cette plante rouge? Elle est très jolie.

4. Vous: _____

Le fleuriste: C'est cent trente francs.

5. Vous: _____

Review Test: Work Units 6–10

I. The words in the following boxes are scrambled. Unscramble them to find a meaningful sentence.

Monique	puces	aux	est	marché
au	Janine	amie	son	avec

II. Choose the correct verb form and write it with its subject.

1. Monsieur et Madame Durant (vend, vendent, vendons) leur maison. _____

2. Le petit chien (romps, rompt, rompent) la grande barrière. _____

3. Le professeur (interrompt, interrompez, interrompent) l'étudiant. _____

4. Janine (rend, rends, rendent) le livre à la bibliothèque. _____

5. Nous (entendons, entendez, entendent) la musique. _____

III. Complete each verb form in the present indicative by adding the correct letter or letters.

1. Nous aim _____ parler français.

2. Odette chant _____ bien.

3. Pauline chois _____ une jolie jupe.

4. J'attend _____ l'autobus.

5. Tu parl _____ bien le français.

6. Les élèves fin _____ les devoirs.

IV. Write the appropriate reflexive pronoun in French.

1. Tous les matins je _____ lave.

2. Joseph, pourquoi ne _____ laves-tu pas?

3. Est-ce que les enfants _____ lavent?

4. Je _____ dépêche pour aller à l'école.

5. Nous _____ amusons quand nous allons au cinéma.

V. Choose the correct answer and write the word in French.

1. Trois et quatre font   (a) cinq   (b) six   (c) sept   (d) huit   _____

2. Six fois deux font   (a) douze   (b) treize   (c) huit   (d) trois   _____ **139**

3. Treize moins neuf font   (a) sept   (b) huit   (c) neuf   (d) quatre   _____

4. Cinquante divisés par deux font
   (a) cinquante-deux   (b) vingt-cinq   (c) trente-cinq   (d) trente   _____

VI. For each clock, write the time shown in French.

A. _____   B. _____   C. _____

D. _____   E. _____   F. _____

VII. Each of the following sentences contains a blank. Of the four choices given, select the one that can be inserted in the blank to form a sensible and grammatically correct sentence and circle the letter of your choice.

1. Quelle est la date aujourd'hui? C'est aujourd'hui _____ février.
   A. l'un   B. le premier de   C. le premier   D. la première

2. Quel jour précède lundi? C'est _____
   A. samedi   B. dimanche   C. mardi   D. jeudi

3. Il y a _____ saisons dans l'année.
   A. cinq   B. quart   C. quatre   D. quarante

4. Les fleurs poussent _____ printemps.
   A. en   B. dans   C. dans le   D. au

5. En général, _____ hiver il fait froid à New York.
   A. en   B. dans   C. dans l'   D. à l'

140

VIII. Write the English for the following commands in French.
Example: **Asseyez-vous!**   You write: **Sit down!**

1. Lavez-vous! _____

2. Asseyons-nous! _____

3. Levez-vous! _____

IX. Fill in the missing letters to form the imperative.
Example: Dance!   Answer: DANSE ____Z____ !

1. Sit down!   A _____ _____ EY _____ _____ - VOUS!

2. Get up!   LEV _____ _____ - VOUS!

3. Choose!   CHOIS _____ _____ _____ _____ _____ !

X. Write in French the questions that would have been asked.
Example: **Elle a vingt-huit ans.** (She is twenty-eight years old.)

You write the question that would have been asked: **Quel âge a-t-elle?**

1. Monsieur Durand a quarante ans. _____

2. J'ai dix-huit ans. _____

3. Il est quatre heures et demie. _____

4. C'est aujourd'hui vendredi. _____

5. C'est le premier janvier. _____

Qu'est-ce que c'est?

Qu'est-ce que c'est?

Qu'est-ce que c'est?

Qu'est-ce que c'est?

Qu'est-ce que c'est?

Qu'est-ce que c'est?

Irregular Verbs in the Present Indicative and Imperative

*Have you ever played guessing games
in English? In French? Here are some
in French.*

Qu'est-ce que c'est?

A brief description is given of something and then you are asked, "Qu'est-ce que c'est?" (What is it?) See how many you can do. The answers are upside down after the last one.

1. C'est quelque chose à boire. Il peut avoir le goût d'orange, ananas, pamplemousse, raisin, ou tomate. Il peut être en boîte ou en bouteille. C'est toujours délicieux. Qu'est-ce que c'est?

2. C'est un meuble. Vous vous asseyez sur ce meuble. Qu'est-ce que c'est?

3. C'est quelque chose à manger. Elle est toujours froide et crémeuse. Elle peut être au chocolat, à la vanille, aux fraises. Elle est toujours délicieuse. Qu'est-ce que c'est?

4. C'est un fruit. Il a la couleur rouge ou jaune ou verte. Qu'est-ce que c'est?

5. C'est une machine qui a un moteur et quatre roues. Elle peut aller vite ou lentement. Elle est dangereuse si le conducteur ne fait pas attention. Elle ne peut pas aller sans essence. Qu'est-ce que c'est?

6. C'est un appareil. Une personne peut parler dans cet appareil et peut entendre une autre personne parler. Quand une personne veut parler, cet appareil sonne. Qu'est-ce que c'est?

7. C'est un animal qui a des plumes et des ailes. Il vole comme un avion. Qu'est-ce que c'est?

8. C'est un appareil. Il sonne tous les matins quand vous dormez et vous vous levez. Qu'est-ce que c'est?

9. C'est une partie du corps humain. Elle a cinq doigts. Qu'est-ce que c'est?

10. C'est un objet d'habillement. C'est pour la tête. Qu'est-ce que c'est?

10. un chapeau

9. une main 8. un réveil 7. un oiseau

6. un téléphone 5. une automobile ou une voiture 4. une pomme

3. une glace 2. une chaise 1. un jus de fruit

143

Vocabulaire

l'aile n. f., the wing
l'ananas n. m., the pineapple
l'appareil n. m., the apparatus, instrument
boire v., to drink
la boîte n., the box, tin can
la bouteille n., the bottle
le conducteur, la conductrice n., the driver
le corps n., body; **le corps humain** the human body
crémeux m., **crémeuse** f., adj., creamy
dangereux m., **dangereuse** f., adj., dangerous
délicieux m., **délicieuse** f., adj., delicious
le doigt n., the finger
entendre v., to hear

l'essence n. f., gasoline
faire attention v., to pay attention, to be careful
la fraise n., the strawberry
froid m., **froide** f., adj., cold
le goût n., the taste, flavor
l'habillement n. m., clothing
jaune adj., yellow
le jus n., juice; **jus d'orange** orange juice
le meuble n., piece of furniture
le moteur n., motor, engine
le pamplemousse n., the grapefruit
la partie n., the part (of a whole)
la personne n., the individual, person

peut v. form of **pouvoir** (can, be able); **elle peut aller** it can go; **il peut avoir** it can have; **il peut être** it can be
qu'est-ce que c'est? what is it?
le raisin n., the grape
la roue n., the wheel
rouge adj., red
sans prep., without
sonner v., to ring
la tomate n., the tomato
la vanille n., vanilla
vert m., **verte** f., adj., green
veut v. form of **vouloir** (to want); **une personne veut** a person wants
la voiture n., the car, automobile
voler v., to fly

Exercises

Review the preceding material before starting these exercises.

I. Choose the correct answer based on the guessing game at the beginning of this unit.

1. Un jus de fruit est quelque chose à   (a) manger.   (b) boire.
(c) conduire.   (d) pouvoir.   _____

2. La glace est toujours   (a) charmante.   (b) froide.   (c) ennuyante.
(d) ronde.   _____

3. Une voiture peut être dangereuse si le conducteur ou la conductrice ne
fait pas   (a) sa leçon.   (b) ses devoirs.   (c) son stylo.   (d) attention.   _____

4. Un téléphone est un   (a) objet d'habillement.   (b) jus.   (c) appareil.
(d) moteur.   _____

5. Un chapeau est un   (a) jus.   (b) goût.   (c) appareil.   (d) objet
d'habillement.   _____

II. Answer the following questions in French in complete sentences. They are personal questions and require answers of your own.

144   **Model answer: Mon fruit favori est l'orange.**

1.   Quel est votre fruit favori? _____

2.   Quel est votre dessert favori? _____

3.   Quel est votre sport favori? _____

III.   Un acrostiche.   Complete the French words in this puzzle.

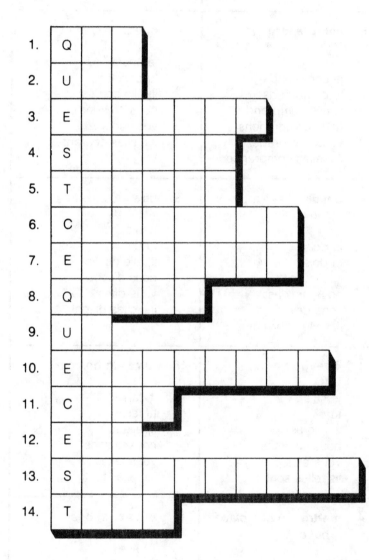

1. Q	1. who
2. U	2. indefinite article *(f., sing.)*
3. E	3. gasoline
4. S	4. to ring
5. T	5. tomato
6. C	6. creamy *(f.)*
7. E	7. annoying *(m.)*
8. Q	8. when
9. U	9. indefinite article *(m., sing.)*
10. E	10. United States
11. C	11. key
12. E	12. water
13. S	13. spectator *(m.)*
14. T	14. head

Structures de la Langue

A. Irregular verbs in the present indicative tense

1. aller *to go* je vais tu vas il, elle va nous allons vous allez ils, elles vont	**2. apprendre** *to learn* j'apprends tu apprends il, elle apprend nous apprenons vous apprenez ils, elles apprennent	**3. avoir** *to have* j'ai tu as il, elle a nous avons vous avez ils, elles ont
4. boire *to drink* je bois tu bois il, elle boit nous buvons vous buvez ils, elles boivent	**5. comprendre** *to understand* je comprends tu comprends il, elle comprend nous comprenons vous comprenez ils, elles comprennent	**6. courir** *to run* je cours tu cours il, elle court nous courons vous courez ils, elles courent
7. devenir *to become* je deviens tu deviens il, elle devient nous devenons vous devenez ils, elles deviennent	**8. devoir** *have to, must, should* je dois tu dois il, elle doit nous devons vous devez ils, elles doivent	**9. dire** *to say, tell* je dis tu dis il, elle dit nous disons vous dites ils, elles disent
10. écrire *to write* j'écris tu écris il, elle écrit nous écrivons vous écrivez ils, elles écrivent	**11. être** *to be* je suis tu es il, elle est nous sommes vous êtes ils, elles sont	**12. faire** *to do, make* je fais tu fais il, elle fait nous faisons vous faites ils, elles font
13. lire *to read* je lis tu lis il, elle lit nous lisons vous lisez ils, elles lisent	**14. mettre** *to put, place, put on* je mets tu mets il, elle met nous mettons vous mettez ils, elles mettent	**15. ouvrir** *to open* j'ouvre tu ouvres il, elle ouvre nous ouvrons vous ouvrez ils, elles ouvrent

16. **partir** to leave, depart	17. **pouvoir** can, to be able	18. **prendre** to take
je pars tu pars il, elle part nous partons vous partez ils, elles partent	je peux or puis tu peux il, elle peut nous pouvons vous pouvez ils, elles peuvent	je prends tu prends il, elle prend nous prenons vous prenez ils, elles prennent
19. **revenir** to come back	20. **savoir** to know (how)	21. **sortir** to go out, leave
je reviens tu reviens il, elle revient nous revenons vous revenez ils, elles reviennent	je sais tu sais il, elle sait nous savons vous savez ils, elles savent	je sors tu sors il, elle sort nous sortons vous sortez ils, elles sortent
22. **venir** to come	23. **voir** to see	24. **vouloir** to want
je viens tu viens il, elle vient nous venons vous venez ils, elles viennent	je vois tu vois il, elle voit nous voyons vous voyez ils, elles voient	je veux tu veux il, elle veut nous voulons vous voulez ils, elles veulent

Exercises

Review the preceding material before starting these exercises.

I. Answer the following questions in the affirmative in complete sentences in French. In answer (a) use **oui**; in answer (b) use **aussi**. Study the models.

Models: (a) **Allez-vous au cinéma?**   You write: (a) **Oui, je vais au cinéma.**
          Et Pierre?   (b) **Il va au cinéma aussi.**

1. (a) Lisez-vous beaucoup? _____

   (b) Et Janine? _____

2. (a) Apprenez-vous le français? _____

   (b) Et Pauline? _____

3. (a) Avez-vous de la glace? _____

   (b) Et Dominique? _____

4. (a) Buvez-vous du jus d'orange? _____

   (b) Et Robert? _____

5. (a) Comprenez-vous la leçon? _____

   (b) Et Joséphine? _____

6. (a) Les garçons courent-ils à l'école? _____

   (b) Et vous et Pierre? _____

7. (a) Hélène et Jeanne doivent-elles écrire des compositions? _____

   _____

   (b) Et vous? _____

8. (a) Monsieur Paquet dit-il la vérité? _____

   (b) Et Madame Paquet et Janine? _____

9. (a) Gabrielle écrit-elle une lettre? _____

   (b) Et Françoise et Béatrice? _____

10. (a) Etes-vous dans le concours de talents à l'école? _____

    _____

    (b) Et Pierre et Janine? _____

II. Answer the following questions in the negative in complete sentences (in French). In answer (a) use **Non**. In answer (b) use **non plus**. Study the models.

| Models: | (a) **Est-ce que Pierre fait attention en classe?** | You write: | (a) **Non, il ne fait pas attention en classe.** |
| | (b) **Et vous?** | | (b) **Je ne fais pas attention en classe non plus.** |

1. (a) Est-ce que Robert lit beaucoup? _____

   (b) Et vous? _____

2. (a) Est-ce que Monique met le vase sur la table? _____

   (b) Et Jacques? _____

3. (a) Est-ce que vous ouvrez la porte? _____

    (b) Et Charles? _____

4. (a) Est-ce que Marie part à huit heures? _____

    (b) Et l'avion? _____

5. (a) Pouvez-vous aller au cinéma ce soir? _____

    (b) Et Madame et Monsieur Paquet? _____

6. (a) Prenez-vous le petit déjeuner à sept heures? _____

    (b) Et Simone? _____

7. (a) Savez-vous quelle heure il est? _____

    (b) Et Pierre? _____

8. (a) Est-ce que Monsieur et Madame Paquet sortent ce soir? _____

_____

    (b) Et Janine? _____

9. (a) Est-ce que vous venez ici tous les jours? _____

    (b) Et votre ami? _____

10. (a) Voyez-vous l'avion dans le ciel? _____

    (b) Et votre amie? _____

III. Change each sentence by replacing the verb in the sentence with the proper form of the verb in parentheses. Keep the same subject, of course. Rewrite the entire sentence in French.

Model: Ouvre-t-il la fenêtre?   (fermer)   **You write: Ferme-t-il la fenêtre?**

1. *Ferme*-t-il la porte?   (ouvrir) _____

2. Est-ce qu'elle *écrit* la lettre?   (lire) _____

3. *Buvez*-vous du café?   (prendre) _____

4. Il ne *comprend* pas la leçon.   (faire) _____

5. *Savez*-vous la date?   (écrire) _____

149

IV. Write the French equivalent for the English words given. Write the entire sentence in French.

    Model: **Marie et Janine** *understand*   **You write:** **Marie et Janine**
             la question.   **comprennent la question.**

1. Henri et Robert *understand* la réponse. _____

2. *I have* beaucoup de devoirs à faire. _____

3. Hélène et Marie *are they* présentes aujourd'hui? _____

4. Michel et Jacques *do they do* leurs leçons? _____

5. *I don't see* un taxi. _____

V. Choose the correct verb form.

1. Nous (vois, voyons, voient) la mer.   _____

2. Je (savez, savent, sais) la réponse.   _____

3. Ils (fait, faisons, font) leur travail.   _____

4. Ils (part, partent, partez) maintenant.   _____

5. Tu (bois, buvez, boivent) du lait.   _____

6. Janine (deviens, devient, deviennent) docteur.   _____

VI. Answer the following questions in complete sentences in the affirmative, substituting the subject pronoun **Ils** or **Elles** for the noun **frères** or **soeurs**. Add **aussi**.

    Model: **François apprend bien. Et**   **You write:** **Ils apprennent bien**
             vos frères?   **aussi.**

1. Pierre comprend bien. Et vos frères? _____

2. Guillaume écrit bien. Et vos soeurs? _____

3. Michel va bien. Et vos frères? _____

4. Guy lit bien. Et vos soeurs? _____

5. Alfred voit bien. Et vos frères? _____

B. The imperative of some common irregular verbs

Infinitive	2d pers. sing. (tu)	2d pers. pl. (vous)	1st pers. pl. (nous)
aller	va *go!*	allez *go!*	allons *let's go!*
apprendre	apprends *learn!*	apprenez *learn!*	apprenons *let's learn!*
avoir	aie *have . . . !*	ayez *have . . . !*	ayons *let's have . . . !*
boire	bois *drink!*	buvez *drink!*	buvons *let's drink!*
dire	dis *say!*	dites *say!*	disons *let's say!*
écrire	écris *write!*	écrivez *write!*	écrivons *let's write!*
être	sois *be . . . !*	soyez *be . . . !*	soyons *let's be . . . !*
faire	fais *do! (or) make!*	faites *do! (or) make!*	faisons *let's do! (or) let's make!*
lire	lis *read!*	lisez *read!*	lisons *let's read!*
mettre	mets *put . . . !*	mettez *put . . . !*	mettons *let's put . . . !*

ouvrir	**ouvre** *open . . . !*	**ouvrez** *open . . . !*	**ouvrons** *let's open . . . !*
partir	**pars** *leave!*	**partez** *leave!*	**partons** *let's leave!*
prendre	**prends** *take!*	**prenez** *take!*	**prenons** *let's take!*
revenir	**reviens** *come back!*	**revenez** *come back!*	**revenons** *let's come back!*
sortir	**sors** *go out!*	**sortez** *go out!*	**sortons** *let's go out!*
venir	**viens** *come!*	**venez** *come!*	**venons** *let's come!*
voir	**vois** *see!*	**voyez** *see!*	**voyons** *let's see!*

Rules and observations:

1. In the boxes above, the 2d person singular (**tu**) and the 2d person plural (**vous**) are right next to each other so that you can compare the forms of the 2d persons. The 1st person plural (**nous**) stands alone at the right.

2. It was pointed out on page 137 that the final **s** drops in the 2d person singular on an **-ER** verb in the imperative. However, when the pronouns **y** and **en** are linked to it, the **s** is retained in all regular **-ER** verbs and in the verb **aller**. Examples: **donnes-en** *(give some!)*; **manges-en** *(eat some!)*; **vas-y** *(go there!)*. The reason for this is that it makes it easier to link the two elements by pronouncing the **s** as a **z**.

Exercises

Review the above material before starting these exercises.

I. Choose the correct verb form in the imperative.

1. Drink! (buvez, partez, faites) _____

2. Come! (pars, viens, vois) _____

3. Say! (dites, faites, voyez) _____

4. Write! (mettez, ayez, écrivez) _____

5. Read! (soyez, sortez, lisez) _____

6. Open! (ouvrons, ouvre, écris) _____

7. Let's go out! (sortez, sortons, voyons) _____

8. Let's be . . . ! (soyez, soyons, ayons) _____

9. Let's drink! (allons, buvons, buvez) _____

10. Come back! (revenez, sortez, venez) _____

Dis la vérité.

II. Change each sentence by replacing the verb in the sentence with the proper from of the verb in parentheses. Keep the imperative form, of course. Rewrite the entire sentence in French. The verb form you write must be in the same person as the one you are replacing.

   Model: Dites la vérité. (écrire)   **You write: Ecrivez la vérité.**

1. *Ecrivez* la phrase. (dire) _____

2. *Prends* le lait. (boire) _____

3. *Venez* tout de suite. (partir) _____

4. *Ouvre* la fenêtre. (fermer) _____

5. *Mets* la valise là-bas. (prendre) _____

6. *Lisons* la lettre. (écrire) _____

7. *Apprenez* le poème. (lire) _____

8. *Partons* maintenant. (sortir) _____

9. *Soyez* à l'heure. (revenir) _____

10. *Voyons* la leçon. (faire) _____

III. Match the following.

1. Close the door.	_____ Donnes-en au garçon.
2. Take your time.	_____ Manges-en si tu veux.
3. Let's open the windows.	_____ Mettez les valises ici.
4. Eat some if you want.	_____ Vas-y.
5. Leave right away.	_____ Ouvrons les fenêtres.
6. Put the suitcases here.	_____ Revenez demain.
7. Give some to the boy.	_____ Ferme la porte.
8. Go there.	_____ Dis la vérité.
9. Come back tomorrow.	_____ Pars tout de suite.
10. Tell the truth.	_____ Prenez votre temps.

IV. For each sentence write a response in the imperative (in French).

   A. Model: Je veux manger maintenant.   You write: Bon! Alors, mangez maintenant!

Je veux partir maintenant.

1. Je veux partir maintenant. _____

2. Je dois ouvrir la fenêtre. _____

3. Je désire faire la leçon. _____

4. Je vais écrire une lettre. _____

5. Je vais lire le journal. _____

    B. Model: Nous voulons boire de   **You write: Bon! Alors, buvez de**
                l'eau maintenant.   **l'eau maintenant!**

1. Nous désirons sortir maintenant. _____

2. Nous voulons être ici à dix heures. _____

3. Nous allons faire le travail ce soir. _____

4. Nous désirons apprendre l'anglais. _____

5. Nous voulons parler français. _____

V. Oral Proficiency. Respond orally in French to the situation described. (Later, you may write your statements for intensive practice.)

Situation: Your French teacher asks you to face all the students in the classroom and to state a few guessing games in French. State the guessing games in French and then ask what it is: *Qu'est-ce que c'est?* Say at least four. You may use your own ideas or ideas suggested in this lesson.

The following is a **summary** of **avoir** and **être** in the present indicative affirmative and negative; and in the interrogative and negative-interrogative with **est-ce que** and the inverted form.

AVOIR	ÊTRE

Affirmative

j'ai	nous avons	je suis	nous sommes
tu as	vous avez	tu es	vous êtes
il *or* elle a	ils *or* elles ont	il *or* elle est	ils *or* elles sont

Negative

je n'ai pas	nous n'avons pas	je ne suis pas	nous ne sommes pas
tu n'as pas	vous n'avez pas	tu n'es pas	vous n'êtes pas
il n'a pas	ils n'ont pas	il n'est pas	ils ne sont pas
elle n'a pas	elles n'ont pas	elle n'est pas	elles ne sont pas

AVOIR	ÊTRE

Interrogative

(a) with est-ce que

Est-ce que j'ai?

Est-ce que tu as?

Est-ce qu'il a?

Est-ce qu'elle a?

Est-ce que nous avons?

Est-ce que vous avez?

Est-ce qu'ils ont?

Est-ce qu'elles ont?

(b) inverted form

ai-je?

as-tu?

a-t-il?

a-t-elle?

avons-nous?

avez-vous?

ont-ils?

ont-elles?

Interrogative

(a) with est-ce que

Est-ce que je suis?

Est-ce que tu es?

Est-ce qu'il'est?

Est-ce qu'elle est?

Est-ce que nous sommes?

Est-ce que vous êtes?

Est-ce qu'ils sont?

Est-ce qu'elles sont?

(b) inverted form

suis-je?

es-tu?

est-il?

est-elle?

sommes-nous?

êtes-vous?

sont-ils?

sont-elles?

AVOIR	ÊTRE
Negative-interrogative	**Negative-interrogative**
(a) with **est-ce que**	(a) with **est-ce que**
Est-ce que je n'ai pas?	Est-ce que je ne suis pas?
Est-ce que tu n'as pas?	Est-ce que tu n'es pas?
Est-ce qu'il n'a pas?	Est-ce qu'il n'est pas?
Est-ce qu'elle n'a pas?	Est-ce qu'elle n'est pas?
Est-ce que nous n'avons pas?	Est-ce que nous ne sommes pas?
Est-ce que vous n'avez pas?	Est-ce que vous n'êtes pas?
Est-ce qu'ils n'ont pas?	Est-ce qu'ils ne sont pas?
Est-ce qu'elles n'ont pas?	Est-ce qu'elles ne sont pas?
(b) **inverted form**	(b) **inverted form**
n'ai-je pas?	ne suis-je pas?
n'as-tu pas?	n'es-tu pas?
n'a-t-il pas?	n'est-il pas?
n'a-t-elle pas?	n'est-elle pas?
n'avons-nous pas?	ne sommes-nous pas?
n'avez-vous pas?	n'êtes-vous pas?
n'ont-ils pas?	ne sont-ils pas?
n'ont-elles pas?	ne sont-elles pas?

Oh! Monsieur! Votre autographe, s'il vous plait! Voici mon programme et voici mon stylo.

The Passé Composé

Have you ever asked someone for an autograph? That's what Janine did while she was at the Paris Opera House during intermission.

L'autographe spécial

Hier soir la famille Paquet est allée à l'opéra. Ils ont vu la représentation de *Faust*. Ils ont quitté la maison à sept heures et demie et ils sont arrivés à l'opéra à huit heures. Ils sont entrés dans le théâtre et ils ont pris leurs places à huit heures et quart. La représentation a commencé à huit heures et demie.

Pendant l'entracte, Madame Paquet est allée parler avec quelques dames. Monsieur Paquet est allé fumer une cigarette, Pierre est allé acheter du chocolat, et Janine est allée boire un jus d'orange.

Madame Paquet a parlé avec les dames et, puis, elle est retournée à sa place. Monsieur Paquet a fumé sa cigarette et il est retourné à sa place aussi. Pierre a mangé son chocolat et il est retourné à sa place. Janine a bu son jus d'orange, mais avant de retourner à sa place, elle a vu un homme et elle a dit:

— Oh! Monsieur! Vous êtes le grand acteur Philippe Jirard!

— Mais . . . mademoiselle . . . a répondu le monsieur.

— Oh! Monsieur! Votre autographe, s'il vous plaît! Voici mon programme et voici mon stylo. Vous pouvez écrire votre autographe sur mon programme, a dit Janine.

— Mais . . . Mais . . . a dit le monsieur.

— Vous êtes très modeste, a dit Janine.

— Mais . . . Ce n'est pas que je suis modeste, mademoiselle . . . Mais si vous insistez . . . Voilà mon autographe! a dit le monsieur.

— Merci, monsieur. Merci mille fois, monsieur! a dit Janine.

Janine est retournée à sa place.

L'opéra se termine et tout le monde quitte le théâtre.

Dehors, Janine a annoncé:

— Regardez mon programme! J'ai l'autographe de Philippe Jirard!

— Philippe Jirard?! Vraiment? Incroyable! a dit la mère.

Janine a donné son programme à sa mère et elle a lu: "Je ne suis pas Philippe Jirard. Je m'appelle Jean Leblanc."

— Ce n'est pas possible! Oh! J'ai fait une bêtise! a dit Janine.

— Ce n'est pas si bête. Tu as l'autographe de Jean Leblanc. Tout le monde n'a pas l'autographe de Jean Leblanc sur un programme! a répondu Pierre.

— Qui est Jean Leblanc? a demandé le père.

— C'est une personne ordinaire, comme toi et moi! a répondu la mère. Maintenant nous avons un autographe spécial!

Et ils ont ri.

Vocabulaire

l'acteur *m.*, **l'actrice** *f.*, *n.*, the actor, the actress

allé *past part. of* **aller** (to go); **la famille Paquet est allée** the Paquet family went

s'appeler *v.*, to be named, to call oneself; **Je m'appelle Jean Leblanc** My name is John Leblanc

arrivé *past part. of* **arriver** (to arrive); **ils sont arrivés** they arrived

bête *adj.*, foolish, dumb; **une bêtise** a foolish mistake

bu *past part. of* **boire** (to drink); **Janine a bu** Janine drank

commencé *past part. of* **commencer** (to begin); **la représentation a commencé** the performance began

la dame *n.*, the lady

dehors *adv.*, outside

demandé *past part. of* **demander** (to ask); **le père a demandé** the father asked

dit *past part. of* **dire** (to say, to tell); **a dit Janine** said

Janine

donné *past part. of* **donner** (to give); **Janine a donné** Janine gave

l'entracte *n. m.*, intermission

entré *past part. of* **entrer** (to enter, to go in); **ils sont entrés** they entered

fait *past part. of* **faire** (to do, to make); **j'ai fait** I did

fumé *past part. of* **fumer** (to smoke); **il a fumé** he smoked

hier *adv.*, yesterday

incroyable *adj.*, unbelievable

insistez *v. form of* **insister** (to insist); **vous insistez** you insist

leurs *poss. adj. pl.* their; **leurs places** their seats

lu *past part. of* **lire** (to read); **elle a lu** she read

mangé *past part. of* **manger** (to eat); **il a mangé** he ate

modeste *adj.*, modest

parlé *past part. of* **parler** (to talk, to speak); **elle a parlé** she talked

pouvez *v. form of* **pouvoir** (can, to be able); **vous**

pouvez écrire you can write

pris *past part. of* **prendre** (to take); **ils ont pris** they took

le programme *n.*, the program

quitté *past part. of* **quitter** (to leave); **tout le monde a quitté le théâtre** everybody left the theater

répondu *past part. of* **répondre** (to reply); **a répondu Pierre** replied Pierre

retourné *past part. of* **retourner** (to return, go back); **elle est retournée** she returned

ri *past part. of* **rire** (to laugh); **ils ont ri** they laughed

si *conj.*, if; *as an adv.*, so

le stylo *n.*, the pen

terminé *past part. of* **terminer** (to end); **l'opéra a terminé** the opera ended

voici here is, here are; **voilà** there is, there are (used when pointing out)

vu *past part. of* **voir** (to see); **elle a vu un homme** she saw a man

Exercises

Review the story and vocabulary before starting these exercises.

I. **Answer the following questions in French in complete sentences. They are based on the story in this unit.**

1. A quelle heure est-ce qu'ils ont quitté la maison pour aller à l'opéra? _____

_____

2. A quelle heure sont-ils arrivés à l'opéra? _____

_____

3. A quelle heure est-ce qu'ils ont pris leurs places? _____

_____

4. A quelle heure la représentation a-t-elle commencé? _____

_____

II. Oui ou Non?

1. Hier soir la famille Paquet est allée à l'opéra. _____

2. Ils ont vu la représentation de *Carmen*. _____

3. Madame Paquet est allée parler avec quelques dames. _____

4. Monsieur Paquet est allé boire un jus d'orange. _____

5. Janine a l'autographe de Philippe Jirard. _____

III. Fill in the blank lines with the past participle in French. **Refer to the story if you have to. The answers are there!**

1. Hier soir la famille Paquet est _____ à l'opéra.

2. Ils ont _____ la représentation de *Faust*.

3. Ils ont _____ la maison à sept heures et demie.

4. Ils sont _____ à l'opéra à huit heures.

5. Ils sont _____ dans le théâtre.

6. Ils ont _____ leurs places.

7. Madame Paquet est _____ parler avec quelques dames.

8. Monsieur Paquet est _____ fumer une cigarette.

9. Pierre est _____ acheter du chocolat.

10. Janine est _____ boire un jus d'orange.

IV. Word Search. Find the past participles *in French* in this puzzle and circle them.

A	L	L	É	T	F	U	M	É	L
P	A	R	L	É	A	L	A	B	U
P	R	I	S	D	I	T	N	T	O
R	Q	U	I	T	T	É	U	R	I
U	R	É	P	O	N	D	U	F	T

1. allé   6. parlé
2. bu   7. pris
3. dit   8. quitté
4. fait   9. répondu
5. lu   10. ri

Structures de la Langue

The Passé Composé (past indefinite *or* compound past)

A. Verbs conjugated with **avoir**

	1st conjugation –ER	2nd conjugation –IR	3rd conjugation –RE
INFINITIVES ⟶	**danser** *to dance*	**finir** *to finish*	**vendre** *to sell*
	I danced, *or* I have danced, *or* I did dance; you danced, *etc.*	I finished, *or* I have finished, *or* I did finish; you finished, *etc.*	I sold, *or* I have sold, *or* I did sell; you sold, *etc.*
SINGULAR			
1. **j'** (I)	**ai dansé**	**ai fini**	**ai vendu**
2. **tu** (you — *familiar only*)	**as dansé**	**as fini**	**as vendu**
3. **il** (he *or* it) **elle** (she *or* it)	**a dansé**	**a fini**	**a vendu**
PLURAL			
1. **nous** (we)	**avons dansé**	**avons fini**	**avons vendu**
2. **vous** (you)	**avez dansé**	**avez fini**	**avez vendu**
3. **ils** **elles** (they)	**ont dansé**	**ont fini**	**ont vendu**

Rules and observations:

1. To form the passé composé of verbs conjugated with **avoir**, use the present indicative of **avoir** plus the past participle of the verb. All verbs are conjugated with **avoir** except: *all reflexive verbs and the 17 verbs listed on page 169*.

2. To form the past participle of a regular **–er** verb, drop the **–er** ending and add **é**.

3. To form the past participle of a regular **–ir** verb, drop the **–ir** ending and add **i**.

162

4. To form the past participle of a regular **-re** verb, drop the **-re** ending and add **u**.

5. The passé composé is used to express an action that was completed in the past. It is used in conversation and in informal writing.

6. The passé composé can be translated into English in three different ways, as noted above.

7. To form the negative, place **n'** in front of the present indicative of **avoir** which, in the passé composé, is called the auxiliary or helping verb. Then put **pas** after it:

1st conjugation	2nd conjugation	3rd conjugation
je **n'**ai **pas** dansé	je **n'**ai **pas** fini	je **n'**ai **pas** vendu
tu **n'**as **pas** dansé	tu **n'**as **pas** fini	tu **n'**as **pas** vendu
il (or) elle **n'**a **pas** dansé	il (or) elle **n'**a **pas** fini	il (or) elle **n'**a **pas** vendu
nous **n'**avons **pas** dansé	nous **n'**avons **pas** fini	nous **n'**avons **pas** vendu
vous **n'**avez **pas** dansé	vous **n'**avez **pas** fini	vous **n'**avez **pas** vendu
ils (or) elles **n'**ont **pas** dansé	ils (or) elles **n'**ont **pas** fini	ils (or) elles **n'**ont **pas** vendu

8. To form the interrogative, use either (a) the **est-ce que** form in front of the subject, or (b) the inverted form, both of which you learned when you formed the present indicative tense:

(a) Est-ce que j'ai dansé?	(b) ai-je dansé?
Est-ce que tu as dansé?	as-tu dansé?
Est-ce qu'il a dansé?	a-t-il dansé?
Est-ce qu'elle a dansé?	a-t-elle dansé?
Est-ce que nous avons dansé?	avons-nous dansé?
Est-ce que vous avez dansé?	avez-vous dansé?
Est-ce qu'ils ont dansé?	ont-ils dansé?
Est-ce qu'elles ont dansé?	ont-elles dansé?

Note: In (b) box above, if you use the inverted form, you need to add **-t-** in the 3rd person singular between the auxiliary verb and the subject pronoun. You already learned to do this when you used the inverted form in the present indicative tense.

STRUCTURES AND VERBS

9. To form the negative-interrogative, use either (a) the **est-ce que** form in front of the subject in the negative form, or (b) the inverted form in the negative:

(a)	(b)
Est-ce que je n'ai pas dansé?	n'ai-je pas dansé?
Est-ce que tu n'as pas dansé?	n'as-tu pas dansé?
Est-ce qu'il n'a pas dansé?	n'a-t-il pas dansé?
Est-ce qu'elle n'a pas dansé?	n'a-t-elle pas dansé?
Est-ce que nous n'avons pas dansé?	n'avons-nous pas dansé?
Est-ce que vous n'avez pas dansé?	n'avez-vous pas dansé?
Est-ce qu'ils n'ont pas dansé?	n'ont-ils pas dansé?
Est-ce qu'elles n'ont pas dansé?	n'ont-elles pas dansé?

Note: In both (a) and (b) boxes above, it is very easy to form the negative-interrogative of a verb in the passé composé. If you just drop, for a minute, the past participle *dansé*, what you have left is actually what you already learned: the negative-interrogative of the present indicative tense of the verb **avoir**. See the summary at the end of work unit eleven.

Exercises

Review the preceding material before starting these exercises.

I. Write the answers to the following in complete sentences in French.

A. Passé composé with **avoir** in the affirmative — answer in the affirmative.

Model: Avez-vous vendu la maison? **You answer: Oui, j'ai vendu la maison.**

1. Avez-vous vendu la voiture? _____

2. Avez-vous acheté la propriété? _____

3. Avez-vous fini les leçons? _____

4. Avez-vous réussi la vente de la propriété? _____

5. Avez-vous fermé les portes et les fenêtres? _____

B. Passé composé with **avoir** in the negative — answer in the negative.

Model: Janine a-t-elle dansé hier soir? **You answer: Non, elle n'a pas dansé hier soir.**

164

Use a pronoun subject in your answer where a noun subject is given in the question.

1.   Janine a-t-elle chanté hier soir? _____

2.   Robert a-t-il choisi une jolie cravate? _____

3.   As-tu mangé l'éclair? _____

4.   Janine et Pierre ont-ils étudié les leçons? _____

5.   Avons-nous fini le travail? _____

C. Passé composé with **avoir** in the interrogative — change to the interrogative in the inverted form.

**Model: Janine a parlé à   You ask: Janine a-t-elle parlé à
           Madame Richy.   Madame Richy?**

1.   Pierre a vu Madame Richy. _____

2.   Hélène a choisi une jolie robe. _____

3.   Coco a mangé l'éclair. _____

Coco a mangé l'éclair.

4.   Suzanne et Georges ont étudié les devoirs. _____

5.   Marie et Betty ont voyagé en France. _____   **165**

D. Passé composé with **avoir** in the interrogative — change to the interrogative with **est-ce que**.

> Model: **Madame Banluc a chanté hier soir.**   You ask: **Est-ce que Madame Banluc a chanté hier soir?**

1. Madame Paquet a acheté un beau chapeau. _____

2. Pierre a perdu sa montre. _____

3. Monsieur Paquet a fumé une cigarette. _____

4. Paul a mangé du chocolat. _____

5. Janine a bu un jus d'orange. _____

E. Passé composé with **avoir** in the negative-interrogative — change into negative-interrogative using the inverted form only.

> Model: **Madame Paquet n'a pas acheté un beau chapeau.**   You ask: **Madame Paquet n'a-t-elle pas acheté un beau chapeau?**

1. Madame Richy n'a pas acheté une automobile. _____

_____

2. Monsieur Richy n'a pas voyagé aux Etats-Unis. _____

_____

3. Madame et Monsieur Armstrong n'ont pas aimé le dessert. _____

_____

4. Mathilde n'a pas entendu la musique. _____

_____

5. Joseph n'a pas choisi une jolie cravate. _____

_____

F. Passé composé with **avoir** in the negative-interrogative — change into negative-interrogative using the **est-ce que** form only.

> Model: **Suzanne n'a pas fini le livre.**   You ask: **Est-ce que Suzanne n'a pas fini le livre?**

1. Robert n'a pas dansé hier soir. _____

2.   Joséphine n'a pas chanté ce matin. _____

3.   Guy et Michel n'ont pas fini leurs leçons. _____

_____

4.   Françoise et Simone n'ont pas entendu la musique. _____

_____

5.   Charles n'a pas perdu son ami. _____

II.   Match the following.

1.   She drank some milk.   _____ Il a vendu sa voiture.

2.   They heard a big noise.   _____ Elles ont fini le travail.

3.   She played in the park.   _____ Il a fermé la fenêtre.

4.   She worked yesterday.   _____ Ils ont oublié de venir.

5.   They lost their dog.   _____ Il a expliqué la leçon.

6.   He explained the lesson.   _____ Elle a joué dans le parc.

7.   He sold his car.   _____ Elles ont perdu leur chien.

8.   He closed the window.   _____ Ils ont entendu un grand bruit.

9.   They forgot to come.   _____ Elle a bu du lait.

10.   They finished the work.   _____ Elle a travaillé hier.

III.   Change the infinitive in parentheses to the past participle.

> **Model: (voir)   Ils ont _____   You write on the blank line: vu**
> **la représentation de Carmen.**

1.   (aimer)   Ils ont _____ la représentation de Carmen.

2.   (quitter)   Ils ont _____ la maison à sept heures et demie.

3.   (prendre)   Ils ont _____ leurs places à huit heures et quart.

4.   (commencer)   La représentation a _____ à huit heures et demie.

5.   (parler)   Madame Paquet a _____ avec les dames.

6.   (fumer)   Monsieur Paquet a _____ sa cigarette.

7.   (manger)   Pierre a _____ son chocolat.

8.   (boire)   Janine a _____ son jus d'orange.

167

9. (voir)   Elle a _____ un homme.

10. (dire)   Elle a _____ . — Oh! Monsieur! Votre autographe!

IV. Give the 3 English translations for each of the following French verb forms in the passé composé. Refer to the chart on page 162.

1. J'ai dansé.   _____ _____ _____

2. Vous avez fini.   _____ _____ _____

3. Nous avons vendu.   _____ _____ _____

V. For each of the following verbs in the passé composé write in French the correct form of **avoir**; in other words, the present indicative tense of **avoir**.

1. J'_____ joué.

2. Tu _____ pleuré.

3. Il _____ fini.

4. Elle _____ choisi.

5. Janine _____ chanté.

6. Nous _____ dansé.

7. Vous _____ perdu.

8. Ils _____ répondu.

9. J'_____ étudié.

10. Il _____ parlé.

11. Robert _____ travaillé.

12. Marie et Bob _____ dîné.

B. Verbs conjugated with **être**

MASCULINE SUBJECTS		FEMININE SUBJECTS	
Singular	Plural	Singular	Plural
je suis allé	nous sommes allés	je suis allée	nous sommes allées
tu es allé	vous êtes allé(s)	tu es allée	vous êtes allée(s)
il est allé	ils sont allés	elle est allée	elles sont allées
English equivalents: I went, *or* I have gone, *or* I did go; you went, *or* you have gone, *or* you did go; *etc., etc., etc.*			

Rules and observations:

1. To form the *passé composé* of verbs conjugated with **être**, use the present indicative of **être** plus the past participle of the verb. All reflexive verbs are conjugated with **être** as are the 17 verbs in the chart below.

2. The past participle of a verb conjugated with **être** agrees in gender (*i.e.*, whether masculine or feminine) and number (*i.e.*, whether singular or plural) with the subject, as shown in the box above. The past participle of a verb conjugated with **être**, therefore, is like an adjective because it describes the subject in some way.

Compare:	**Elle est jolie.**	**Elle est partie.**
	She is pretty.	She has left.

3. To form the negative, interrogative, and negative-interrogative, do the same as you did for verbs conjugated with **avoir** in the passé composé. The word order is the same. See the summary at the end of work unit eleven.

C. The 17 verbs conjugated with être*

1. **aller** to go

2. **arriver** to arrive

3. ***descendre** to go down, come down

   Elle est descendue vite.
   She came down quickly.

   BUT: *Elle a descendu la valise.*
   She brought down the suitcase.

4. **devenir** to become

5. **entrer** to enter, go in, come in

6. ***monter** to go up, come up

   Elle est montée lentement.
   She went up slowly.

   BUT: *Elle a monté l'escalier.*
   She went up the stairs.

7. **mourir** to die

8. **naître** to be born

9. **partir** to leave

10. ***passer** to go by, pass by

    Elle est passée chez moi.
    She came by my house.

BUT: *Elle m'a passé le sel.*
She passed me the salt.

AND: *Elle a passé un examen.*
She took an exam.

11. ***rentrer** to go in again,
    to return (home)

    Elle est rentrée tôt.
    She returned home early.

    BUT: *Elle a rentré le chat dans la maison.*
    She brought (took) the cat into the house.

12. **rester** to remain, stay

13. **retourner** to return, go back

14. **revenir** to come back

15. ***sortir** to go out

    Elle est sortie hier soir.
    She went out last night.

    BUT: *Elle a sorti son mouchoir.*
    She took out her handkerchief.

16. **tomber** to fall

17. **venir** to come

*Some of these verbs, as noted above, are conjugated with **avoir** if the verb is used in a transitive sense and has a direct object.*

D. Some irregular past participles

INFINITIVE	PAST PARTICIPLE	INFINITIVE	PAST PARTICIPLE
1. **apprendre** _to learn_	**appris**	16. **naître** _to be born_	**né**
2. **avoir** _to have_	**eu**	17. **ouvrir** _to open_	**ouvert**
3. **boire** _to drink_	**bu**	18. **paraître** _to appear, seem_	**paru**
4. **comprendre** _to understand_	**compris**	19. **permettre** _to permit_	**permis**
5. **couvrir** _to cover_	**couvert**	20. **pouvoir** _to be able, can_	**pu**
6. **croire** _to believe_	**cru**	21. **prendre** _to take_	**pris**
7. **devenir** _to become_	**devenu**	22. **promettre** _to promise_	**promis**
8. **devoir** _to owe, have to, should_	**dû**	23. **recevoir** _to receive_	**reçu**
9. **dire** _to say, tell_	**dit**	24. **revenir** _to come back_	**revenu**
10. **écrire** _to write_	**écrit**	25. **rire** _to laugh_	**ri**
11. **être** _to be_	**été**	26. **savoir** _to know_	**su**
12. **faire** _to do, make_	**fait**	27. **tenir** _to hold_	**tenu**
13. **lire** _to read_	**lu**	28. **venir** _to come_	**venu**
14. **mettre** _to put, place_	**mis**	29. **voir** _to see_	**vu**
15. **mourir** _to die_	**mort**	30. **vouloir** _to want_	**voulu**

Exercises

Review the preceding material before starting these exercises.

I.   Write the answers to the following in complete sentences in French.

A.   Passé composé with **être** in the affirmative — answer the questions in the affirmative.

Drill on aller

REMEMBER TO WATCH FOR AN AGREEMENT OF THE PAST PARTICIPLE WITH THE SUBJECT IN THE PASSÉ COMPOSÉ WHEN THE VERB IS CONJUGATED WITH **être**!

Model: **Madame Paquet est-elle allée à l'opéra?**   **You answer:**   **Oui, Madame Paquet est allée à l'opéra.**

1.   Janine est-elle allée au cinéma? _____

2.   Monique est-elle allée à l'école? _____

3.   Robert est-il allé au théâtre? _____

4.   Pierre et Raymond sont-ils allés au parc? _____

5.   Anne et Béatrice sont-elles allées au Canada? _____

_____

6.   Jacques et Jeanne sont-ils allés à l'aéroport? _____

_____

7.   Monsieur et Madame Beaupuy sont-ils allés aux Etats-Unis? _____

_____

8.   La mère est-elle allée dans le garage? _____

9.   Le père est-il allé dans la cuisine? _____

10.   La jeune fille est-elle allée à la pharmacie? _____

_____

B. Passé composé with **être** in the negative — answer the questions in the negative.

| Model: | Janine est-elle arrivée à l'opéra à huit heures et demie? | You answer: | Non, elle n'est pas arrivée à l'opéra à huit heures et demie. |

> Use a pronoun subject in your answer where a noun subject is given in the question.

1. Madame Paquet est-elle arrivée à l'opéra à huit heures et demie? _____

_____

2. Est-ce qu'ils sont entrés dans le théâtre à huit heures? _____

_____

3. Monsieur et Madame Paquet sont-ils partis de bonne heure? _____

_____

4. Est-ce qu'il est resté à la maison? _____

5. Simone est-elle sortie ce soir? _____

C. Passé composé with **être** in the interrogative — change to the interrogative in the inverted form.

| Model: | Monique est tombée dans la rue. | You ask: | Monique est-elle tombée dans la rue? |

1. Yolande est venue ce soir. _____

2. François est retourné à midi. _____

3. Les garçons sont restés dans l'école. _____

4. Les jeunes filles sont descendues vite. _____

5. Monsieur et Madame Paquet sont rentrés à minuit. _____

_____

D. Passé composé with **être** in the interrogative — change to the interrogative with **est-ce que**.

| Model: | Madame Banluc est née à la Martinique. | You ask: | Est-ce que Madame Banluc est née à la Martinique? |

1.   John James Audubon est né aux Cayes à Haïti. _____

   _____

2.   Napoléon Bonaparte est mort à Sainte-Hélène. _____

   _____

3.   Marie-Antoinette est née à Vienne. _____

4.   Valéry Giscard d'Estaing est devenu Président de la République française en 1974. ___

   _____

5.   Joséphine est née à la Martinique. _____

Joséphine est née à la Martinique.

6. Marie-Antoinette est morte à Paris. _____

7. Joséphine est devenue impératrice en 1804. _____

_____

E. Passé composé with **être** in the negative-interrogative — change the following negative sentences into negative-interrogative using the inverted form only.

   Model: Tu n'es pas sorti hier soir.   **You ask: N'es-tu pas sorti hier soir?**

1. Tu n'es pas resté à la maison. _____

2. Elle n'est pas tombée dans le jardin. _____

3. Il n'est pas parti ce matin. _____

4. Vous n'êtes pas arrivé à dix heures. _____

5. Elles ne sont pas allées à l'école aujourd'hui. _____

_____

II. Match the following.

1. She has left.   _____ Il a bu du vin.

2. They have read some books. _____ Elle est partie.

3. They died.   _____ Ils ont lu des livres.

4. He drank some wine.   _____ Elles sont mortes.

5. We went into the living room. _____ Vous avez appris la leçon.

6. You went to the restaurant. _____ Nous sommes entrés dans le salon.

7. He has had an accident.   _____ Tu es allée au restaurant.

8. She has been sick.   _____ Vous êtes devenu médecin.

9. You became a doctor.   _____ Il a eu un accident.

10. You learned the lesson.   _____ Elle a été malade.

III. Give the 3 English translations for each of the following French verb forms in the passé composé. Refer to the chart on page 162.

1. Je suis allé au cinéma. _____ _____ _____

2. Elle est partie. _____ _____ _____

174 3. Nous sommes arrivés. _____ _____ _____

IV. For each of the following verbs in the passé composé write in French the correct form of **être**.

1. Je _____ allé.

2. Tu _____ venu.

3. Il _____ arrivé.

4. Elle _____ partie.

5. Jean _____ sorti.

6. Nous _____ entrés.

7. Vous _____ tombé.

8. Ils _____ montés.

9. Elles _____ allées.

10. Je _____ descendu.

11. Michel _____ rentré.

12. Elle _____ morte.

V. Un acrostiche. Finish writing the past participle (in French) for each of the following verbs.

1. lire   1. L

2. avoir   2. E

3. prendre   3. P

4. arriver   4. A

5. rire   5. R

6. tenir   6. T

7.   7. I

8. croire   8. C

9.   9. I

10. promettre   10. P

11. écrire   11. E

12. pouvoir   12. P

13. aller   13. A

14. savoir   14. S

15. sortir   15. S

16. être   16. É

VI. For each of the following verbs in the passé composé write (in French) the correct form of either **avoir** or **être**, depending on which is required.

1. Suzanne _____ parlé.

2. Il _____ monté.

3. Elle _____ sortie.

4. Elle _____ compris.

5. Nous _____ arrivés.

6. Vous _____ dit.

7. Elles _____ lu.

8. Tu _____ fait.

9. Robert _____ resté.

10. Ils _____ ri.

11. Je _____ allé.

12. Madame Paquet _____ bu.

VII. Identify the following past participles by writing the infinitive form (in French). These past participles are all irregular.

Model: dit   **You write: dire**

1. appris _____
2. devenu _____
3. eu _____
4. couvert _____
5. cru _____
6. compris _____
7. permis _____
8. reçu _____
9. promis _____
10. voulu _____
11. dû _____
12. vu _____
13. dit _____
14. venu _____
15. écrit _____
16. été _____
17. bu _____
18. fait _____
19. tenu _____
20. lu _____
21. ouvert _____
22. mis _____
23. su _____
24. mort _____
25. ri _____
26. né _____
27. revenu _____
28. paru _____
29. pu _____
30. pris _____

VIII. Write the past participle (in French) for each of the following verbs. Some are regular, some are irregular.

Model: vendre   **You write: vendu**

1. avoir _____
2. être _____
3. faire _____
4. finir _____
5. savoir _____
6. lire _____
7. apprendre _____
8. défendre _____
9. choisir _____

176

10. aller _____   13. aider _____   16. voir _____

11. sortir _____   14. bâtir _____   17. danser _____

12. saisir _____   15. jouer _____   18. vendre _____

IX. Some verbs in French are conjugated with **avoir** to form the passé composé and some verbs are conjugated with **être**. For each of the following verbs write on the blank line either **avoir** or **être**, depending on which is required to form the passé composé.

Models: aller   **You write: être**

          parler   **You write: avoir**

1. rester _____   8. chanter _____   15. partir _____

2. danser _____   9. mourir _____   16. chercher _____

3. finir _____   10. donner _____   17. retourner _____

4. vendre _____   11. dire _____   18. choisir _____

5. arriver _____   12. naître _____   19. avoir _____

6. entrer _____   13. aller _____   20. être _____

7. aimer _____   14. étudier _____   21. venir _____

X. Change from the passé composé to the present indicative tense.

Model: Il a bu du lait.   **You write: Il boit du lait.**

1. Il a lu un bon livre. _____

2. J'ai vendu la voiture. _____

3. Elle est allée à l'opéra. _____

4. Nous avons écrit des lettres. _____

5. Vous êtes arrivé de bonne heure. _____

XI. Change from the present indicative tense to the passé composé.

Model: Monsieur Paquet a une   **You write: Monsieur Paquet a eu une**
         belle voiture grise.   **belle voiture grise.**

1. Madame Paquet a un beau chapeau rouge. _____

177

2. Janine boit un jus d'orange. _____

3. Pierre mange du chocolat. _____

4. Monique va au cinéma. _____

5. Jeanne et Joséphine entrent dans le théâtre. _____

XII. Fill in the ending of the past participle with the appropriate agreement, if needed. If none is needed, write a dash (—). Refer to the story at the beginning of this unit if you have to. The answers are there!

> **Model: La famille Paquet est**   **You fill in the ending of the past participle if**
> **allé_____ à l'opéra.**   **an agreement is needed: é or s**

1. La famille Paquet est allé_____ à l'opera.

2. Monsieur Paquet est retourné_____ à sa place.

3. Madame Paquet est retourné_____ à sa place.

4. Janine est retourné_____ à sa place.

5. Ils sont arrivé_____ à l'opéra à huit heures.

6. Ils sont entré_____ dans le théâtre.

7. Pierre est retourné_____ à sa place.

XIII. On the blank line, write the appropriate past participle of the verb in parentheses. Refer to the story at the beginning of this unit if you have to. The answers are there!

> **Model: (aller)   La famille Paquet**   **You write on the blank line: allée**
> **est _____ à l'opéra.**

1. (aller)   La famille Paquet est _____ à l'opéra.

2. (arriver)   Ils sont _____ à l'opéra à huit heures.

3. (entrer)   Ils sont _____ dans le théâtre.

4. (aller)   Madame Paquet est _____ parler avec quelques dames.

5. (aller)   Monsieur Paquet est _____ fumer une cigarette.

6. (aller)   Pierre est _____ acheter du chocolat.

7. (aller)   Janine est _____ boire un jus d'orange.

8. (retourner)   Madame Paquet est _____ à sa place.

9. (retourner)   Monsieur Paquet est _____ à sa place.

10. (retourner)   Janine est _____ à sa place.

XIV.   Oral Proficiency. Respond orally in French to the situation described. (Later, you may write your responses for intensive practice.) Review this unit for ideas or words to use. You may use your own ideas or the vocabulary suggested in the situation. You must use the **passé composé** tense.

Situation: You have just seen a French comedy on stage. On your way out of the theater a friend of yours sees you in the lobby, rushes over to you, and asks why you look angry: *Pourquoi as-tu l'air fâché?* Give some reasons why. You may use your own ideas or ideas suggested by the following: *aimer, détester, perdre, vendre, finir, mauvais, boire, voir, rire.*

The Opera House, Paris.
Reprinted with permission of French Cultural Services, New York.

Here's a recipe in French for a stew.
Try making it yourself. It's fun!

RAGOÛT DE MOUTON À L'IRLANDAISE (IRISH STEW)

Pour 6 personnes   cuisson: 2 heures, 35 min.

1500 grammes de mouton coupé
     en morceaux
3 grosses pommes de terre
300 grammes d'oignons
sel, poivre, blanc de céleri,
     et 3 gousses d'ail
3 cuillères à soupe de farine blanche

1. Disposez dans une cocotte:
   (a) une couche d'oignons hachés
   (b) une grosse pomme de terre coupée en lamelles
   (c) un tiers des morceaux de mouton
   (d) du sel, du poivre
   (e) une gousse d'ail haché (si vous désirez)
2. Répétez en disposant une deuxième couche d'oignons hachés, une grosse pomme de terre coupée en lamelles, un tiers des morceaux de mouton, du sel, du poivre, une gousse d'ail haché.
3. Répétez en disposant une troisième couche d'oignons hachés, une grosse pomme de terre coupée en lamelles, un tiers des morceaux de mouton, du sel, du poivre, une gousse d'ail haché.
4. Ajoutez une tasse et demie d'eau chaude.
5. Faites bouillir pendant 5 min.
6. Laissez cuire doucement, à couvert, pendant 1 heure 30 min.
7. Après une heure et demie, si le mélange est épais, ajoutez un peu d'eau chaude. Maintenant, mettez dans la cocotte le céleri coupé en petits morceaux.
8. Laissez cuire doucement pendant 1 heure.
9. Maintenant, ajoutez 3 cuillères à soupe de farine blanche, lentement, pendant que vous remuez le mélange.
10. Bonne chance! Ne le brûlez pas!

Direct Object Pronouns, including en

Let's see how the family stew turns out.

A chacun son goût

Ce soir Pierre a servi le dîner pour la famille et les voisins, Monsieur et Madame Richy. Il a servi un ragoût de mouton à l'irlandaise. La recette pour le ragoût est sur la page d'en face.

Pierre:	Voici le ragoût! Je vais le servir maintenant. A table, s'il vous plaît!

(Tout le monde va s'asseoir à table: Monsieur et Madame Paquet, Janine, Pierre, Monsieur et Madame Richy.)

Janine:	Oh! Il sent bon!
Monsieur Paquet:	Et comment! Il sent très bon. Moi, j'ai grand faim.
Madame Paquet:	Il est magnifique, n'est-ce pas? . . . Excusez-moi, je vais dans la cuisine. Vous pouvez commencer sans moi.

(Madame Paquet se lève. Elle quitte la table pour aller dans la cuisine.)

Madame Richy:	Vraiment extraordinaire!
Monsieur Richy:	J'adore les ragoûts.
Madame Richy:	Moi aussi. Pierre, tu es un bon garçon!
Pierre:	Alors, qui va commencer?
Monsieur Paquet:	Après toi, Pierre. Tu peux commencer si tu veux.
Janine:	Vas-y, Pierre! Tu goûtes le premier.
Pierre:	Bon. Alors, je vais commencer . . . Maintenant, je goûte le ragoût . . .
Janine:	Je vais le goûter aussi . . . Oh! Oh! Il est brûlé! C'est dégoûtant. Je vais être malade. Il est brûlé! Goûtez-en!

(Janine se lève et quitte la table.)

Pierre:	Oui. Il est brûle. Janine a raison. Il est brûle. Je ne l'aime pas. Je vais être malade aussi. Goûtez-en!

(Pierre se lève et quitte la table.)

Monsieur Paquet: Je vais le goûter aussi . . . Oui. Il est brûlé. Janine et Pierre ont raison. Je ne l'aime pas.

(Monsieur Paquet se lève pour quitter la table.)

Monsieur Richy: Moi, je vais le goûter maintenant . . . Ce ragoût est délicieux! Il est bien cuit, comme le ragoût de ma mère. Bien cuit! Excellent . . . Chérie, pourquoi ne fais-tu pas un ragoût si bien cuit aussi?

Madame Richy: Tu as raison, chéri. La prochaine fois je vais le faire trop cuire. Je vais le brûler pour toi et tu peux le manger seul. Tiens! Mange toute la cocotte!

(Madame Richy se lève. Monsieur Richy reste seul à la table avec la cocotte de ragoût brûlé devant lui.)

(Madame Paquet rentre dans la salle à manger avec le dessert.)

Madame Paquet: Alors, est-ce que tout le monde aime mon ragoût? J'ai un dessert que j'ai fait aussi. Qui veut en goûter?

Vocabulaire

à couvert covered

à table to (at) the table, come to the table!

l'ail *n. m.*, garlic; **une gousse d'ail** a clove of garlic

aime *v. form of* **aimer**; **Je ne l'aime pas!** I don't like it!

ajouter *v.*, to add

avoir faim *v.*, to be hungry; **avoir raison** to be right; **J'ai grand faim** I'm very hungry; **Janine et Pierre ont raison!** Janine and Pierre are right!

blanc *m.*, **blanche** *f.*, *adj.*, white

bouillir *v.*, to boil

brûler *v.*, to burn; **brûlé** burned; **ne le brûlez pas!** don't burn it!

le céleri *n.*, celery; **le blanc de céleri** celery stalk

chacun *pron.*, each one; **à chacun son goût** to each his/her own (taste)

la chance *n.*, chance, luck; **bonne chance!** good luck!

chaud *m.*, **chaude** *f.*, *adj.*, hot

la cocotte *n.*, the stewing pot; **toute la cocotte** the whole pot

comment *adv.*, how

connaît *v. form of* **connaître** to know (someone), to be acquainted with (someone); **Est-ce que Pierre connaît Madeleine?** Does Pierre know Madeleine? (pres. indicative: **je connais, tu connais, il (elle) connaît, nous connaissons, vous connaissez, ils (elles) connaissent)**

la couche *n.*, layer

couper *v.*, to cut; **coupé** sliced

la cuillère *n.*, the spoon; **cuillère à soupe** soup spoon

cuire *v.*, to cook; **cuit** cooked; **cuisson** cooking time; **bien cuit** well done (cooked); **trop cuit** overdone (overcooked)

dégoûtant *adj.*, disgusting, revolting

devant *prep.*, in front of;

devant lui in front of him

disposer *v.*, to dispose, to arrange; **en disposant** arranging

doucement *adv.*, gently (low flame)

en *partitive*, some; **goûtez-en!** taste some!

épais *m.*, **épaisse** *f.*, *adj.*, thick

la faim *n.*, hunger; **avoir faim** to be hungry

faire bouillir *v.*, to boil; **faire trop cuire** to overcook

la farine *n.*, flour

goûter *v.*, to taste; **le goût** the taste; **Qui veut en goûter?** Who wants to taste some? **Goûtez-en!** Taste some!

le gramme *n.*, the gram (metric unit of measurement); 1 gram equals about .035 ounce; 500 grams equal about 1.1 lbs.; 300 grams equal about 10 oz.

gros *m.*, **grosse** *f.*, *adj.*, big, fat, large

hacher *v.*, to chop (up);

haché chopped

irlandais *m.*, **irlandaise** *f.*, *adj.*, Irish; **à l'irlandaise** Irish style

le kilogramme *n.*, kilogram (1,000 grams; 1 kilo equals about 2.2 lbs.)

laisser *v.*, to let, to allow

la lamelle *n.*, the thin slice

malade *adj.*, sick

le mélange *n.*, the mixture

mettez *v. form of* **mettre** (to put, to place)

le morceau *n.*, the piece, morsel

le mouton *n.*, the mutton

l'oignon *n. m.*, the onion

la page *n.*, the page; **page d'en face** opposite page

pendant *prep.*, during; **pendant que** *conj.*, while

peux *v. form of pouvoir*; **tu peux commencer** you can begin

le poivre *n.*, the pepper

la pomme de terre *n.*, the potato

prochain *m.*, **prochaine** *f.*, *adj.*, next; **la prochaine fois** the next time

le ragoût *n.*, the stew

la raison *n.*, the reason; **avoir raison** to be right

la recette *n.*, the recipe

remuer *v.*, to stir

le sel *n.*, the salt

sent *v. form of* **sentir** (to smell, to feel); **il sent très bon!** it smells very good!

servir *v.*, to serve; **je vais le servir maintenant** I'm going to serve it now.

seul *m.*, **seule** *f.*, *adj.*, alone

tiens! *exclam.*, here!

un tiers one-third

vas-y! go to it!

veux *v. form of* **vouloir** (to want); **si tu veux** if you want

le voisin, la voisine *n.*, the neighbor

Exercises

Review the story and vocabulary before starting these exercises.

I. Answer the following questions in complete sentences (in French). They are based on the story, "Chacun son goût."

1. Qui a servi le dîner ce soir? _____

2. Pour qui a-t-il servi le dîner? _____

3. Qui commence à goûter le ragoût? _____

4. Qui aime le ragoût? _____

5. Pourquoi aime-t-il le ragoût? _____

6. Qui a fait le ragoût? _____

II. Answer the following questions in complete sentences (in French). They are personal questions and require answers of your own.

1. Aimez-vous manger du ragoût? _____

2. Savez-vous faire un ragoût? _____

3. Aimez-vous le ragoût brûlé? _____

III. Comment dit-on en français . . . ? Find these statements in the story and write them in French.

1. And how! It smells very good. I'm very hungry. _____

   _____

2. Janine is right. It's burned. I don't like it. Taste some! _____

   _____

3. I'm going to taste it. _____

4. Mrs. Paquet comes back into the dining room with the dessert. _____

   _____

5. Does everybody like my stew? I have a dessert that I made also. Who wants to taste some?

   _____

   _____

Structures de la Langue

A. Direct object pronouns

	Singular		Plural
me or **m'**	me	**nous**	us
te or **t'**	you (familiar)	**vous**	you (sing. polite or plural)
le or **l'**	him, it	**les**	them (persons or things)
la or **l'**	her, it		

person or thing (braces grouping le/la)

Rules and observations:

1. A direct object **pronoun** takes the place of a direct object **noun**.

2. A direct object noun ordinarily comes after the verb, but a direct object pronoun is ordinarily placed *in front of* the verb.

3. The vowel **e** in **me**, **te**, **le** and the vowel **a** in **la** drop and an apostrophe is added if the verb right after it starts with a vowel or a silent *h; e.g.,* **je l'aime**. (I like it.)

4. You might say that the direct object "receives" the action of the verb.

5. Study the direct object pronouns in the above box and the model sentences in the boxes below.

184

B. Direct object pronoun referring to a thing in the present indicative

The noun as direct object of the verb	The pronoun in place of the noun
(a) **Janine lit le poème.** *Janine is reading the poem.*	(a) **Janine le lit.** *Janine is reading it.*
(b) **Pierre lit la lettre.** *Pierre is reading the letter.*	(b) **Pierre la lit.** *Pierre is reading it.*
(c) **Janine apprend le poème.** *Janine is learning the poem.*	(c) **Janine l'apprend.** *Janine is learning it.*
(d) **Pierre écrit la lettre.** *Pierre is writing the letter.*	(d) **Pierre l'écrit.** *Pierre is writing it.*
(e) **Janine lit les poèmes.** *Janine is reading the poems.*	(e) **Janine les lit.** *Janine is reading them.*

Rules and observations:

1. The direct object pronoun must agree in gender and number with the noun it is replacing. Gender means masculine or feminine. Number means singular or plural.

2. Actually, what you do is drop the noun direct object. The definite article that remains becomes the pronoun direct object. Put it *in front of* the verb. If the verb starts with a vowel or a mute *h*, drop the **e** in **le** and the **a** in **la** and add an apostrophe.

(a) From: **Janine lit le poème.** You get: **Janine le lit.**	Janine lit le poème.
(b) From: **Pierre lit la lettre.** You get: **Pierre la lit.**	Pierre lit la lettre.
(c) From: **Janine apprend le poème.** You get: **Janine l'apprend.**	Janine apprend le poème.

(d) From: **Pierre écrit la lettre.** You get: **Pierre l'écrit.**	Pierre ⌐écrit (la) lettre.
(e) From: **Janine lit les poèmes.** You get: **Janine les lit.**	Janine ⌐lit (les) poèmes.

C. Direct object pronoun referring to a person in the present indicative

Pierre **me** connaît.	Pierre knows *me.*
te	*you. (familiar)*
le	*him.*
la	*her.*
nous	*us.*
vous	*you. (sing. polite or plural)*
les	*them.*

Rules and observations:

1. Direct object pronouns, whether they refer to persons or things, are ordinarily placed *in front of* the verb.

2. If the verb is negative, put **ne** *in front of the direct object pronoun* and **pas** *after* the verb, as in the examples in the box below.

Pierre ne **me** connaît pas.	Pierre does not know *me.*
ne **te** pas.	*you. (familiar)*
ne **le** pas.	*him.*
ne **la** pas.	*her.*
ne **nous** pas.	*us.*
ne **vous** pas.	*you. (sing. polite or plural)*
ne **les** pas.	*them.*

186

D. Direct object pronoun in the affirmative and negative command

Affirmative command		Negative command	
with noun direct object	with pronoun direct object	with noun direct object	with pronoun direct object
Apprenez le poème!	**Apprenez-le!**	N'apprenez pas le poème.	**Ne l'apprenez pas!**
Ecrivez la lettre!	**Ecrivez-la!**	N'écrivez pas la lettre.	**Ne l'écrivez pas!**
Etudiez les leçons!	**Etudiez-les!**	N'étudiez pas les leçons.	**Ne les étudiez pas!**

Rules and observations:

1. In the affirmative command, a direct object pronoun is placed *right after* the verb and joined with a hyphen.

2. In the negative command, a direct object pronoun is placed *in front of* the verb, where it ordinarily goes.

3. In the negative command, the **ne** is placed *in front of* the direct object pronoun and the **pas** *after* the verb.

E. Direct object pronoun as object of an infinitive

(a) **Monsieur Richy veut goûter le ragoût.** ⟶ **Monsieur Richy veut le goûter.**

 (*Mr. Richy wants to taste the stew.*)   (*Mr. Richy wants to taste it.*)

(b) **Janine veut apprendre le poème.** ⟶ **Janine veut l'apprendre.**

 (*Janine wants to learn the poem.*)   (*Janine wants to learn it.*)

(c) **Pierre ne veut pas écrire la lettre.** ⟶ **Pierre ne veut pas l'écrire.**

 (*Pierre does not want to write the letter.*)   (*Pierre does not want to write it.*)

Rules and observations:

1. A pronoun as object of an infinitive is placed *in front of* the infinitive.

187

2. In a negative statement with a pronoun as object of an infinitive, **ne** is placed in front of the verb and **pas** after it (as is usual) and the pronoun as object of the infinitive still remains in front of the infinitive.

3. The point is that the verb can be made negative and it has nothing to do with the logical position of the pronoun as object of an infinitive.

F. Direct object pronoun with a verb in the passé composé

The noun as direct object of the verb	The pronoun in place of the noun
(a) **Marie a préparé le dîner.** (Mary prepared the dinner.)	(a) **Elle l'a préparé.** (She prepared it.)
(b) **Robert a préparé la salade.** (Robert prepared the salad.)	(b) **Il l'a préparée.** (He prepared it.)
(c) **Jean a préparé les dîners.** (John prepared the dinners.)	(c) **Il les a préparés.** (He prepared them.)
(d) **Anne a préparé les salades.** (Anne prepared the salads.)	(d) **Elle les a préparées.** (She prepared them.)

Rules and observations:

1. The verb form **a préparé** is in the passé composé, 3d person, singular tense. Review how to form the passé composé in the preceding work unit.

2. You still put the direct object pronoun *in front of* the verb form (**a préparé**), just as you put it *in front of* the simple verb form in the present indicative. Review the position of the direct object pronoun in the present indicative on pages **185 and 186.**

3. There is one new thing to be learned here: the past participle (**préparé**) of the verb in the passé composé must agree in gender (masculine or feminine) and number (singular or plural) with the *preceding* direct object pronoun, if there is one.

4. If the *preceding* direct object pronoun is **le** (masculine, singular), there is no agreement required on the past participle.

5. If the *preceding* direct object pronoun is **la** (feminine, singular), you must add **e** to the past participle.

6. If the *preceding* direct object pronoun is **les** (masculine, plural), you must add **s** to the past participle.

7. If the *preceding* direct object pronoun is **les** (feminine, plural), you must add **es** to the past participle.

8. To sum it up: There must be an agreement in both gender and number in the past participle of a verb conjugated with **avoir** with the *preceding* direct object pronoun if there is one. There is no agreement if the direct object is a *noun* and it follows the verb. Compare the column on the right and the column on the left in the above box.

9. A reminder: When we conjugate a verb with **être**, there is an agreement between the past participle and the subject, *e.g.,* **Janine est allée au théâtre**. See pages **168** and **169**.

G. Meanings and positions of **en** as an object pronoun

(a) Avez-vous **du café?** (Have you *any coffee?*) (Have you *some coffee?*)	Oui, j'**en** ai. (Yes, I have *some* [*of it*].)
(b) Buvez-vous **de l'eau?** (Do you drink *any water?*)	Oui, j'**en** bois. (Yes, I drink *some.*)
(c) Mangez-vous **de la glace?** (Do you eat *any ice cream?*)	Oui, j'**en** mange. (Yes, I eat *some* .)
(d) Mangez-vous **des pommes?** (Do you eat *any apples?*)	Oui, j'**en** mange. (Yes, I eat *some* .)
(e) Avez-vous **des soeurs?** (Do you have *any sisters?*)	Oui, j'**en** ai deux. (Yes, I have two [*of them*].)
(f) Vient-il **de Paris?** (Does he come *from Paris?*)	Oui, il **en** vient. (Yes, he comes *from there* .)
(g) Avez-vous peur **des serpents?** (Are you afraid *of snakes?*)	Oui, j'**en** ai peur. (Yes, I'm afraid *of them* .)
(h) Buvez **du café!** (Drink *some coffee!*)	Buvez-**en!** (Drink *some!*)
(i) Ne buvez pas **de café!** (Don't drink *any coffee!*)	N'**en** buvez pas! (Don't drink *any* [*of it*]*!*)

189

Rules and observations:

1. The pronoun **en** has more than one translation in English, as you can see from the model sentences in the above box.

2. **En** is used to replace a noun preceded by the preposition **de** or any combination of **de**; for example, **du**, **de l'**, **de la**, **des**.

3. **En** is used to refer to persons or things if the noun is used in a partitive sense.

4. **En** is used to refer to places and things but not to persons, if the noun is not used in a partitive sense. See (f) and (g) above.

5. In the affirmative imperative, **en** is placed *right after* the verb and joined with a hyphen. In the negative imperative, **en** is placed in front of the verb, where it is ordinarily placed, e.g., **Goûtez-en!** (Taste some!), **N'en goûtez pas!** (Don't taste any!)

Exercises

I. Change the following sentences by substituting a pronoun as object of the verb in place of the noun object. Rewrite the entire sentence.

   Model: Janine lit *le poème.*   You write: Janine le lit.

1. Pierre lit *la lettre.* _____

2. Janine écrit *la leçon.* _____

3. Michel apprend *l'espagnol.* _____

4. Christophe fait *les devoirs.* _____

5. Alexandre écoute *la musique.* _____

6. Yolande prononce *le mot.* _____

7. Théodore voit *l'hôtel.* _____

8. Monique dit *la phrase.* _____

9. Joséphine attend *l'autobus.* _____

10. Anne mange *les gâteaux.* _____

II. Answer the following questions in the affirmative, substituting a pronoun as object of the verb in place of the noun object. Also, substitute a pronoun in place of the noun subject. Rewrite the entire sentence.

> **Model: Janine écrit-elle *la leçon?***   **You write: Oui, elle l'écrit.**

1. Monique dit-elle *la phrase?* _____

2. Joséphine attend-elle *l'autobus?* _____

3. Pierre lit-il *la lettre?* _____

4. Michel mange-t-il *les gâteaux?* _____

5. Yolande écoute-t-elle *la musique?* _____

III. Answer the following questions in the negative, substituting a pronoun as object of the verb in place of the noun object. Also, substitute a pronoun in place of the noun subject. Rewrite the entire sentence.

> **Model: Est-ce que Janine boit le   You write: Non, elle ne le boit pas.**
> **jus d'orange?**

1. Est-ce que Pierre mange la saucisse? _____

2. Est-ce que Joséphine prononce le mot? _____

3. Est-ce qu'Henri aime le saucisson? _____

4. Est-ce que Georges lit la lettre? _____

5. Est-ce que Georgette apporte les gâteaux? _____

IV. Answer the following questions in complete sentences in the affirmative, substituting a direct object pronoun for the noun object.

> **Model: Apprenez-vous le français   You answer: Oui, je l'apprends**
> **maintenant?   maintenant.**

1. Comprenez-vous la leçon aujourd'hui? _____

2. Dites-vous toujours la vérité? _____

3. Faites-vous les devoirs maintenant? _____

4. Lisez-vous le journal tous les jours? _____

5. Ecrivez-vous la phrase en ce moment? _____ **191**

V. Answer the following questions in the affirmative in complete sentences, substituting a direct object pronoun for the noun object. Also, substitute a pronoun for the noun subject.

Model: **Est-ce que Pierre connaît**   You answer: **Oui, il la connaît.**
        Madeleine?

1. Est-ce que Janine connaît Monique? _____

2. Est-ce que Monique connaît Robert? _____

3. Est-ce que Robert connaît Pierre et Hélène? _____

4. Est-ce que Marie connaît Monsieur et Madame Paquet? _____

5. Est-ce qu'Henri connaît Anne et Françoise? _____

VI. Answer the following questions in the affirmative.

Model: **Est-ce qu'elle vous voit?**   You answer: **Oui, elle me voit.**

1. Est-ce qu'elle vous connaît? _____

2. Est-ce qu'il te voit? _____

3. Est-ce qu'elle nous aime? _____

4. Est-ce qu'ils les attendent? _____

5. Est-ce qu'il l'adore? _____

VII. Answer the following questions in the affirmative.

Model: **Est-ce que vous m'aimez bien?**   You answer: **Oui, je vous aime bien.**

1. Est-ce que tu m'aimes bien? _____

2. Est-ce que vous l'aimez bien aussi? _____

3. Est-ce que tu l'aimes bien aussi? _____

4. Est-ce qu'il vous aime bien? _____

5. Est-ce qu'elle vous aime bien aussi? _____

VIII. Answer the following questions in the affirmative.

Model: **Est-ce que vous m'aimez?**   You answer: **Oui, je vous aime.**

1. Est-ce que tu m'aimes? _____

192   2. Est-ce qu'il vous aime? _____

3. Est-ce que vous l'aimez aussi? _____

4. Est-ce qu'il t'aime? _____

5. Est-ce qu'elle vous aime? _____

IX. For each statement write a response in French in the affirmative imperative. Use a pronoun object in place of the noun object.

   Model: Je veux apprendre le poème!   You answer: **Bon! Alors, apprenez-le!**

1. Je veux écrire la lettre! _____

2. Je veux étudier les leçons! _____

3. Je veux lire le livre! _____

4. Je veux boire le lait! _____

5. Je veux faire les devoirs! _____

X. For each statement write a response in French in the negative imperative. Use a pronoun object in place of the noun object.

   **Model: Je ne veux pas apprendre   You answer: Bon! Alors, ne l'apprenez
   le poème!   pas!**

1. Je ne veux pas écrire la lettre! _____

2. Je ne veux pas étudier les leçons! _____

3. Je ne veux pas lire le livre! _____

4. Je ne veux pas boire le lait! _____

5. Je ne veux pas faire les devoirs! _____

XI. Change the following sentences by substituting a pronoun as object of the infinitive in place of the noun object. Rewrite the entire sentence.

   Model: Janine veut lire *la lettre*.   You write: **Janine veut la lire.**

1. Pierre veut lire *le livre*. _____

2. Madeleine veut apprendre *le poème*. _____

3. Paul ne veut pas écrire *la lettre*. _____

4. Philippe ne veut pas manger *la saucisse.* _____

5. Gertrude ne veut pas apporter *les gâteaux.* _____

XII. Answer the following questions in the affirmative, substituting **en** as a pronoun object of the verb in place of the words indicated.

Model: Avez-vous du café? **You answer: Oui, j'en ai.**

1. Avez-vous *du lait?* _____

194   **As-tu du lait?**

2. Buvez-vous *de l'eau?* _____

3. Mangez-vous *de la glace?* _____

4. Mangez-vous *des pommes?* _____

5. Avez-vous *des soeurs?* _____

6. Avez-vous *des frères?* _____

7. Vient-il *de Paris?* _____

8. Avez-vous peur *des serpents?* _____

9. Mangez-vous *du rosbif?* _____

10. Buvez-vous *du vin?* _____

XIII. Answer the following questions in the negative, substituting **en** as a pronoun object of the verb in place of the words indicated.

   Model: Avez-vous *du vin?*   **You answer: Non, je n'en ai pas.**

1. Avez-vous *du café?* _____

2. Avez-vous *de l'eau?* _____

3. Avez-vous *de la glace?* _____

4. Avez-vous *des gâteaux?* _____

5. Avez-vous *des frères?* _____

XIV. For each statement write a response in French in the affirmative imperative, substituting **en** in place of the words indicated.

   Model: Je veux boire *du café!*   **You answer: Bon! Alors, buvez-en!**

1. Je veux boire *du vin!* _____

2. Je veux manger *du gâteau!* _____

3. Je veux écrire *des lettres!* _____

4. Je veux boire *de l'eau!* _____

5. Je veux manger *de la salade!* _____

195

XV. For each statement write a response in French in the negative imperative, substituting **en** in place of the words indicated.

Model: **Je ne veux pas boire de café!**   **You answer:** **Bon! Alors, n'en buvez pas!**

1. Je ne veux pas boire *de vin!* _____

2. Je ne veux pas manger *de gâteau!* _____

3. Je ne veux pas écrire *de lettres!* _____

XVI. Change the following sentences in the passé composé by substituting a pronoun as object of the verb in place of the noun object. Rewrite the entire sentence. Watch for agreement of the past participle with a preceding direct object pronoun.

Model: **Pierre a préparé *la leçon*.**   **You write:** **Pierre l'a préparée.**

1. Madame Paquet a préparé *le dîner.* _____

2. Monsieur Richy a mangé *le ragoût.* _____

3. Pierre a servi *le dîner.* _____

4. Janine a préparé *les devoirs.* _____

5. Monsieur Paquet a préparé *les salades.* _____

XVII. Answer the following questions in the affirmative, substituting a pronoun as object of the verb in place of the noun object. Also, substitute a pronoun in place of the noun subject. Rewrite the entire sentence. Watch for agreement on the past participle!

Model: **Est-ce que Pierre a préparé *la salade?***   **You write:** **Oui, il l'a préparée.**

1. Est-ce que Pierre a servi *le dîner?* _____

2. Est-ce que Madame Paquet a préparé *le dîner?* _____

3. Est-ce que Monsieur Richy a mangé *le ragoût?* _____

4. Est-ce que Janine a écrit *la lettre?* _____

5. Est-ce que Christophe a fait *les devoirs?* _____

XVIII. Answer the following questions in the negative, substituting a pronoun as object of the verb in place of the noun object. Also, substitute a pronoun in place of the noun subject. Rewrite the entire sentence. Watch for agreement on the past participle!

> **Model: Est-ce que Pierre a préparé   You write: Non, il ne l'a pas préparé.**
> **le dîner?**

1. Est-ce que Guy a préparé *la salade?* _____

2. Est-ce que Pierre a fait *le dîner?* _____

3. Est-ce que Janine a lu *le poème?* _____

4. Est-ce que Madame Richy a mangé *le ragoût?* _____

5. Est-ce que Robert a fait *les devoirs?* _____

XIX.   Oral Proficiency. Respond orally in French to the situation described. (Later, you may write your responses for intensive practice.)

Situation: You prepared dinner for your friends. One friend says that he likes a dish you made and would like the recipe. In four or five sentences, tell your friend how to make the dish. Start with *Je suis content que tu aimes le* _____ . (I'm glad that you like the _____ .) You may use your own idea or ideas suggested by the following: *préparé, brûlé, poulet, cuire, la recette, mettre, trop de sel* (too much salt), *servir, oignon.*

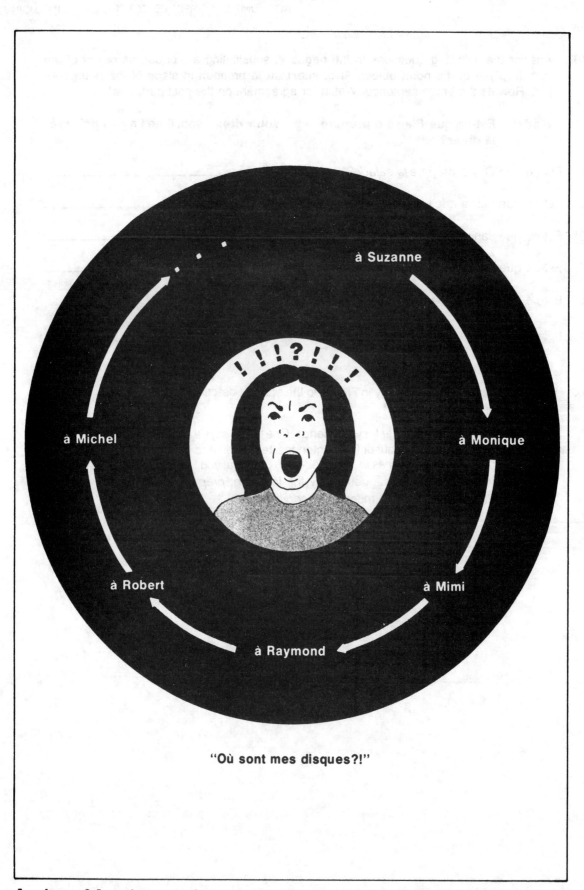

"Où sont mes disques?!"

Les disques? *Je ne les ai pas, Janine. Je les ai donnés à Monique. Je lui ai donné tes disques.*

Indirect Object Pronouns, including y

*Round and round the records go and
where do they end up? Who knows?*

La ronde

Janine a prêté ses disques à son amie Suzanne au mois de septembre. C'est aujourd'hui le premier décembre. Janine veut reprendre ses disques pour les écouter pendant les fêtes de Noël. Elle va voir son amie Suzanne et elle lui dit:

Janine: Suzanne, je t'ai prêté mes disques au mois de septembre et aujourd'hui c'est le premier décembre. Je veux les jouer pendant les fêtes de Noël. Veux-tu me rendre mes disques, s'il te plaît?

Suzanne: Je ne les ai pas, Janine. Je les ai donnés à Monique. Va la voir. Je lui ai donné les disques.

(Janine va voir Monique.)

Janine: Monique, j'ai prêté mes disques à Suzanne et elle m'a dit que vous les avez maintenant. Je lui ai donné mes disques au mois de septembre.

Monique: Je ne les ai pas, Janine. Je les ai prêtés à Mimi. Va la voir. Je lui ai donné les disques.

(Janine va voir Mimi.)

Janine: Mimi, as-tu mes disques? Tu les as, je sais. Je les ai prêtés à Suzanne, elle les a donnés à Monique et Monique m'a dit que vous les avez maintenant.

Mimi: Oh! Les disques! Quels disques? Les disques d'Edith Piaf? de Maurice Chevalier? de Lily Pons? de Judy Garland?

Janine: Oui, C'est ça.

Mimi: Non. Je ne les ai pas. Je les ai donnés à Raymond. Va le voir. Je lui ai donné les disques.

(Janine va voir Raymond.)

Janine: Raymond, j'ai prêté mes disques à Suzanne au mois de septembre et aujourd'hui c'est le premier décembre. Suzanne m'a dit qu'elle les a donnés à Monique. Monique m'a dit qu'elle les a donnés à Mimi. Mimi m'a dit que vous les avez

Raymond: Oh! Les disques. Je les ai donnés à Robert, et Robert les a donnés à Michel, et Michel les a donnés à . . .

Vocabulaire

l'ami *m.*, **l'amie** *f.*, *n.*, the friend
le disque *n.*, the phonograph record
écouter *v.*, to listen (to)
les *direct obj. pron.*, them
lui *indirect obj. pron.*, to her, to him
me *indirect obj. pron.*, to me

mes *poss. adj. pl.*, my
le mois *n.*, the month; **au mois de** in the month of
le Noël *n.*, Christmas
prêté *past part. of* **prêter** (to lend)
rendre *v.*, to return (something), to give back
reprendre *v.*, to take back,

get back
la ronde *n.*, the round
ses *poss. adj. pl.*, his, her
s'il te plaît please *(fam. use);* **s'il vous plaît** *(polite use)*
te *indirect obj. pron.*, to you *(fam.);* **t'** is a contraction of **te**

Exercises

Review the story and vocabulary before starting these exercises.

I. Answer the following questions in French in complete sentences. They are all based on the dialogue in this unit, "La ronde."

1. Qui a prêté ses disques à Suzanne? _____

2. Pourquoi Janine veut-elle reprendre ses disques? _____

   _____

3. Est-ce que Janine reprend ses disques? _____

II. Comment dit-on en français . . . ? Refer to the dialogue in this unit if you have to.

1. She said to me that you have them now. _____

2. Today is December first. _____

3. I don't have them. I gave the records to her. Go see her. _____

   _____

4. I gave the records to Mimi. Mimi gave them to Raymond. _____

   _____

5. I gave the records to him. Go see him. _____

III.   Unscramble the French words listed below and write them in the appropriate squares.

1.   ELS

2.   UA

3.   RÊTPÉ

4.   ÉNODN

5.   ĔLON

6.   QUESID

7.   SEM

Structures de la Langue

A.   Indirect object pronouns

Singular		Plural	
me or **m'**	to me	**nous**	to us
te or **t'**	to you *(familiar)*	**vous**	to you *(sing. polite or plural)*
lui	to him, to her, to it	**leur**	to them

Rules and observations:

1.   An indirect object pronoun takes the place of an indirect object noun.

2.   You might say that an indirect object "receives" the direct object because it is usually a matter of something "going" to someone; for example, *to me, to you, to him, to her, to it, to us, to them.* Sometimes the *to* is not mentioned in English: *I am giving him the book;* what we really mean to say is, *I am giving the book to him.* Then, too, there are some verbs in French that take an indirect object pronoun because the verb takes the preposition **à** *(to);* for example, **Je lui réponds** can be translated into English as: *I am answering her (or) him,* or, *I am responding to her (or) to him.*

201

3. An indirect object pronoun is ordinarily placed *in front of* the verb.

4. Study the indirect object pronouns in the above box and the model sentences in the box below.

Pierre **me** donne le gâteau.	Peter is giving the cake *to me.*
te	*to you.*
lui	*to him.*
lui	*to her.*
lui	*to it.*
nous	*to us.*
vous	*to you.*
leur	*to them.*

5. To make the verb negative, put **ne** *in front of the indirect object pronoun* and **pas** after the verb, as you did for the direct object pronouns:

> **Pierre ne me donne pas le gâteau.**
>
> *(Peter is not giving the cake to me.)*

Note: Double object pronouns are not ordinarily introduced in a Level One curriculum.

6. In the affirmative imperative, do the same as you did for the direct object pronouns. The indirect object pronoun is put *right after* the verb and joined with a hyphen:

> **Donnez-lui le gâteau!**   (Give the cake to him/her.)

7. In the affirmative imperative, **me** changes to **moi** when it is tacked on to the verb and joined with a hyphen:

> **Donnez-moi le gâteau!**   (Give me the cake!)

8. In the negative imperative, do the same as you did for the direct object pronouns. Put the indirect object pronoun *in front of* the verb, where it ordinarily goes:

> **Ne me donnez pas le gâteau!**   (Don't give me the cake!)
>
> **Ne lui donnez pas le gâteau!**   (Don't give her/him the cake!)

9. If the indirect object pronoun is the object of an infinitive, do the same as you did for the direct object pronouns. Put the indirect object pronoun *in front of* the infinitive:

> **Janine veut leur parler.**   (Janine wants to talk to them.)

10. Remember that there is *no agreement* between the past participle of a verb conjugated with **avoir** in the passé composé if there is an indirect object. However, there *must be an agreement* (both in gender and in number) *if there is a preceding direct object.* Compare:

> **Je lui ai donné les disques.**   **Je les ai donnés à Mimi.**
>
> (I *gave* the records *to her.*)   (I *gave them* to Mimi.)

B. Y is an indirect object form that is used to refer to places or to things. It ordinarily replaces a noun preceded by the preposition **à**, or **dans**, or **sur**:

> (a) Allez-vous **à la bibliothèque**?   Oui, j'**y** vais.
>
>   (Are you going *to the library*?)   (Yes, I'm going *there.*)
>
> (b) Les gants sont-ils **dans le tiroir**?   Oui, ils **y** sont.
>
>   (Are the gloves *in the drawer*?)   (Yes, they are *there.*)
>
> (c) Est-ce que le chapeau est **sur la commode**?   Oui, il **y** est.
>
>   (Is the hat *on the dresser*?)   (Yes, it is *there.*)
>
> (d) Aimez-vous aller **au cinéma**?   Oui, j'aime **y** aller.
>
>   (Do you like going *to the movies*?)   (Yes, I like going *there.*)

Exercises

Review the preceding material before starting these exercises.

I. Change the following sentences by substituting an indirect object pronoun in place of the nouns. Put the indirect object pronoun in its proper position. Rewrite the entire sentence.

Model: Pierre donne le gâteau à *Janine*.   You write: **Pierre lui donne le gâteau.**

1. Janine donne le journal *à Pierre.* _____

2. Madeleine donne le livre à *Mathilde.* _____

3. Gloria donne la fleur à *Hélène.* _____

4. Robert donne la balle *aux garçons.* _____

5. Monique donne les stylos *à Marie et à Henri.* _____

II. Answer the following questions in complete sentences (in French), using an appropriate indirect object pronoun in place of the words in parentheses.

A. Model: A qui parlez-vous? (à la jeune fille)   You write: **Je lui parle.**

1. A qui parlez-vous? (à la femme) _____

2. A qui parlez-vous? (au garçon) _____

3. A qui parlez-vous? (à Madeleine) _____

4. A qui parlez-vous? (à l'ami) _____

5. A qui parlez-vous? (à Robert) _____

B. Model: A qui donnez-vous les fleurs? (aux femmes)   You write: **Je leur donne les fleurs.**

1. A qui donnez-vous les gâteaux? (aux garçons) _____

2. A qui donnez-vous les livres? (à Marie et à Robert) _____

3. A qui donnez-vous le ragoût brûlé? (aux chiens) _____

4. A qui donnez-vous les lettres? (à la mère et au père) _____

5. A qui donnez-vous le jus? (à Janine et à Pierre) _____

III. Answer the following questions in the affirmative using an indirect object pronoun in each answer.

 Model: **Est-ce que vous me parlez?**   **You answer: Oui, je vous parle.**

1. Est-ce que vous me parlez? _____

2. Est-ce que vous lui parlez? _____

3. Est-ce que vous nous parlez? _____

IV. For each statement write a response in French in the affirmative imperative. Use an indirect object pronoun in place of the words indicated.

 Model: **Je veux donner le ragoût**   **You answer: Bon! Alors, donnez-lui le**
 à Pierre.   **ragoût!**

1. Je veux donner le gâteau à *Marie*. _____

2. Je veux donner le parapluie à *la femme*. _____

3. Je veux donner le bonbon à *l'enfant*. _____

4. Je veux donner le jus de fruit à *Robert*. _____

5. Je veux donner le ragoût brûlé à *Monsieur Richy*. _____

V. For each statement write a response in French in the negative imperative. Use an indirect object pronoun in place of the words indicated.

 Model: **Je ne veux pas donner les**   **You answer: Bon! Alors, ne leur donnez**
 bonbons *aux enfants*.   **pas les bonbons!**

1. Je ne veux pas donner le chocolat *aux garçons*. _____

2. Je ne veux pas donner les devoirs à *la maîtresse*. _____

3. Je ne veux pas donner le billet à *Françoise*. _____

VI. For each statement write a response in French in the affirmative imperative. Use an indirect object pronoun in your response.

 Model: Je veux vous parler.   **You write: Bon! Alors, parlez-moi!**

1. Je veux vous parler. _____

2. Je veux lui parler. _____

3. Je veux leur parler. _____

205

VII. For each statement write a response in French in the negative imperative. Use an indirect object pronoun in your response.

    Model: **Je ne veux pas vous parler.**   **You write:** **Bon! Alors, ne me parlez pas!**

1. Je ne veux pas vous parler! _____

2. Je ne veux pas lui parler! _____

3. Je ne veux pas leur parler! _____

VIII. Match the following.

1. He is giving the assignments to them.   _____ Elle me donne le gâteau.

2. She is giving him the hat.   _____ Il te donne le livre.

3. She is giving you the juice.   _____ Elle lui donne le chapeau.

4. She is giving me the cake.   _____ Il nous donne le chocolat.

5. He is giving you the book.   _____ Elle vous donne le jus.

6. He is giving us the chocolate.   _____ Il leur donne les devoirs.

IX. Answer the following questions in the affirmative using **y** in your answer to take the place of the words indicated.

    Model: **Allez-vous *à la bibliothèque?***   **You write:** **Oui, j'y vais.**

1. Allez-vous à *la maison?* _____

2. Allez-vous *au cinéma?* _____

3. Allez-vous à *l'aéroport?* _____

X. The words in the following boxes are scrambled. Unscramble them to find a meaningful sentence. Write the sentence on the line.

Model:

donne	me	ragoût
Pierre	le	

You write: *Pierre me donne le ragoût.*

1.

lui	parlez	Bon!	Alors,

_____

2.

leur	parler
veut	Janine

_____

XI. **Oral Proficiency.** Respond orally in French to the situation described. (Later, you may write your responses for intensive practice.)

Situation: You are in school and while walking to your next class, a friend stops you in the hall and says: _Où sont mes cassettes?_ (Where are my cassettes?) _Je te les ai données la semaine passée_ (I gave them to you last week). Respond to your friend by stating at least three things that happened to the cassettes. You may use any or all of the following: _avoir, prêter, donner, aller, voir, les, lui, demander, penser._

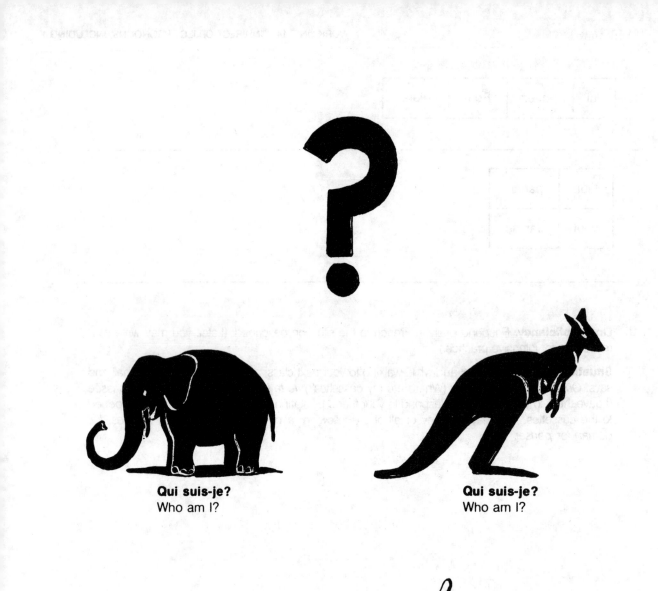

Qui suis-je?
Who am I?

Qui suis-je?
Who am I?

Qui suis-je?
Who am I?

Que suis-je?
What am I?

Qu'est-ce que je suis?
What am I?

Interrogative Pronouns

Have you ever guessed any riddles in English? In French? Here are fifteen riddles in French; some are easy, some are not so easy. The answers are upside down after the last one.

Quinze devinettes

1. Je porte toujours un chapeau mais je n'ai pas de tête. Que suis-je?

2. Je vole comme un oiseau. Qu'est-ce que je suis?

3. J'ai un cou très, très long et je peux voir les autres animaux de très haut. Qui suis-je?

4. Je suis toujours au milieu de Paris. Que suis-je?

5. J'habite dans l'eau. J'ai des yeux mais je n'ai pas de paupières. Qui suis-je?

6. J'ai des jambes et j'ai des bras mais je n'ai pas de mains. Qu'est-ce que je suis?

7. Je vais, je viens, je sors, je retourne, sans quitter ma maison. Qui suis-je?

8. Je n'ai pas de pieds et de jambes. J'ai seulement deux aiguilles. Que suis-je?

9. Je suis un animal qui porte mes petits enfants dans ma poche. Qui suis-je?

10. Je suis jaune dedans et blanc dessus. Qu'est-ce que je suis?

11. Quand je quitte la maison, je ne sors jamais par la porte et jamais par la fenêtre. Je sors par la cheminée. Que suis-je?

12. J'entre le premier dans la maison. Qu'est-ce que je suis?

13. Je peux traverser une vitre sans la casser. Que suis-je?

14. Je suis le plus sale de la maison. Qu'est-ce que je suis?

15. Je tourne sans tourner. Que suis-je?

1. un champignon	6. un fauteuil	11. la fumée
2. un avion	7. une tortue	12. une clef
3. une girafe	8. un réveil	13. la lumière
4. la lettre "r"	9. un kangourou	14. un balai
5. un poisson	10. un œuf	15. le lait

Vocabulaire

l'aiguille *n. f.*, the needle, hand of a clock

l'animal *n. m.*, **les animaux** *pl.*, the animal, the animals

l'avion *n. m.*, the airplane

le balai *n.*, the broom

le bras *n.*, the arm

casser *v.*, to break; **sans la casser** without breaking it

le champignon *n.*, the mushroom

la cheminée *n.*, the chimney

la clef *n.*, the key

le cou *n.*, the neck

deviner *v.*, to guess; **une devinette** a riddle

le fauteuil *n.*, the armchair

la fenêtre *n.*, the window

la fumée *n.*, the smoke

la girafe *n.*, the giraffe

habite *v. form of* **habiter** (to live, reside, inhabit)

haut *adv.*, high

jamais *adv.*, ever; **ne ... jamais** never

la jambe *n.*, the leg

le kangourou *n.*, the kangaroo

le lait *n.*, the milk

la lumière *n.*, the light

la main *n.*, the hand

le milieu *n.*, the middle; **au milieu de** in the middle of

l'oeuf *n. m.*, the egg

la paupière *n.*, the eyelid

peux *v. form of* **pouvoir** (to be able, may, can); **je peux** I can

le pied *n.*, the foot

la poche *n.*, the pocket

le poisson *n.*, the fish

porte *v. form of* **porter** (to wear, carry)

que *interrog. pron.*, what; **que suis-je?** what am I?

qu'est-ce que je suis? am I?

qui suis-je? who am I?

quitter *v.*, to leave; **sans quitter** without leaving

le réveil *n.*, the alarm clock

sale *adj.*, dirty, soiled; **le plus sale de la maison** the dirtiest in the house

sors *v. form of* **sortir** (to go out); **je sors** I go out; **je ne sors jamais** I never go out

suis *v. form of* **être** (to be); **je suis** I am

la tortue *n.*, the turtle

tourner *v.*, to turn, to turn sour

traverser *v.*, to cross, to go through

viens *v. form of* **venir** (to come); **je viens** I come

la vitre *n.*, the window-pane (glass)

Exercises

Review the preceding material before starting these exercises.

I. Fill in the blank lines after each picture by writing the French word for it. Use the indefinite article. They are based on the riddles in this unit.

Model:

U N E   M A I S O N

1. __ __ __ __ __ __ __ __ __ __ __

2. __ __ __ __ __ __ __ __ __ __

3. __ __ __ __ __ __ __ __

4. _ _ _ _ _ _ _ _

5. _ _ _ _ _ _ _ _ _ _ _

II. Complete the following statements by writing the appropriate words in French. They are based on the fifteen riddles in this unit.

1. Je suis un kangourou. Je _____ mes petits enfants dans ma poche.

2. Je suis un poisson. J'ai des _____ , mais je _____ de paupières.

3. Je suis un balai et je _____ le plus sale de la maison.

4. Je suis un fauteuil. J'ai deux bras mais je _____ de mains.

5. Je suis une girafe. J'ai un cou très, très _____ et je _____ voir les autres animaux de très haut.

III. Fill in the squares by writing the French words across for the English words in the list.

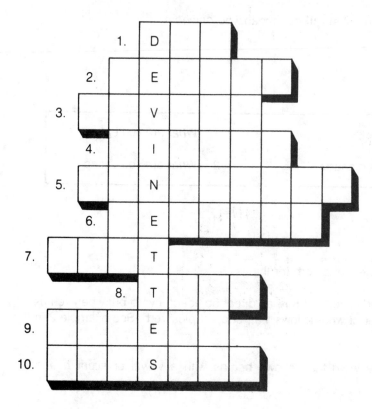

1. D
2. E
3. V
4. I
5. N
6. E
7. T
8. T
9. E
10. S

1. ten
2. I am
3. alarm clock
4. giraffe
5. kangaroo
6. window
7. milk
8. very
9. I can
10. fish

Structures de la Langue

A. Interrogative pronouns

1. Qui

1. **Qui** parle?	1. *Who* is talking?
2. **Qui** aimez-vous?	2. *Whom* do you love?
3. **A qui** parlez-vous?	3. *To whom* are you talking?
4. **De qui** parlez-vous?	4. *About whom* are you talking?

Rules and observations:

1. **Qui** is used as a subject. See example 1 in the above box.

2. **Qui** is used as a direct object and is translated into English as *whom*. See example 2 in the above box.

3. **Qui** is used as an object of a preposition. See example 3 in the above box (**qui** is object of the preposition *à*).

4. In example 4 in the above box, **qui** is used as object of the preposition *de*.

5. The *i* in **qui** never drops. Note that **qui** can mean *who* or *whom*.

2. Que and Qu'est-ce que

1. **Que** mangez-vous?	1. *What* are you eating?
2. **Qu'est-ce que** vous mangez?	2. *What* are you eating?

Rules and observations:

1. **Que** is used as a direct object of a verb for things.

2. **Qu'est-ce que** can be used instead of **que** as direct object of a verb but when you use it, keep the normal word order of what follows, *i.e.*, subject plus verb. See example 2 in the above box.

3. The **e** in **que** drops if the word that follows begins with a vowel or silent *h* and an apostrophe replaces it.

212

Exercises

Review the preceding material before starting these exercises.

I. **Match the following.**

1. De qui parlez-vous?   _____ Who is talking?

2. Que dites-vous?   _____ Whom do you love?

3. Qui aimez-vous?   _____ Whom are you talking to?

4. Qu'est-ce que vous mangez?   _____ About whom are you talking?

5. A qui parlez-vous?   _____ What are you eating?

6. Qui parle?   _____ What are you saying?

II. **Fill in the missing words with either qui, que, or qu'est-ce que, as required.**

1. _____ parle?   6. _____ vous mangez?

2. _____ est à la porte?   7. _____ dites-vous?

3. A _____ parlez-vous?   8. _____ vous dites?

4. De _____ parlez-vous?   9. _____ arrive?

5. _____ mangez-vous?   10. _____ faites-vous?

III. **Write the question in French that must have been asked for each of the following answers. In your question use qui, que, or qu'est-ce que, as indicated in parentheses.**

     Model: Robert parle. (qui)   **You write: Qui parle?**

1. Monsieur Richy mange une pomme. (qui) _____

2. Je bois du lait. (que) _____

3. Monique parle à Roger. (qui) _____

4. Je dis la réponse. (qu'est-ce que) _____

5. Janine a écrit une lettre. (qu'est-ce que) _____

6. J'ai lancé la balle. (qui) _____

7. Elle lit un livre. (que) _____

8. Je mange une orange. (qu'est-ce que) _____

9. Pierre a servi la salade. (qu'est-ce que) _____

10. Madame Paquet a fait le ragoût. (qui) _____

213

IV. **Oral Proficiency.** You are bringing a package to the post office in Paris to send it to the United States (**aux Etats-Unis**). Complete the conversation.

le paquet/package, **lourd**/heavy, **indiquer**/to indicate, **l'employé**/employee

L'employé: Ce paquet est lourd!

1. Vous: _____

   L'employé: Mais vous n'avez pas indiqué ça sur votre déclaration pour la douane.

2. Vous: _____

   L'employé: Vous voulez l'envoyer par avion?

3. Vous: _____

   L'employé: Cela va coûter cent vingt francs.

4. Vous: _____

   L'employé: Alors, qu'est-ce que vous voulez faire?

5. Vous: _____

Review Test: Work Units 11–15

I. How many French words can you find hidden in the word **MAISON**? Find at least eight.

> **MAISON**

1. _____
2. _____
3. _____
4. _____

5. _____
6. _____
7. _____
8. _____

II. Now, take the same French word, **MAISON**, scramble all the letters and find another French word that has the same letters. Hint: It's a verb form in the imperative.

III. There are five French words hidden in this clock. Note that for most of the words, the first letter is the same as the last letter of the previous word. This clock has no hands because it's a "word clock!" Write the missing letters on the lines.

CLUES: From 12 to 4, give the French for the word "when".
From 4 to 5, give the French for the word "of" or "from".
From 5 to 7, give the French for the word "water".
From 7 to 8, give the indefinite article, masculine, singular.
From 8 to 11, give the French for the word "nine".

STRUCTURES AND VERBS

IV. Choose the verb form that would make sense in the statement or question.

1. Est-ce que vous _____ beaucoup de livres?
   a. venez   b. pouvez   c. lisez   d. partez

2. Les étudiants _____ -ils le francais?
   a. vendent   b. apprennent   c. ouvrent   d. boivent

3. Janine aime beaucoup _____ du jus d'orange.

   a. boire   b. dire   c. lire   d. devoir

V. Choose the correct imperative form of the verb that would make sense in each statement.

1. _____ les livres sur la table, s'il vous plaît.
   a. Buvez   b. Mettez   c. Soyez   d. Venez

2. _____la leçon pour demain, s'il vous plaît!
   a. Faites   b. Revenez   c. Partez   d. Buvez

3. _____ au cinéma ce soir!
   a. Prenons   b. Prêtons   c. Allons   d. Pouvons

4. _____ cette belle pâtisserie, s'il te plaît!
   a. Mangez   b. Mange   c. Sois   d. Bois

5. _____ ici à cinq heures, s'il vous plaît!
   a. Soyez   b. Sois   c. Comprenez   d. Entendez

VI. Choose the verb form that could replace the underlined verb and make sense in the statement.

1. Pour demain, préparez, les pages cinq à dix.
   a. ayez   b. soyez   c. lisez   d. partez

2. S'il vous plaît, Joseph, ouvrez la fenêtre.
   a. apprenez   b. fermez   c. écrivez   d. allez

3. Hier, j'ai reçu une lettre de mon ami.
   a. j'ai lu   b. j'ai écrit   c. je suis allé   d. je suis venu

4. Nous avons fait les devoirs à l'école.
   a. avons parlé   b. avons fini   c. avez écrit   d. ont lu

5. Mes parents sont sortis à huit heures ce soir.
   a. avons ri   b. ai parlé   c. sont devenus   d. sont partis

VII. Write the infinitive in French for each of the following past participles.

Example: **vu**   You write: voir

1. eu _____   4. dit _____   7. compris _____
2. été _____   5. lu _____   8. mis _____
3. fait _____   6. su _____   9. ri _____

216

VIII. For each of the following verbs in the passé composé write in French the correct form of either **avoir** or **être** (whichever is required) in the present indicative.

Example: Hier, Monsieur Dufy _____ allé au Canada. You write: <u>est</u>

1. Les enfants _____ allés à l'école.
2. J' _____ mangé du chocolat.
3. Je _____ allé au cinéma hier soir.
4. Janine _____ chanté.

5. Robert _____ parti.
6. Claire _____ parlé avec les dames.
7. Pierre _____ bu un café.
8. Marie _____ sortie.

IX. In the second sentence, choose the correct direct object pronoun to take the place of the direct object noun stated in the first sentence.

1. Jacqueline lit le livre. Jacqueline _____ lit.
   a. le   b. la   c. les   d. l'

2. Robert écrit la lettre. Robert _____ écrit.
   a. les   b. la   c. l'   d. le

3. Odette apprend la leçon. Odette _____ apprend.
   a. l'   b. la   c. le   d. les

4. Je mange les gâteaux. Je _____ mange.
   a. la   b. le   c. les   d. l'

5. Tu fais la leçon. Tu _____ fais.
   a. le   b. l'   c. les   d. la

X. In the second sentence, choose the correct indirect object pronoun to take the place of the indirect object noun stated in the first sentence.

1. Ma mère donne l'argent à mon père. Elle _____ donne l'argent.
   a. lui   b. leur   c. me   d. vous

2. Madame Durand parle aux élèves. Elle _____ parle.
   a. leur   b. lui   c. les   d. la

3. Odette veut écrire à Jacques. Elle veut _____ écrire.
   a. lui   b. le   c. leur   d. l'

4. Robert pose une question à Marie. Il _____ pose une question.
   a. le   b. lui   c. l'   d. leur

5. L'élève répond au professeur. Il _____ répond.
   a. lui   b. le   c. les   d. leur

XI. On the black line, write the interrogative pronoun in French for the English word under the line.

1. _____ parle?
   (who)

2. _____ aimez-vous?
   (whom)

3. A _____ parlez-vous?
   (whom)

4. De _____ parle-t-il?
   (whom)

5. _____ manges-tu?
   (what)

6. _____ dites-vous?
   (what)

— *Madame, il est trois heures. La leçon est finie!*

Demonstrative Pronouns — *ceci, cela, ça*

*Do you like answering true-false
questions? Let's see how Mrs. Ravel's
students make out.*

Vrai ou faux?

Madame Ravel est professeur de géographie. Elle pose des questions à la classe.

Madame Ravel:	Paris est la capitale de la France. Marie, ceci est vrai ou faux?
Marie:	Cela est vrai, madame.
Madame Ravel:	Bravo, Marie! Maintenant, Suzanne. Marseille est un port sur la Méditerranée. Suzanne, ceci est vrai ou faux?
Suzanne:	Cela est faux, madame.
Madame Ravel:	Non! Non! Non! Ceci est vrai: Marseille est un port sur la Méditerranée . . . Maintenant, Georges. La Seine est un fleuve. Georges, ceci est vrai ou faux?
Georges:	Cela est vrai, madame. La Seine est un fleuve.
Madame Ravel:	Bravo, Georges! C'est ça!

(La Directrice de l'école entre dans la salle de classe.)

La Directrice:	Madame Ravel, on vous demande au téléphone dans mon bureau.
Madame Ravel:	Oh! Merci, madame. Je viens tout de suite.

(La Directrice quitte la salle de classe.)

Madame Ravel:	Marie, tu es chargée de continuer la leçon. Viens ici devant la classe.

(Madame Ravel quitte la salle et Marie va devant la classe.)

Tous les élèves:	Paris est la capitale de la France. Ceci est vrai ou faux, Madame Marie? Oh, cela est vrai! Oh, bravo, Madame Marie! Tu as du génie! Quelle intelligence!

(Tous les élèves rient.)

(Robert lance un avion en papier contre l'horloge.)

Robert:	J'ai lancé un avion en papier contre l'horloge. Ceci est vrai ou faux, Madame Marie? Oh, cela est vrai! Oh, bravo, Madame Marie! Quel génie! Quelle intelligence!

Marie:	Silence! Silence! Robert, tu es insolent!
Robert:	Cela est vrai? Je suis insolent?? Oh! pardonnez-moi, Madame Marie!

(Madame Ravel rentre dans la salle de classe.)

Madame Ravel:	Bon! Merci, Marie. Tu peux t'asseoir. Nous allons continuer la leçon . . . Hélène, pose une question à Raymond.
Hélène:	Raymond, où se trouve la Grande Bretagne?
Raymond:	Près de la petite Bretagne!

(Tous les élèves rient.)

Madame Ravel:	Raymond, ta réponse est ridicule! . . . Suzanne, pose une question à Georges.
Suzanne:	Georges, qui habite le pôle nord?
Georges:	Un bonhomme de neige!

(Tous les élèves rient.)

Madame Ravel:	Georges, ta réponse est absurde!
Georges:	Peut-être le Père Noël? Ho! Ho! Ho!

(Tous les élèves rient.)

Madame Ravel:	Ça suffit! . . . Soyons sérieux! Paulette, où est Nancy?
Paulette:	Elle est absente!
Madame Ravel:	Je ne parle pas de Nancy. Je parle de Nancy. Je parle de Nancy, la ville en France. Oh! Quelle classe!
Hélène:	Madame Ravel, j'ai une question à poser à Robert. Robert, où est Cadillac?
Robert:	Dans le garage de mon père!

(Tous les élèves rient.)

Madame Ravel:	Oh! Quelle classe! Je deviens folle!
Robert:	Madame, il est trois heures. La leçon est finie! C'est vrai ou faux, madame?
220 *Madame Ravel:*	C'est superbe!

Vocabulaire

le bonhomme de neige n., the snowman

le bureau n., the office

ça dem. pron., that (**ça** is short for **cela**)

ceci dem. pron., this

cela dem. pron., that

c'est ça! that's right!

contre prep., against

demander v., to ask (for); **on vous demande au téléphone** you're wanted on the phone

deviens v. form of **devenir** (to become); **je deviens folle!** I'm going crazy!

le directeur, la directrice n., the director, the principal

faux m., **fausse** f., adj., false

le fleuve n., the river

le génie n., genius

la Grande Bretagne n., Great Britain

l'horloge n., the clock

lancer v., to throw, fling

la Méditerranée n., the Mediterranean (Sea)

la neige n., the snow; **un bonhomme de neige** a snowman

le nord n., the north; **le pôle nord** the North Pole

la papier n., paper

pardonner v., to pardon, to forgive; **pardonnez-moi** forgive me

le Père Noël n., Santa Claus

peut-être adv., maybe, perhaps

poser une question to ask a question

près (de) adv., near

quel génie! what genius!

quelle classe! what a class!

rentrer v., to return

la réponse n., the answer; **ta réponse est ridicule!** your answer is ridiculous!

rient v. form of **rire** (to laugh); **tous les élèves rient** all the students laugh

sérieux m., **sérieuse** f., adj., serious; **soyons sérieux!** let's be serious!

suffit v. form of **suffire** (to suffice, to be enough); **ça suffit** that's enough

trouver v., to find; **se trouver** to be located

viens v. form of **venir** (to come); **je viens tout de suite** I'm coming right away; **viens ici!** come here!

vrai m., **vraie** f., adj., true

Exercises

Review the story and vocabulary before starting these exercises.

I. Vrai ou faux? On the blank line write **vrai** if the statement is *true* or **faux** if the statement is *false*.

1. Paris est la capitale de la France. _____

2. Marseille est un port sur la Méditerranée. _____

3. La Seine est un fleuve. _____

4. Madame Ravel est professeur de mathématiques. _____

5. La directrice de l'école n'entre pas dans la classe. _____

6. Suzanne est chargée de continuer la leçon. _____

7. Robert a lancé un avion en papier contre la fenêtre. _____

8. Il est trois heures, la leçon est finie, et Madame Ravel est heureuse. _____

II. Complete the following statements by writing the appropriate words in French.

1. Madame Ravel est _____ de _____.

2. La capitale de la France est _____.

3. Marseille est un _____ sur la Méditerranée.

4. La Seine est un _____ .

5. La directrice de l'école entre _____ la salle de _____ .

6. Madame Ravel, on vous demande _____ téléphone dans mon _____ .

7. Marie, tu est chargée de _____ la _____ .

8. J'ai une question à _____ à Robert.

III. Answer the following questions in complete sentences (in French).

1. Qui est Madame Ravel? _____

2. Qui entre dans la salle de classe? _____

3. Quand Madame Ravel quitte la salle, où va-t-elle? _____

   _____

4. Qui a lancé un avion en papier contre l'horloge? _____

   _____

5. A quelle heure est-ce que la leçon finit? _____

   _____

Structures de la Langue

A. Demonstrative pronouns: ceci, cela, ça

1. **Ceci** est vrai.	1. *This* is true.
2. **Cela** est faux.	2. *That* is false.
3. C'est **ça**!	3. *That's* right!
4. Je fais **cela**.	4. I do *that*.
5. Je fais **ceci**.	5. I do *this*.

Rules and observations:

1. Ça is a contraction of **cela**.

2. **Ceci** and **cela** are demonstrative pronouns in a neuter sense. They usually refer to a general or indefinite concept, to an idea or to a statement. As pronouns, they do not refer to any particular masculine or feminine noun.

3. **Ceci** or **cela** can be used as the subject of a sentence. See examples 1 and 2 in the above box. They can also be used as the direct object of a verb. See examples 4 and 5 in the above box. They can also be used as the object of a preposition: **Elle parle toujours de cela.** (She always talks about that.)

Exercises

Review the preceding material before doing these exercises.

I. Match the following.

1. Je fais ceci.   _____ This is true.

2. C'est ça.   _____ That is true.

3. Je fais cela.   _____ That's right.

4. Cela est vrai.   _____ I do this.

5. Ceci est vrai.   _____ I do that.

II. Answer the following questions in French, using **Oui** in your answer and a complete statement.

    Model: Cela est vrai?   **You write: Oui, cela est vrai.**

1. Cela est faux? _____

2. Ceci est vrai? _____

3. C'est ça? _____

III. Find the following demonstrative pronouns in the squares and circle them.

E	C	E	L
C	E	I	C
E	C	A	E
I	I	Ç	L
L	C	A	A

1. ceci

2. cela

3. ça

IV. **Oral Proficiency.** Respond orally in French to the situation described. (Later, you may write your responses for intensive practice.)

Situation: You are in French class. Each student has to make one statement in French followed by **Cela est vrai?** (Is that true?) and **Cela est faux?** (Is that false?) It's your turn. Make at least three statements and then ask if that's true or false. You may use any or all of the following: **être, capitale de la France, la Seine, un fleuve, Marseille, un port, la Méditerranée, les Alpes, en France.** You may use the **passé composé** tense or the present, or both.

223

— *Nous sommes très heureux de vous voir.*

Disjunctive Pronouns

*Monsieur and Madame Paquet received
an invitation for dinner at the home of
some neighbors. Are they in for a
big surprise!*

R.S.V.P.

Monsieur et Madame Paquet ont recu une invitation à dîner chez leurs voisins, Monsieur Madame Berger. Voici l'invitation:

> Madame Berger
> vous invite à dîner
> vendredi, 15 avril 20h.
>
> 21, rue des Jardins
> R.S.V.P.   Paris

Madame Paquet: Eh bien, François, est-ce que nous y allons ou est-ce que nous n'y allons pas? Il faut répondre à l'invitation.

Monsieur Paquet: Claire, tu sais que je ne veux pas aller chez eux parce que je ne les aime pas. Lui et elle sont des snobs.

Madame Paquet: Tu as raison. Quand je l'ai vue au supermarché hier, elle m'a parlé, mais elle m'a regardée d'un air supérieur.

Monsieur Paquet: D'ailleurs, ils sont ennuyants.

Madame Paquet: Oui. Ils m'ennuient aussi. Mais tu sais que si nous refusons l'invitation, tout est fini entre eux et nous.

Monsieur Paquet: Il faut accepter pour rester amis avec eux.

Claire accepte l'invitation. Quand ils arrivent pour dîner chez les Berger, ils entrent dans le foyer. Ils voient d'autres voisins chez eux. Tout le monde crie: Surprise! Surprise!

— Nous sommes très heureux de vous voir. Ce dîner est en votre honneur, leur dit **Madame Berger**.

— Pour nous?! En notre honneur?! s'exclament Claire et François.

— Oui, répond Monsieur Berger.

— Mais pourquoi? Qu'est-ce que nous avons fait? leur demande Claire.

— Parce que vous êtes bons! Et vous êtes aimables et gentils! répond Madame Berger.

— Merci, merci, disent les Paquet.

Tout le monde a mangé, bu, chanté, et dansé jusqu'à minuit. Claire et François Paquet sont rentrés contents chez eux.

Quand ils arrivent chez eux, Monsieur Paquet dit à sa femme:

— Tu sais, Claire, j'ai toujours dit que les Berger sont très aimables et gentils. **Je les aime beaucoup.**

— Moi aussi, j'ai toujours dit cela, François.

Vocabulaire

d'ailleurs adv., besides
aimable adj., likeable
chez prep., at (to) the home (place) of; **chez eux** at their house; **chez moi** at my house; **chez leurs voisins** at the home of their neighbors; **chez les Berger** at the Bergers
ennuient v. form of **ennuyer** (to bore, annoy); **ils m'ennuient** they bore me;

ennuyants adj. m. pl., boring
entre prep., between; **entre eux et nous** between them and us
eux disj. pron., them; **avec eux** with them
faut v. form of **falloir**; **il faut** it is necessary
gentil m., **gentille** f., adj., nice, kind
h. abbrev. for **heures**; **20 h.** is 8 o'clock in the evening

l'honneur n. m., honor
leur dit Madame Berger Mrs. Berger says to them
pour prep., for, in order (to)
R.S.V.P., please reply (Répondez, **s**'il vous plaît.)
reçu past part. of **recevoir** (to receive); **ils ont reçu** they received
refusons v. form of **refuser** (to refuse); **si nous refusons** if we refuse
rester v., to remain, to stay

Exercises

Review the story and vocabulary before starting these exercises.

I. Complete the dialogue in French between Mr. and Mrs. Paquet. They are deciding whether or not to accept a dinner invitation. Refer to the story if you have to.

Madame Paquet: Eh bien, François, est-ce que nous acceptons l'invitation pour dîner chez les Berger?

Monsieur Paquet: _____

Madame Paquet: Pourquoi?

Monsieur Paquet: _____

Madame Paquet: Oui. Tu as raison. Ils m'ennuient aussi.

226 *Monsieur Paquet:* _____

II. Complete the following statements in French by writing the appropriate words from among these:

(a) à l'invitation (b) chez eux (c) je ne les aime pas (d) entre eux et nous
(e) vous voir

1. Si nous refusons l'invitation, tout est fini _____.

2. Nous sommes très heureux de _____.

3. Ils voient d'autres voisins _____.

4. Je ne veux pas y aller parce que _____.

5. Il faut répondre _____.

III. Choose the correct answer based on the story in this unit.

1. M. et Mme. Paquet ont reçu (a) un balai. (b) une voiture. (c) un ami. (d) une invitation. _____

2. M. Paquet ne veut pas aller chez les Berger parce qu' (a) il est malade. (b) il est heureux. (c) il est aimable. (d) il ne les aime pas. _____

3. M. et Mme. Berger sont très heureux (a) de recevoir les Paquet. (b) d'aller dîner. (c) d'accepter l'invitation. (d) d'aller au super-marché. _____

Structures de la Langue

A. Disjunctive pronouns (also known as stressed pronouns or tonic pronouns)

Singular		Plural	
moi	me *or* I	**nous**	us *or* we
toi	you *(familiar)*	**vous**	you *(formal singular or plural)*
soi	oneself	**eux**	them, they *(masculine)*
lui	him *or* he	**elles**	them, they *(feminine)*
elle	her *or* she		

Rules and observations:

1. The disjunctive pronoun is used when it is the object of a preposition:
   Elle parle avec moi.   (She is talking with me.)
   Nous allons chez eux.   (We are going to their house.)

2. The disjunctive pronoun is used in a compound subject:
   Lui et elle sont intelligents.   (He and she are intelligent.)

3. The disjunctive pronoun is used in a compound object:
   Je vous connais — toi et lui.   (I know you — you and him.)

4. You may use **à** with a disjunctive pronoun to express possession only if the verb is **être** and if the subject is a noun, personal pronoun or a demonstrative pronoun:
   Ce livre est à moi.   (This book is mine.)
   Ces livres sont à elles.   (These books are theirs.)
   Ces livres sont à eux.   (These books are theirs.)

5. The disjunctive pronoun **moi** is used instead of **me** in the affirmative imperative when it is tacked on to the verb and joined with a hyphen; example:
   Excusez-moi.   (Excuse me.)

6. A disjunctive pronoun is also known as a *stressed* or a *tonic* pronoun.

Exercises

Review the preceding material before starting these exercises.

I. **On the blank line write the disjunctive pronoun (in French) that expresses possession as needed, according to what is given in English in parentheses.**

   Model: Les livres sont à _____ (mine).   **You write: moi.**

   1. Le parapluie est à _____ (mine).   4. La maison est à _____ (ours).

   2. Les balles sont à _____ (his).   5. La voiture est à _____ (yours, *pl.*).

   3. L'orange est à _____ (hers).   6. Les gâteaux sont à _____ (theirs, *m.*).

II. **On the blank line write in French the proper disjunctive pronoun for the English given in parentheses.**

   Model: (me)   Elle parle avec _____ .   **You write: Elle parle avec moi.**

Elle parle avec moi.

1. (him) Je suis allée au cinéma avec _____.

2. (me) Il va partir sans _____.

3. (he) Madeleine et _____ sont intelligents.

4. (she) Marie et _____ écrivent les leçons.

5. (us) Le ragoût est pour _____.

6. (you, *formal singular*) Elle va partir avec _____.

7. (you, *familiar singular*) Nous allons sortir avec _____.

8. (them, *masculine*) Ce gâteau est pour _____.

9. (them, *feminine*) Ces petits fours sont pour _____.

10. (he and I) _____ nous allons au cinéma.

III. **Fill in the missing pronouns in French. They are not all disjunctive!**

Monsieur Paquet annonce: J'ai les billets pour le théâtre. Ces quatre billets

sont pour _____ . Ce billet est pour _____ , ce billet est pour
              (us)   (me)

_____ , Claire; et ces deux billets sont pour _____ deux,
    (you)   (you)

Janine et Pierre. Prenez-_____ .
                         (them)

Madame Paquet dit: François, ne _____ donne pas les billets. Je
                                 (to them)

préfère _____ mettre dans ma poche.
       (them)

Monsieur Paquet répond: Non, Claire, ne _____ mets pas dans ta
                                    (them)

poche. Je veux _____ garder sur _____ .
           (them)   (me)

Janine demande: Papa, est-ce que nous allons au théâtre ce soir?

Monsieur Paquet répond: Oui, nous _____ allons ce soir.
                               (there)

IV. **Oral Proficiency.** You are a tourist in Paris. A man gives you directions as he points to a **métro** (subway) map on the wall. Make up a conversation between the two persons.

       Monsieur: Quelle rue cherchez-vous?

1. Touriste: _____

       Monsieur: Il faut prendre la ligne Opéra, puis il faut changer pour les Jardins du Luxembourg, puis il faut changer pour Odéon.

2. Touriste: _____

       Monsieur: Quoi? Vous ne comprenez pas le français?

3. Touriste: _____

       Monsieur: Vous êtes américain?

4. Touriste: _____

       Monsieur: I speak English. I will explain to you in English.

5. Touriste: _____

SUR LE PONT D'AVIGNON

Sur le pont d'A _ vi _ gnon L'on y dan _ se, l'on y

dan _ se; Sur le pont d'A _ vi _ gnon L'on y dan _ se tout en rond Les

Fin

beaux messieurs font comm' ça Et puis en _ cor' comm' ça. Sur le

Sur le pont d'Avignon,
L'on y danse, l'on y danse;
Sur le pont d'Avignon,
L'on y danse tout en rond.
Les bell's dames font comm' ça,
Et puis encor' comm' ça.

Sur le pont d'Avignon,
L'on y danse, etc.
Les blanchisseuses font comm'ça,
Et puis encor' comm 'ça.

Sur le pont d'Avignon,
L'on y danse, etc.
Les cordonniers font comm'ça,
Et puis encor' comm'ça.

Non! Non! Es-tu fou?

Adjectives

*Janine and her brother Pierre have
nothing to do. They get into mischief
when Pierre persuades her to look under
the hood of their father's car. In this scene
Pierre does something foolish despite his
sister's objections.*

Tour d'écrou

Quelle voiture! La famille Paquet a une belle voiture grise qui ne leur donne jamais de problèmes. Même les grosses voitures neuves ne sont pas meilleures que la voiture de la famille Paquet.

Aujourd'hui Pierre fait quelque chose de bête. Il regarde dans le moteur de la voiture de leur père.

Pierre: Janine, donne-moi le tournevis.

Janine: Pourquoi? Que vas-tu faire, Pierre?

Pierre: Je dis, donne-moi le tournevis.

Janine: Quel tournevis? Il y en a beaucoup.

Pierre: Le plus petit.

Janine: Mais, que vas-tu faire, Pierre?

Pierre: Je vais engager le tournevis dans cette vis et je vais tourner.

Janine: Non! Non! Non!

Pierre: Maintenant je tourne le tournevis . . . là . . . là . . . là . . . J'enlève la vis et l'écrou. Ils ne sont pas utiles. Maintenant je les mets dans la poubelle.

Janine: Non! Es-tu fou?

Pierre: C'est fait.

Quand Monsieur Paquet veut aller faire des courses dans sa voiture, il va au garage, il monte dans sa voiture, et il tourne la clef pour mettre le moteur en marche. Il entend du bruit et le moteur ne marche pas.

Il appelle la station-service et le garagiste arrive; il emporte la voiture de Monsieur Paquet au garage de service.

Le lendemain, le garagiste téléphone à Monsieur Paquet et il lui dit: Le montant à payer est de 200 francs, monsieur. Voici le problème: Il y a une vis dans le moteur qui manque!

233

Vocabulaire

appeler v., to call

beau m., **belle** f., adj., beautiful

bête adj. m. f., foolish, dumb

le bruit n., the noise

c'est fait it's done

la couleur n., the color; **de quelle couleur est . . .** what color is . . .

l'écrou n. m., nut that fits on a screw or bolt

emporter v., to take (carry) away

engager v., to engage, to put (machinery) in gear

enlever v., to remove, to take off

entendre v., to hear

faire des courses to do (go) shopping

fou m., **folle** f., adj., crazy

le garagiste n., the garage mechanic

gris m., **grise** f., adj., gray

il y a there is, there are; **il y en a beaucoup** there are many (of them)

là adv., there

le lendemain n., the following day

manquer v., to miss, to be missing, to be lacking something; **il y a une vis dans le moteur qui manque!** there is a screw in the motor that is missing!

marcher v., to walk, to run (a motor or apparatus); **mettre en marche** to put into operation

meilleur m., **meilleure** f., adj., better

même adv., even

le montant n., total amount (of an account)

monter v., to climb, to mount, to get into

le moteur n., the motor, the

engine

neuf m., **neuve** f., adj., new

petit m., **petite** f. adj., small; **plus petit, plus petite** smaller; **le plus petit, la plus petite** the smallest

la poubelle n., the garbage can

que conj., than, that; pron., what

quel m., **quelle** f., interrog. adj., what, which; **quel tournevis?** which screwdriver? **quelle voiture!** what a car!

qui pron., which, who

le tour n., the turn; **tour d'écrou** turn of the nut

le tournevis n., the screwdriver

utile adj., useful

la vis n., the screw

la voiture n., the car, automobile

Exercises

Review the story and vocabulary before starting these exercises.

I. Answer the following questions in complete sentences (in French). They are based on the story, "Tour d'écrou."

1. Qui a une belle voiture grise? _____

2. Est-ce que les grosses voitures neuves sont meilleures que la voiture de Monsieur Paquet?

   _____

3. Pourquoi Pierre veut-il le tournevis? _____

4. Où est-ce que Pierre met la vis et l'écrou? _____

II. Answer the following questions in French in complete sentences. They are personal questions and require answers of your own.

1. Est-ce que votre famille a une voiture? _____

2. Allez-vous faire des courses dans la voiture de votre famille? _____

_____

3. De quelle couleur est la voiture de votre famille? _____

III. Oui ou Non?

1. La voiture de la famille Paquet est belle. _____

2. Pierre fait quelque chose de bête. _____

3. Janine met le tournevis dans le moteur. _____

4. Pierre met la vis et l'écrou dans la poubelle. _____

Structures de la Langue

A. Agreement and position of descriptive adjectives

Masculine	Feminine
un chapeau **gris**	une voiture **grise** (gray)
des chapeaux **gris**	des voitures **grises**
un passage **étroit**	une rue **étroite** (narrow)
des passages **étroits**	des rues **étroites**
un homme **libre**	une femme **libre** (free)
des hommes **libres**	des femmes **libres**

Rules and observations:

1. Most descriptive adjectives *follow* the noun in French.

2. Here are some common adjectives that normally *precede* the noun: **autre, beau, bon, chaque, gros, jeune, joli, long, mauvais, petit, plusieurs, vieux,** and **grand** (exception: **un homme grand**, a tall man; **un grand homme**, a great man).

3. Adjectives must agree in gender and number with the nouns they modify.

235

B. Formation of masculine descriptive adjectives in the plural

1. To form the plural of a masculine singular adjective, ordinarily add **s**.

2. If a masculine singular adjective ends in **s**, it remains the same in the plural: **gris**.

3. If a masculine singular adjective ends in **x**, it remains the same in the plural: **dangereux**.

4. If a masculine singular adjective ends in **al**, it ordinarily changes to **aux** in the plural: **loyal**, **loyaux**.

C. Formation of regular feminine descriptive adjectives

1. To form the feminine singular of an adjective, ordinarily add **e** to the masculine singular, e.g., **gris**, **grise**.

2. If the masculine singular adjective ends in **e**, the feminine singular is the same, .e.g, **libre**.

3. To form the feminine plural of an adjective, ordinarily add **s**, e.g., **grises**.

D. Formation of irregular feminine descriptive adjectives

Masculine		Feminine	
Singular	Plural	Singular	Plural
neuf	**neufs**	**neuve**	**neuves**
furieux	**furieux**	**furieuse**	**furieuses**
dernier	**derniers**	**dernière**	**dernières**
ancien	**anciens**	**ancienne**	**anciennes**
bon	**bons**	**bonne**	**bonnes**
cruel	**cruels**	**cruelle**	**cruelles**
muet	**muets**	**muette**	**muettes**

Rules and observations:

1. A masculine singular adjective that ends in **-f** changes to **-ve** to form the feminine singular: **neuf**, **neuve**.

2. A masculine singular adjective that ends in **-eux** changes to **-euse** to form the feminine singular: **furieux**, **furieuse**.

3. A masculine singular adjective that ends in **-ier** changes to **-ière** to form the feminine singular: **dernier, dernière**.

4. Some adjectives double the final consonant in the masculine singular to form the feminine singular, then an **e** is added: **ancien, ancienne**.

E. Other irregular feminine forms of descriptive adjectives

Masculine		Feminine	
Singular	Plural	Singular	Plural
beau	beaux	belle	belles
frais	frais	fraîche	fraîches
sec	secs	sèche	sèches
gros	gros	grosse	grosses
long	longs	longue	longues
blanc	blancs	blanche	blanches
favori	favoris	favorite	favorites
public	publics	publique	publiques
doux	doux	douce	douces

Exercises

I. Answer the following questions in French, substituting the appropriate form of the descriptive adjective in parentheses for the one indicated. Use **non** in your answer, but write your sentence in the affirmative.

Model: Avez-vous une voiture grise? (blanc)   **You write: Non, j'ai une voiture blanche.**

1. Avez-vous une maison blanche? (gris) _____

2. Avez-vous un bon stylo? (mauvais) _____

3. Avez-vous une grosse pomme? (beau) _____

4. Avez-vous une pêche fraîche? (doux) _____

5. Avez-vous un joli chapeau? (vieux) _____

II. Answer the following questions in the affirmative in complete French sentences. In answer (a) use **oui**. In answer (b) use **aussi**. Write the appropriate form of the descriptive adjective in your answers. Use subject pronouns in your answers. Study the models.

Model: (a) **Est-ce que Monsieur Paquet est bon?** You answer: (a) **Oui, il est bon.**

(b) **Et Madame Paquet?** You answer: (b) **Elle est bonne aussi.**

1. (a) Est-ce que Janine est petite? _____

(b) Et Pierre? _____

2. (a) Est-ce que Monsieur Paquet est furieux? _____

(b) Et Madame Paquet? _____

3. (a) Est-ce que Monique est gentille? _____

(b) Et Pierre? _____

4. (a) Est-ce que Janine et Monique sont belles? _____

(b) Et Pierre et Robert? _____

5. (a) Est-ce que la maison est neuve? _____

(b) Et les voitures? _____

III. Answer the following questions in the negative in complete French sentences. In answer (a) use **non**. In answer (b) use **non plus**. Write the appropriate form of the descriptive adjective in your answers. Use subject pronouns in your answers. Study the models.

Model: (a) **Est-ce que Madame Paquet est cruelle?** You answer: (a) **Non, elle n'est pas cruelle.**

(b) **Et Monsieur Paquet?** You answer: (b) **Il n'est pas cruel non plus.**

1. (a) Est-ce que Madame Paquet est petite? _____

(b) Et Monsieur Paquet? _____

2. (a) Est-ce que le professeur de français est mauvais? _____

(b) Et le professeur d'espagnol? _____

3. (a) Est-ce que le maître d'italien est gros? _____

(b) Et la maîtresse d'allemand? _____

4. (a) Est-ce que le petit garçon est muet? _____

(b) Et la petite fille? _____

5. (a) Est-ce que les passages sont étroits? _____

(b) Et les rues? _____

IV. Choose the form of the adjective that does not belong in the group.

    Model: **(a) beau**   **(b) sec**   **(c) gros**   **(d) longue**   __d__

1. (a) neuf   (b) ancien   (c) bon   (d) cruelle   _____

2. (a) muets   (b) cruels   (c) dernière   (d) beaux   _____

3. (a) neuve   (b) furieuse   (c) étroits   (d) bonne   _____

4. (a) belles   (b) grise   (c) fraîches   (d) blanches   _____

5. (a) beau   (b) longs   (c) sec   (d) blanc   _____

F. Possessive adjectives

Masculine			
Singular		Plural	
mon livre	my book	**mes livres**	my books
ton stylo	your pen	**tes stylos**	your pens
son ballon	his (her, its) balloon	**ses ballons**	his (her, its) balloons
notre parapluie	our umbrella	**nos parapluies**	our umbrellas
votre sandwich	your sandwich	**vos sandwichs**	your sandwiches
leur gâteau	their cake	**leurs gâteaux**	their cakes

Feminine			
Singular		Plural	
ma robe	my dress	**mes robes**	my dresses
ta jaquette	your jacket	**tes jaquettes**	your jackets
sa balle	his (her, its) ball	**ses balles**	his (her, its) balls
notre maison	our house	**nos maisons**	our houses
votre voiture	your car	**vos voitures**	your cars
leur soeur	their sister	**leurs soeurs**	their sisters

239

Rules and observations:

1. A possessive adjective agrees in gender and number *with the noun* it modifies, *not with the possessor.*

2. Some possessive adjectives do not agree with the gender of the noun *in the singular.* They are all the same, whether in front of a masculine or feminine singular noun: **notre, votre, leur.**

3. Some possessive adjectives do not agree with the gender of the noun *in the plural.* They are all the same, whether in front of a masculine or feminine plural noun: **mes, tes, ses, nos, vos, leurs.**

4. What you have to be aware of are the following possessive adjectives: **mon** or **ma, ton** or **ta, son** or **sa.**

5. In front of a *feminine singular noun* beginning with a vowel or silent *h,* the masculine singular forms are used: **mon, ton, son** — instead of **ma, ta, sa.**

mon adresse	my address	**son** amie	his (or her) friend
ton opinion	your opinion	**mon** habitude	my habit (custom)

6. Since **son, sa** and **ses** can mean *his* or *her,* you may add **à lui** or **à elle** to make the meaning clear.

sa maison à lui	his house	**son livre à elle**	her book
sa maison à elle	her house	**ses livres à lui**	his books
son livre à lui	his book	**ses livres à elle**	her books

7. If there is more than one noun, a possessive adjective must be used in front of each noun: **ma mère et mon père** (my mother and father).

8. Use the definite article instead of the possessive adjective when referring to parts of the body if it is clear who the possessor is.

J'ai de l'argent **dans la main.**	(I have some money *in my hand.*)

Exercises

Review the preceding material before starting these exercises.

I. Answer the following questions in French in the affirmative, using the appropriate form of the possessive adjective. Use **oui** in your answer.

    Model: **Aimes-tu ta robe grise?**   **You answer:** **Oui, j'aime ma robe grise.**

1. Aimes-tu ta petite voiture neuve? _____

2. Aimez-vous mon parapluie rouge? _____

3. Aimez-vous notre maison blanche? _____

4. Aimes-tu mon amie Monique? _____

5. Aimez-vous ses grosses pommes? _____

6. Aimes-tu ma jolie soeur? _____

7. Aimez-vous mes jaquettes? _____

8. Aimes-tu mes robes? _____

9. Aimez-vous leurs gâteaux? _____

10. Aimez-vous votre livre? _____

II. Answer the following questions in French in the affirmative, using the appropriate form of the possessive adjective. Use **oui** in your answer.

    Model: **Est-ce votre maison?**   **You answer:** **Oui, c'est ma maison.**

1. Est-ce votre voiture? _____

2. Est-ce ton chapeau? _____

3. Est-ce son livre à lui? _____

4. Est-ce votre maîtresse de français? _____

5. Est-ce leur maison? _____

III. Answer the following questions in French in the affirmative, using the appropriate form of the possessive adjective. Use **oui** in your answer.

    Model: **Ce sont vos livres?**   **You answer:** **Oui, ce sont mes livres.**
    (Are they your books?)   (Yes, they are my books.)

1. Ce sont vos stylos? _____

2. Ce sont leurs crayons? _____

3. Ce sont tes gâteaux? _____

4. Ce sont mes pommes? _____

5. Ce sont nos pêches? _____

IV. Fill in the missing words in French, using the appropriate form of a possessive adjective so that the rest of the sentence and dialogue will make sense.

Madame Paquet: Bonjour, Madame Richy! Oh! Vous avez un joli chapeau! J'aime beaucoup

_____ chapeau.

Madame Richy: Merci! J'ai aussi une nouvelle robe. Aimez-vous _____ nouvelle

robe rouge?

Madame Paquet: Oui, j'aime beaucoup _____ nouveau chapeau et _____

nouvelle robe rouge. J'adore _____ vêtements!

Madame Richy: Mon mari a une nouvelle jaquette. J'aime beaucoup _____ nouvelle

jaquette.

Madame Paquet: Et mon mari a un nouveau complet. J'aime beaucoup _____

nouveau complet.

Madame Richy: Alors, _____ maris ont de nouveaux vêtements. Nous aimons

beaucoup _____ nouveaux vêtements.

V. Answer in a complete sentence in French, using the appropriate form of a possessive adjective. In your answer, use the noun given in parentheses.

Model: Que mangez-vous? (pomme) **You answer: Je mange ma pomme.**

1. Que mangez-vous? (pêche) _____

2. Que mange-t-il? (sandwich) _____

3. Que mangent-ils? (chocolat) _____

4. Que mangent-elles? (soupe) _____

5. Que mangez-vous? (petits fours) _____

VI. Oral Proficiency. Your friend Michelle is on the telephone inviting you to go to the movies with her. Complete the conversation.

Michelle: Il y a un bon film français au cinéma ce soir. Veux-tu y aller avec moi?

1. Vous: _____

Michelle: C'est *Un homme et une femme.* C'est un nouveau film de Paris.

2. Vous: _____

Michelle: Tu veux demander à Jeanne et à Suzy de venir avec nous?

3. Vous: _____

Michelle: Tu sais, le film commence à huit heures.

4. Vous: _____

Michelle: Qu'est-ce que nous allons faire après le film?

5. Vous: _____

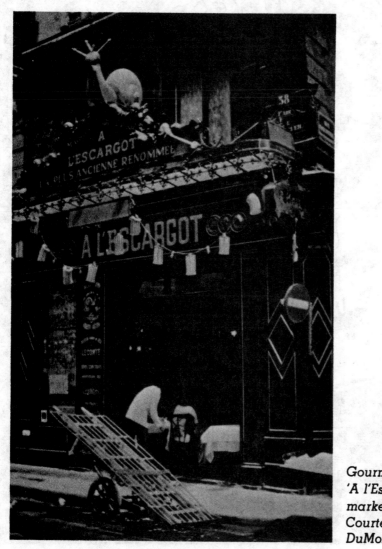

*Gourmet restaurant
'A l'Escargot' in the
market hall quarter, Paris.
Courtesy of
DuMont Buchverlag, Köln.*

Les Signes du Zodiaque.

Adjectives (Continued)

*Let's see what Pierre's horoscope reveals
for today. What does yours say?*

Zodiaque

Pierre lit le journal dans la cuisine. Il a la page de l'horoscope devant lui.

 I **Le Bélier** (Aries)

(21 mars – 20 avril)

Vous êtes le meilleur juge de vos actions.

 II **Le Taureau** (Taurus)

(21 avril – 21 mai)

Votre qualité la plus forte est la patience. Attendez des nouvelles!

 III **Les Gémeaux** (Gemini)

(22 mai – 21 juin)

La personne qui vous aime le plus attend une lettre de vous.
Ecrivez-lui.

 IV **Le Cancer** (Cancer)

(22 juin – 23 juillet)

Méfiez-vous des obstacles dangereux.

 V **Le Lion** (Leo)

(24 juillet – 23 août)

Demain va être un jour parfait pour finir vos projets.

 VI **La Vierge** (Virgo)

(24 août – 23 septembre)

Méfiez-vous des petites automobiles vertes.

VII **La Balance** (Libra)

(24 septembre – 23 octobre)

Quelle chance! Vous allez voir un grand changement.

VIII **Le Scorpion** (Scorpio)

(24 octobre – 22 novembre)

Vous avez un esprit inventif. Soyez prudent!

IX **Le Sagittaire** (Sagittarius)

(23 novembre – 21 décembre)

Votre qualité la plus forte est l'imagination.

X **Le Capricorne** (Capricorn)

(22 décembre – 20 janvier)

Ne sortez pas aujourd'hui. Restez dans votre maison. Il y a du danger dans les rues.

XI **Le Verseau** (Aquarius)

(21 janvier – 19 février)

Il faut profiter du moment. Quelle semaine! Bonnes nouvelles!

XII **Les Poissons** (Pisces)

(20 février – 20 mars)

N'allez pas à la plage aujourd'hui. Il y a un requin affamé dans l'eau.

Le téléphone sonne. Voici la conversation entre Pierre et Monique:

Monique: C'est toi, Pierre? Ici Monique.

Pierre: Oui, c'est moi. Comment vas-tu?

Monique: Ça va. Écoute, Pierre. Il y a une grande soirée chez moi ce soir. Nous allons danser et chanter. Ma mère a préparé un gâteau délicieux. Nous allons beaucoup nous amuser. Henri va venir, ainsi que Paul, Robert, Raymond, Suzanne, Hélène, ta soeur Janine, et d'autres amis. Veux-tu venir?

Pierre: Attends, Monique. Je vais regarder dans le journal. Je n'ai pas lu mon horoscope pour aujourd'hui.

Pierre regarde l'horoscope dans le journal. Il lit sous son signe du Zodiaque, Le Capricorne. Il retourne au téléphone.

Pierre: Monique, mon horoscope dit qu'il faut rester à la maison aujourd'hui parce qu'il y a du danger dans les rues.

Monique: Es-tu superstitieux? Tu es fou!

Pierre: Écoute. Je vais venir tout de même.

Plus tard, Pierre quitte la maison pour aller à la soirée chez Monique. Quand il traverse la rue, il voit un grand camion venant à toute vitesse. Pierre _____

_____

_____ .

(Note to the student: Write your own ending to this story in one or two sentences, in French, of course!)

Vocabulaire

affamé *adj.*, starved, famished

ainsi que *conj.*, (just) as

amuser *v.*, to amuse; **s'amuser** *refl. v.*, to have a good time, to amuse oneself; **nous allons beaucoup nous amuser** we are going to have a very good time; **amusez-vous bien!** have a good time!

ça va *interj.*, I'm fine, it's fine, it's okay

le changement *n.*, the change, alteration

comment vas-tu? how are you?

écrivez *v. form of* **écrire**; **écrivez-lui** write to him/to her

fort *m.*, **forte** *f.*, *adj.*, strong; **votre qualité la plus forte** your strongest quality

ici *adv.*, here; **ici Monique** this is Monique here

intelligent *m.*, **intelligente** *f.*, *adj.*; **l'élève le plus intelligent de la classe** the most intelligent student in the class

inventif *m.*, **inventive** *f.*, *adj.*, inventive; **un esprit inventif** an inventive spirit

lit *v. form of* **lire**; **il lit** he is reading (he reads); **lu** *past part.*; **je n'ai pas lu** I haven't read

lui *disj. pron.*, him; **devant lui** in front of him; *as an indir. obj. pron.*, to him/to her

méfiez-vous *v. form (imperative) of* **se méfier** (to beware); **méfiez-vous des obstacles dangereux** beware of dangerous obstacles

meilleur *m.*, **meilleure** *f.*, *adj.*, better; **le meilleur, la meilleure** the best

même *adj.*, same; **tout de même** all the same, just the same

la nouvelle *n.*, (piece of)

news; **bonnes nouvelles** good news

la plage *n.*, the beach

plus *adv.*, more; **le plus** the most

profiter *v.*, to profit, to take advantage (of); **il faut profiter du moment** you must take advantage of the moment

la qualité *n.*, the quality; **la qualité la plus forte** the strongest quality

le requin *n.*, the shark

le signe *n.*, the sign; **les signes du Zodiaque** the signs of the Zodiac

le soir *n.*, the evening; **ce soir** this evening, tonight; **une soirée** an evening party

sortez *v. form (imperative) of* **sortir**; **ne sortez pas** don't go out

soyez *v. form (imperative) of* **être**; **soyez prudent!** be prudent!

Exercises

Review the story and vocabulary before starting these exercises.

I. Complete the following statements by writing the appropriate words in French. They are all in the story. Refer to it if you have to.

1. Pierre _____ le journal dans la cuisine. Il a la page _____ devant

_____ .

2. Vous êtes _____ juge de vos actions.

3. Votre qualité la _____ est la patience.

4. La personne qui vous aime _____ attend une lettre de vous.

5. Il faut profiter _____. Quelle _____! Bonnes _____!

II. Vrai ou faux?

1. Pierre lit le journal dans le salon. _____

2. Pierre parle au téléphone avec Monique. _____

3. Il y a une grande soirée chez Monique. _____

4. Pierre reste dans la maison. _____

5. Quand Pierre traverse la rue, il voit un grand camion. _____

III. Unscramble the words to find a meaningful sentence. Write it on the blank line. Refer to the story in this unit if you have to.

1. Pierre / horoscope / son / lit. _____

2. Demain / parfait / jour / être / va / un. _____

   _____

3. Une / personne / aime / vous / beaucoup. _____

4. Il / a / y / requin / un / l'eau / dans. _____

5. Téléphone / sonne / le. _____

Structures de la Langue

A. Forms of the interrogative adjective **Quel**

Masculine		Feminine	
Singular	Plural	Singular	Plural
quel (what, which)	**quels**	**quelle** (what, which)	**quelles**

Rules and observations:

1. The interrogative adjective **quel** agrees in gender and number with the noun it modifies.

2. Here are four examples to illustrate each form:

   1. **Quel livre** lisez-vous?　　　*Which (what) book* are you reading?
   2. **Quels fruits** aimez-vous?　　*Which (what) fruits* do you like?
   3. **Quelle leçon** étudiez-vous?　*Which (what) lesson* are you studying?
   4. **Quelles phrases** écrivez-vous?　*Which (what) sentences* are you writing?

3. In exclamations, **quel** and **quelle** mean *what a . . .!*

Quel homme!

　　　Quel homme!　　*What a* man!
　　　Quelle femme!　　*What a* woman!
　　　Quelle semaine!　　*What a* week!

4. When the verb **être** is used, the form of **quel** is not ordinarily in front of the noun it modifies:

　　　Quel est votre nom?　　*What* is your name?
　　　Quelle est votre adresse?　　*What* is your address?

249

Exercises

Review the preceding material before starting these exercises.

I. Write in French the questions that must have been asked.

    Model: Il est dix heures et quart.   You write the question: Quelle heure est-il?

    1. Mon nom est Pierre Paquet. _____

    2. Mon adresse est 17, rue de Rivoli. _____

    3. J'ai vingt ans. _____

II. Answer the following questions in complete sentences (in French). They are personal questions and require answers of your own.

    1. Quel est votre nom? _____

    2. Quelle est votre adresse? _____

    3. Quel âge avez-vous? _____

III. Write the appropriate form of **quel** on the blank line.

    1. Vous lisez un livre! _____ livre lisez-vous?

    2. Vous écrivez des phrases! _____ phrases écrivez-vous?

    3. Vous aimez les fruits! _____ fruits aimez-vous?

    4. Vous étudiez une leçon! _____ leçon étudiez-vous?

IV. Match the following.

    1. Quel homme!   ____ What a car!

    2. Quelle femme!   ____ What a stew!

    3. Quel ragoût!   ____ What a man!

    4. Quel livre!   ____ What a book!

250   5. Quelle voiture!   ____ What a woman!

V. Find the four different forms of **quel** and circle them.

Q	A	C	I	A	D	B
E	U	E	L	L	S	E
Q	U	E	L	S	U	Q
E	U	Q	L	U	E	U
Q	U	E	L	L	E	S
U	E	A	M	E	E	U

B. Demonstrative adjectives

1. **ce** garçon	1. this (that) boy
2. **cet** arbre	2. this (that) tree
3. **cet** homme	3. this (that) man
4. **cette** femme	4. this (that) woman
5. **cette** église	5. this (that) church
6. **ces** femmes	6. these (those) women
7. **ces** hommes	7. these (those) men

Rules and observations:

1. **Ce** is used before a masculine singular noun that begins with a consonant. See example 1 in the above box.

2. **Cet** is used before a masculine singular noun that begins with a vowel or silent *h*. See examples 2 and 3 in the above box.

3. **Cette** is used before *all* feminine singular nouns.

4. **Ces** is used in front of *all* nouns in the plural.

251

5. These demonstrative adjectives can means *this* or *that* in the singular, depending on the meaning intended. **Ces** can mean *these* or *those*.

6. If there is any doubt as to the meaning (*this, that, these, those*), just add **-ci** to the noun to give it the meaning of *this* or *these*. Actually, **-ci** is a shortening of **ici**, which means *here*. Add **-là** (which means *there*) to the noun to give it the meaning of *that* or *those*. Examples:

ce livre-ci	*this book*	**cette page-ci**	*this page*
ce livre-là	*that book*	**cette page-là**	*that page*
ces livres-ci	*these books*	**ces pages-ci**	*these pages*
ces livres-là	*those books*	**ces pages-là**	*those pages*

7. If there is more than one noun, a demonstrative adjective must be used in front of each noun: **cette dame et ce monsieur** (*this lady and gentleman*).

Exercises

Review the preceding material before starting these exercises.

I. Substitute the noun in parentheses for the noun in italics. Rewrite the sentence, using the appropriate form of the demonstrative adjective given.

   Model: Je mange ce *fruit*.   (pomme)   **You write: Je mange cette pomme.**

   A. Je mange cette *soupe*.

   1. (pêche) _____

   2. (gâteau) _____

   3. (petits fours) _____

   4. (ananas) _____

   5. (tomate) _____

   B. Etudiez-vous ce *vocabulaire*?

   1. (leçon) _____

   2. (livre) _____

3. (pages) _____

4. (phrases) _____

5. (poème) _____

C. Nous allons au cinéma avec ces *garçons.*

1. (jeunes filles) _____

2. (ami) _____

3. (amie) _____

4. (jeune homme) _____

5. (étudiants) _____

II. For each imperative that is given, write a response indicating that you are doing what you are told to do.

    Model: Donnez-moi ce livre!   **You write: Bien! Je vous donne ce livre!**

1. Donnez-moi ce journal! _____

2. Donnez-lui cette pomme! _____

3. Donnez-leur ces pommes frites! _____

III. Change the demonstrative adjective and the noun, which are in italics, to the singular or plural, depending on what is given. Rewrite the sentence.

    Model: Je vais lire *ces livres* et   **You write: Je vais lire ce livre et**
           **   *cette lettre.***   **ces lettres.**

1. Je vais manger *ces ananas* et *cette tomate.* _____

   _____

2. Je vais écrire *ces leçons* et *cette phrase.* _____

   _____

3. Je vais boire *ce vin* et *cette bière.* _____

4. Je vais envoyer *ces lettres.* _____

5. Je vais acheter *ces livres.* _____   **253**

C. Regular comparative and superlative adjectives

Adjective *masc. and fem.*	Comparative	Superlative
grand tall	**plus grand (que)** taller (than)	**le plus grand (de)** (the) tallest (in)
grande tall	**plus grande (que)** taller (than)	**la plus grande (de)** (the) tallest (in)
grand tall	**moins grand (que)** less tall (than)	**le moins grand (de)** (the) least tall (in)
grande tall	**moins grande (que)** less tall (than)	**la moins grande (de)** (the) least tall (in)
grand tall	**aussi grand (que)** as tall (as)	
grande tall	**aussi grande (que)** as tall (as)	
intelligent intelligent	**plus intelligent (que)** more intelligent (than)	**le plus intelligent (de)** (the) most intelligent (in)
intelligente intelligent	**plus intelligente (que)** more intelligent (than)	**la plus intelligente (de)** (the) most intelligent (in)
intelligent intelligent	**moins intelligent (que)** less intelligent (than)	**le moins intelligent (de)** (the) least intelligent (in)
intelligente intelligent	**moins intelligente (que)** less intelligent (than)	**la moins intelligente (de)** (the) least intelligent (in)
intelligent intelligent	**aussi intelligent (que)** as intelligent (as)	
intelligente intelligent	**aussi intelligente (que)** as intelligent (as)	

Rules and observations:

1. In making a comparison in English, we ordinarily add **-er** to the adjective (*tall, taller*) or we place *more* or *less* in front of the adjective (*more intelligent, less intelligent*). In French, we use **plus** or **moins** in front of the adjective. See the examples in the above box.

2. In order to express *as . . . as* in French, we use **aussi . . . que**.

3. The adjective must agree in gender and number with the noun it modifies. Example: Marie est plus **intelligente** que son frère. (Mary is more intelligent than her brother.)

4. In making a comparison, we use **que** in French to express *than;* we also use **que** in French to express *as*.

5. If the adjective is one that ordinarily is placed in front of the noun, then it remains in front of the noun when making a comparison. If the adjective is one that ordinarily is placed after the noun, then it remains after the noun when making a comparison. Examples:

   > **une jolie robe, une plus jolie robe, la plus jolie robe**
   > a pretty dress, a prettier dress, the prettiest dress

   > **une personne intelligente, une personne plus intelligente, la personne la plus intelligente**
   > an intelligent person, a more intelligent person, the most intelligent person

D.   Irregular comparative and superlative adjectives

Adjective (masc.)	Comparative	Superlative
bon, *good*	**meilleur,** *better*	**le meilleur,** *(the) best*
mauvais, *bad*	**plus mauvais,** *worse*	**le plus mauvais,** *(the) worst*
	pire, *worse*	**le pire,** *(the) worst*
petit, *small*	**plus petit,** *smaller (in size)*	**le plus petit,** *(the) smallest*
	moindre, *less (in importance)*	**le moindre,** *(the) least*

Rules and observations:

1. Actually, there are no rules that apply to these irregular adjectives of comparison. Just study them and make observations of your own.

2. Observe that **mauvais** and **petit** have regular and irregular comparisons.

3. Note that **de** is used (and not **dans**) to express *in* when using the superlative.

Exercises

Review the preceding material before starting these exercises.

I. Answer the following questions in French, substituting the appropriate forms of the words in parentheses for the ones indicated. Use **non** in your answer, but write your sentence in the affirmative. Also, use a pronoun subject in place of the noun subject.

Model: Est-ce que Paul est *plus*   You answer: **Non, il est moins grand**
grand que son frère?   (moins)   **que son frère.**

1. Est-ce que Pierre est *plus* grand que sa mère? (moins) _____

   _____

2. Est-ce que Janine est *plus* grande que son père? (moins) _____

   _____

3. Est-ce que Monique est *plus* intelligente que Janine? (moins) _____

   _____

II. Answer the following questions in complete sentences (in French). Use the noun in parentheses in your answer. Make all required changes in the forms of the adjectives.

Model: Qui est plus grand que   You answer: **Janine est plus grande que**
Robert? (Janine)   **Robert.**

1. Qui est plus grand que Janine? (Madame Paquet) _____

   _____

2. Qui est moins grand que Pierre? (Janine) _____

   _____

3. Qui est plus petit que Monique? (Mathilde) _____

   _____

4. Qui est moins petit que Joseph? (Suzanne) _____

   _____

5. Qui est aussi grand que Monsieur Paquet? (Monsieur Richy) _____

   _____

6. Qui est aussi petit que Madame Banluc? (Madame Paquet) _____

   _____

III. For each statement that is given, write in French a response contradicting the **statement.** Begin your response with **Non, ce n'est pas vrai.** Then use the name in parentheses in your answer in place of the noun subject in the statement, which is in italics. Make all required changes in agreement.

Model: *Monique* **est la plus** **intelligente du cours** **d'anglais.   (Joseph)**

You write: **Non, ce n'est pas vrai. Joseph** **est le plus intelligent du cours** **d'anglais.**

1. *Raymond* est le plus intelligent du cours de mathématiques. (Janine) _____

_____

2. *Bob* est le plus grand du cours de français. (Suzanne) _____

_____

Michel est le moins grand de la famille.

3. *Michel* est le moins grand de la famille. (Simone) _____

_____

4. *Béatrice* est la plus belle du groupe. (Charles) _____

_____

5. *Henri* est le plus petit. (Hélène) _____

_____

IV. Answer the following questions in the affirmative in complete French sentences. In answer (a) use **oui** and write a complete sentence. In answer (b) write a complete answer and add **aussi**. Make the required changes in the adjectives.

Models:	(a) **Ce livre est-il plus long que les autres?**	You write:	(a) **Oui, ce livre est plus long que les autres.**
	(b) **Et cette lettre?**	You write:	(b) **Cette lettre est plus longue que les autres aussi.**

1. (a) Cette phrase est-elle moins facile que les autres? _____

_____

   (b) Et ces questions? _____

2. (a) Ce poème est-il plus difficile que les autres? _____

_____

   (b) Et cette leçon? _____

3. (a) Cette voiture est-elle plus belle que les autres? _____

_____

   (b) Et ces maisons? _____

4. (a) Ce garçon est-il plus beau que les autres? _____

_____

   (b) Et ces jeunes filles? _____

5. (a) Cette banane est-elle plus délicieuse que les autres? _____

_____

   (b) Et ces gâteaux? _____

V. On the blank line write the French equivalent for the English words in parentheses.

1. (more)   Simone est _____ intelligente que sa soeur.

2. (tall)   Alain est aussi _____ que sa mère.

3. (as)   Monique est _____ petite que son père.

4. (prettier)   Anne est _____ que Suzanne.

5. (the least)   Michel est _____ grand.

VI. Le Mot Mystère. (Mystery Word). In order to find the mystery word, you must first find and circle in the puzzle the French words given under it. The letters that remain in the puzzle are scrambled. Unscramble them to find **le mot mystère**.

E	M	A	R	C	H	E	E	T	R
N	V	Q	U	I	O	T	T	O	F
A	M	I	E	I	L	U	A	U	A
G	E	B	R	U	I	T	Y	R	I
R	M	Ê	M	E	I	P	N	N	R
I	D	A	N	S	À	L	O	E	E
S	P	A	Y	E	R	U	N	V	T
E	U	Q	U	E	L	S	E	I	S
P	O	U	B	E	L	L	E	S	O
B	E	A	U	C	O	U	P	N	

à	grise	poubelle
amie	il	quel
au	marche	qui
beaucoup	me	se
bruit	même	son
dans	non	tournevis
en	payer	tu
et	plus	y
faire		

VII. Oral Proficiency. Respond orally in French to the situation described. (Later, you may write your responses for intensive practice.)

Situation: You are a salesclerk in a UNISEX shop. A customer comes in to buy a few articles of clothing. Greet the customer by saying: *Bonjour! Vous désirez?* The customer wants to buy a few things, for example, a shirt, blouse, socks, necktie, and other items. After your opening statement, show the customer a few items and ask questions. You may use any or all of the following: *ce, cet, cette, ces, quel, quelle, quels, quelles; regarder, joli, meilleur, une soirée, aimer, préférer, plus joli(e) que, plus beau (belle) que, plus grand(e) que.*

259

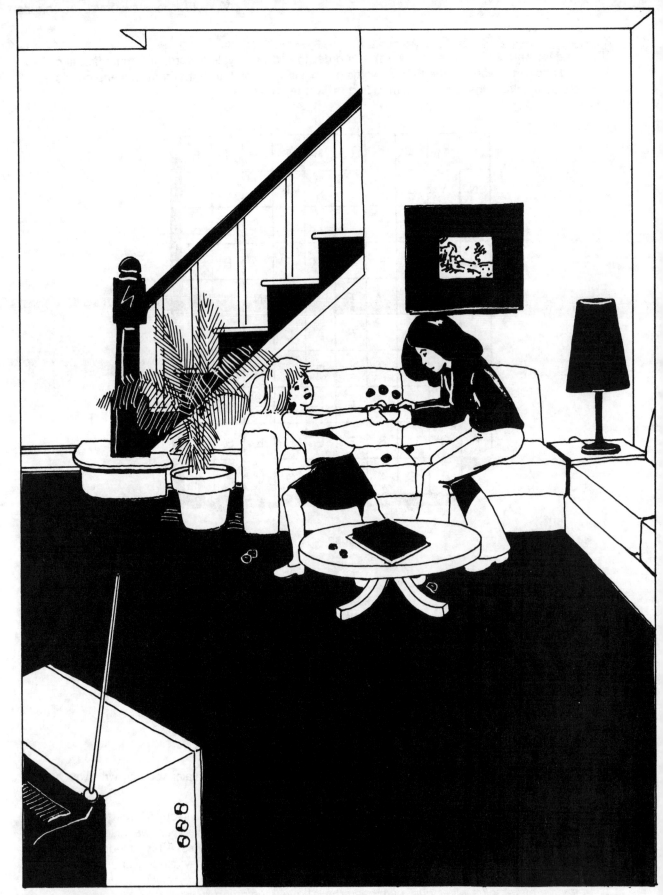

Donne-moi la bôite de chocolats!

Adverbs and Tag Questions – *n'est-ce pas?*

Janine receives a phone call from a neighbor, Madame Bédier. She wants her to babysit with Renée, her five-year-old daughter, while she and her husband are at the movies. What do you suppose happens to the box of chocolates while they are out?

La boîte de chocolats

C'est samedi. Janine n'a rien à faire. Elle est à la fenêtre dans sa chambre. Elle regarde les oiseaux sur les branches du pommier dans le jardin.

Le téléphone sonne.

— Janine! C'est pour toi, dit sa mère.

Janine quitte sa chambre et descend l'escalier.

— C'est Madame Bédier, dit sa mère. Elle va au cinéma ce soir avec son mari et elle a besoin de toi.

— Allô! J'écoute. Ici Janine . . . . Comment allez-vous, madame? . . . . Très bien, merci . . . . Je ne fais rien ce soir . . . . Vous allez au cinéma . . . Ah! Bon! . . . . D'accord . . . . Oui, je peux venir chez vous ce soir et rester avec Renée . . . . Oui, je sais . . . . Oh, elle a déjà cinq ans! . . . . Oui, elle est grande pour son âge . . . . Oui, je sais qu'elle est capricieuse . . . . Oui, je sais qu'elle parle plus vite que les autres enfants . . . . Oui, je sais qu'elle marche moins vite que les autres enfants . . . . Bon! . . . . D'accord! A six heures et demie . . . . A ce soir, madame.

A six heures vingt, Janine quitte la maison pour aller chez les Bédier qui habitènt à côté de la maison des Paquet.

— Ah! Janine! s'exclame Madame Bédier. Philippe! C'est Janine! La meilleure gardienne d'enfants du voisinage! N'est-ce pas, Philippe?

Monsieur et Madame Bédier ont mis leurs chapeaux, manteaux, et gants. Avant de sortir, Madame Bédier dit:

— Renée, sois sage! A huit heures et demie tu vas te coucher, n'est-ce pas? Janine, tu sais où est la chambre de Renée, n'est-ce pas? La boîte de chocolats est là-bas sur la petite table ronde. Seulement une pièce pour Renée. Elle en a mangé trois aujourd'hui. Janine, tu peux en avoir deux pièces si tu veux parce que tu es plus grande que Renée. Il y a une comédie à la télévision ce soir. Nous allons voir le film *La Lettre* au Bijou. A tout à l'heure!

261

Ils partent.

— Janine, je veux ma pièce de chocolat maintenant, dit Renée. J'aime mieux la cerise à la crème. Quelle pièce est la cerise à la crème, Janine? demande Renée.

— Je ne sais pas! J'aime beaucoup les chocolats et mon favori est le nougat. Quelle pièce est le nougat, Renée? demande Janine.

— Je ne sais pas! . . . . Ah! . . . . je sais comment savoir!

— Comment? demande Janine.

— Je vais écraser chaque pièce avec le doigt, répond Renée.

— Non! Renée! Non! Tu vas les abîmer! s'exclame Janine.

— Ça ne fait rien. Laisse-moi! crie Renée.

Renée arrache vigoureusement la boîte de chocolats des mains de Janine et elle commence à piquer chaque pièce avec son doigt.

— Voilà, Janine! Voilà la cerise à la crème pour moi et le nougat pour toi!

— Oh! Toutes les pièces de chocolats sont écrasées! Tout est abîmé! Qu'est-ce que je vais dire à tes parents? s'exclame Janine.

Renée quitte le salon avec la boîte de chocolats. Après quelques minutes, elle revient dans le salon et elle dit:

— Janine, ne t'inquiète pas. J'ai jeté la boîte de chocolats dans la poubelle avec les ordures! Maintenant, tu n'as pas besoin d'expliquer à mes parents.

— Ta mère a raison, lui dit Janine. Tu es vraiment capricieuse. Méchante! Va te coucher! Vite!

Trois heures plus tard, Monsieur et Madame Bédier rentrent à la maison. Madame entre dans le salon et dit:

— Janine, tu peux avoir toute la boîte de chocolats. Emporte la boîte avec toi. Bonsoir, et merci!

Vocabulaire

à tout à l'heure! see you in a little while!
abîmer v., to spoil, to ruin
l'accord n. m., the agreement; **d'accord** okay, agreed
allô interj., hello (used when answering the telephone)
arracher v., to pull away, to pull out

avant prep., before; **avant de sortir** before going out
le besoin n., the need; **avoir besoin de** to have need of, to need
la boîte n., the box
bonsoir salutation, good evening
ça ne fait rien! that doesn't matter!

capricieux m., **capricieuse** f., adj., capricious, whimsical
la cerise n., the cherry
chaque adj., each
le côté n., the side; **à côté de** next to
déjà adv., already; **elle a déjà cinq ans!** she is already five years old!

262

descendre v., to descend, to come (go) down
écraser v., to crush
en pron., partitive, of them; **elle en a mangé trois!** she ate three (of them)
l'escalier n. m., the staircase
le gant n., the glove
le gardien, la gardienne n., the guardian; **gardien (gardienne) d'enfants** babysitter

s'inquiéter refl. v., to worry, to be upset; **ne t'inquiète pas!** don't worry!
jeter v., to throw
laisse-moi! let me!
le manteau n., the coat
méchant m., **méchante** f., adj., mean, nasty, naughty
mieux adv., better; **j'aime mieux** I prefer, I like better
mignon m., **mignonne** f., adj., darling, cute

l'oiseau n. m., the bird
l'ordure n. f., garbage, rubbish
la pièce n., the piece
piquer v., to poke, to puncture
le pommier n., the apple tree
sois v. form of **être**; **sois sage!** be good!
va te coucher! go to bed! (v. form of **aller se coucher**)
le voisinage n., the neighborhood

Exercises

Review the story and vocabulary before starting these exercises.

I. Oui ou Non?

1. Janine est dans sa chambre; elle regarde les oiseaux sur les branches du pommier dans le jardin.   _____

2. Madame Bédier va au cinéma avec son mari; et elle a besoin de Janine.   _____

3. Renée a dix ans.   _____

4. Janine écrase toutes les pièces de chocolats.   _____

5. Renée a mangé tous les chocolats.   _____

II. Choose the correct answer.

1. Janine est à la fenêtre dans   (a) le salon.   (b) la cuisine.   (c) la salle de bains.   (d) sa chambre.   _____

2. Madame et Monsieur Bédier vont   (a) au cinéma.   (b) à l'église. (c) au théâtre.   (d) à l'opéra.   _____

3. Renée a jeté la boîte de chocolats   (a) par la fenêtre.   (b) dans la rue.   (c) dans la poubelle.   (d) contre le mur.   _____

4. La boîte de chocolats est   (a) dans le tiroir.   (b) sur la petitie table ronde.   (c) dans la cuisine.   (d) sous le lit.   _____

5. Renée est   (a) très mignonne.   (b) très gentille.   (c) capricieuse. (d) fatiguée.   _____   263

III. Write in the missing words in French. Refer to the story if you have to.

1. Renée, à huit heures et demie tu vas _____ , n'est-ce pas?

2. J'ai _____ la boîte de chocolats dans la poubelle avec les ordures.

3. Janine, tu peux avoir _____ la boîte de chocolats!

4. Janine est la _____ gardienne d'enfants du voisinage.

5. Renée parle _____ vite que les autres enfants.

6. Renée marche _____ vite que les autres enfants.

Structures de la Langue

A. Position of an adverb

---

1. Janine aime **beaucoup** les chocolats.   (Janine likes chocolates *very much*.)

2. Madame Bédier a parlé **distinctement.**   (Mrs. Bédier spoke *distinctly*.)

3. Madame Bédier a **bien** parlé.   (Mrs. Bédier spoke *well*.)

Rules and observations:

1. An adverb is a word that describes a verb, an adjective, or another adverb.

2. In French, an adverb ordinarily *follows* the simple verb it modifies, as in the first model sentence in the above box.

3. If a verb is compound, as in the passé composé (model sentence 2), the adverb generally *follows* the past participle only if it is a long adverb. The adverb **distinctement** is long.

4. If a verb is compound, as in the passé composé (model sentence 3), *short common adverbs* (like **beaucoup**, **bien**, **déjà**, **encore**, **mal**, **mieux**, **souvent**, **toujours**) *must precede* the past participle.

B. Formation of some adverbs

1. Many adverbs are formed in French by adding the ending **-ment** to the *feminine singular* form of an adjective. This is similar to adding *-ly* to an adjective in English to form an adverb: *quick/quickly.*

seule/seulement	**furieuse/furieusement**
(alone/only)	(furious/furiously)

2. Ordinarily, adjectives that end in **-ant** are transformed into adverbs by dropping **-ant** and adding **-amment**.

constant/constamment	(constant/constantly)

3. Ordinarily, adjectives that end in **-ent** are transformed into adverbs by dropping **-ent** and adding **-emment**.

patient/patiemment	(patient/patiently)

C. Regular comparison of adverbs

Adverb	Comparative	Superlative
vite (quickly)	**plus vite (que)** *more quickly (than)* *faster (than)*	**le plus vite** *(the) most quickly* *(the) fastest*
	moins vite (que) *less quickly (than)*	**le moins vite** *(the) least quickly*
	aussi vite (que) *as quickly (as)* *as fast (as)*	

D. Tag question: n'est-ce pas?

The phrase *n'est-ce pas?* is tagged to a statement when the speaker expects the listener to agree. It can be translated into English in any number of ways: *isn't that right? isn't that so? etc.* The appropriate translation into English depends on the meaning of the statement in French.

> Renée a cinq ans, **n'est-ce pas**?   (Renée is five years old, *isn't she*?)

Exercises

Review the preceding material before starting these exercises.

I. Change the following adjectives to adverbs in French.

Model: furieuse   furieusement

1. distincte _____   4. constant _____

2. seule _____   5. patient _____

3. courageuse _____   6. fière _____

II. Rewrite each sentence in French, adding the adverb in parentheses in its proper position.

Model: Madame Coty aime le   You write: Madame Coty aime beaucoup
café. (beaucoup)   le café.

1. Monsieur Richy aime le ragoût brûlé. (beaucoup) _____

_____

2. Le professeur a parlé. (bien) _____

3. Janine a parlé. (constamment) _____

4. Elle est partie. (déjà) _____

5. Pierre a mangé. (beaucoup) _____

III. Write the French adverb for the English in italics.

Model: Pierre marche aussi *quickly* que son père.   **You write: vite**

266   1. Janine parle aussi *well* que sa mère. _____

2. Joseph mange *more* vite que son frère. _____

3. Bob marche *as* lentement *as* son cousin. _____ _____

4. Raymond étudie *more* souvent *than* Michel. _____ _____

5. Mathilde parle *less* vite que sa soeur. _____

6. François travaille *the least* vite. _____

IV. Le Mot Mystère (Mystery Word). In order to find the *mystery word*, you must first find and circle in this puzzle the French words given under it. The letters that remain in the puzzle are scrambled. Unscramble them to find *le mot mystère.*

A	E	M	V	P	Y	G	R	I	S
U	N	O	O	L	A	L	L	E	R
T	F	I	I	U	A	L	A	C	A
O	J	N	T	S	A	U	S	S	I
M	O	S	U	G	A	R	Ç	O	N
O	L	P	R	R	F	E	M	M	E
B	I	E	E	A	N	E	P	A	S
I	R	T	B	N	N	L	U	I	E
L	I	I	O	D	L	U	N	D	I
E	L	T	N	O	P	É	R	A	S

à	garçon	moins petit
aller	gris	ne
aussi	il	opéras
automobile	joli	pas
bon	la	plus grand
en	lui	voiture
femme	lundi	y

V. **Oral Proficiency.** Respond orally in French to the situation described. (Later, you may write your responses for intensive practice.) Review this lesson for ideas or words to use.

Situation: You are babysitting in your neighbor's house next door. They have two children, Robert who is five years old, and Debbie who is seven. They are quarreling with each other about what to watch on TV. You do your best to settle the argument. They are behaving badly and it's your job to restore a pleasant atmosphere. In five sentences resolve the quarrel and restore order. You may use your own ideas or ideas suggested by the following: *avoir, être, sois (soyez) sage(s), avoir besoin de, capricieux, capricieuse, abîmer, laisse-moi! jeter, méchant(e), va te coucher! vite* (quickly).

Review Test: Work Units 16–20

I. Complete this crossword puzzle **(mots-croisés).**

I. *Mots-croisés* (Crossword Puzzle)

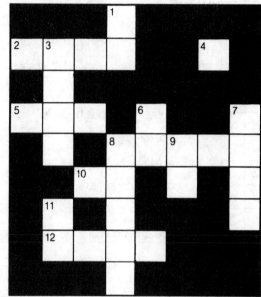

Verticalement

1. 1st person singular direct and indirect object pronoun.
3. 3d person plural indirect object pronoun.
6. Preposition used with adverbs of quantity, e.g., *beaucoup, trop.*
7. Masculine plural demonstrative pronoun.
8. Masculine singular demonstrative pronoun.
9. 3d person masculine singular direct object pronoun.
11. Pronoun that takes the place of the partitive and serves as a direct object.

Horizontalement

2. Feminine singular subject pronoun.
4. Pronoun commonly used in an interrogative sentence, as in *Est-ce qu'il...a?*
5. 3d person singular indirect object pronoun.
8. Feminine singular demonstrative pronoun.
10. 1st person singular subject pronoun.
12. 1st person plural direct and indirect object pronoun.

II. Dans le potage(in the soup). In this word puzzle, find the verb form in the present indicative tense for each verb in the sentences below. When you find them, draw a line around each one. The verb form in the present tense of *faire* in the first statement given below is *faites*, and it has already been done to get you started. The words are written horizontally, vertically, diagonally, or backwards.

A	I	M	E	B	A	L	I	T	A
C	D	A	L	O	S	E	T	I	D
O	O	E	F	I	O	A	E	G	I
U	I	E	A	A	L	L	O	N	S
R	S	V	S	I	O	U	E	A	U
S	A	I	R	E	U	Ê	T	E	S
I	L	N	A	P	S	U	V	L	O
A	E	I	P	E	U	V	E	N	T
E	O	N	T	N	E	D	N	E	V
L	U	I	A	L	L	E	Z	O	N
F	A	T	E	Z	V	A	V	A	I
F	I	N	I	S	S	O	N	S	S

Que (faire)-vous ce soir?

Que me (dire)-vous?

J' (aimer) danser.

Moi, je (aller) chez moi.

Les garçons (avoir)-ils assez d'argent pour aller au cinéma?

Nous (aller) en France l'été prochain.

Quand (partir)-tu?

Et vous, (être)-vous heureux?

Tes parents (pouvoir)-ils venir avec nous?

Que (devoir)-tu faire maintenant?

Pourquoi (courir)-tu?

(Vendre)-ils leur maison?

Est-ce que nous (finir) le travail aujourd'hui?

III. Mots-croisés. This activity tests your knowledge of the **passé composé** tense. The missing words are the present tense of *avoir* or *être* or the correct form of the past participle, or a subject pronoun.

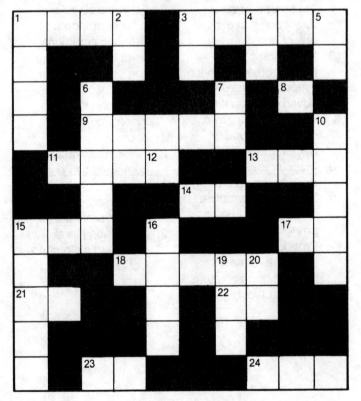

Horizontalement

1. Hier, je _____ allé au cinéma.
3. Martine est _____ (aller) aux grands magasins.
8. Pierre _____ lu un livre.
9. Ils ont _____ (vouloir) partir.
11. _____ avez parlé assez.
13. La lettre? Je l'ai _____ (lire).
14. Pierre s'est _____ (taire).
15. J'ai _____ (mettre) du sucre dans le café.

17. J'ai _____ (devoir) (à l'envers)* partir.
18. Les lettres? Je les ai _____ (mettre) sur le bureau.
21. Nous avons bien _____ (rire).
22. Avez-vous _____ (savoir) la réponse?
23. Paul a-t-_____ compris?
24. Qu'a-t-elle _____ (dire)?

* à l'envers   backwards

Verticalement

1. Je _____ tombé en montant dans le bus.
2. J'ai _____ (savoir) la réponse.
3. Hier soir, j'_____ beaucoup mangé.
4. Ma camarade a _____ (lire) un livre intéressant.
5. Ce matin j'ai _____ (avoir) un petit accident.
6. Nous _____ pris le train.
7. Les enfants ont _____ (pouvoir) manger.

10. Nous avons _____ (vendre) la maison.
12. A-t-il _____ (savoir) (à l'envers)* répondre à la question?
15. Madame Durand est _____ (mourir) la semaine dernière.
16. Tu as _____ (finir) la leçon?
19. Jacqueline _____ restée à la maison.
20. Tu as _____ (savoir) cela, n'est-ce pas?

*A l'envers/backwards

IV. Complete the paragraph in French about Colette, writing the appropriate form of the adjective. Make all required changes for agreement with the noun.

Colette occupe la _____ place dans la _____ salle de classe.
                   1. premier   2. grand

Elle est une _____ amie de _____ le monde. Elle ne fait
                   3. bon   4. tout

jamais de _____ choses. Elle prépare toujours _____ les
              5. mauvais   6. tout

leçons de français. Elle est une très _____ étudiante. Elle est
                          7. excellent

toujours trés _____ . Elle porte une _____ jupe
             8. studieux   9. joli

et une blouse _____ .
          10. blanc

V. Change the following adjectives into adverbs using the *-ment* ending in French.

1. gentil _____

2. franc _____

3. affreux _____

4. amer _____

VI. Write at least ten common adverbs in French that do not end in *-ment*.

1. _____   3. _____   5. _____   7. _____   9. _____

2. _____   4. _____   6. _____   8. _____   10. _____

VII. In this dialogue, Yvette and you are talking about the exams in June and your summer vacation. Complete the conversation by choosing the appropriate French adverb from the following: *bien, rapidement, déjà, toujours, aussi.*

Yvette: Es-tu prêt pour tes examens?

Vous: Oui, je suis _____ prêt pour mes examens.
                                  1.

Yvette: Demain j'ai encore un autre examen, et puis les vacances commencent.

Vous: Les jours de vacances vont passer _____ .
                                              2.

Yvette: Nous avons passé l'été passé dans les montagnes.

Vous: Ma famille et moi allons _____ dans les montagnes.
                                     3.

Yvette: En juillet nous allons faire un voyage en Australie.

Vous: Ma famille et moi _____ ! Nous allons à Melbourne!
                              4.

Yvette: Si tu me donnes ton adresse, je vais t'envoyer une carte postale de Sydney.

Vous: Mais je t'ai _____ donné mon adresse! L'as-tu perdue?

Le Docteur: Il est ridicule de croire qu'il faut manger pour vivre.

Negations and Other Structures of the Language

Mrs. Paquet has been sick since
yesterday. She has indigestion. What do
you think of the doctor's advice? Would
you do what he says or what she does?

Manger pour vivre ou vivre pour manger?

Madame Paquet est malade depuis hier. Elle a mangé quelque chose qui lui a donné mal à l'estomac. Elle est souffrante dans son lit. Son mari a appelé le docteur pour lui donner un médicament. Le docteur va venir dans quelques minutes. Madame Paquet l'attend patiemment depuis vingt minutes.

Le docteur est arrivé. Il est dans la chambre de Madame Paquet depuis quinze minutes. Il l'examine. Monsieur Paquet est avec eux.

Monsieur Paquet:	Dites-moi, docteur, faut-il appeler une ambulance pour transporter ma femme à l'hôpital?
Le Docteur:	Non, monsieur. Il n'est pas nécessaire de la transporter à l'hôpital. Elle peut rester ici dans son lit. Elle n'est pas gravement malade. Les ambulances rendent grand service, mais dans ce cas votre femme peut rester où elle est.
	J'insiste, chère madame. Prenez ce médicament et ne mangez rien.
Madame Paquet:	Rien manger?!
Le Docteur:	Absolument rien!
Madame Paquet:	Pas même un oeuf à la coque?
Le Docteur:	Pas même un oeuf à la coque!
Monsieur Paquet:	Mais, docteur, soyez raisonnable.
Madame Paquet:	Oui, docteur, soyez raisonnable! Rien à manger?
Le Docteur:	Pendant au moins deux jours.
Madame Paquet:	Je vais mourir de faim! Soyez raisonnable, docteur.
Le Docteur:	Je suis raisonnable, madame.
Madame Paquet:	Pas même un petit morceau de pain grillé?

Le Docteur:	Pas même un petit morceau de pain grillé!
Madame Paquet:	. . . sans beurre . . . sans confiture . . .?
Le Docteur:	Pas de pain grillé, pas de beurre, pas de confiture. Rien. Il est ridicule de croire qu'il faut manger pour vivre. Rappelez-vous, madame, qu'une personne ne se nourrit pas seulement par le pain. Manger est mauvais pour la santé. Tout le monde mange mal. La chimie du corps ne peut pas tolérer les aliments modernes . . . Excusez-moi maintenant. Je dois partir parce que je vais dîner au Coq d'or: du poisson . . .
Madame Paquet:	Du poisson! Ah!
Le Docteur:	Un beau filet mignon . . .
Madame Paquet:	Ah!
Le Docteur:	Une belle salade . . .
Madame Paquet:	Ah!
Le Docteur:	Rappelez-vous, aussi, que quand j'ai pris le serment d'Hippocrate, j'ai promis de remplir mes devoirs.

Le docteur va à la porte.

Madame Paquet:	Hippocrate ou hypocrite?! Docteur, n'oubliez pas le proverbe: ''Dis-moi ce que tu manges et je te dirai ce que tu es!''

Le docteur sort.

Madame Paquet:	François, y a-t-il quelque chose à manger dans le réfrigérateur? Et donne-moi mon médicament.

Vocabulaire

absolument *adv.*, absolutely

l'aliment *n. m.*, the food

la chimie *n.*, chemistry

le Coq d'or Golden Cock (name of a restaurant)

la coque *n.*, the shell (of an egg); **un oeuf à la coque** soft-boiled egg

depuis *adv., prep.*, since; **depuis quand** since when; **depuis combien de temps** since how long (a time); **Madame Paquet est malade depuis hier** Mrs. Paquet has been sick since yesterday

dîner *v.*, to dine, to have dinner

dis-moi ce que tu manges et je te dirai ce que tu es! tell me what you eat and I'll tell you what you are!

dois *v. form of* **devoir** (ought to, have to, must); **je dois** I have (to)

l'estomac *n. m.*, the stomach

griller *v.*, to grill, to toast; **grillé** toasted

Hippocrate *n. m.*, Hippocrates (Ancient Greek physician)

le mal *n.*, pain, ache; **mal à l'estomac** stomach ache

malade *adj.*, sick, ill

manger *v.*, to eat

le médicament *n.*, medicine

moins *adv.*, less; **au moins** at least

le morceau *n.*, morsel, piece

mourir *v.*, to die

nourrir *v.*, to nourish; **se nourrir** *refl. v.*, to nourish oneself

l'oeuf *n. m.*, the egg

le pain *n.*, the bread; **pain grillé** toast

pas de pain no bread; **pas de beurre** no butter; **pas même** not even

patiemment *adv.*, patiently
pour *prep.*, for, in order (to)
prenez *v. form (imperative) of*
   prendre; prenez take
pris *past part. of* **prendre** (to
   take)
promis *past part. of*
   promettre (to promise)
quelque *adj.*, some;
   quelques a few; **quelque**

chose something
rappelez-vous *v. form*
   (imperative) of **se rappeler**
   (to remember)
rendre service to perform a
   service
le serment *n.*, oath; **le**
   serment d'Hippocrate
   Hippocratic Oath (a code
   of medical ethics imposed

by Hippocrates upon his
   students of medicine)
souffrir *v.*, to suffer;
   souffrant *m.*, **souffrante**
   f., *adj.*, sick
soyez *v. form (imperative)*
   of **être**; **soyez**
   raisonnable!
   be reasonable!
vivre *v.*, to live

Exercises

Review the story and vocabulary before starting these exercises.

I. Answer the following questions in complete sentences (in French). They are based on the
   story in this unit.

1. Qui est malade? _____

2. Pourquoi est-elle malade? _____

3. Depuis quand est-elle malade? _____

4. Qui lui donne du médicament? _____

5. Pourquoi le docteur doit-il partir? _____

II. **Comment dit-on en français...?** Write the French equivalent for the English given. Refer
   to the story in this unit if you have to.

1. Mrs. Paquet has been sick since yesterday. _____

2. Absolutely nothing! _____

3. Not even a soft-boiled egg! _____

4. Tell me what you eat and I'll tell you what you are! _____

   _____

5. Take this medicine and don't eat anything! _____   277

III. The words in the following boxes are scrambled. Unscramble them to find a meaningful sentence. Write the sentence in French on the line provided.

Model:

le	est
arrivé	docteur

You write: ___Le docteur est arrivé.___

1.

le	est	n'
arrivé	docteur	pas

_____

2.

est	Madame Paquet	hier
depuis	malade	n'est-ce pas?

_____

3.

est	la	dans	quinze
chambre	il	depuis	minutes

_____

IV. Mots-croisés. (Crossword Puzzle). Give the French words for the English.

Verticalement

1. 3d pers. sing., pres. indicative of **devoir**

2. to call

5. butter

6. year

7. since

8. bed

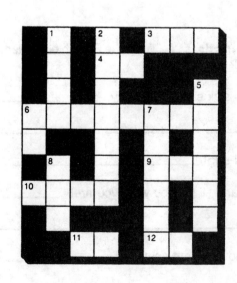

Horizontalement

3. _____ à l'estomac

4. past part. of **pouvoir**

6. to wait

9. by

10. yesterday

11. past part of **lire**

12. reflexive pronoun

278

Structures de la Langue

A.   Negations: **ne . . . pas / ne . . . jamais / ne . . . rien**

Present Indicative	Passé Composé
1. Je **ne** fume **pas**. (I do not smoke.)	4. Je **n'ai pas** fumé. (I did not smoke.)
2. Je **ne** fume **jamais**. (I never smoke.)	5. Je **n'ai jamais** fumé. (I have never smoked.)
3. Elle **ne** mange **rien**. (She's eating nothing. or: She's not eating anything.)	6. Elle **n'a rien** mangé. (She has eaten nothing. or: She hasn't eaten anything.)

Rules and observations:

1.   To make a sentence negative in the present indicative (as you already know from experience in previous work units), merely put **ne** in front of the verb and **pas** after it.

2.   If you want to negate the verb by saying **never** in the present indicative, merely put **ne** in front of the verb and **jamais** after it.

3.   If you want to negate a verb by saying **nothing** in the present indicative, merely put **ne** in front of the verb and **rien** after it.

4.   In the passé composé, put **ne** in front of the auxiliary (or helping) verb and either **pas** or **jamais** or **rien** after it.

5.   If the first letter of the verb is a vowel, drop **e** in **ne** and add an apostrophe: **Je n'ai . . .**

B.   Subordination with **quand, parce que,** and **que**

1.   **Quand** j'ai faim, je mange.
(*When* I'm hungry, I eat.)

2.   Madame Paquet est dans son lit **parce qu'**elle est malade.
(Mrs. Paquet is in her bed *because* she is sick.)

3.   Je sais **que** vous êtes intelligent.
(I know *that* you are intelligent.)

279

Rules and observations:

1. Each sentence in the above box contains two clauses: a main clause and a subordinate clause. In model sentence 1, the main clause is **je mange** and the subordinate clause is **quand j'ai faim**. As a main clause, **je mange** can stand alone. However, **quand j'ai faim** cannot stand alone; it is incomplete and subordinate to the main clause.

2. In model sentence 2, the main clause is **Madame Paquet est dans son lit** and the subordinate clause is **parce qu'elle est malade**. As a main clause, **Madame Paquet est dans son lit** can stand alone and make sense. However, **parce qu'elle est malade** cannot stand alone; it is incomplete and subordinate to the main clause. Of course, subordinate clauses are used frequently as fragmentary replies to questions or statements in conversation and informal writing. Nevertheless, a subordinate clause is not a complete sentence.

3. In model sentence 3, the main clause is **Je sais** and the subordinate clause is **que vous êtes intelligent**.

C. **Dans** and a duration of time

> Le docteur va venir **dans quelques minutes**.
>
> (The doctor is going to come *in a few minutes*.)

Rules and observations:

1. **Dans** and a duration of time indicates a definite time in the future when something will happen.

2. In the model sentence above, **dans quelques minutes** means *at the end of a few minutes*. If that is what you mean, use **dans** for *in*.

3. **Dans** and a duration of time can be at the beginning or the end of a sentence, but future time must be implied.

D. **En** and a duration of time

> **En une heure,** le docteur est venu.
>
> (*In one hour,* the doctor came.)

Rules and observations:

1. **En** and a duration of time indicates the completion of an action at any time *within* that period of time.

2. In the model sentence above, **en une heure** means *in* or *within* one hour; in other words, any time before the one hour is up. If that is what you mean, use **en** for *in*.

3. **En** and a duration of time must be at the beginning of a sentence if the action has already been completed (as a general rule).

E. **Depuis** and a duration of time

> 1. **Depuis quand** Madame Paquet **est**-elle malade?
>
>   (*Since when has* Mme. Paquet been sick?)
>
> 2. Madame Paquet est malade **depuis hier**.
>
>   (Mme. Paquet has been sick *since yesterday.*)
>
> 3. **Depuis combien de temps** Mme. Paquet **attend**-elle le docteur?
>
>   (*How long has* Mme. Paquet *been waiting* for the doctor?)
>
> 4. Madame Paquet **attend** le docteur **depuis vingt minutes**.
>
>   (Mme. Paquet *has been waiting* for the doctor *for twenty minutes.*)

Rules and observations:

1. In model sentence 1 in the above box, **depuis quand** is used in the question to express *since when;* in other words, at what point in the past. When you use this structure, you must use the present indicative tense of the verb.

2. In model sentence 2, which is the answer to 1, **depuis hier** is used to express *since yesterday* and the verb is still in the present indicative tense. (Note the verb tense in English in the question and in the answer in both model sentences: *has been.*) In French, however, we use the simple present tense because the thought expressed in the verb still holds right *now* in the present.

3. In model sentences 3 and 4, **depuis combien de temps** has a slightly different meaning. It asks: for how long. The answer to the question asked in this type of sentence structure usually requires a certain length of time to be stated, *e.g.,* twenty minutes, three hours, a month, and so forth. Note here, too, that in French we use the verb in the present tense because the action of the verb (in this case, waiting) is carried on right up to the present.

Exercises

I. Answer the following questions in French in the negative using **ne . . . pas**.

Model: Fumez-vous?   **You answer: Non, je ne fume pas.**

1. Dansez-vous bien? _____

2. Votre père chante-t-il souvent? _____

3. Votre mère lit-elle beaucoup? _____

4. Vos amis écrivent-ils bien? _____

5. Fumes-tu? _____

II. Answer the following questions in French in the negative using **ne . . . jamais**.

> **Model: Mangez-vous beaucoup?**   You answer: **Non, je ne mange jamais beaucoup.**

1. Parlez-vous beaucoup? _____

2. Votre père boit-il beaucoup de lait? _____

3. Votre soeur travaille-t-elle beaucoup? _____

4. Ton ami étudie-t-il beaucoup? _____

5. Buvez-vous beaucoup d'eau? _____

III. Answer the following questions in French in the negative using **ne . . . rien**.

> **Model: Est-ce que Madame Paquet mange quelque chose?**   You answer: **Non, Madame Paquet ne mange rien.**

1. Lucille mange-t-elle quelque chose? _____

2. Guy écrit-il quelque chose? _____

3. Lis-tu quelque chose? _____

4. Madame Paquet fait-elle quelque chose? _____

5. Étudiez-vous quelque chose? _____

IV. Answer the following questions in French in the negative, using the negation requested.

(A) Use **ne . . . rien** in your answers.

> **Model: Avez-vous mangé quelque chose?**   You answer: **Non, je n'ai rien mangé.**

1. Avez-vous dit quelque chose? _____

2. Janine a-t-elle bu quelque chose? _____

3. Vos amis ont-ils étudié quelque chose? _____

4. Avez-vous lu quelque chose? _____

5. Avez-vous écrit quelque chose? _____

6. As-tu bu quelque chose? _____

7. Julie et Lucille ont-elles mangé quelque chose? _____

(B) Use **ne . . . jamais** in your answers.

Model: **Avez-vous jamais voyagé**   **You answer:**   **Non, je n'ai jamais**
            en France?   **voyagé en France.**

> NOTE THAT SOME OF THESE VERBS IN THE PASSÉ
> COMPOSÉ ARE CONJUGATED WITH **AVOIR**, SOME
> WITH **ÊTRE**. BE CAREFUL!

1. Avez-vous jamais voyagé en Angleterre? _____

2. Êtes-vous jamais allé au Canada? _____

3. Avez-vous jamais vu un film français? _____

4. Juliette est-elle jamais allée à l'opéra? _____

5. Robert a-t-il jamais lu un journal français? _____

6. Monsieur et Madame Paquet sont-ils jamais allés en Espagne? _____

_____

7. Lucille et Marie-Louise ont-elles jamais mangé un éclair? _____

_____

V. The words in the following boxes are scrambled. Unscramble them to find a meaningful sentence. Write the sentence in French on the line provided.

Model:

sais	vous	que
êtes	intelligent	je

You write: **Je sais que vous êtes intelligent.** _____

1.

êtes	malade	je
sais	vous	que

2.

dans	est	lit	elle	est
son	Madame Paquet,	parce qu'	malade	n'est-ce pas?

_____

3.

j'ai	je	faim
mange	quand	

_____

4.

venir	va	quelques
le docteur	minutes	dans

_____

5.

heure	le docteur	est
une	venu	en

_____

VI. Identify the following verb forms by giving the infinitive for each. They are all in the story in this unit.

Model: dis   **You write: dire**

1. est _____   4. attend _____

2. a _____   5. dites _____

3. va _____   6. prenez _____

VII. Answer the following questions in complete sentences (in French). Use the French words in parentheses in your answers. Use a pronoun in place of the noun as subject.

Model: Depuis quand Madame Paquet   **You answer: Elle est malade depuis**
est-elle malade?   (hier)   **hier.**

1. Depuis quand Pierre est-il absent? (lundi) _____

2. Depuis combien de temps Madame Paquet attend-elle le docteur? (vingt minutes) _____

_____

3. Depuis combien de temps attendez-vous l'autobus? (dix minutes) _____

284 _____

4. Depuis quand travaillez-vous ici? (le premier avril) _____

   _____

5. Depuis combien de temps lisez-vous ce livre? (une heure) _____

   _____

6. Depuis quand lisez-vous ce livre? (ce matin) _____

   _____

VIII. Answer the following questions in the affirmative in complete sentences in French.

   Model: Faut-il manger pour vivre?   **You answer: Oui, il faut manger pour vivre.**

1. Faut-il boire pour vivre? _____

2. Faut-il étudier pour apprendre? _____

3. Faut-il parler français dans la classe de français? _____

   _____

4. Faut-il parler espagnol dans la classe d'espagnol? _____

   _____

5. Faut-il faire les devoirs pour apprendre? _____

   _____

IX. Oral Proficiency. You and your friend Pierre are talking about your plans for the summer vacation. Imagine a conversation between yourself and him.

   Pierre: Dis-moi, est-ce que tu as l'intention de chercher du travail pour l'été prochain?

1. Vous: _____

   Pierre: Où est-ce que tu vas travailler?

2. Vous: _____

   Pierre: Tu as de la chance. Moi, je n'ai pas trouvé de travail.

3. Vous: _____

   Pierre: Tu crois que je peux travailler avec toi?

4. Vous: _____

   Pierre: Alors, je vais parler avec lui tout de suite.

5. Vous: _____

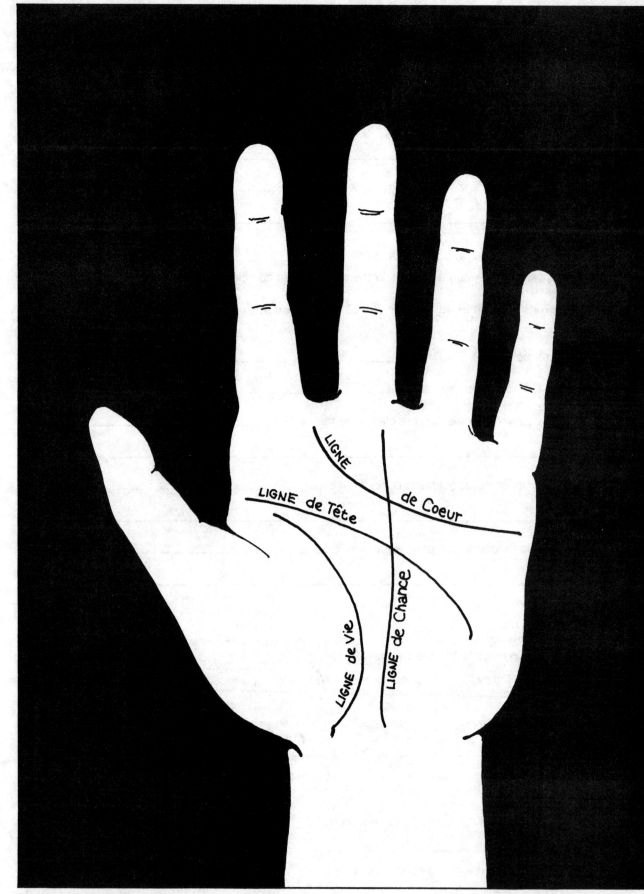

Les secrets de votre main

Orthographical Changing Verbs in the Present Indicative and Other Structures of the Language

Some people like to have their palms read. It can be fun—believe it or not.

Les secrets de votre main

Claire et François Paquet sont allés à la foire samedi. Là, ils se sont bien amusés. Ils ont vu des expositions, ils ont acheté des souvenirs, et ils sont entrés chez une chiromancienne pour se faire lire les lignes de la main.

— Tiens! François! Une chiromancienne! s'exclame Claire.

— Où? lui a demandé François.

— Là, devant nous. Ne vois-tu pas?

> Madame Sétou,
> chiromancienne,
>
> révèle les secrets de votre main.

— François, je vais me faire lire les lignes de la main. Veux-tu aussi? lui a demandé Claire.

— Oui, je veux bien aussi. Mais, tu sais que je n'y crois pas, dit François.

Ils entrent chez la chiromancienne.

— Est-ce que nous vous dérangeons, madame?

— Mais non, pas du tout! Entrez! Entrez! répond Madame Sétou.

— Je veux me faire lire les lignes de la main. Et mon mari aussi, dit Claire.

— Bon! répond la chiromancienne. Asseyez-vous et donnez-moi la main.

Madame Sétou regarde fixement la main de Claire et elle commence à lire les lignes:

— Ah! Je vois dans votre ligne de chance que vous allez faire un voyage aux États-Unis avec un homme, s'exclame Madame Sétou.

— C'est curieux! dit Claire. Mon mari et moi, nous commençons à faire des préparations pour un autre voyage aux États-Unis.

— Maintenant, dit Madame Sétou, je regarde votre ligne de cœur. Je vois que vous êtes amoureuse d'un homme.

— C'est curieux! dit Claire. Vous avez raison. Je suis amoureuse de mon mari!

— Maintenant, monsieur, asseyez-vous et donnez-moi la main, dit Madame Sétou.

François Paquet lui donne la main.

— Ah! Je vois dans votre ligne de chance que vous allez faire un voyage aux États-Unis avec une femme, s'exclame Madame Sétou.

— C'est curieux! dit François. Ma femme et moi, nous commençons à faire des préparations pour un autre voyage aux États-Unis.

— Maintenant, dit Madame Sétou, je regarde votre ligne de coeur. Je vois que vous êtes amoureux d'une femme.

— C'est curieux! dit François. Vous avez raison. Je suis amoureux de ma femme! La main révèle tout, n'est-ce pas?

— Oui, monsieur, la main révèle les secrets dans votre vie. Ça fait dix francs pour les révélations.

François lui paye les dix francs.

Dehors, Claire dit à François:

— Madame Sétou sait tout, n'est-ce pas?

— Oui, Madame Sétou sait tout, mais je n'ai rien appris de nouveau. Et toi?

— Moi non plus. Nous savons déjà que nous voyageons aux États-Unis et que nous sommes amoureux!

Vocabulaire

l'amour n. m., love; **amoureux** m., **amoureuse** f., adj., in love; **nous sommes amoureux** we are in love
s'amuser refl. v., to have a good time; **ils se sont bien amusés** they had a good time
appris past part. of **apprendre; je n'ai rien appris de nouveau** I didn't learn anything new
asseyez-vous imperative of s'asseoir (to sit down)
la chance n., luck, fortune, chance
le chiromancien, la

chiromancienne, n., the palm reader
le coeur n., the heart
crois v. form of **croire** (to believe); **je n'y crois pas** I don't believe in it
curieux m., **curieuse** f., adj., curious, odd
déranger v., to disturb
donnez-moi la main give me your hand
fixement adv., intently, fixedly
la foire n., the fair
la ligne n., the line; **se faire lire les lignes de la main** to have one's palm read (to have the lines of one's hand read)

pas du tout not at all
plus adv., more; **non plus** neither; **moi non plus** me neither
révéler v., to reveal
sais v. form of **savoir; tu sais** you know
veux v. form of **vouloir; veux-tu?** do you want to?; **je veux bien** I'd like to; **je veux me faire lire les lignes de la main** I want to have my palm read
vois v. form of **voir; ne vois-tu pas?** don't you see?
voyager v., to travel
y advl. pron., **je n'y crois pas** I don't believe in it

288

Exercises

Review the story and vocabulary before starting these exercises.

I. Vrai ou faux? On the blank line write **vrai** if the statement is true or **faux** if the statement is false.

1. Claire et François Paquet sont allés à une foire. _____

2. François refuse de se faire lire les lignes de la main. _____

3. Claire et François n'ont rien appris de nouveau chez la chiromancienne. _____

II. Write appropriate responses in French on the blank lines. The following is a conversation between Claire and François Paquet who are about to have their palms read.

Claire: Tiens! François! Une chiromancienne!

François: _____

Claire: Là, devant nous. Je vais me faire lire les lignes de la main. Veux-tu?

François: _____

Claire: Madame Sétou sait tout, n'est-ce pas?

François: _____

Claire: Je n'ai rien appris de nouveau. Et toi?

François: _____

III. Write complete sentences in French using the cue words given below. Change the infinitives where necessary to either the present tense or the passé composé, whichever you prefer. Supply other words as needed.

Model: Claire et François Paquet / aller / la foire.

You write: Claire et François Paquet sont allés à la foire.

or: Claire et François Paquet vont à la foire.

1. Joseph et Joséphine / aller / cinéma / samedi.

_____

2. Ils / entrer / chez / chiromancienne.

_____

3. Ils / ne / apprendre / rien / chez / chiromancienne.

_____

4. François Paquet / lui / payer / francs / pour / révélations.

_____

Structures de la Langue

A. Orthographical changing verbs in the present indicative

<table>
<tr><td colspan="2" align="center">appeler (to call)</td></tr>
<tr><td>Singular</td><td>Plural</td></tr>
<tr><td>j'appelle</td><td>nous appelons</td></tr>
<tr><td>tu appelles</td><td>vous appelez</td></tr>
<tr><td>il, elle, on appelle</td><td>ils, elles appellent</td></tr>
</table>

Rules and observations:

1. An orthographical changing verb is a verb that changes in spelling.

2. In the box above, **appeler** doubles the **l** in the three persons of the singular and in the third person plural. This is done because the stress falls on the syllable that contains the **l** when pronounced. The letter **l** does not double in the first and second persons of the plural because the stress is on the final syllable (**-ons** and **-ez**).

3. There are other verbs that double the consonant in the same persons as above. For example: **jeter** (to throw) and **rappeler** (to recall, to call (someone) back).

<table>
<tr><td colspan="2" align="center">employer (to use, employ)</td></tr>
<tr><td>Singular</td><td>Plural</td></tr>
<tr><td>j'emploie</td><td>nous employons</td></tr>
<tr><td>tu emploies</td><td>vous employez</td></tr>
<tr><td>il, elle, on emploie</td><td>ils, elles emploient</td></tr>
</table>

4. For verbs ending in **-oyer** or **-uyer** you must change the **y** to **i** before a silent **e**, as noted in the above box.

5. Other verbs that end in **-oyer** or **-uyer** are: **nettoyer** (to clean), **envoyer** (to send), **ennuyer** (to bore, to bother), **essuyer** (to wipe).

6. Verbs ending in **-ayer** may change the **y** to **i** or may keep the **y** before silent **e**. Two examples are: **essayer** (to try, to try on) and **payer** (to pay, to pay for).

---

manger (to eat)

Singular	Plural
je mange	nous mangeons
tu manges	vous mangez
il, elle, on mange	ils, elles mangent

---

7. For verbs ending in **-ger**, add a silent **e** after the **g** if the vowels **a** or **o** follow **g**. This is done in order to preserve the soft sound of **g** as it is pronounced in the infinitive. If a silent **e** were not inserted between **g** and **a** or **g** and **o**, the **g** would then have to be pronounced hard, as in the English word *go*.

8. Other verbs ending in **-ger** that are treated in the same way are:

> **arranger** (to arrange); **changer** (to change); **corriger** (to correct); **déranger** (to disturb); **nager** (to swim); **obliger** (to oblige); **songer** (to think, to dream); **voyager** (to travel).

---

prononcer (to pronounce)

Singular	Plural
je prononce	nous prononçons
tu prononces	vous prononcez
il, elle, on prononce	ils, elles prononcent

---

9. For verbs ending in **-cer**, change **c** to **ç** before the vowels **a, o, u**. This is done in order to preserve the soft sound of **c** (like *s*) as it is pronounced in the infinitive. The little mark under the **c** (**ç**) is called *une cédille*. Actually, it is the lower half of consonant *s* and indicates that **ç** should be pronounced as *s*.

10. Other verbs ending in **-cer** that are treated in the same way are:

> **annoncer** (to announce); **avancer** (to advance); **commencer** (to begin); **effacer** (to efface, to erase); **lancer** (to hurl, to lance, to launch); **menacer** (to threaten, to menace); **placer** (to place, to put, to set); **remplacer** (to replace).

---

acheter (to buy)

Singular   *Plural*

j'achète   nous achetons

tu achètes   vous achetez

il, elle, on achète   ils, elles achètent

---

11. If there is a silent e in the syllable just before the infinitve ending (as in acheter above), it changes to è in a verb form — provided that the syllable right after it contains another silent e. Study the changes in spelling in the above box.

12. Other verbs that change in the same way are: **lever** (to lift, to raise), **se lever** (to get up), and **enlever** (to remove, to take off).

Exercises

Review the preceding material before starting these exercises.

I. Answer the following questions in complete sentences (in French) in the affirmative. Substitute *nous* as the subject pronoun in place of "Et vous et votre soeur?" Also, substitute an object pronoun for the noun direct object, as shown in these two models:

Model: **Bob arrange les fleurs.**   You answer: **Nous les arrangeons aussi.**
            Et vous et votre soeur?

Model: **Simone efface le tableau.**   You answer: **Nous l'effaçons aussi.**
            Et vous et votre soeur?

1. Hélène change la phrase. Et vous et votre soeur? _____

_____

2. Yves corrige le devoir. Et vous et votre soeur? _____

_____

3. Monique appelle les garçons. Et vous et votre soeur? _____

_____

4. Guy emploie le dictionnaire. Et vous et votre soeur? _____

_____

5. Lucille achète les roses. Et vous et votre soeur? _____

292

_____

II. **Do the same here as you did above, substituting** *nous* **as the subject pronoun in place of "Et vous et votre frère?"**

1. Paulette lance la balle. Et vous et votre frère? _____

   _____

2. René avance les mains. Et vous et votre frère? _____

   _____

3. Renée lève les fenêtres. Et vous et votre frère? _____

   _____

4. Suzanne paye l'addition. Et vous et votre frère? _____

   _____

5. Charles mange les bananes. Et vous et votre frère? _____

   _____

Charles mange les bananes.

III. Change to the passé composé.

> **Model:** **Claire et François Paquet**   **You write:** **Claire et François Paquet**
> **vont à la foire.**   **sont allés à la foire.**

1. Janine et Monique vont au cinéma. _____

2. Nous voyageons aux États-Unis. _____

3. Madame Sétou regarde fixement la main de Madame Paquet. _____

   _____

4. Madame Sétou révèle les secrets de votre main. _____

   _____

5. Claire et François Paquet achètent des souvenirs. _____

   _____

IV. Change to the present indicative.

> **Model:** **Nous avons mangé les pommes.**   **You write:** **Nous mangeons les**
>   **pommes.**

1. Nous avons arrangé les fleurs. _____

2. Il a acheté une cravate. _____

3. Ils ont appelé la police. _____

4. Tu as employé le dictionnaire. _____

5. Nous avons prononcé le mot. _____

B. **Aller** in the present indicative with an infinitive

Je vais faire mes devoirs.   **Il va voir** ses amis.

(*I'm going to do* my homework.)   (*He's going to see* his friends.)

Rule: It is customary to use **aller** in the present indicative with an infinitive form of a verb, as we do in English.

C. **Vouloir** in the present indicative with an infinitive

Elle **veut acheter** une nouvelle robe.   Monsieur Paquet **veut vendre** son auto.

(She *wants to buy* a new dress.)   (Mr. Paquet *wants to sell* his car.)

Rule: It is customary to use **vouloir** in the present indicative with an infinitive form of a verb, as we do in English.

D. The use of **il y a, y a-t-il . . .?, voici,** and **voilà**

(a) **Il y a** un bon restaurant près d'ici.   (*There is* a good restaurant near here.)

(b) **Il y a** dix étudiants dans cette classe.   (*There are* ten students in this class.)

(c) J'ai vu Janine **il y a deux heures**.   (I saw Janine *two hours ago*.)

(d) **Y a-t-il** un arrêt d'autobus près d'ici?   (*Is there* a bus stop near here?)

(e) **Est-ce qu'il y a** des fruits sur la table?   (*Are there* fruits on the table?)

(f) **N'y a-t-il pas** de sel dans la soupe?   (*Isn't there* any salt in the soup?)

(g) Non, **il n'y a pas** de sel dans la soupe.   (No, *there isn't* any salt in the soup.)

(h) Je l'ai vue **il y a un an**.   (I saw her *a year ago*.)

(i) **Voici** ma mère et **voilà** mon père!   (*Here's* my mother and *there's* my father!)

(j) **Voici** un taxi et **voilà** un taxi!   (*Here is* a taxi and *there is* a taxi!)

(k) **Me voici!**   **Le voici!**   **Vous voilà!**   **Les voilà!**   **La voici!**

(*Here I am!*)   (*Here he is!*   (*There you are!*)   (*There they are!*)   (*Here she is!*
                 Here it is!)   *Here it is!*)

Rules and observations:

1. **Il y a** is used simply to mention the existence of something which may or may not be known to the listener. It may be about people, things, or facts. Its equivalent in English is *there is* or *there are*.

2. **Il y a** also means *ago* when a length of time is stated right after it. See models (c) and (h) in the above box

3. The interrogative form of **il y a** is given in models (d) and (e) above.

4. The negative form of **Il y a** is given in model sentence (g) above.

5. The negative-interrogative form of **Il y a** is given in model sentence (f) above. **Est-ce qu'Il n'y a pas** is also a correct form.

6. **Voici** and **voilà** have a demonstrative characteristic. They are used to point out, to call attention to someone or something. They are based on **vois + ici (+ là)**. If you analyze the word, it actually means: *See (look) here! See (look) there!* See models (i) and (j) above.

7. If you regard **voici** or **voilà** as a "verb form," you will understand why the object pronoun is placed in front of it, as in the model sentences in (k) above.

Exercises

Review the preceding material before starting these exercises.

I. Answer the following questions in the affirmative in complete sentences (in French).

    Model: Allez-vous faire vos devoirs?   **You answer: Oui, je vais faire mes devoirs.**

1. Allez-vous faire un voyage au Canada? _____

2. Va-t-elle écrire une lettre? _____

3. Est-ce qu'il va jouer dans le parc? _____

4. Vont-ils voyager en Angleterre? _____

5. Allons-nous répondre à la question? _____

II. Answer the following questions in the negative in complete sentences (in French).

    Model: Voulez-vous acheter un   **You answer: Non, je ne veux pas acheter**
                   nouveau chapeau?   **un nouveau chapeau.**

1. Voulez-vous acheter une nouvelle voiture? _____

    _____

2. Le professeur de français veut-il corriger les devoirs? _____

    _____

3. L'étudiant veut-il prononcer le mot? _____

4. Janine veut-elle employer le dictionnaire? _____

5. Monsieur Paquet veut-il fumer une cigarette? _____

III. Match the following.

1. There you are! _____ Me voici!   4. Here I am! _____ Le voilà!

2. Here she is! _____ Vous voilà!   5. There it is! _____ La voici!

3. Here they are! _____ Les voici!

IV. Change to the negative.

**Model: Il y a un bon restaurant   You write: Il n'y a pas un bon restaurant
près d'ici.   près d'ici.**

1. Il y a un grand parc dans cette ville. _____

2. Y a-t-il un arrêt d'autobus ici? _____

3. Est-ce qu'il y a dix garçons dans la classe? _____

_____

V. Answer the following questions in the affirmative in complete sentences, using French for the English in parentheses.

**Model: Avez-vous vu Janine?   You answer: Oui, j'ai vu Janine il y a deux
(two hours ago)   heures.**

1. Avez-vous lu *Le livre de mon ami* d'Anatole France? (three months ago) _____

_____

2. A-t-il vu Pierre? (ten minutes ago) _____

3. Êtes-vous allé en Californie? (a year ago) _____

4. Sont-elles arrivées? (a half hour ago) _____

5. Est-elle partie? (an hour ago) _____

VI. Oral Proficiency. Respond orally in French to the situation described. (Later, you may write your responses for intensive practice.)

Situation: You are the president of the French Club. There are several new students present at the first meeting and they are trying to decide whether or not to join the club. They want to know primarily what everybody does in the club. As president, you must tell them what you all do from time to time. Of course, you must use the first person plural of the verbs (the *nous* form) in the present tense. State at least six activities that all the members take part in, including yourself. You may use your own ideas or ideas suggested by the following: *appeler, employer, manger, corriger, arranger, commencer, danser, parler, voyager, il y a, à présent, avoir besoin de, effacer, placer.*

297

Papa! Papa! Attends! Attends!

Prepositions and Infinitives and Other Structures of the Language

In this story, the Paquet family is celebrating the wedding anniversary of Mr. and Mrs. Paquet. After a festive lunch, they attempt to play some music on their brand new stereo that Mr. Paquet had bought as a present for his wife.

Le beau cadeau

C'est aujourd'hui samedi.

Monsieur Paquet est allé acheter une radio stéréo. C'est un cadeau pour sa femme à l'occasion de leur vingtième anniversaire de mariage. Madame Paquet est allée chez le coiffeur pour une nouvelle coiffure. Janine a préparé un grand déjeuner toute la matinée dans la cuisine, et Pierre est allé aux grands magasins acheter un petit cadeau pour sa mère de la part de lui et de sa soeur. Il est allé, aussi, chez un confiseur pour acheter une boîte de chocolats et chez un fleuriste pour acheter des fleurs.

Après un déjeuner délicieux, Monsieur Paquet dit:

— Et maintenant nous allons écouter un peu de musique. Elle est belle, cette radio stéréo, n'est-ce pas?

Monsieur Paquet essaye d'allumer la radio, mais il n'y a pas de musique! Il n'y a pas de son! Il n'y a rien!

— Zut, alors! J'ai horreur de réparer des radios! dit-il.

— D'abord, le téléviseur il y a un an! Et maintenant, une nouvelle radio stéréo qui ne marche pas! Incroyable! Ces appareils gouvernent notre vie! s'exclame Madame Paquet.

Monsieur Paquet va téléphoner au magasin où il a acheté la radio stéréo.

— Il faut appeler le magasin, dit-il.

A ce moment-là, Pierre s'exclame:

—Papa! Papa! Attends! Attends! Tu n'as pas branché la stéréo sur la prise de courant!

Vocabulaire

agréable *adj.*, pleasant

l'anniversaire *n. m.*, anniversary, birthday

brancher *v.*, to plug in, to connect (an electrical apparatus)

le cadeau *n.*, the gift, present

le coiffeur, la coiffeuse *n.*, the hairdresser; **une coiffure** *n.*, a hair style

le confiseur, la confiseuse *n.*, the confectioner, candy maker; **une confiserie** a candy store

d'abord *advl. phrase*, at first, first

essayer *v.*, to try

la fleur *n.*, the flower

le fleuriste, la fleuriste *n.*, the florist

gouverner *v.*, to govern, to rule, to direct

l'horreur *n. f.*, horror; **J'ai horreur de** + *inf.* I hate + *pres. part.*

le magasin *n.*, the store; **le grand magasin** the department store

le mariage *n.*, the marriage

le matin *n.*, the morning; **la matinée** the morning (long); **toute la matinée** all morning long

l'occasion *n. f.*, the occasion

la part *n.*, part, behalf; **de la part de lui** on his behalf

peu *adv.*, little

la prise *n.*, hold, grip; **une prise de courant** electric outlet (in the wall)

le son *n.*, the sound

299

Exercises

Review the story and vocabulary before starting these exercises.

I. Answer the following questions in complete sentences in French. They are all based on the story in this unit.

1. Où Monsieur Paquet est-il allé? _____

2. Qui a préparé un grand déjeuner? _____

3. Qui est allé chez le coiffeur? _____

4. Qui a acheté une boîte de chocolats? _____

5. Pourquoi la radio stéréo ne marche-t-elle pas d'abord? _____

_____

II. Oui ou Non?

1. Madame Paquet a acheté une radio stéréo. _____

2. Pierre a acheté une boîte de chocolats chez un confiseur. _____

3. Monsieur Paquet a horreur de réparer des radios. _____

4. Monsieur Paquet va téléphoner au fleuriste. _____

5. La radio stéréo ne marche pas d'abord parce que Monsieur Paquet n'a pas branché l'appareil sur la prise de courant. _____

III. Write short sentences in French using the cue words in each group. They are all based on the story in this work unit. Use the present indicative or the passé composé, whichever you prefer. Supply other words as needed.

1. Monsieur Paquet / acheter / radio stéréo.

_____

2. Janine / préparer / déjeuner.

_____

3. Pierre / aller / confiseur / chocolats.

_____

Structures de la Langue

A. The use of **de** with an infinitive after certain idiomatic expressions

1. **avoir besoin de + inf.**
   (to need + inf.)

2. **avoir envie de + inf.**
   (to feel like + pres. part.)

3. **avoir horreur de + inf.**
   (to hate, to detest + pres. part. or inf.)

4. **avoir peur de + inf.**
   (to be afraid + inf.)

5. **avoir raison de + inf.**
   (to be right + inf.)

6. **avoir tort de + inf.**
   (to be wrong + inf.)

Models:

1. **J'ai besoin d'aller** chez le dentiste. (*I need to go* to the dentist.)

2. **Tu as envie de dormir.** (*You feel like sleeping.*)

3. **Il a horreur de réparer** des radios. (*He hates repairing (to repair)* radios.)

4. **Nous avons peur de traverser** la mer. (*We are afraid to cross* the sea.)

5. **Vous avez raison d'avoir** peur. (*You are right to be* afraid.)

6. **Vous avez tort d'avoir** peur. (*You are wrong to be* afraid.)

Rule: The above idiomatic expressions take **de + infinitive form**. Note that in English we sometimes use a present participle (or gerund) instead of an infinitive, as in model sentences 2 and 3 in the above box.

B. The use of **Il est** + adjective + **de** + infinitive

1. **Il est agréable d'aller** à un bal. (*It is pleasant to go (going)* to a dance.)

2. **Il est amusant d'aller** à un cirque. (*It is fun to go (going)* to a circus.)

3. **Il est désagréable d'aller** chez le dentiste. (*It is unpleasant to go (going)* to the dentist.)

4. **Il est impossible de lire** ce gros livre en une heure. (*It is impossible to read* this thick book within an hour.)

5. **Il est intéressant d'aller** à un musée. (*It is interesting to go (going)* to a museum.)

Rule: Use **Il est** (not **C'est**) + adjective + de + infinitive.

C. The use of **à** after certain verbs + infinitive

---

1. **J'apprends à lire** en français. (*I am learning to read* in French.)

2. **Je commence à écrire** en français. (*I am beginning to write* in French.)

3. **J'hésite à sortir** parce qu'il pleut. (*I hesitate going (to go) out* because it's raining.)

Rule: In French, some verbs take **à** between the verb form and the infinitive. Study the above models.

D. The use of **pour, sans, avant de, au lieu de,** and **afin de** + infinitive

---

1. Il est parti **pour aller** voir ses amis. (He left *to go* see his friends.)

2. Elle est sortie **sans dire** un mot. (She went out *without saying* a word.)

3. Nous mangeons et buvons **pour vivre.** (We eat and drink *(in order) to live.*)

4. Ils sont allés au cinéma **avant de finir** leurs devoirs. (They went to the movies *before finishing* their homework.)

5. Elles sont sorties **au lieu de rester** à la maison. (They went out *instead of staying* home.)

6. Il est revenu **afin de voir** ses amis. (He came back *in order to see* his friends.)

Rule: The infinitive form of the verb is used *after* prepositions and prepositional phrases, except after **en**.

E. The use of no preposition after certain verbs + infinitive

1. **J'aime aller** au cinéma.   (*I like to go (going) to the movies.*)

2. **Tu aimes mieux aller** au théâtre.   (*You prefer to go (going) to the theater.*)

3. **Il déteste aller** chez le dentiste.   (*He hates to go (going) to the dentist.*)

4. **Elle veut aller** au Canada.   (*She wants to go to Canada.*)

5. **Nous pensons aller** en Angleterre.   (*We intend to go (going) to England.*)

6. **Vous pouvez aller** à l'opéra ce soir.   (*You can go to the opera tonight.*)

7. **Ils veulent aller** en Australie.   (*They want to go to Australia.*)

8. **Elles doivent aller** à la bibliothèque.   (*They have to go to the library.*)

ALSO MAKE A NOTE OF THE IMPERSONAL EXPRESSION **Il faut**, as in:

Il faut étudier pour apprendre.   (*It is necessary to study in order to learn.*)

Rule: No preposition is needed between the verb form and the infinitive when you use the above verbs.

F. The use of **de** after certain verbs + infinitive

1. **J'ai oublié de fermer** la fenêtre.   (*I forgot to close the window.*)

2. **Je promets de venir** chez vous.   (*I promise to come to your house.*)

3. **Elle a refusé de sortir** hier soir.   (*She refused to go out last night.*)

4. **Je tâche de faire** mes devoirs.   (*I try to do my homework.*)

Rule: The above verbs require **de** + infinitive.

Exercises

Review the preceding material before starting these exercises.

I. Write the appropriate preposition in French, either **à** or **de**, on the blank line. If no preposition is needed, write a dash (—).

Model: **Elle a oublié ____de____ fermer la porte.**

1. Tu as envie _____ jouer, n'est-ce pas?

2. Elle apprend _____ lire l'espagnol.

3. J'aime _____ aller au cinéma.

4. Il a besoin _____ travailler.

5. Nous commençons _____ écrire le français.

6. Veux-tu _____ aller au Canada?

7. J'aime mieux _____ prendre du thé.

8. Elle hésite _____ fumer.

9. Vous avez raison _____ partir.

10. Nous avons tort _____ rester.

II. Answer the following questions in the affirmative in complete French sentences. In answer (a) use **oui**. In answer (b) use **aussi**. Study the models.

Models: (a) **Avez-vous envie de sortir?**

(b) **Et Robert?**

You answer: (a) **Oui, j'ai envie de sortir.**

(b) **Il a envie de sortir aussi.**

> USE SUBJECT PRONOUNS IN YOUR ANSWERS.

1. (a) As-tu envie d'aller au cinéma? _____

   (b) Et tes amis? _____

2. (a) Madame Paquet a-t-elle besoin d'aller au supermarché? _____

   _____

   (b) Et Louise et Antoinette? _____

3. (a) Êtes-vous sorti sans dire un mot? _____

   (b) Et Joséphine? _____

4. (a) Apprenez-vous à lire le français? _____

   (b) Et Robert? _____

5. (a) Avez-vous horreur de manger dans un restaurant sale? _____

   _____

304 (b) Et Michel et Marie? _____

9 ETAGES 9 FLOORS

à votre service. at your service.

Super-terrasse en plèin ciel. Bar.	Roof-garden. Bar.
Tissus d'ameublement. Tapis. Meubles de cuisine.	Furnishing materials. Carpets. Kitchen furniture.
Jouets. Camping. Bagages.	Toys. Camping. Luggage.
Restaurant. Salon de thé. Cadeaux : "La Maîtrise".	Restaurant. Tea-room. Gifts: "La Maîtrise".
Confection féminine. Pull-overs. Chemisiers. Sportswear.	Women's ready-to-wear. Pullovers. Sportswear.
Salon de Beauté. Salon de Coiffure. Lingerie féminine. Tout pour l'enfant.	Beauty-salon. Hairdressers. Lingerie. Everything for children.
Bureau de voyages. Locations théâtre. Chaussures pour femmes. Tissus. Linge de maison.	Travel agency. Theatre agency. Women's shoes. Materials, household linen.
Interprètes. Taxiphones. Journaux. Parfums. Bijoux. Souvenirs de Paris. Radio. Télévision.	Interpreters. Taxiphones. Newspapers. Perfumes. Jewelry. Souvenirs of Paris. Radio. Television.
Bar rapide. Verrerie. Porcelaine. Orfèvrerie.	Snack-bar. Glass-ware. China-ware. Silver.
EVERSMART Vêtements et accessoires pour Hommes.	EVERSMART. Men's clothes and accessories.

BUREAU INFORMATION

III. **Choose the correct answer after studying the picture on the preceding page.**

1. Un jouet est généralement pour (a) une dame. (b) un monsieur.
(c) un enfant. (d) un agent de police. _____

2. Si vous avez faim, vous allez au (a) salon de coiffure. (b) bureau
de voyages. (c) salon de beauté. (d) restaurant. _____

3. Si vous voulez prendre de la pâtisserie et du thé, vous allez (a) au salon
de beauté. (b) aux tapis. (c) aux interprètes. (d) au salon de thé. _____

IV. **Match the following after studying the picture on the preceding page.**

1. everything for children _____ chaussures pour femmes

2. carpets _____ bar rapide

3. women's shoes _____ tout pour l'enfant

4. toys _____ tapis

5. snack-bar _____ jouets

V. **After studying the picture on the preceding page, choose the word that does not belong in the group.**

1. (a) pull-over (b) chemisiers (c) vêtements (d) parfums _____

2. (a) verrerie (b) porcelaine (c) lingerie (d) orfèvrerie _____

3. (a) linge de maison (b) tapis (c) super-terrasse (d) meubles
de cuisine _____

VI. **Oral Proficiency.** In this conversation you and a friend of yours are talking about the basketball team at your school. Complete the conversation.

Robert: Tu es allé au match de basket-ball hier soir?

1. Vous: _____

Robert: Nous avons une bonne équipe, n'est-ce pas?

2. Vous: _____

Robert: Albert est notre meilleur joueur.

3. Vous: _____

Robert: Nous jouons notre dernier match la semaine prochaine.

4. Vous: _____

Robert: Est-ce que tu vas venir?

5. Vous: _____

CONGRATULATIONS! YOU HAVE JUST FINISHED THE 23 WORK UNITS.

Review Test: Work Units 21–23

I. Write the following sentences in the negative.
Example: **Je mange.**   You write: Je ne mange pas.

1. Je fume. _____

2. Madame Paquet est grande. _____

3. Nous allons au cinéma. _____

II. Read the following sentences and write either **quand, parce qu', or que** on the line where they belong.

1. Je mange _____ j'ai faim.

2. Monsieur Bernard est dans son lit _____ il est malade.

3. Vous savez _____ mon professeur de francais est très intelligent.

III. Write the missing word in French.

1. Depuis quand Madame Paquet est- _____ malade?

2. Madame est malade _____ hier.

3. Depuis combien de _____ Madame Paquet attend-elle le docteur?

4. Madame Paquet _____ le docteur depuis vingt minutes.

IV. Choose the verb form that is correct and makes sense in each statement.

1. Nous _____ pour vivre.
   a. prononçons   b. mangeons   c. avancez   d. obligent

2. Jeanne veut_____ une nouvelle robe rouge.
   a. acheter   b. achète   c. effacer   d. effaçons

V. Write the following sentences in French.

1. I have to go to the dentist._____

2. You are right and I am wrong. _____

3. We are not afraid to cross the street. _____

4. I feel like sleeping. _____

5. It is interesting to go to a museum. _____

VI. Match the following statements.

1. I am learning to read in French.   _____ Nous mangeons et buvons pour vivre.

2. I am beginning to write in French.   _____ Elle est partie pour aller voir ses amis.

3. I hesitate going out because it's raining. _____ J'apprends à lire en français.

4. She left to go see her friends.   _____ J'hésite à sortir parce qu'il pleut.

5. We eat and drink in order to live.   _____ Je commence à écrire en français.

307

APPENDIX

French Idioms

With ALLER

aller to feel (health); **Comment allez-vous?**

aller à la rencontre de qqn to go to meet someone

aller à pied to walk, to go on foot

aller chercher to go get

allons donc! nonsense! come on, now!

With AVOIR

avoir...ans to be...years old; **Quel âge avez-vous? J'ai dix-sept ans.**

avoir à + inf. to have to, to be obliged to + inf.

avoir affaire à qqn to deal with someone

avoir beau + inf. to be useless + inf., to do something in vain; **Vous avez beau parler; je ne vous écoute pas** / You are talking in vain; I am not listening to you.

avoir besoin de to need, to have need of

avoir bonne mine to look well, to look good (persons)

avoir chaud to be (feel) warm (persons)

avoir congé to have a day off, a holiday

avoir de la chance to be lucky

avoir envie de + inf. to feel like, to have a desire to

avoir faim to be (feel) hungry

avoir froid to be (feel) cold (persons)

avoir hâte to be in a hurry

avoir honte to be ashamed, to feel ashamed

avoir l'air + adj. to seem, to appear, to look + adj.; **Vous avez l'air malade** / You look sick.

avoir l'air de + inf. to appear + inf.; **Vous avez l'air d'être malade** / You appear to be sick.

avoir l'habitude de + inf. to be accustomed to, to be in the habit of; **J'ai l'habitude de faire mes devoirs avant le dîner** / I'm in the habit of doing my homework before dinner.

avoir l'idée de + inf. to have a notion + inf.

avoir l'intention de + inf. to intend + inf.

avoir la bonté de + inf. to have the kindness + inf.

avoir la parole to have the floor (to speak)

avoir le temps de + inf. to have (the) time + inf.

avoir lieu to take place

avoir mal to feel sick

avoir mal à + (place where it hurts)   to have a pain or ache in...;**J'ai mal à la jambe** / My leg hurts; **J'ai mal au dos** / My back hurts; **J'ai mal au cou** / I have a pain in the neck.

avoir mauvaise mine   to look ill, not to look well

avoir peine à + inf.   to have difficulty in + pres. part.

avoir peur de   to be afraid of

avoir raison   to be right (persons)

avoir soif   to be thirsty

avoir sommeil   to be sleepy

avoir tort   to be wrong (persons)

With ETRE

être à l'heure   to be on time

être à qqn   to belong to someone; **Ce livre est à moi** / This book belongs to me.

être à temps   to be in time

être au courant de   to be informed about

être bien   to be comfortable

être bien aise (de)   to be very glad, happy (to)

être d'accord avec   to agree with

être de retour   to be back

être en état de + inf.   to be able + inf.

être en retard   to be late, not to be on time

être en train de + inf.   to be in the act of + pres. part., to be in the process of, to be busy + pres. part.

être en vacances   to be on vacation

être enrhumé   to have a cold, to be sick with a cold

être le bienvenu (la bienvenue)   to be welcomed

être pressé(e)   to be in a hurry

être sur le point de + inf.   to be about + inf.

être temps de + inf.   to be time + inf.

Quelle heure est-il?   What time is it? **Il est une heure** / It is one o'clock; **Il est deux heures** / It is two o'clock.

y être   to be there, to understand it, to get it; **J'y suis!** / I get it! / I understand it!

Il était une fois...   Once upon a time there was (there were)...

With FAIRE

Cela ne fait rien   That doesn't matter / That makes no difference.

Comment se fait-il?   How come?

en faire autant   to do the same, to do as much

faire + inf.   to have something done

faire à sa tête   to have one's way

faire attention (à)   to pay attention (to)

faire beau   to be pleasant, nice weather

faire bon accueil   to welcome

faire chaud   to be warm (weather)

faire de son mieux   to do one's best

faire des emplettes; faire des courses; faire du shopping   to do or to go shopping

faire des progrès   to make progress

faire du bien à qqn   to do good for someone; **Cela lui fera du bien** / That will do her (or him) some good.

faire face à   to oppose

faire faire qqch   to have something done or made; **Je me fais faire une robe** / I'm having a dress made (BY SOMEONE) for myself.

faire froid   to be cold (weather)

faire jour   to be daylight

faire la connaissance de qqn   to make the acquaintance of someone, to meet someone for the first time, to become acquainted with someone

faire la cuisine   to do the cooking

faire la queue   to line up, to get in line, to stand in line, to queue up

faire le ménage   to do housework

faire le tour de   to take a stroll, to go around

faire mal à qqn   to hurt, to harm someone

faire nuit   to be night(time)

faire part à qqn   to inform someone

faire part de qqch à qqn   to let someone know about something, to inform, to notify someone of something

faire partie de   to be a part of

faire peur à qqn   to frighten someone

faire plaisir à qqn   to please someone

faire savoir qqch à qqn   to inform someone of something

faire semblant de + inf.   to pretend + inf.

faire ses adieux   to say good-bye

faire son possible   to do one's best

faire un tour   to go for a stroll

faire un voyage   to take a trip

faire une partie de   to play a game of

faire une promenade   to take a walk

faire une promenade en voiture   to go for a drive

faire une question   to ask, to pose a question

faire une visite   to pay a visit

faire venir qqn   to have someone come; **Il a fait venir le docteur** / He had the doctor come.

Faites comme chez vous!   Make yourself at home!

Que faire?   What is to be done?

Quel temps fait-il?   What's the weather like?

Review of Basic Vocabulary by Topics

L'École (School)

le banc *n.*, the seat, the bench
la bibliothèque *n.*, the library
le bureau *n.*, the desk, the office
le cahier *n.*, the notebook
le calendrier *n.*, the calendar
le carnet *n.*, the small notebook
la carte *n.*, the map
la classe *n.*, the class; **la classe de français** French class
le congé *n.*, leave, permission; **jour de congé** day off (from school or work)
la cour *n.*, the playground, the courtyard
la craie *n.*, the chalk
le crayon *n.*, the pencil; **le crayon feutre** the crayon
les devoirs *n. m.*, homework assignments
la dictée *n.*, the dictation
le drapeau *n.*, the flag

l'école *n. f.*, the school
écrire *v.*, to write
l'élève *n. m. f.*, the pupil
l'encre *n. f.*, the ink
étudier *v.*, to study; **les études** *n. f. pl.*, the studies
l'étudiant *m.*, **l'étudiante** *f.*, *n.*, the student
l'examen *n. m.*, the examination
l'exercice *n. m.*, the exercise
expliquer *v.*, to explain
la faute *n.*, the mistake
la leçon *n.*, the lesson; **leçon de français** French lesson
le livre *n.*, the book
le livret d'exercices *n.*, the workbook
le lycée *n.*, the high school
le maître *m.*, **la maîtresse** *f.*, *n.*, the teacher
le papier *n.*, the paper; **une feuille de papier** a sheet of paper
passer *v.*, to pass; **passer un examen** to take an exam

poser *v.*, to pose; **poser une question** to ask a question
le professeur *m.*, **la professeur-dame, une femme professeur** *f.*, *n.*, the professor
le pupitre *n.*, the desk (student's)
la règle *n.*, the rule, the ruler
répondre *v.*, to respond, to answer, to reply
la réponse *n.*, the answer
réussir *v.*, to succeed; **réussir à un examen** to pass an exam
la salle *n.*, the room; **la salle de classe** the classroom
le stylo *n.*, the pen
le tableau noir *n.*, the blackboard, the chalkboard
l'université *n. f.*, the university
le vocabulaire *n.*, the vocabulary

Les Jours de la semaine, les mois de l'année, les saisons, et les jours de fête
(Days of the Week, Months of the Year, Seasons, and Holidays)

Les jours de la semaine

le dimanche, Sunday
le lundi, Monday
le mardi, Tuesday
le mercredi, Wednesday
le jeudi, Thursday
le vendredi, Friday
le samedi, Saturday

Les saisons

le printemps, spring
l'été *(m.),* summer
l'automne *(m.),* autumn, fall
l'hiver *(m.),* winter

Les mois de l'année

janvier, January
février, February
mars, March
avril, April
mai, May
juin, June
juillet, July
août, August
septembre, September
octobre, October
novembre, November
décembre, December

Les jours de fête

fêter *v.,* to celebrate a holiday; **bonne fête!** happy holiday!
l'anniversaire *m.,* anniversary, birthday; **bon anniversaire!** happy anniversary! *or* happy birthday!
le Jour de l'An, New Year's Day
Bonne année! Happy New Year!
les Pâques, Easter; **Joyeuses Pâques,** Happy Easter
la Pâque, Passover
le quatorze juillet (Bastille Day), July 14, French "Independence Day"
les grandes vacances, summer vacation
la Toussaint, All Saints' Day (le premier novembre)
le Noël, Christmas; **Joyeux Noël!** Merry Christmas!
à vous de même! the same to you!

Les légumes, les poissons, les viandes, les produits laitiers, les desserts, les fromages et les boissons
(Vegetables, Fish, Meats, Dairy Products, Desserts, Cheeses, and Beverages)

Les légumes

l'aubergine *f.*, the eggplant
la carotte, the carrot
le champignon, the mushroom
les épinards *m.*, the spinach
les haricots verts *m.*, the string beans
le maïs, the corn
l'oignon *m.*, the onion
les petits pois *m.*, the peas
la pomme de terre, the potato

Les viandes

l'agneau *m.*, the lamb; **la côte d'agneau,** the lamb chop
le biftek, the steak
le jambon, the ham
le porc, the pork
le poulet, the chicken
le rosbif, the roast beef
le veau, the veal; **la côte de veau,** the veal chop

Les poissons

le maquereau, the mackerel
la morue, the cod
le saumon, the salmon
la sole, the sole
la truite, the trout

Les produits laitiers

le beurre, the butter
la crème, the cream
le fromage, the cheese
le lait, the milk
l'oeuf *m.*, the egg

Les desserts

le fruit, the fruit
le gâteau, the cake; **le gâteau sec,** the cookie
la glace, the ice cream
la pâtisserie, the pastry

Les fromages

le brie
le camembert
le gruyère
le petit suisse
le port-salut
le roquefort

Les boissons

la bière, the beer
le cacao, the cocoa
le café, the coffee
le chocolat chaud, the hot chocolate
le cidre, the cider
l'eau minérale *f.*, the mineral water
le jus, the juice; **le jus de tomate,** the tomato juice
le thé, the tea
le vin, the wine

Les animaux, les fleurs, les couleurs, les arbres et les fruits
(Animals, Flowers, Colors, Trees, and Fruits)

Les animaux

l'âne *m.*, the donkey
le chat *m.*, **la chatte** *f.*, the cat
le cheval, the horse
le chien *m.*, **la chienne** *f.*, the dog
le cochon, the pig
le coq, the rooster
l'éléphant *m.*, the elephant
le lapin, the rabbit
le lion, the lion
l'oiseau *m.*, the bird
la poule, the hen
le poulet, the chicken
le renard, the fox
la souris, the mouse
le tigre, the tiger
la vache, the cow

Les fleurs

l'iris *m.*, the iris
le lilas, the lilac
le lis, the lily
la marguerite, the daisy
l'oeillet *m.*, the carnation
la rose, the rose
la tulipe, the tulip
la violette, the violet

Les couleurs

blanc, white
bleu, blue
brun, brown
gris, gray
jaune, yellow
noir, black
rouge, red
vert, green

Les arbres

le bananier, the banana tree
le cerisier, the cherry tree
le citronnier, the lemon tree
l'oranger *m.*, the orange tree
le palmier, the palm tree
le pêcher, the peach tree
le poirier, the pear tree
le pommier, the apple tree

Les fruits

la banane, the banana
la cerise, the cherry
le citron, the lemon; **citron vert,** lime
la fraise, the strawberry
la framboise, the raspberry
l'orange *f.*, the orange
le pamplemousse, the grapefruit
la pêche, the peach
la poire, the pear
la pomme, the apple
le raisin, the grape
la tomate, the tomato

315

Le corps humain, les vêtements, la toilette
(The Human Body, Clothing, Washing and Dressing)

Le corps humain

la bouche, mouth
le bras, arm
les cheveux m., hair
le cou, neck
les dents f., teeth
le doigt, finger; **doigt de pied,** toe
l'épaule f., shoulder
l'estomac m., stomach
le genou, knee
la jambe, leg
la langue, tongue
les lèvres f., lips
la main, hand
le menton, chin
le nez, nose
l'oeil m., eye; **les yeux,** eyes
l'oreille f., ear
la peau, skin
le pied, foot
la poitrine, chest
la tête, head
le visage, face

La toilette

se baigner v., to bathe oneself
la baignoire n., the bathtub
le bain n., the bath
la brosse n., the brush; **brosse à dents,** toothbrush
brosser v., to brush; **se brosser les dents,** to brush one's teeth
la cuvette n., the toilet bowl
le dentifrice n., the toothpaste
le déodorant n., deodorant
déshabiller v., to undress; **se déshabiller,** to undress oneself
la douche n., the shower; **prendre une douche,** to take a shower
enlever v., to remove, to take off
le gant de toilette n., the washcloth
la glace n., the hand mirror
s'habiller v., to dress oneself
le lavabo n., the washroom, washstand
laver v., to wash; **se laver,** to wash oneself
mettre v., to put on
le miroir n., the mirror
ôter v., to take off, to remove
le peigne n., the comb; **se peigner les cheveux,** to comb one's hair
porter v., to wear
la salle de bains n., the bathroom
le savon n., the soap
la serviette n., the towel
le shampooing n., the shampoo

Les vêtements

le bas, stocking
le béret, beret
la blouse, blouse, smock
le blouson, jacket (often with zipper)
le chandail, sweater
le chapeau, hat
la chaussette, sock
la chaussure, shoe
la chemise, shirt
le complet, suit
le costume, suit
la cravate, necktie
l'écharpe f., scarf
le gant, glove
la jupe, skirt
le maillot de bain, swim suit
le manteau, coat
le pantalon, trousers, pants
la pantoufle, slipper
le pardessus, overcoat
la poche, pocket
le pullover, pullover or long-sleeved sweater
la robe, dress
le soulier, shoe
le veston, (suit) coat

La famille, la maison, les meubles (Family, Home, Furniture)

La famille

le cousin, la cousine, cousin
l'enfant *m. f.,* child
l'époux *m.,* **l'épouse** *f.,* spouse (husband/wife)
la femme, wife
la fille, daughter
le fils, son
le frère, brother; **le beau-frère,** brother-in-law
la grand-mère, grandmother
le grand-père, grandfather
les grands-parents, grandparents
le mari, husband
la mère, la maman, mother; **la belle-mère,** mother-in-law
le neveu, nephew
la nièce, niece
l'oncle *m.,* uncle
le père, le papa, father; **le beau-père,** father-in-law
le petit-fils, grandson
la petite-fille, granddaughter
les petits-enfants, grandchildren
la soeur, sister; **la belle-soeur,** sister-in-law
la tante, aunt

La maison

la cave, the cellar
la chambre, the room; **chambre à coucher,** bedroom
la cheminée, the fireplace, chimney
la cuisine, the kitchen
l'escalier *m.,* the stairs, staircase
la fenêtre, the window
le mur, the wall
la pièce, the room
le plafond, the ceiling
le plancher, the floor
la porte, the door
la salle, the room; **la salle à manger,** the dining room; **la salle de bains,** bathroom
le salon, the living room
le toit, the roof

Les meubles

l'armoire *f.,* the wardrobe closet
le bureau, the desk
le canapé, the sofa, couch
la chaise, the chair
la commode, the dresser, chest of drawers
la couchette, the bunk
l'évier *m.,* the kitchen sink
le fauteuil, the armchair
le four, the oven
la fournaise, the furnace
le fourneau, the kitchen stove, range
la lampe, the lamp
le lit, the bed
le phonographe, the phonograph
le piano, the piano
la radio stéréophonique, the stereophonic radio
la table, the table
le tapis, the carpet
le téléphone, the telephone
le téléviseur, the television (set)

La ville, les bâtiments, les magasins, les divers modes de transport
(The City, Buildings, Stores, Various Means of Transportation)

La ville

l'avenue *f.*, the avenue
la boîte aux lettres, the mailbox
la bouche de métro, the subway entrance
le boulevard, the boulevard
le bruit, the noise
la chaussée, the road
défense d'afficher, post no bills
les feux *m.*, the traffic lights
le parc, the park
la pollution, the pollution
la rue, the street
le trottoir, the sidewalk
la voiture de police, the police car

Les bâtiments

la banque, the bank
la bibliothèque, the library
le bureau de poste, the post office
la cathédrale, the cathedral
la chapelle, the chapel
le château, the castle
le cinéma, the movie theatre
l'école *f.*, the school
l'église *f.*, the church
la gare, the railroad station
la grange, the barn

le gratte-ciel, the skyscraper
l'hôpital *m.*, the hospital
l'hôtel *m.*, the hotel
l'hôtel de ville, the city hall
la hutte *f.*, the hut, cabin
l'immeuble d'habitation, the apartment building
le musée, the museum
le palais, the palace
la synagogue, the synagogue
le temple, the temple
le théâtre, the theatre
l'usine *f.*, the factory

Les divers modes de transport

l'autobus *m.*, the city bus
l'autocar *m.*, the interurban bus
l'automobile *f.*, the car
l'avion *m.*, the plane
le bateau, the boat
la bicyclette, the bicycle
le camion, the truck
le chemin de fer, the railroad
le métro, the subway
la moto, the motorcycle
le train, the train
le transatlantique, the ocean liner
le vélo, the bike
la voiture, the car

Les magasins

la bijouterie, the jewelry shop
la blanchisserie, the laundry
la boucherie, the butcher shop
la boulangerie, the bakery (mostly for bread)
la boutique, the (small) shop
le bureau de tabac, the tobacco shop
le café, the café
la charcuterie, the pork store, delicatessen
la crémerie, the dairy store
l'épicerie *f.*, the grocery store
le grand magasin, the department store
la librairie, the bookstore
le magasin, the store
la pâtisserie, the pastry shop
la pharmacie, the drugstore
le supermarché, the supermarket

Les métiers et les professions, les langues, les pays et les continents
(Trades and Professions, Languages, Countries, and Continents)

Les métiers et les professions

l'acteur m., **l'actrice** f., actor, actress

l'agent de police m., police officer

l'auteur, author (of a book) or composer (of a song) or painter (of a picture)

l'avocat m., **la femme-avocat** f., lawyer

le bijoutier, la bijoutière, jeweler

le blanchisseur, la blanchisseuse, launderer

le boucher, la bouchère, butcher

le boulanger, la boulangère, baker

le charcutier, la charcutière, pork butcher

le chauffeur, driver, chauffeur

le coiffeur, la coiffeuse, hairdresser, barber

le, la dentiste, dentist

l'épicier, l'épicière, grocer

le facteur, letter carrier

le fermier, la fermière, farmer

le, la libraire, bookseller

le maître, la maîtresse, teacher

le marchand, la marchande, merchant

le médecin, la femme-médecin, doctor

le pâtissier, la pâtissière, pastry chef

le pharmacien, la pharmacienne, pharmacist

le professeur, la femme-professeur, professor

le sénateur, senator

le serveur, la serveuse, waiter, waitress

le tailleur, la tailleuse, tailor

le vendeur, la vendeuse, salesperson

Les langues
(all are masculine)

allemand, German

anglais, English

chinois, Chinese

danois, Danish

espagnol, Spanish; **castillan,** Castilian (Spanish)

français, French

grec ancien, Ancient Greek

grec moderne, Modern Greek

hébreu, Hebrew

italien, Italian

japonais, Japanese

latin, Latin

norvégien, Norwegian

portugais, Portuguese

russe, Russian

suédois, Swedish

Les pays, les continents

l'Allemagne f., Germany; **l'Allemagne de l'Ouest,** West Germany; **l'Allemagne de l'Est,** East Germany

l'Angleterre f., England

l'Australie f., Australia

la Belgique, Belgium

le Canada, Canada

la Chine, China

le Danemark, Denmark

l'Espagne f., Spain

les États-Unis m., United States

l'Europe f., Europe

la France, France

la Grande-Bretagne, Great Britain

la Grèce, Greece

la Hollande, Holland

l'Irlande f., Ireland

l'Israël m., Israel

l'Italie f., Italy

le Japon, Japan

le Luxembourg, Luxembourg

le Mexique, Mexico

la Norvège, Norway

la Pologne, Poland

le Porto Rico, Puerto Rico

le Portugal, Portugal

la Russie, Russia; **U.R.S.S.,** Union des républiques socialistes soviétiques (U.S.S.R)

la Suède, Sweden

la Suisse, Switzerland

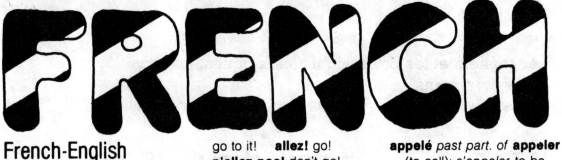

French-English

A

à *prep.* at, to; **à bientôt** see you soon; **à ce moment-là** at that moment; **à couvert** covered; **à tout à l'heure** see you in a little while

a *v. form of* **avoir; il, elle a**/he, she, it has; **a eu** *v. form,* passé composé *of* **avoir**

abîmer *v.* to spoil, to damage

accepté *past part. of* **accepter** (to accept)

achat *n. m.* purchase; **achète** *v. form of* **acheter** (to buy); **acheté** *past part.*

addition *n. f.* bill, check

adieu *n. m.* farewell, good-bye

Afrique *n. f.* Africa

agent de police *n. m.* policeman

agréable *adj.* pleasant

ai *v. form of* **avoir; j'ai**/I have; **je n'ai pas**/I don't have

aidé *past part. of* **aider** (to help)

ail *n. m.* garlic

aile *n. f.* wing

aime *v. form of* **aimer** (to love, to like); **aimé** *past part.;* **aimer bien** to like; **aimer mieux** to prefer, to like better

ainsi que *conj.* as well as, (just) as

ajoute, ajoutez *v. forms of* **ajouter** (to add)

aliment *n. m.* **alimentation** *n. f.* food, nourishment

allé *past part. of* **aller** (to go); **allez, allons** *v. forms of* **aller; allez-y!** go there!

go to it! **allez!** go! **n'allez pas!** don't go! **allons!** let's go!

allemand *n. m.* German (language); **Allemagne** *n. f.* Germany

allô *interj.* hello (used when answering a telephone)

allumer *v.* to turn on, switch on (an apparatus), to light

alors *adv.* so, then, well

américain *n. m.* American (language); **l'Amérique** *n. f.* America

ami *n. m.* **amie** *n. f.* friend; **amitié** *n. f.* friendship

amour *n. m.* love; **amoureux, amoureuse** *adj. m. f.* in love; **amoureuse de** in love with; **nous sommes amoureux** we are in love

amusant, amusante *adj.* amusing, enjoyable; **amuser** *v.* to amuse; **s'amuser** *refl. v.* to have a good time, amuse oneself, enjoy oneself; **nous allons beaucoup nous amuser** we are going to have a very good time; **amusez-vous bien!** have a good time! **ils se sont bien amusés** they had a very good time

an *n. m.* **année** *n. f.* year

ananas *n. m.* pineapple

ancien *adj. m. s.* **ancienne** *adj. f. s.* ancient, old, former

anglais *n. m.* English (language)

Angleterre *n. f.* England

animaux *n. m. pl.* animals

anniversaire *n. m.* birthday, anniversary

annoncé *past part. of* **annoncer** (to announce)

août *n. m.* August

appareil *n. m.* apparatus (telephone)

appelé *past part. of* **appeler** (to call); *s'appeler* to be called, be named; **Comment vous appelez-vous?** *What is your name?* **Je m'appelle Janine**/My name is Janine

apporte *v. form of* **apporter** (to bring); **apporté** *past part.;* **apporte!**/bring!

apprendre *v.* to learn; **appris** *past part.;* **Je n'ai rien appris de nouveau**/I didn't learn anything new

s'approcher (de) *refl. v.* to approach, come (go) near

après *prep.* after; **après-midi** *n. m.* afternoon; **l'après-midi** in the afternoon

arbre *n. m.* tree

arc-en-ciel *n. m.* rainbow

argent *n. m.* money

armoire *n. f.* closet

arracher *v.* to pull (away)

arrêt *n. m.* stop; **arrêt d'autobus** bus stop; **arrêté** *past part. of* **arrêter** (to arrest), **s'arrêter** (to stop)

arrivent *v. form of* **arriver** (to arrive); **arrivé** *past part.*

as *v. form of* **avoir** (to have); **tu as**/you have; **as-tu?**/do you have?

s'assembler *refl. v.* to gather together

s'assied *v. form of* **s'asseoir** (to sit down); **assis** *past part.;* **assis(e)** *adj.* seated, sitting; **assieds-toi!**/sit down! **asseyez-vous!**/ sit down!

assiette *n. f.* plate, dish

assister à *v.* to attend, be present at

assourdissant(e) *adj. m. (f.)* *s.* deafening (very loud)

attendre *v.* to wait (for), expect

attention *n. f.* **à** watch out for

attraper *v.* to catch

au (combining of **à** + **le**) at the, to the, in the, with; **au caissier**/at the cashier's; **au courant**/in the know; **au four**/in the oven; **au guichet**/at the ticket window; **au lit**/in bed; **au mois de**/in the month of; **au régime**/on a diet; **au revoir**/good-bye, until we meet again

aujourd'hui *adv.* today

aussi *adv.* also, too, as

auteur *n. m.* author, writer

autobus *n. m.* city bus; **autocar** *n. m.* interurban bus

automne *n. m.* autumn, fall

autour *adv.* around

autre(s) *adj., pron.* other(s), another; **l'autre** the other one; **un (une) autre** another one

aux (combining of **à** + **les**) to the, in the, at the, with; **aux États-Unis** to (in) the United States

avancer *v.* to advance

avant *prep.* before; **avant de sortir** before going out

avec *prep.* with; **avec eux** with them

avez *v. form of* **avoir** (to have); **vous avez** you have, you do have

avion *n. m.* airplane

avis *n. m.* opinion; **avisé** *adj.* shrewd, smart

avocat *n. m.* lawyer

avoir *v.* to have

avoué *n. m.* attorney, lawyer

B

bague *n. f.* ring

se baigner *v. refl.* to bathe oneself

bal *n. m.* dance

balai *n. m.* broom

balançoire *n. f.* swing, see-saw

balle *n. f.* ball, bullet

ballon *n. m.* ball, balloon, football

banc *n. m.* bench (seat)

bar *n. m.* **rapide** snack-bar

barrière *n. f.* fence

bas *n. m.* stocking; *adj.* low; *adv.* low, down; **les plus bas** the lowest

basse *adj. f.* low

bat *v. form of* **battre** (to beat)

bâti *past part. of* **bâtir** (to build); **bâtiment** *n. m.* building

bâton *n. m.* wand, stick, baton

beau *adj. m. s.* beautiful, handsome; **beaux** *pl.*

beaucoup (de) *adv.* much, a lot, many

beauté *n. f.* beauty

bébé *n. m.* baby

belge *adj.* Belgian; **Belgique** *n. f.* Belgium; **Il est Belge, Elle est Belge**/He (She) is Belgian

belle *adj. f. s.* beautiful

bercer *v.* to rock, lull

besoin *n. m.* need

bête *adj.* foolish, dumb; **bêtise** *n. f.* foolish thing, dumb thing

beurre *n. m.* butter

bibliothèque *n. f.* library

bien *adv.* well; **bien sûr** of course; **bientôt** *adv.* soon

bière *n. f.* beer

billet *n. m.* ticket

blanc *adj. m. s.* **blanche** *adj. f. s.* white

blé *n. m.* wheat

blesser *v.* to hurt, injure

bleu *n. m., adj. m. sing.* **bleus** *adj. m. pl.* blue

boire *v.* to drink

bois *n. m.* woods

boisson *n. m.* drink, beverage

boit *v. form of* **boire**

boîte *n. f.* tin can, box

bon *adj. m. s.,* **bons** *pl.;* **bonne** *adj. f. s.,* **bonnes** *pl.* good

bon voyage! have a good trip! **bon retour!** have a good return trip!

bonbon *n. m.* candy

bonheur *n. m.* happiness

bonhomme *n. m.* **de neige** snowman

bonjour *n. m.* hello, good day, good morning, good afternoon

bonne *adj. f. s.* good; **bonne chance!** good luck! **de bonne heure** early; **bonnes nouvelles!** good news!

bonsoir *n. m.* good night, good evening

bouche *n. f.* mouth

boucher *n. m.* butcher; **boucherie** *n. f.* butcher shop

bouillir *v.* to boil

boulanger *n. m.* baker; **boulangerie** *n. f.* bakery

bouteille *n. f.* bottle

boutique *n. f.* boutique, small shop

bras *n. m.* arm

brave *adj. m.* good, fine, honest (when **brave** follows a noun, it means *brave:* **c'est un homme brave** he's a brave man; **c'est une femme brave** she's a brave woman)

briller *v.* to shine

brosse *n. f.* brush

bruit *n. m.* noise

brûler *v.* to burn; **brûlé** burned

bu *past part. of* **boire**

buffet *n. m.* china closet, hutch, sideboard

bureau *n. m.* desk, office

but *n. m.* goal

C

ça *dem. pron.* that (**ça** is short for *cela*); **Ça ne fait rien!** That doesn't matter! **Ça va!** (I'm) fine!

caché *adj. m. s.* hidden

cadeau *n. m.* present, gift

café *n. m.* coffee, café (coffee house)

cahier *n. m.* notebook

caisse *n. f.* cash box (register); **caissier** *n. m.* **caissière** *n. f.* cashier

camarade *n. m. f.* comrade, buddy, pal, mate

camembert *n. m.* camembert (name of a cheese)

camion *n. m.* truck; **camionneur** *n. m.* truck driver

campagne *n. f.* countryside

Canada *n. m.* Canada; **Il est Canadien**/He is Canadian; **Elle est Canadienne**/She is Canadian

canne *n. f.* cane

carte *n. f.* map, menu

cas *n. m.* case

casser *v.* to break; **sans la casser** without breaking it

cave *n. f.* cellar

ce *dem. adj. m. s.* this, that; **ce n'est pas** . . . it isn't . . . . **ce que** *pron.* that which, what; **ce qui** *pron.* that which; **ce soir** tonight; **ce sont** . . . they are . . . or it's . . .

ceci *dem. pron.* this; **cela** *dem. pron.* that; **Cela n'a pas d'importance** That has no importance; That's not important.

céleri *n. m.* celery; **blanc de céleri** celery stalk

cent *adj.* one hundred

cerise *n. f.* cherry

ces *dem. adj. m. f. pl.* these, those

cesse *n. f.* ceasing, stopping

c'est . . . he's . . . she's . . . it's . . . **c'est aujourd'hui le premier décembre** today is December 1st; **c'est ça!** that's right! **c'est bien ça!** that's quite right! **c'est fait!** it's done! **c'est fini!** it's finished

cet *dem. adj. m. s.* **cette** *f. s.* this

chacun *pron.* each one; **chacune** *fem.*

chaise *n. f.* chair

chambre *n. f.* room; **chambre à coucher** bedroom

champ *n. m.* field

champignon *n. m.* mushroom

chance *n. f.* luck, chance, fortune

changement *n. m.* change

chanté *past part. of* **chanter**

(to sing); **chanteur** *n. m.*, **chanteuse** *n. f.* singer

chapeau *n. m.* hat

chapelle *n. f.* chapel

chaque *adj.* each

charmante *adj. f.* charming

chasser *v.* to chase away, hunt

chat *n. m.*, **chatte** *n. f.* cat

château *n. m.* castle

chaud, chaude *adj. m. f.* hot

chaussettes *n. f.* socks; **chaussure** *n. f.* shoe

cheminée *n. f.* chimney

chemise *n. f.* shirt

cher, chère *adj. m. s., f. s.* dear; **cher** *adj., adv.* expensive; **chéri, chérie** *n. m. f.* darling, honey

cherché *past part. of* **chercher** to look (for), search (for), get

cheval *n. m.* horse

cheveux *n. m. pl.* hair

chez *prep.* at (to) the home (place) of; **chez moi** at my house; **chez le dentiste** to (at) the dentist's; **chez le coiffeur** to (at) the hairdresser's, barber's; **chez le médecin** to (at) the doctor's; **chez vous** to (at) your house (place)

chien *n. m.* dog

choisi *past part. of* **choisir** (to choose, select)

choisit, choisissez *v. forms of* **choisir; il choisit** he chooses; **choisissez!** choose!

chose *n. f.* thing

chuchoter *v.* to whisper

ciel *n. m.* sky

cigale *n. f.* cicada

cinéma *n. m.* movies

cinq *adj.* five; **cinquième** fifth; **cinquante** fifty

clair *adj. m. s.* clear

clef *n. f.* key

client *n. m.* customer

cloche *n. f.* bell

coeur *n. m.* heart

coiffeur *n. m.* hairdresser, barber; **coiffure** *n. f.* hair style: **se coiffer** *v. refl.* to comb one's hair, style one's hair

coin *n. m.* corner

combien *adv.* how many, how much

comme *adv.* like, as; **comme il faut** as it should be, proper and correct

commencé *past part. of* **commencer** (to begin, commence)

comment *adv.* how

commode *n. f.* dresser

comprendre *v.* to understand; **compris** *past part.* understood

confiture *n. f.* jam, preserves

congé see **jour de congé**

connaissez-vous . . . ? *v. form of* **connaître** (to know someone, be acquainted with); do you know . . . ? **Est-ce que Pierre connaît Robert?** Does Pierre know Robert? (pres. indicative: **je connais, tu connais, il (elle) connaît, nous connaissons, vous connaissez, ils (elles) connaissent**)

conte *n. m.* story, tale

contraire *n. m., adj.* contrary, opposite

contre *prep.* against

contrôleur *n. m.* ticket taker, train conductor

cordiaux *adj. m. pl.* cordial

corps *n. m.* body

corriger *v.* to correct

côté *n. m.* side; **à côté de** next to

cou *n. m.* neck

couché *adj.* lying down; **se coucher** *v.* to go to bed

couleur *n. f.* color; **de quelle couleur est** . . . ? what color is . . . ?

couloir *n. m.* hallway, corridor

se couper *v. refl.* to cut oneself

courent, court *v. forms of* **courir** (to run)

cours *n. m.* course; **cours de français** French course

court, courte *adj. m. s., f. s.* short

couteau *n. m.* knife

coûter v. to cost

couvert past part. of **couvrir** (to cover)

craie n. f. chalk

cravate n. f. necktie

crayon n. m. pencil

crémeux adj. m. creamy

crie, crient v. forms of **crier** (to shout, to cry out)

crois v. form of **croire** (to believe); **je n'y crois pas.** I don't believe in it.

croix n. f. cross

cru past part. of **croire**

cuiller, cuillère n. f. spoon; **cuillère à soupe** soup spoon

cuire v. to cook; **cuit** past part.

cuisine n. f. kitchen, cooking (food)

cuisson n. f. cooking (time)

D

d' prep. (contraction of **de**)

d'abord advl. expr. at first, first

d'accord agreed, okay

d'ailleurs adv. besides

dame n. f. lady

dangereux adj. m., **dangereuse** adj. f. dangerous

dans prep. in

dansé past part. of **danser** (to dance); **danseur** n. m., **danseuse** n. f. dancer

davantage adj. more

de prep. of, from, with; **de bonne heure** adv. early

de quelle couleur est . . . what color is . . .

de rien you're welcome

debout adv. standing

décembre n. m. December

déchirer v. to tear

décision n. f. decision

décréter v. to decree, to enact, to give an executive order

dedans adv. inside

défendre v. to defend, forbid; **défendu,** past part.

dégoûtant adj. m. s. disgusting, revolting

dehors adv. outside

déjà adv. already

déjeuner v. to have lunch, to eat lunch, to lunch; n. m. lunch; **le petit déjeuner** breakfast

délicieux adj. m. s. pl., **délicieuse** adj. f. s. delicious

demain adv. tomorrow

demander v. to ask (for); **demandé** past part.

demeurer v. to live, reside, inhabit, stay, remain

demi m., **demie** f., adj. half

d'en face opposite

dent n. f. tooth

se dépêcher refl. v. to hurry

depuis adv., prep. since

déranger v. to disturb

dernier m., **dernière** f., adj. last; **la dernière mise** the last bid

derrière adv., prep. behind

descendre v. to go down, come down; **descendu** past part.

désir n. m. desire; **désirer** v. to desire

désobéir v. to disobey

dessert n. m. dessert

dessus adv. on top, above

détail n. m. detail

détective n. m. detective

détester v. to detest, to hate

deux n. m., adj. two; **tous les deux** both

deuxième n. m. f., adj. second

devant prep. before, in front of

devenir v. to become; **devenu** past part.

deviens, devient v. forms of **devenir**; **je deviens folle! je deviens fou!** I'm going crazy!

devinette n. f. riddle

devoir v. to owe, ought to, must, have to

devoirs n. m. pl. homework, assignments, duties

dictionnaire n. m. dictionary

Dieu n. m. God

difficile adj. m. f. difficult

diligent adj. m. diligent, industrious

dîné past part. of **dîner**

dîner v. to dine, to have dinner; n. m. dinner

dire v. to say, to tell; **dire des histoires** to tell stories, make up stories, fibs

directeur n. m., **directrice** n. f. director, principal

dis, disent v. forms of **dire**; **je dis** I say; **tu dis** you say; **ils, elles disent** they say; **dis-moi** tell me

disposer v. to dispose, arrange, prepare

disque n. m. phonorecord, disc, recording

distinctement adv. distinctly

dit v. form of **dire**; **il/elle dit** he/she says, tells; also past part. of **dire**

dites-moi tell me; **dites-nous** tell us

divers adj. diverse, different

dix n. m., adj. ten

docteur n. m. doctor

dodo n. m. sleep; **fais dodo** go to sleep (child's language)

doigt n. m. finger

dois, doit, doivent v. forms of **devoir**; **je dois** I have to; **il/elle doit** he/she has to; **ils/elles doivent** they have to

domestique adj. domestic; **domestiqué** adj. domesticated

donne v. form of **donner**; **donne!** give! **donne-moi/donnez-moi** give me; **donné** past part. of **donner**

donner v. to give

dormir v. to sleep; **dors** v. form of **dormir**

dos n. m. back

dossier n. m. brief, file of papers

douane n. f. customs (duty or tax on imported goods)

douce adj. f. sweet, soft

doucement adv. softly, sweetly, gently (low flame)

douche n. f. shower

doute n. m. doubt; **sans doute** undoubtedly, without a doubt

doux *adj. m.* sweet, soft

drapeau *n. m.* flag

droite *n. f.* right (*as opposed to left*); **à droite, à la droite** to (on) the right

drôle *adj. m. f.* funny, droll

dû *past part.* of **devoir**

du (*contraction of* **de** + **le**)

E

eau *n. f.* water

échapper *v.* to escape, to get away; **le chapeau échappé** the hat that got away

éclair *n. m.* eclair

éclairant *pres. part.* of **éclairer** illuminating

éclairer *v.* to illuminate, to light up

école *n. f.* school

écouter *v.* to listen (to)

écraser *v.* to crush

écrire *v.* to write

écrit, écrivent, écrivez *v. forms of* **écrire**

écrivain *n. m.* writer, author

effacer *v.* to erase

église *n. f.* church

eh bien! *exclam.* well now!

élève *n. m. f.* pupil, student

elle *per. pron. f.* she, her, it; **elles** *per. pron. f. pl.* they, them; **avec elles**/with them

embarras *n. m.* embarrassment, hindrance, fuss, distress

émission *n. f.* TV program, show

emplette *n. f.* purchase

employer *v.* to use, to employ

emporter *v.* to take along, to take (carry) away

en *prep.* in, into, on, while; *as pron.*, some (of it, of them), of them; *see* Work Unit 13

en arrivant on (upon) arriving; **en courant** running; **en disposant** arranging; **en forme** in good shape; **en tenue d'exercice** in a gym suit;

en ville downtown, into town

enchère *n. f.* bid, bidding

encore *adv.* again; **encore une fois** once more, yet, still

endroit *n. m.* place

enfant *n. m. f.* child

enfin *adv.* finally, at last, in short

engager *v.* to apply to, to put into gear

enlever *v.* to remove, to take off

ennuyer *v.* to annoy, to bore; **ennuyant** annoying, boring

enseignement *n. m.* teaching, instruction

enseigner *v.* to teach

ensemble *adv.* together

ensuite *adv.* then, after, next

entendre *v.* to hear; **entendu** *past part.*

entracte *n. m.* intermission

entraîneur *n. m.* coach, sports instructor

entre *prep.* between; **entre eux et nous** between them and us

entrer (dans) *v.* to enter, to go (into), to come in; **entré** *past part.*; **entrée** *n. f.* entrance

envoyer *v.* to send

épais *adj.* thick

épaule *n. f.* shoulder

épicerie *n. f.* grocery store; **épicier** *m.* **épicière** *f.*, grocer

épingle *n. f.* pin

épouse *n. f.* wife; **époux** *n. m.* husband

équipe *n. f.* team

érection *n. f.* construction, erection

erreur *n. f.* error, mistake

es *v. form of* **être**; **tu es** you are (familiar use); **es-tu . . . ?** are you . . . ?

espagnol *n. m.* Spanish

espérer *v.* to hope

esprit *n. m.* spirit

essayer *v.* to try

essence *n. f.* gasoline

est *v. form of* **être**; **il/elle est** he/she/it is

est-ce . . . ? is it . . . ?

estomac *n. m.* stomach

et *conj.* and

étage *n. m.* floor (of a building designated by number)

étais *v. form of* **être** (*imperfect indicative*); **j'étais** I was

États-Unis *n. m. pl.* United States; **aux États-Unis** in (to) the United States

été *n. m.* summer; *also past part.* of **être** (been); **j'ai été** I was, I have been

éteindre *v.* to extinguish, to snuff out

êtes *v. form of* **être**; **vous êtes** you are

être *v.* to be

étroit *adj. m. s.* narrow

étudiant *n. m.* **étudiante** *n. f.*, student

étudié *past part.* of **étudier**

étudier *v.* to study

eu *past part.* of **avoir**; **j'ai eu** I had, I have had

eux *disj. pron. m. pl.* them

éviter *v.* to avoid

exactement *adv.* exactly

examiner *v.* to examine

exclamer, s'exclamer *v., refl. v.* to exclaim

excuser *v.* to excuse

expliquer *v.* to explain

exposition *n. f.* exhibit

extraordinaire *adj. m. f. s.* extraordinary, unusual

extrêmement *adv.* extremely

F

fable *n. f.* fable

fâché *adj.* angry; **se fâcher** *refl. v.* to get angry

facile *adj.* easy; **facilement** *adv.* easily

façon *n. f.* way; **de façon à** so as to

facteur *n. m.* mailman, postman

faible *adj.* weak

faim *n. f.* hunger; **avoir faim** to be hungry; **j'ai faim** I'm hungry

faire *v.* to do, to make; **faire**

bouillir to boil; **faire connaissance** to meet, to become acquainted with; **faire de la gymnastique** to do gymnastics, to do exercises; **faire la toilette** to wash and dress oneself; **se faire lire les lignes de la main** to have one's palm read, to have the lines of one's hand read; **se faire mal** to hurt oneself; **faire réparer** to have repaired; **faire trop cuire** to overcook; **faire visite** to visit, to pay a visit

fais, fait, faites v. forms of **faire; fais dodo** go to sleep (child's langauge); **il/elle fait** he/she/it does (makes); **c'est fait** it's done, it's finished; **fait** past part. of **faire; elle a fait la leçon** she did (has done) the lesson; **faites le travail!** do the work! **faites bouillir l'eau, s'il vous plaît!** boil the water, please!

famille n. f. family
farine n. f. flour
fatigué m. **fatiguée** f., adj. tired
faut v. form of **falloir** (to be necessary, must); **il faut** it is necessary, you must, you have to, one must, we must, we have to, etc., etc. (This is an impersonal verb and the subject is always **il**); **faut-il?** is it necessary?
faute n. f. mistake, error
fauteuil n. m. armchair
faux adj. false
favori m. **favorite** f., adj. favorite
femme n. f. woman, wife
fenêtre n. f. window
ferme n. f. farm
fermé past part. of **fermer** (to close)
fête n. f. holiday, feast, birthday
feu n. m. fire, traffic light

feuille n. f. leaf; **feuille de papier** sheet of paper
figure n. f. face
filer v. to go (away) quickly (used familiarly); **filez!** go away! beat it!
filet n. m. net
fille n. f. daughter; **une jeune fille** a girl
film n. m. film, movie
fils n. m. son
fin n. f. end
fini m., **finie** f. adj. finished; **fini** past part. of **finir** (to finish)
finis, finissent, finissons, finit v. forms of **finir; finissons!** let's finish!
fixement adv. intently, fixedly
fleur n. f. flower; **fleuriste** n. m. f. florist
fleuve n. m. river
foire n. f. fair (as at a county or state fair)
fois n. f. time; **une fois** one time, once; **deux fois** two times, twice, etc.; **mille fois** a thousand times; **la prochaine fois** the next time
folle adj. f. s. crazy; **fou** adj. m. s.
font v. form of **faire**
football n. m. soccer (in the U.S.A.)
forme n. f. form, shape
formidable adj. terrific
fort m. **forte** f., adj. strong; **votre qualité la plus forte** your strongest quality; **le (la) plus fort (forte)** the strongest
fou adj. m. s. crazy
four n. m. oven
fourchette n. f. fork
fourmi n. f. ant
foyer n. m. foyer
frais m. s. pl., **fraîche** f. s. adj. fresh; **il fait frais** it's cool
fraise n. f. strawberry
franc n. m. franc (6 francs equal about $1)
français n. m. French (language); **Il est Français**/He is French;

Elle est Française/She is French; **Je parle français**/I speak French
France n. f. France
fréquence n. f. frequency
frère n. m. brother
froid n. m., adj., **froide** f., adj. cold
fromage n. m. cheese
fumé past part. of **fumer** (to smoke); **la fumée** the smoke
furieux m. s. pl., **furieuse** adj. f. s. furious

G

gagner v. to win
galant m., **galante** f., adj. gallant
gant n. m. glove
garagiste n. m. auto mechanic
garçon n. m. boy; **garçon (de restaurant);** (Nowadays, a customer addresses a waiter as Monsieur, not garçon; address a waitress as Mademoiselle or Madame)
garder v. to guard, keep
gardien n. m. guard; **un gardien (une gardienne) d'enfants** babysitter; **un gardien (une gardienne) de but** goalie
gare n. f. station (bus, train, etc.)
gâteau n. m. cake
gauche n. f. left (as opposed to right); **à gauche** on (to) the left
généralement adv. generally
généreux adj., m. s. pl. generous
génie n. m. genius
genou n. m. knee
gentil adj., m. s., **gentille** adj., f. s. nice, kind
géographie n. f. geography
gilet n. m. vest
girafe n. f. giraffe
glace n. f. ice, ice cream, mirror; **glacé** adj., m. s., **glacée** adj., f. s. glazed, frosted

gousse *n. f.* clove; **une gousse d'ail** clove of garlic

goût *n. m.* taste, flavor; **goûter** *v.* to taste; **goûtez-en!** taste some!

gouverner *v.* to govern

grain *n. m.* grain

gramme *n. m.* gram; 1 gram = about .035 ounce; 500 grams = about 1.1 lbs.

grand *adj., m. s.,* **grande** *adj., f. s.* great, big, large, tall; **grand faim (J'ai grand faim** I'm very hungry); **grand magasin** *n. m.* department store; **grand prix** *n. m.* grand prize

Grande Bretagne *n. f.* Great Britain

grande salle *n. f.* auditorium

grange *n. f.* barn

grave *adj., m. f.* grave, serious; **gravement** *adv.* seriously, gravely

grillé *adj., m. s.,* **grillée** *adj., f. s.* toasted, grilled

gris *adj., m. s. pl.,* **grise** *adj., f. s.* gray

gros *adj., m. s. pl.,* **grosse** *adj., f. s.* big, huge, large, fat

groupe *n. m.* group

guérir *v.* to cure

gueule *n. f.* mouth (of an animal)

guichet *n.m.* ticket window

gymnase *n. m.* gymnasium, gym; **gymnastique** *n. f.* gymnastics

H

habillement *n. m.* clothing; **s'habiller** *refl. v.* to get dressed, to dress

habit *n. m.* clothing, attire (habit, *i.e.,* robe and hood of a monk)

habitant *n. m.* inhabitant

habite *v. form of* **habiter** (to live, to reside, to inhabit)

halte! *interj.* halt! stop!

haut *adv.* high, tall; **à haute voix** in a loud voice; **un**

chapeau haut de forme top hat

herbe *n. f.* grass

heure *n. f.* hour; **heureux, heureuse** *adj., m. f.* happy

hideux *adj. m. s. pl.* hideous

hier *adv.* yesterday

histoire *n. f.* story, history

hiver *n. m.* winter; **en hiver** in winter

homme *n. m.* man

honneur *n. m.* honor

honte *n. f.* shame, disgrace

hôpital *n. m.* hospital

horizontalement *adv.* horizontally

horloge *n. f.* clock

horreur *n. f.* horror

hôtel *n. m.* hotel

huile *n. f.* oil

huit *adj.* eight

humain, humaine *adj.* human

humble *adj.* humble

hutte *n. f.* hut

I

ici *adv.* here; **ici Monique** this is Monique here

idée *n. f.* idea

identifier *v.* to identify

il *pron.* he *or* it; **il faut** it is necessary; **il y a** there is *or* there are; **il y en a beaucoup** there are many of them; **il n'y a pas (de) . . .** there isn't *or* aren't (any) . . . **il y a un an** a year ago

ils *pron. m.* they

image *n. f.* picture

immédiatement *adv.* immediately

immeuble *n. m.* building

incertain, incertaine *adj.* uncertain

incroyable *adj.* unbelievable

inquiet, inquiète *adj.* upset

s'inquiéter *refl. v.* to worry, to be upset; **ne t'inquiète pas!** don't worry!

insister *v.* to insist

insolent, insolente *adj., m. f.* insolent

intelligent, intelligente *adj., m. f.* intelligent; **l'élève le (la) plus intelligent (intelligente) de la classe** the most intelligent student in the class

intéressant, intéressante *adj., m. f.* interesting

interroger *v.* to interrogate, to question

inventif, inventive *adj., m. f.* inventive

invitation *n. f.* invitation

inviter *v.* to invite

irlandais, irlandaise *adj., m. f.* Irish

italien, italienne *adj., m. f.* Italian

J

j' (je) *per. pron.* I; **j'ai** I have; **j'ai grand faim** I'm very hungry; **j'ai seize ans** I'm sixteen years old

jamais *adv.* never, ever

jambe *n. f.* leg

jambon *n. m.* ham

jaquette *n. f.* jacket

jardin *n. m.* garden

jaune *n. m.* yellow

je *per. pron.* I; **je n'ai rien à faire** I have nothing to do; **je ne fais rien ce soir** I'm not doing anything tonight

jeter *v.* to throw

jeune *adj. m. f. s.* young; **jeune fille** *n. f.* girl

jeunesse *n. f.* youth

joli *adj. m. s.,* **jolie** *adj. f. s.* pretty

jouer *v.* to play; **joué** *past part.*

jouet *n. m.* toy

joueur *n. m.,* **joueuse** *n. f.* player

jour *n. m.* day; **jour de congé** day off (no school, no work); **Jour de la Bastille** Bastille Day (le 14 juillet)

journal *n. m.* newspaper

journée *n. f.* day; **toute la journée** all day long

joyeux, joyeuse *adj.* joyous, happy

juge *n. m.* judge
juillet *n. m.* July
jupe *n. f.* skirt
jus *n. m.* juice
jusque *prep.* until; **jusqu'à, jusqu'aux** until, up to; **jusqu'au printemps** until spring
juste *adj.* accurate, correct, exact

K

kangourou *n. m.* kangaroo
kilogramme *n. m.* kilogram; **1 kilogramme** = about 2.2 lbs.
kilomètre *n. m.* kilometer; **1 kilomètre** = about 0.621 mile

L

l' (le, la) *def. art. m., f.* the; *also, dir. obj. pron.* **Je la vois** (I see her *or* I see it.)
là *adv.* there; **là-bas** *adv.* over there
laideur *n. f.* ugliness
laisser *v.* to let, allow, leave (something behind); **laisse-moi!** let me!
lait *n. m.* milk
lamelle *n. f.* thin slice
lampe *n. f.* lamp
lancer *v.* to throw
langue *n. f.* language, tongue
lapin *n. m.* rabbit
large *n. m.* width, breadth; *adj.* wide
laver *v.* to wash; **se laver** *refl. v.* to wash oneself
le *def. art. m. s.* the; *also, dir. obj. pron.* **Je le vois** (I see him *or* I see it.)
leçon *n. f.* lesson
légume *n. m.* vegetable
lendemain *adv.* following day, next day
lentement *adv.* slowly
les *def. art. m. or f. pl.* the; *also, dir. obj. pron.* **Je les vois** (I see them.)

lettre *n. f.* letter
leur *indir. obj. pron.* (to) them; *also, poss. adj.* their; **Je leur parle** (I'm talking to them.); **J'aime leur voiture** (I like their car); **J'aime leurs amis** (I like their friends.)
lever *v.* to raise, lift; **se lever** *refl. v.* to get up; **elle lève la main** (she raises her hand); **levez-vous!** get up! **lève-toi!** get up!
libéré *adj. m.* **libérée** *adj. f.*, liberated
liberté *n. f.* liberty
lieu *n. m.* place
ligne *n. f.* line
lire *v.* to read
lis, lit *v. forms of* **lire**
lit *n. m.* bed; **au lit** in bed
livre *n. m.* book; *n. f.*, pound
loi *n. f.* law
loin *adv.* far
long *adj. m. s.*, **longue** *adj. f. s.* long
Louisiane *n. f.* Louisiana
lu *past part. of* **lire**; **Je n'ai pas lu le livre.** (I haven't read the book/I didn't read the book.)
lui *indir. obj. pron.* (to) him, (to) her; *also, disj. pron.* him; **avec lui** with him; **avec elle** with her
lumière *n. f.* light
lunaire *adj.* lunar
lune *n. f.* moon
lunettes *n. f. pl.* eye glasses
lustre *n. m.* chandelier

M

m' (me) *refl. pron., dir. and indir. obj. pron.* myself, me, to me
ma *poss. adj. f. sing.* my **(ma maison)**
madame *n. f.* (*pl.* **mesdames**) Mrs., madam
mademoiselle *n. f.* (*pl.* **mesdemoiselles**) Miss
magasin *n. m.* store; **grand magasin** department store
magazine *n. m.* magazine

magicien *n. m.*, **magicienne** *n. f.* magician
magnifique *adj.* magnificent, wonderful
maillot *n. m.* **de bain** swim suit
main *n. f.* hand
maintenant *adv.* now
mais *conj.* but; **mais non!** of course not! why, no! **mais oui!** of course!
maison *n. f.* house
maître *n. m.*, **maîtresse** *n. f.* teacher
mal *n. m.* pain, harm; *adv.* badly, poorly; **se faire mal** to hurt oneself
malade *adj.* sick, ill
malheur *n. m.* unhappiness, misfortune
malheureux *adj. m.*, **malheureuse** *adj. f.* unhappy
malle *n. f.* trunk (luggage)
maman *n. f.* mama, mom
manche *n. f.* sleeve; **La Manche** English Channel
manger *v.* to eat; **mangeant** *pres. part.* **en mangeant** while eating
manquer *v.* to miss, be missing (lacking)
manteau *n. m.* coat
marchand *n. m.*, **marchande** *n. f.* merchant
marchandise *n. f.* merchandise, goods
marché *n. m.* market; **le marché aux puces** flea market
marcher *v.* to walk; to work, run (an apparatus or machine)
mari *n. m.* husband; **le mariage** marriage
match *n. m.* game, match (sport)
mathématiques *n. f. pl.* mathematics
matin *n. m.* morning; **le matin** in the morning
matinée *n. f.* morning (all morning long); early afternoon theater performance
mauvais *adj. m.*, **mauvaise** *adj. f.* bad

me *refl. pron., dir. and indir. obj. pron.* myself, me, to me

méchant *adj. m.,* **méchante** *adj. f.* mean, nasty

mécontent *adj. m.* **mécontente** *adj. f.* unhappy, discontent, malcontent

médecin *n. m.* doctor

médicament *n. m.* medicine

Méditerranée *n. f.* Mediterranean (Sea)

se méfier *refl. v.* to beware; **méfiez-vous de . . .** beware of . . .

meilleur, meilleure *adj.* better; **le meilleur, la meilleure** the best

mélange *n. m.* mixture

même *adj.* same, self; **moi-même** myself; **la même chose** the same thing; **tout de même** all the same, just the same; **pas même** not even

ménagère *n. f.* housewife

mensonge *n. m.* lie, untruth, falsehood

merci *n. m.* thanks, thank you

mère *n. f.* mother

merveilleux, merveilleuse *adj., m. f.* marvelous, wonderful

mes *poss. adj. pl.* my (**mes livres**)

mesdames *n. f. pl.* ladies

mesdemoiselles *n. f. pl.* young ladies, Misses

messieurs *n. m. pl.* gentlemen

mesure *n. f.* measure

met *v. form of* **mettre; elle met** she puts

métal *n. m.* metal

métier *n. m.* trade, occupation

métro, (métropolitain) *n. m.* subway

mettez *v. form of* **mettre** *v.* to put (on), place, wear; **mettre en marche** to put into operation, to start (a machine, apparatus)

meuble(s) *n. m.* furniture

midi *n. m.* noon; **le Midi** southern France

mieux *adv.* better; **j'aime mieux** I prefer, I like better

mignon, mignonne *adj., m. f.* darling, cute

milieu *n. m.* middle; **au milieu de** in the middle of

mille *adj.* thousand

minéral, minérale *adj., m. f.* mineral

minuit *n. m.* midnight

mis *past part. of* **mettre** (to put on); **ils ont mis . . .** they put on . . .

misérable *adj., m. or f.* miserable

mode *n. m.* method, mode, kind

modeste *adj.* modest

moi *stressed per. pron.* me (**avec moi**)

moine *n. m.* monk

moins *adv.* less; **le moins, la moins . . .** the least; **au moins** at least; *see also idioms with* **au** *in Part III, Unit 1*

mois *n. m.* month; **au mois de** in the month of

mon *poss. adj. m. sing.* my (**mon livre**)

monde *n. m.* world; **tout le monde** everybody

monsieur *n. m.* sir, gentleman, Mr., mister

monstrueux, monstrueuse *adj., m. f.* monstrous

montant *n. m.* amount, sum

monté *past part. of* **monter** (to get in, go up, come up)

montre *n. f.* watch (wrist)

montrer *v.* to show

se moquer de *v. refl.* to make fun of

morceau *n. m.* piece, morsel

mort *past part. of* **mourir** (to die)

mot *n. m.* word; **un petit mot** a note

moteur *n. m.* motor

mouche *n. f.* fly (insect)

mouchoir *n. m.* handkerchief

mourir *v.* to die

mouton *n. m.* mutton

mouvement *n. m.* action, movement

muet, muette *adj.* mute

mur *n. m.* wall

musée *n. m.* museum

musique *n. f.* music

N

nager *v.* to swim

naissance *n. f.* birth; **l'anniversaire** (*n. m.*) **de naissance** birthday

naître *v.* to be born

nappe *n. f.* tablecloth

naturellement *adv.* naturally

né *past part. of* **naître**

ne mangez rien don't eat anything

ne pas + *inf.* not to; **de ne pas révéler** not to reveal

nécessaire *adj.* necessary

neige *n. f.* snow; **neiger** *v.* to snow

n'est-ce pas? isn't that so? isn't it? *see Work Unit 20*

nettoyer *v.* to clean

neuf *adj.* nine; **neuf, neuve** *adj., m. f.* new

neveu *n. m.* nephew

nez *n. m.* nose

Noël *n. m.* Christmas

noir, noire *adj.* black

nom *n. m.* name

nombre *n. m.* number; **nombreux, nombreuse** *adj., m. f.* numerous

non *adv.* no; **non plus** neither; **moi non plus** me neither

notre *poss. adj.* our; *pl.,* **nos** (**nos livres**)

nourriture *n. f.* nourishment, food

nous *per. pron.* we, us

nouveau, nouveaux *adj.* new; **Je n'ai rien appris de nouveau**/I didn't learn anything new; **un nouveau livre** (a new book)

nouvel, nouvelle *adj.* new; **un nouvel étudiant, une nouvelle étudiante**/ a new student

Nouvelle-Orléans *n. f.* New Orleans

nouvelles *n. f. pl.* news; **bonnes nouvelles!** good news!

nuage n. m. cloud; **nuageux, nuageuse** adj. cloudy

nuire v. to harm, hurt

O

obéir v. to obey

objet n. m. object, article

obscur, obscure adj. dark, obscure

observer v. to observe

occasion n. f. occasion

oeil n. m. eye; **yeux** pl.

oeuf n. m. egg; **oeuf à la coque** soft-boiled egg

oeuvre n. f. work; **une oeuvre d'art** a work of art

offre v. form of **offrir** (to offer); past part. **offert**

oignon n. m. onion

oiseau n. m. bird; **oiseaux** pl.

on indef. per. pron. one, people, you; someone, they; **On vous demande au téléphone**/You're wanted on the phone.

oncle n. m. uncle

ont v. form of **avoir** (to have); **ils (elles) ont** they have, they do have

opéra n. m. opera

orage n. m. storm

ordures n. f. pl. garbage

oreille n. f. ear

ou conj. or; **où** adv. where

oublié past part. of **oublier** (to forget)

oui adv. yes

ouvert, ouverte adj., m. f. open; also past part. of **ouvrir** (to open)

ouvre v. form of **ouvrir; elle ouvre** she opens

P

page n. f. page

pain n. m. bread; **pain grillé** toast

paisible adj. peaceful

paix n. f. peace

palme n. f. palm branch

palmier n. m. palm tree

pamplemousse n. m. grapefruit

panier n. m. basket

papa n. m. papa, daddy, dad

papier n. m. paper; **une feuille de papier** a sheet of paper

par prep. by, through; **par terre** on the floor, on the ground

paraître v. to appear, seem

parapluie n. m. umbrella

parc n. m. park

parce que conj. because

par-dessous adv. underneath, below

par-dessus adv. over, above; **pardessus** n. m. coat, overcoat

parfait, parfaite adj., m. f. perfect

parle v. form of **parler** (to talk, to speak); **Qui parle?** Who is talking? **parlé** past part.

part n. f. part, behalf; **de la part de lui**/on his behalf (from him)

part v. form of **partir** (to leave, to go away); **tout le monde part** everybody is leaving; **parti** past part. of **partir**

participe n. m. participle

partie n. f. part

partir v. to leave, to go away; **partons-nous?** are we leaving?

partout adv. everywhere

paru past part. of **paraître**

pas adv. not, none, no; **pas loin** not far; **pas du tout** not at all; **pas même** not even; see also **ne pas**; **Je n'ai pas de bananes**/I haven't any bananas, I don't have any bananas, I have no bananas

passage n. m. passage, passage way; **passage clouté** n. m. crosswalk

passé n. m. past; also past part. of **passer**

passe-moi le pain, passez-moi le beurre/pass me the bread, pass me the butter

passer v. to spend (time), to pass by, to go by

pâte n. f. dough, paste, "pasta" (macaroni, spaghetti, etc.)

patiemment adv. patiently

pâtisserie n. f. pastry, pastry shop

pâtissier, pâtissière n. m. f. pastry cook

patrie n. f. country (nation)

paupière n. f. eyelid

pauvre adj. poor

payer v. to pay, to pay for; **payé** paid for

pays n. m. country (nation)

paysage n. m. countryside

peau n. f. skin

pêche n. f. peach

se peigner v. refl. to comb one's hair

peindre v. to paint; **peint** past part.

pendant prep. during; **pendant que** conj. while

perdre v. to lose; **perdu** past part.

père n. m. father; **Père Noël** n. m. Santa Claus

permettre v. to permit, to allow; **permis** past part.

personne n. f. person

petit, petite, petits, petites adj. small, little; **le plus petit, la plus petite, les plus petits, les plus petites** the smallest, the littlest; **le petit déjeuner** breakfast; **le petit four** little cake (usually square in shape with icing); **petits pois** n. m. pl. peas

peu adv. little, few, not much

peuple n. m. people (of a nation)

peur n. f. fear

peut v. form of **pouvoir**

peut-être adv. maybe, perhaps

peux v. form of **pouvoir**

pharmacie n. f. pharmacy, drug store

pharmacien, pharmacienne n. pharmacist, druggist

photo n. f. photo

phrase n. f. sentence, phrase

pièce n. f. room, piece

pied n. m. foot

pinceau n. m. artist's brush

piquer v. to poke, puncture

piste n. f. track

pistolet n. m. pistol

place n. f. place, seat, plaza

plafond n. m. ceiling

plage n. f. beach

plainte n. f. lamentation

plaire v. to please

plaisir n. m. pleasure

plaît v. form of **plaire; s'il vous plaît** please (if it is pleasing to you)

plat n. m. plate, dish

pleurer v. to cry, to weep

pleut v. form of **pleuvoir** (to rain); **il pleut** it's raining, it rains

pluie n. f. rain

plume n. f. feather

plus adv. more; **le plus, la plus, les plus** the most; **plus petit, plus petite** smaller; **plus tard** later; **ne . . . plus**/no . . . longer, no . . . more

plusieurs adv. several

poche n. f. pocket

poème n. m. poem

poète, poétesse (femme poète) n. poet

poids n. m. weight

poire n. f. pear

pois n. m. pea; **les petits pois** peas

poisson n. m. fish

poivre n. m. pepper

pôle nord n. m. North Pole

pomme n. f. apple; **une pomme de terre** potato

pommes frites n. f. pl. French fries

pommier n. m. apple tree

porc n. m. pork

port n. m. port

porte n. f. door

porte v. form of **porter** (to wear, to carry)

poser v. to pose, to place; **poser une question** to ask a question

poubelle n. f. rubbish can

poulet n. m. chicken; **une poule** a hen

pour prep. for, in order (to)

pourquoi adv. why;

pourquoi pas? why not?

pouvez, pouvons v. forms of **pouvoir** (can, to be able, may); **pu** past part.; **vous pouvez**/you can; **vous pouvez être**/you can be; **pouvez-vous?** can you?

précéder v. to precede

préféré past part. of **préférer** (to prefer)

premier, première adj., m. f. first

prendre v. to take, to have (a meal); **Que prenez-vous pour le petit déjeuner?** What do you have for breakfast?

préparatoire adj. preparatory, preliminary

préparé past part. of **préparer** (to prepare); **se préparer** to prepare oneself

près (de) adv. near

présent n. m. present

presque adv. almost

prêt, prête adj. ready, prepared

prêté past part. of **prêter** (to lend)

prêtre, prêtresse n. priest, priestess

prier v. to beg, to request, to ask

printemps n. m. spring (season)

pris past part. of **prendre**

prise n. f. **de courant** electric outlet (wall)

prix n. m. price, prize; **le grand prix** the first prize

probablement adv. probably

prochain, prochaine adj. next; **la prochaine fois**/the next time

produits laitiers n. m. pl. dairy products

professeur, professeur-dame n. professor, teacher

profession n. f. profession

profiter v. to profit, to take advantage (of); **il faut profiter du moment**/you (one) must take advantage of the moment

programme n. m. program

projet n. m. project

se promener v. refl. to go for (to take) a walk, to stroll

promettre v. to promise; **promis** past part.

prononcer v. to pronounce

propriété n. f. property

proverbe n. m. proverb

pu past part. of **pouvoir**

public n. m. public; **public, publique** adj. public

puce n. f. flea; **le marché aux puces** flea market

puis adv. then

punit v. form of **punir** (to punish); **il punit**/he punishes

pupitre n. m. desk (pupil's)

Q

qualité n. f. quality; **la qualité la plus forte**/the strongest quality

quand adv. when

quatorze adj. fourteen

que conj. than, that; interrog. pron. what

quel adj. m. s. what, which; **quel sport?**/what (which) sport? **quel âge ont les enfants?**/how old are the children? what (a) . . . ! what (an) . . . ! **quel déjeuner!**/what a lunch! **quel embarras!**/what an embarrassment!

quelle adj. f. s. what, which; **quelle maison?**/what (which) house? what (a) . . . ! what (an) . . . ! **quelle classe!**/what a class! **quelle idée!**/what an idea! **Quelle heure est-il?**/What time is it? **Quelle est la date aujourd'hui?**/What's the date today? **De quelle couleur est . . . ?** What color is . . . ?

quelles adj. f. pl. what, which; **quelles maisons?**/what (which) houses? **quelles idées!**/what ideas!

quelque adj. some;

quelques some, a few; **quelque chose**/ something

quelquefois adv. sometimes

quels adj. m. pl. what, which; **quels livres?**/what (which) books?

qu'est-ce que c'est? what is it?

qu'est-ce que je suis? or **que suis-je?** what am I?

question n. f. question

qui pron. who, whom, which, that; in proverbs he who/she who **Qui suis-je?**/Who am I? **Avec qui sortez-vous?**/With whom are you going out? **Le livre qui est sur la table est à moi**/The book which (that) is on the table is mine.

quinze adj. fifteen; **J'ai quinze ans**/I am fifteen years old.

quitte, quittent v. forms of **quitter** (to leave); **quitté** past part.; **Elle a quitté la maison à huit heures**/ She left the house at 8 o'clock.

quoi pron. what; **Quoi?!**/ What?! **Quoi de neuf?** What's new?

R

R.S.V.P. Répondez, s'il vous plaît/Reply, please.

raconter v. to tell, to relate

ragoût n. m. stew

raisin n. m. grape

raison n. f. reason; **avoir raison**/to be right; **Vous avez raison**/You are right; **Tu as raison**/You (fam. sing.) are right.

raisonnable adj. reasonable

rang n. m. rank, row

rapide adj. rapid; **rapidement** adv. rapidly, fast, quickly

se rappeler v. to remember, to recall

rare adj. rare; **rarement** adv. rarely

rayonner v. to radiate symmetrically

recette n. f. recipe

recevoir v. receive; **reçu** past part.

refuser v. to refuse

regarder v. to look, to look at, to watch; **Regarde!**/Look! **Regardez!**/Look! **se regarder** (l'un à l'autre) v. to look at each other

régime n. m. diet

règle n. f. rule, ruler

regretter v. to regret, to be sorry

religieuse n. f. nun (sister); adj. religious

religieux n. m. monk, friar; adj. religious

rembourser v. to reimburse

remercier v. to thank; **Je vous remercie**/I thank you.

remplir v. to fill, fulfill

remuer v. to stir

rendez-vous n. m. appointment

rendre v. return (something), give back; **Rendez-moi mes disques**/Give me back my (phono) records.

rendre visite à quelqu'un to visit someone

rentrer v. to go in again, to return (home)

réparer v. to repair

repas n. m. meal

répéter v. to repeat

répondre v. to answer, to reply, to respond; **répondu**, past part.

réponse n. f. answer, response, reply

repos n. m. rest, repose (sleep); **au repos** at rest

se reposer v. refl. to rest

reprendre v. to take back, get back, to resume

représentation n. f. presentation, show, performance

requin n. m. shark

se ressembler v. refl. to resemble each other, to look alike

restaurant n. m. restaurant

reste n. m. rest, remainder

rester v. to remain, to stay; **resté** past part.; **restons-nous?**/are we staying?

retard n. m. delay; **être en retard**/to be late

retentir v. to resound, to ring

retourner v. to return, to go back

réussir v. to succeed

réveil n. m. alarm clock

révéler v. to reveal

revenir v. to return, to come back; **revenu,** past part.

rêver v. to dream

reviens, revient, reviennent v. forms of **revenir**

revoir v. to see again; **au revoir** good-bye

ri past part. of **rire**

riche adj. rich

ridicule adj. ridiculous

rien indef. pron. nothing; **ne . . . rien** nothing; **Je n'étudie rien**/I study nothing (I don't study anything); **de rien** you're welcome

rient, rira v. forms of **rire**; **Tous les élèves rient**/All the students laugh.

rire v. to laugh

risquer v. to risk

rit v. form of **rire**; **Il rit tout le temps**/He laughs all the time.

robe n. f. dress

rompre v. to break

rond, ronde adj. round; **ronde** n. f. round, roundelay

rosbif n. m. roast beef

rose n. f. rose

roue n. f. wheel

rouge adj. red

rougit v. form of **rougir** (to blush); **Pierre rougit**/Peter blushes.

route n. f. road

ruban n. m. ribbon

rue n. f. street

rumeur n. f. stir, stirring, muffled din, hum

S

s' contraction of **se**, refl. pron.

sa poss. adj., f. sing. his, her, its, one's; **sa voiture**/his (her, etc.) car

sagesse n. f. wisdom, discretion

sais v. form of **savoir; je sais**/I know, **tu sais**/you know, **vous savez**/you know; **je ne sais pas**/I don't know.

saisir v. to seize, to grasp

saison n. f. season

sait v. form of **savoir; elle (il, on), sait**/she (he, one) knows

sale adj. soiled, dirty; **le plus sale**/the dirtiest

salle n. f. (large) room; **une salle des ventes**/ auction sales room; **une salle à manger**/dining room; **une salle de bains**/bathroom; **une salle de classe**/classroom; **une grande salle**/auditorium

salon n. m. living room

samedi n. m. Saturday

sans prep. without; **sans doute**/ without doubt, undoubtedly; **sans la casser**/without breaking it

santé n. f. health

satisfaire v. to satisfy

saucisse n. f. sausage; **saucisson** n. m. bologna

sauter v. to jump, to leap

sauvage adj. wild, savage

savent, savez, savons v. forms of **savoir**

savoir v. to know (how), to find out; **savez-vous lire?**/ do you know how to read?

scrupuleux, scrupuleuse adj. scrupulous

se refl. pron. himself, herself, oneself, themselves; (reflexive verbs are not alphabetized in this vocabulary under the refl. pron. **se**; they are alphabetized under the first letter of the verb, e.g. **se dépêcher** is listed under the **D**'s)

sec adj. m. s. dry; **sèche** f.

Seine n. f. Seine River (flows through Paris)

séjour n. m. stay, visit

sel n. m. salt

semaine n. f. week

sénateur n. m. senator

sent v. form of **sentir** (to smell); **Il sent bon!** It smells good!

sentiment n. m. feeling

serpent n. m. snake

service n. m. service

servir v. to serve; **se servir (de)** to serve oneself, to use

ses poss. adj. pl. his, her, its, one's; (**ses livres, ses parents**)

seul adj. m. s. alone, single

seulement adv. only

si adv. so; **si** conj. if

s'il te plaît please (fam. use); **s'il vous plaît** (polite use)

silence n. m. silence

snob n. m. snob

soeur n. f. sister

soif n. f. thirst

soigneusement adv. carefully

soir n. m. evening; **ce soir** tonight; **le soir** in the evening

soirée n. f. evening party

sois v. form of **être; Sois sage!** Be good!

soixante adj. sixty

sol n. m. ground, soil

soldat n. m. soldier

soleil n. m. sun

sommeil n.m. slumber, sleep

sommes v. form of **être; nous sommes** we are

son n. m. sound

son poss. adj. m. s. his, her, its, one's; (**son livre**)

sonne v. form of **sonner** (to ring); **la cloche sonne** the bell rings

sont v. form of **être; ils, elles sont** they are

sors, sort v. forms of **sortir** (to go out, to leave); **Je sors** I go out/I do go out/I am going out; **Je ne sors**

jamais I never go out.

sortez v. form (Imperative) of **sortir; Ne sortez pas!** Don't go out!

sorti past part. of **sortir**

sortie n. f. exit

sortir v. to go out, to leave

souffrante adj. f. s. sick

souffrir v. to suffer

soulier n. m. shoe

soupe n. f. soup

sourire n. m. smile; as a v. to smile

souris n. f. mouse

sourit v. form of **sourire**

sous prep. under

souvent adv. often

soyez, soyons v. forms of **être** (Imperative); **Soyez à l'heure!** Be on time! **Soyez prudent!** Be prudent! **Soyons sérieux!** Let's be serious!

spécial, spéciale adj. special

spectacle n. m. show (entertainment, e.g., movie, theater)

spectateur, spectatrice n. spectator (person in an audience)

splendide adj. splendid

sport n. m. sport

stade n. m. stadium

stupéfié(e) adj. stupefied, dumbfounded

stylo n. m. pen

su past part. of **savoir**

suffit v. form of **suffire** (to suffice, to be enough)

suis v. form of **être; je suis**/I am; **je ne suis pas**/I am not

suisse adj. Swiss; **la Suisse** Switzerland

suit v. form of **suivre** (to follow); **Il suit la route**/He is following the route.

supermarché n. m. supermarket

superstitieux, superstitieuse adj. superstitious

sur prep. on, upon

sûr, sûre adj. sure, certain

sûrement adv. surely

surtout adv. especially, above all

T

t' *contraction of* **te,** *refl. pron.;* (**Est-ce que tu t'appelles Janine?** Is your name Janine?)

ta *poss. adj., f. sing.* your (*fam. use*); **ta maison** your house

tableau *n. m.* chalk board, picture, painting

tablier *n. m.* apron

tambour *n. m.* drum

tante *n. f.* aunt

tapis *n. m.* carpet, rug

tard *adv.* late; **plus tard** later

tarte *n. f.* tart

tasse *n. f.* cup; **une tasse de café** a cup of coffee; **une tasse à café** a coffee cup

te *refl. pron., dir. and indir. obj. pron. (fam.)* yourself, you, to you

tel, telle *adj.* such

télégramme *n. m.* telegram

téléphone *n. m.* telephone; **au téléphone** to the telephone, on the telephone

téléviseur *n. m.* television set (apparatus)

télé *n. f.* TV; **la télévision** television; **à la télévision** on television

temps *n. m.* tense, time (duration), weather; **Quel temps fait-il?** What's the weather like? **Il a beaucoup de temps**/He has a lot of time.

tendrement *adv.* tenderly

tenir *v.* to hold

tenu *past part. of* **tenir**

tenue *n. f.* suit, attire; **en tenue d'exercice** in a gym suit

terminé *past part. of* **terminer** (to terminate, to end, to finish)

terrasse *n. f.* terrace; **une terrasse de café** a sidewalk café

tes *poss. adj. pl (fam.)* your; (**tes livres**/your books)

tête *n. f.* head

théâtre *n. m.* theater

tiennent *v. form of* **tenir**

tiens! here! look!

tiens *v. form of* **tenir**

tiers one third (1/3)

tigre *n. m.* tiger

tinte *v. form of* **tinter** (to ring, to toll)

tiroir *n. m.* drawer

toi *pron. (fam.)* you; **avec toi** with you; **toi que voilà . . .** you there . . .

toilette *n. f.* washing and dressing; **faire sa toilette** to groom oneself (wash and dress)

toit *n. m.* roof

tolérer *v.* to tolerate

tomate *n. f.* tomato

tombé *past part. of* **tomber** (to fall)

tombeau *n. m.* tombe, grave

ton *poss. adj. m. sing.* your (*fam. use*); (**ton stylo**/your pen)

tort *n. m.* wrong; **vous avez tort** you are wrong

tortue *n. f.* turtle

tôt *adv.* early

toujours *adv.* always, still

tour *n. m.* turn, tour; **un tour de force** trick

tourner *v.* to turn, to turn sour

tournevis *n. m.* screw driver

tous *adj. m. pl.* all; **tous les deux** both; **toutes les deux** (*fem.*) both; **tous les élèves** all the pupils; **tous les élèves rient** all the pupils laugh; **tous les enfants** all the children; **tous les matins** every morning; **tous les soirs** every evening

tout *adj., pron., adv.* all, everything, every; **tout de même** just the same, all the same; **tout de suite** immediately; **tout d'un coup** all of a sudden; **Tout est bien qui finit bien!** All's well that ends well! **tout le monde** everybody; **tout l'été** all summer

toute, toutes *adj., f.* all; **toute la classe** the whole class; **toutes les jeunes filles** all the girls; **toute la bôite de chocolats** the whole box of chocolates; **toute la cocotte!** the whole pot! **toute la journée** the whole day, all day long; **toute la matinée** all morning long, the whole morning

tranquille *adj.* calm, quiet, tranquil

tranquillement *adv.* calmly, peacefully, quietly

transporter *v.* to transport

travail *n. m.* work

travaillé *past part. of* **travailler** (to work)

traverser *v.* to cross, to go through, to traverse; **à travers** through, across

très *adv.* very (*Note: never use* **très** *with* **beaucoup**)

tricolore *n. m. adj.* tricolor (French flag, consisting of 3 vertical bands of blue, white, red)

triompher *v.* to triumph

triste *adj. m. f.* sad, unhappy

trois *adj.* three; **troisième** *adj.* third

trop *adv.* too, too much, too many; **trop facile**/too easy; **il travaille trop**/he works too much; **il a trop d'argent**/he has too much money; **il fait trop de fautes**/he makes too many mistakes; (*Note: never say* **trop beaucoup**)

trottoir *n. m.* sidewalk

trouve *v. form of* **trouver** (to find); **il trouve**/he finds; **se trouver** to be located; **la bibliothèque se trouve près du parc**/the library is located near the park

tu *per. pron. fam.* you

tulipe *n. f.* tulip

U

un, une *adj.* one; *also, indef. art.* a, an; **J'ai un père**/I have a (one) father; **j'ai une mère**/I have a (one) mother; **j'ai un livre**/I have a (one) book; **j'ai une pomme**/ I have an (one) apple

usine *n. f.* factory

usuel, usuelle *adj.* usual

utile *adj.* useful

V

va *v. form of* **aller;** **il, elle va**/ he, she, it goes, does go, is going; **va te coucher!** go to bed! (*fam. use*)

vache *n. f.* cow

vais *v. form of* **aller; je vais**/I'm going, I do go, I go; **je vais me faire lire les lignes de la main**/I'm going to have my palm read

valeur *n. f.* value

valise *n. f.* suitcase, valise

valoir *v.* to be worth

vanille *n. f.* vanilla; **j'aime la glace à la vanille**/I like vanilla ice cream

vas *v. form of* **aller; tu vas**/you go, you do go, you are going (*fam. use*); **comment vas-tu?**/how are you? (*fam. use*)

vase *n. m.* vase

vas-y! go to it!/go there!

vaut *v. form of* **valoir; il vaut mieux**/it is better

veau *n. m.* veal

vélo *n. m.* bike

venant *v. form of* **venir**

vend, vends, vendez, vendu *v. forms of* **vendre**

vendeur, vendeuse *n. m. f.* salesman, saleslady

vendre *v.* to sell

vendu *past part. of* **vendre**

venez *v. form of* **venir** (to come)

vent *n. m.* wind

vente *n. f.* sale; **une vente aux enchères** auction

venu *past part. of* **venir**

vérité *n. f.* truth

vermisseau *n. m.* small worm

verra *v. form of* **voir; il, elle verra**/he, she will see

verre *n. m.* glass (drinking); **je bois un verre de lait**/I'm drinking a glass of milk

vers *prep.* toward

vert *n. m., adj.* green; **aimez-vous le vert?**/do you like green? **j'aime les petites automobiles vertes**/I like small green cars.

verticalement *adv.* vertically

veste *n. f.* vest (worn under a suit coat)

veston *n. m.* coat (of a suit)

vêtements *n. m. pl.* clothing

veut, veux *v. forms of* **vouloir** (to want); **je veux, tu veux, il** *ou* **elle** *ou* **on veut**/I want, you (*fam.*) want, he *or* she *or* it wants

viande *n. f.* meat

vie *n. f.* life

vieille *adj. f. s.* old; **une vieille dame**/an old lady; **vieux** *adj. m. s. pl.* old

viens, vient *v. forms of* **venir** (to come)

vigueur *n. f.* force

ville *n. f.* town, city

vin *n. m.* vine

vingt *adj.* twenty; **vingtième** twentieth

violence *n. f.* violence

vis *n. f.* screw

visage *n. m.* face

visite *n. f.* visit; **rendre visite à quelqu'un** to visit someone

visiter *v.* to visit

vite *adv.* quickly, fast

vitesse *n. f.* speed; **à toute vitesse** at full speed, quickly

vitre *n. f.* window (glass) pane

vive, vivent *v. forms of* **vivre** (to live); **Vive le quatorze juillet!**/Hurrah for the 14th of July! **Vive la France!**/Long live France! **Vive l'Amérique!**/Long live America!

vivra *v. form of* **vivre; il** *ou* **elle vivra**/he *or* she will live

vivre *v.* to live

vocabulaire *n. m.* vocabulary

voici here is, here are; **voici les livres!**/here are the books! **voici Robert!**/Here's Robert!

voient *v. form of* **voir** (to see); **ils** *ou* **elles voient**/they see

voilà there is, there are; **voilà les livres!**/there are the books! **voilà Robert!**/There's Robert!

voir *v.* to see

voisin, voisine *n. m., f.* neighbor

voisinage *n. m.* neighborhood

voit *v. form of* **voir; il** *ou* **elle voit**/he *or* she sees, does see, is seeing

voiture *n. f.* car, automobile

voix *n. f.* voice; **à voix basse**/in a low voice, softly; **à haute voix**/in a loud voice

vol *n. m.* flight

voler *v.* to fly, to steal

vont *v. form of* **aller; ils** *ou* **elles vont**/they go, do go, are going

vos *poss. adj. pl.* your; **Voici vos livres!**/Here are your books!

votre *poss. adj. s.* your; **Voici votre livre!**/Here's your book!

voudrais *v. form (Conditional) of* **vouloir** (to want); **je voudrais une tasse de café**/I would like a cup of coffee

voulez *v. form of* **vouloir; Voulez-vous aller au cinéma avec moi?**/Do you want to go to the movies with me?

vouloir *v.* to want; **vouloir dire** to mean, to signify; **Que veut dire ce mot?**/What does this word mean?

voulu *past part. of* **vouloir**

vous *per. pron.* you; **vous deux**/you two

voyage *n. m.* trip; **faire un voyage** to take a trip

voyageons *v. form of* **voyager; nous voyageons**/we are travelling

voyager *v.* to travel

voyez-vous? do you see?

vrai *adj. m.,* **vraie** *f.* true, real

vraiment *adv.* really, truly

vu *past part. of* **voir** (to see); **Avez-vous vu Janine?**/Have you see Janine?

Y

y *advl. pron., adv. of place* there ; **il y a** there is, there are; **il y a vingt élèves**

dans cette classe/there are 20 pupils in this class; **y a-t-il vingt étudiants dans cette classe?**/are there 20 students in this class? **Il y a quelqu'un à la porte**/there is someone at the door.

yeux *n. m. pl.* eyes; **l'oeil** *n. m. s.* the eye

Z

zèbre *n. m.* zebra
zodiaque *n. m.* zodiac
zut *interj.* darn it!

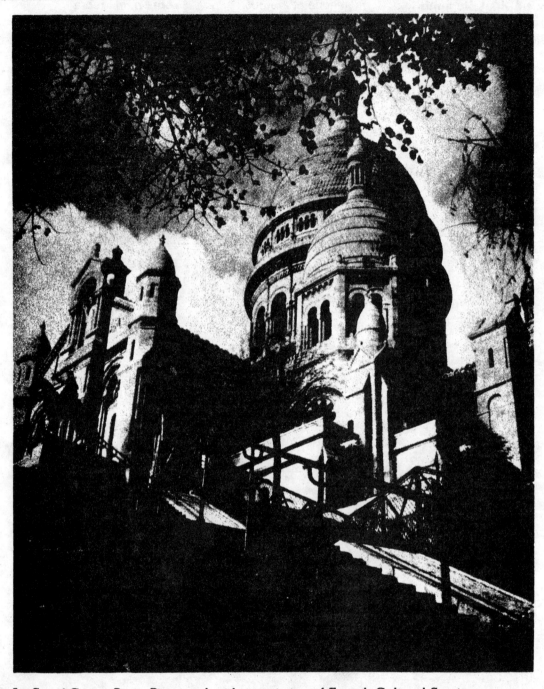

Le Sacré-Coeur, Paris. Reprinted with permission of French Cultural Services, New York City.

ENGLISH

English-French

A

a **un, une; un homme**/a man; **une femme**/a woman
above **au-dessus, en haut**
absolutely **absolument**
to accept **accepter**
accident **un accident**
acrostic **un acrostiche**
actor, actress **un acteur, une actrice**
to add **ajouter**
address **une adresse**
to adore **adorer**
to advance **avancer**
to affirm **affirmer**
after **après**; afternoon/**un après-midi**; in the afternoon/**l'après-midi**
again **encore, de nouveau**
age **un âge**
agreed **d'accord**
airplane **un avion**
airport **un aéroport**; air terminal/**une aérogare**
alarm clock **un réveil**
all **tout, toute, toutes, tous**; all of a sudden/**tout d'un coup**; All's well that ends well/**Tout est bien qui finit bien**; all summer/**tout l'été**; all day long/**toute la journée**; all morning long/**toute la matinée**; all the girls/**toutes les jeunes filles**; all the boys/**tous les garçons**
to allow **permettre** (past part., **permis**)
almost **presque**
already **déjà**
also **aussi**
always **toujours**

American (language) **l'américain** n. m.; He is American, She is American/**Il est Américain, Elle est Américaine**
to amuse **amuser**; to amuse oneself/**s'amuser**
amusing **amusant, amusante**
an **un, une; un tablier**/an apron; **une pomme**/an apple
ancient **ancien, ancienne**
and **et**
angry **fâché, fâchée**; to get angry/**se fâcher**
animal **un animal**; animals/**animaux**
to announce **annoncer**
to annoy **ennuyer**
annoying **ennuyant, ennuyante**
another **un autre, une autre**
answer **une réponse**; to answer/**répondre** (past part., **répondu**)
ant **une fourmi**
apparatus **un appareil**
appetite **un appétit**
apple **une pomme**
apple tree **un pommier**
appointment **un rendez-vous**
to appreciate **apprécier**
to approach **s'approcher (de)**
arm **un bras**
armchair **un fauteuil**
around **autour**; he is traveling around the world/**il voyage autour du monde**; it is around two o'clock/**il est vers deux heures**

to arrange **arranger, disposer**
arrested **arrêté**
to arrive **arriver**
art **l'art,** m.
artist **l'artiste,** m. f.
as **comme**
as well as (just as) **ainsi que**
to ask (for) **demander**
to ask a question **poser une question**
aspirin **une aspirine**
to assert **affirmer**
assignments **les devoirs,** m.
astronomer **un astronome**
at **à**
at first **d'abord**
at last **enfin**
at that moment **à ce moment-là**
to attend **assister à**
auditorium **une grande salle**
August **août,** m.
aunt **une tante**
author **un auteur, une femme auteur**
auto mechanic **un garagiste, une garagiste**
autograph **un autographe**
automobile **une automobile, une voiture**
autumn **l'automne,** m.
to avoid **éviter**

B

baby **un bébé**
babysitter **une gardienne d'enfants, un gardien d'enfants**
bad **mauvais, mauvaise**

337

badly **mal**

baker **un boulanger, une boulangère**

bakery **une boulangerie**

ball **une balle, un ballon**

balloon **un ballon**

banana **une banane**

barber **un coiffeur, une coiffeuse**

basket **un panier**

Bastille Day **Le Jour de la Bastille**

to bathe **baigner;** to bathe oneself **se baigner**

bathroom **une salle de bains**

baton **un bâton**

to be **être**

to be able **pouvoir** (*past part.,* **pu**)

to be born **naître** (*past part.,* **né**)

to be late **être en retard**

to be located **se trouver**

to be present at **assister à, être présent(e) à**

to be right **avoir raison**

to be sorry **regretter**

to beat **battre** (*past part.,* **battu**)

beautiful **beau, beaux, bel, belle, belles** (**un beau cadeau, de beaux cadeaux, un bel arbre, une belle femme, de belles femmes**)

beauty **la beauté**

because **parce que**

to become **devenir**

bedroom **une chambre à coucher**

before **avant;** before going out/**avant de sortir**

to beg **prier**

to begin **commencer (â + inf.); je commence à travailler**/I'm beginning to work.

behind **derrière** (*in back of*)

Belgian **belge;** He is Belgian, She is Belgian/**Il est Belge, Elle est Belge**

Belgium **la Belgique**

to believe **croire** (*past part.,* **cru**)

below **par-dessous, au-dessous**

bench (seat) **un banc**

besides **d'ailleurs**

better *as an adj.,* **meilleur, meilleure;** *as an adv.,* **mieux;** the best **le meilleur, la meilleure, les meilleurs, les meilleures; cette pomme est meilleure**/this apple is better; **cette pomme est la meilleure**/this apple is the best; **Paul travaille mieux que Robert**/Paul works better than Robert.

between **entre; entre eux et nous**/between them and us

beverage **un boisson**

to beware **se méfier de; méfiez-vous des obstacles dangereux/** beware of dangerous obstacles

bid, bidding **une enchère**

bike **un vélo; une bicyclette**/a bicycle

bill **une addition**

bird **un oiseau**

birth **une naissance;** birthday/**un anniversaire de naissance**

black **noir, noire, noirs, noires**

blue **bleu, bleue, bleus, bleues**

body **un corps**

to boil **bouillir, faire bouillir**

book **un livre**

to bore **ennuyer**

boring **ennuyant, ennuyante**

to be born **naître;** *past part.,* **né**

both **tous les deux, toutes les deux**

bottle **une bouteille**

boutique **une boutique**

box **une boîte**

boy **un garçon**

to break **briser, casser, rompre**

breakfast **le petit déjeuner**

to bring **apporter**

broom **un balai**

brother **un frère**

to brush **brosser, se brosser; je brosse le manteau**/I'm brushing the coat; **je me brosse les**

dents/I brush my teeth

brush **une brosse**

to build **bâtir**

building **un bâtiment, un immeuble**

to burn **brûler**

bus **un autobus** (city bus); **un autocar** (interurban, long distance bus)

but **mais**

butcher **un boucher, une bouchère**

butcher shop **une boucherie**

butter **le beurre**

to buy **acheter**

by **par**

C

cake **un gâteau, des gâteaux**

to call **appeler;** to be called, to be named **s'appeler; j'appelle le médecin**/I'm calling the doctor; **je m'appelle Janine, je m'appelle Pierre**/My name is Janine, my name is Peter.

can (may) **pouvoir; vous pouvez entrer**/you can (may) come in

Canada **le Canada**

Canadian **canadien, canadienne; Canadien, Canadienne; un livre canadien**/a Canadian book; **Madame Dupont est Canadienne**/Mrs. Dupont is Canadian.

candy **un bonbon**

capital **une capitale**

capricious **capricieux, capricieuse**

car **une voiture, une automobile**

carefully **soigneusement**

carpet **un tapis**

to carry **porter**

to carry away **emporter**

cash box (register) **une caisse**

cashier **un caissier, une caissière**

castle **un château**

cat **un chat, une chatte**

to catch **attraper**

ceiling **un plafond**

to celebrate **célébrer**

cellar **une cave**

center **un centre**

certain **certain, certaine, sûr, sûre**

chair **une chaise**

chalk **une craie**

change **un changement**

chapel **une chapelle**

charming **charmant, charmante**

to chase, to chase away **chasser**

check (bill) **une addition**

cheese **un fromage**

cherry **une cerise**

chicken **un poulet**

child **un enfant, une enfant**

chimney **une cheminée**

chocolate **un chocolat**

to choose **choisir**

Christmas **le Noël**; Merry Christmas/**Joyeux Noël**

church **une église**

city **une ville**

class **une classe**; classroom/**une salle de classe**; a French class/**une classe de français**

to clean **nettoyer**

clear **clair, claire**

clock **une horloge**; alarm clock/**un réveil**

to close **fermer**

closet **une armoire**

clothing **un vêtement, des vêtements**

cloud **un nuage**; cloudy/**nuageux, nuageuse**; a cloudy sky/**un ciel nuageux**

coat (overcoat) **un manteau, un pardessus**

coffee **le café**

cold **froid, froide**; the cold/**le froid**; j'ai froid/I'm cold, I feel cold; **il fait froid ici**/It's cold here.

color **la couleur**; what color is . . ./**de quelle couleur est . . .**

comb **un peigne**; to comb one's hair/**se peigner les cheveux**

to come **venir**; to come back/**revenir**

to come down **descendre**

to come in **entrer (dans)**

to confess **confesser**

contrary **contraire**

to cook **cuire, faire la cuisine**

to correct **corriger**

to cost **coûter**

country **un pays, une nation**

countryside **un paysage**

courageous **courageux, courageuse**

course **un cours**; a French course/**un cours de français**

cousin **un cousin, une cousine**

to cover **couvrir**; *past part.,* **couvert**

cow **une vache**

crazy **fou, fol, folle**

cross **une croix**; to cross/**traverser**

cruel **cruel, cruelle**

to crush **écraser**

to cry **pleurer**; to cry out/**crier**

cup **une tasse**; a coffee cup/**une tasse à café**; a cup of coffee/**une tasse de café**

curious **curieux, curieuse**

customer **un client, une cliente**

to cut **couper**; to cut oneself/**se couper**; **j'ai coupé le pain**/I cut the bread; **je me suis coupé le doigt**/I cut my finger.

cute **mignon, mignonne,** *adj. m. f.*

D

dad, daddy **un papa**

dance **un bal**; to dance/**danser**

dancer **un danseur, une danseuse**

dangerous **dangereux, dangereuse**

dark **obscur, obscure**

darling **chéri, chérie**

darn it! **zut alors!**

daughter **une fille**

day **un jour, une journée**; all day long/**toute la journée**

dear **cher, chère**

December **le décembre**

decision **une décision**

to defend **défendre**

delicious **délicieux, délicieuse**

department store **un grand magasin**

desire **un désir**; to desire/**désirer**

desk **un bureau**; desk (pupil's, student's)/**un pupitre**

dessert **un dessert**

detail **un détail**

detective **un détective**

to detest **détester**

dictionary **un dictionnaire**

to die **mourir**; *past part.,* **mort**

diet **un régime**; on a diet/**au régime**

difficult **difficile**

to dine **dîner**

dining room **une salle à manger**

dinner **le dîner**

dirty **sale**

disk (record) **un disque**

disgusting **dégoûtant, dégoûtante**

dish **un plat, une assiette**

to disobey **désobéir (à)**

to dispose **disposer**

distinctly **distinctement**

to disturb **déranger**

to do **faire**

to do gymnastics **faire de la gymnastique**

doctor **un docteur, un médecin, une femme docteur, une femme médecin**

dog **un chien, une chienne**

door **une porte**

doubt **un doute**; to doubt/**douter, se douter**

dream **un rêve**; to dream/**rêver**

dress **une robe**; to dress/**s'habiller**

drink **un boisson**; to drink/**boire**; *past part.,* **bu**

drug store **une pharmacie**
druggist **un pharmacien,
une pharmacienne**
drum **un tambour**
dry **sec, sèche**
dumb **bête**; a dumb (stupid,
foolish) thing/**une bêtise**
during **pendant**

E

each **chaque**; each one
chacun, chacune
ear **une oreille**
early **de bonne heure, tôt**
easily **facilement**
easy **facile**
to eat **manger**
egg **un oeuf**; soft-boiled
egg/**un oeuf à la coque**
eight **huit**
to employ **employer**
to end **finir, terminer**; the
end/**la fin**
English (language)
l'anglais, n. m. He is
English, She is English/**Il
est Anglais, Elle est
Anglaise**
English Channel **La Manche**
to enjoy oneself **s'amuser**
enjoyable **amusant,
amusante**
to enter (in, into) **entrer
(dans)**
entrance **une entrée**
to erase **effacer**
error **une faute, une erreur**
to escape **échapper,
s'échapper**
evening **le soir**; in the
evening/**le soir**; this
evening, tonight/**ce soir**;
every evening/**tous les
soirs**
evening party **une soirée**
everybody **tout le monde**
everything **tout, toutes les
choses**
everywhere **partout**
exactly **exactement**
to examine **examiner**
to exclaim **exclamer,
s'exclamer**
to excuse **excuser,
s'excuser**

exhibit **une exposition**
to expect **attendre**
to explain **expliquer**
extraordinary **extraordinaire**
extremely **extrêmement**
eye **un oeil**; eyes/**les yeux**
eye glasses **les lunettes**, f.
eyelid **la paupière**

F

face **le visage, la figure**
to fall **tomber**
false **faux, fausse**
family **la famille**
far **loin**
farewell **adieu**
farm **la ferme**
fast **vite, rapidement**
father **le père**
favorite **favori, favorite**
fear **la peur**; to have fear, to
be afraid/**avoir peur**
feast **la fête**
feel hungry **avoir faim**
fifteen **quinze**
to fill **remplir**
film **le film**
finally **enfin**
to find **trouver**
finger **le doigt**
to finish **finir, terminer**
fire **le feu**
first **premier, première**; at
first/**d'abord**
fish **le poisson**
flag **le drapeau**
flea **la puce**; flea market/**le
marché aux puces**
floor **le plancher**; floor (of a
building designated by a
number)/**un étage**;
ground floor/**le rez de
chaussée**; the first floor/**le
premier étage**
florist **le, la fleuriste**
flour **la farine**
flower **la fleur**
fly (insect) **la mouche**
to fly **voler**
to follow **suivre**
food **la nourriture,
l'aliment,** m.,
l'alimentation, f.
foolish **bête**; a foolish
thing/**une bêtise**

foot **le pied**
football **un ballon; jouer au
football**/to play soccer
for **pour**
to forbid **défendre**
to forget **oublier**
fork **la fourchette**
fourteen **quatorze**
franc **un franc** (6 francs
equal about $1)
French (language) **le
français**; He is French,
She is French/**Il est
Français, Elle est
Française**
French fries **les pommes
frites,** f.
fresh **frais, fraîche**
friend **un ami, une amie**
friendship **une amitié**
from **de**
to fulfill **remplir**
funny **drôle**
furious **furieux, furieuse**
furniture **le meuble**

G

game **le match**
garage **le garage**
garbage **les ordures,** f.
garden **le jardin**
garlic **l'ail,** m.
gasoline **l'essence,** f.
generally **généralement**
generous **généreux,
généreuse**
genius **un génie**
gentleman **le monsieur; les
messieurs,** pl.
geography **la géographie**
German (language)
l'allemand, m.
to get angry **se fâcher**
to get away **échapper,
s'échapper**
to get dressed **s'habiller**
girl **la jeune fille**
to give **donner**
to give back **rendre**
glass (drinking) **un verre**
glove **le gant**
to go **aller**
to go away **partir, s'en aller**
to go back **retourner**
to go by **passer**

to go down **descendre**
to go for a walk **se promener**
to go in (into) **entrer dans**
to go out **sortir**
to go through **traverser**
to go to bed **se coucher**; go to bed!/**va te coucher! allez vous coucher!**
goalie **le gardien de but, la gardienne de but**
God **le Dieu**
good **bon, bonne**
good afternoon, good day, good morning **bonjour**
good-bye **au revoir**
good evening, good night **bonsoir**
good luck **bonne chance**
grape **le raisin** (raisin/**le raisin sec**)
grapefruit **le pamplemousse**
Great Britain **la Grande Bretagne**
green **vert, verte**
grocer **un épicier, une épicière**
grocery store **une épicerie**
group **un groupe**
to guard **garder**
guard **un gardien, une gardienne**

H

hair **les cheveux**, m.
hairdresser **le coiffeur, la coiffeuse**
half **demi, demie**
ham **le jambon**
hand **la main**
handkerchief **le mouchoir**
handsome **bel, beau, beaux; un bel homme**/a handsome man
happiness **le bonheur**
happy **heureux, heureuse, joyeux, joyeuse**
to harm **nuire**
harm **le mal**
hat **le chapeau**
to hate **détester**
to have **avoir**
to have a good time **s'amuser**; have a good

time!/**amusez-vous bien!**
have a good trip! **bon voyage!**
have a good return trip! **bon retour!**
to have a meal **prendre un repas**
to have dinner **dîner**
to have lunch **déjeuner**
to have to **devoir**
he **il**
head **la tête**
health **la santé**
to hear **entendre**
heart **le coeur**
hello **bonjour; allô** (used when answering the telephone)
to help **aider**
her as a poss. adj., **son, sa, ses** (**Alice a son livre**/Alice has her book; **Hélène lit sa leçon**/Helen is reading her lesson; **Marie a ses livres**/Mary has her books); as a dir. obj. pron., **la** (**Voyez-vous Marie? Oui, je la vois**/Do you see Mary? Yes, I see her); as obj. of a prep., **elle** (**avec elle**/with her); as an indir. obj. pron., **lui**/to her (**Je lui donne le livre**/I'm giving [to] her the book)
here **ici**
here is, here are **voici** (**Voici Robert!**/Here's Robert!); (**Voici les livres!**/Here are the books!)
herself **se** (**Monique se lave**/Monique is washing herself)
to hide **cacher**
him as a direct obj. pron., **le** (**Je le vois**/I see him); as obj. of a prep., **lui** (**avec lui**/with him); as an indir. obj. pron., **lui**/to him (**Je lui donne le livre**/I'm giving [to] him the book)
himself **se** (**Robert se lave**/Robert is washing himself)
his **son, sa, ses** (**Robert a son livre**/Robert has his book; **Henri lit sa leçon**/Henry is reading his

lesson; **Raymond a ses livres**/Raymond has his books)
to hold **tenir**
holiday **la fête**
homework **le devoir, les devoirs**
honor **l'honneur**, m.
to hope **espérer**
horse **le cheval**
hospital **l'hôpital**, m.
hot **chaud, chaude**
hotel **l'hôtel**, m.
hour **l'heure**, f.
house **la maison**
how **comment**
how many, how much **combien (de)**
human **humain, humaine**
hunger **la faim**; to be hungry/**avoir faim**
to hunt **chasser**
to hurry **se dépêcher**
to hurt **blesser, nuire**; to hurt oneself/**se faire mal, se blesser**
husband **le mari, l'époux**, m.

I

ice **la glace**
ice cream **la glace**; vanilla ice cream/**la glace à la vanille**; chocolate ice cream/**la glace au chocolat**
idea **l'idée**, f.
if **si**
ill **malade**
to illuminate **éclairer**
immediately **tout de suite, immédiatement**
in **dans**
in front of **devant**
in love **amoureux, amoureuse**; in love with/**amoureux de, amoureuse de**
in order (to) **pour**
industrious **diligent, diligente, industrieux, industrieuse**
inhabit **demeurer, habiter**
to injure **blesser**
inside **dedans**

341

instruction **l'enseignement,** *m.*

intermission **l'entracte,** *m.*

Irish **irlandais, irlandaise;** Irish style/**à l'irlandaise**

isn't it? isn't that so? **n'est-ce pas?** *see also* Work Unit 20

it *per. pron. f., as subj.,* **elle** (**elle est ici**); *per. pron. m., as subj.,* **il** (**il est ici**); *as obj. of prep., m.,* **lui** (**avec lui**); *f.,* **elle** (**avec elle**); *dir. obj. pron. f.,* **la** (**Voyez-vous la maison? Oui, je la vois**); *dir. obj. pron. m.,* **le** (**Voyez-vous le garage? Oui, je le vois**)

it is necessary **il faut, il est nécessaire (de)**

it's (it is) **C'est . . .** (**C'est samedi**/It's Saturday)

its **son, sa, ses,** *poss. adj.* (**Le petit chat a son jouet, sa nourriture, et ses rubans**/The little cat has its toy, its food, and its ribbons)

Italian (language) **l'italien,** *m.; as an adj.,* **italien, italienne**

J

jacket **la jaquette**

joyous **joyeux, joyeuse**

juice **le jus**

July **juillet,** *m.*

to jump **sauter**

just as **ainsi que**

K

kangaroo **le kangourou**

to keep **garder**

key **la clef**

kilogram **le kilogramme** (1 kilogram equals about 2.2 lbs.)

kilometer **le kilomètre** (1 kilometer equals about 0.621 miles)

kind **gentil, gentille**

kitchen **la cuisine**

knee **le genou, les genoux**

knife **le couteau, les couteaux**

to know (how) **savoir; Savez-vous lire?**/Do you know how to read? **Savez-vous la leçon?**/Do you know the lesson?

to know (to be acquainted with) **connaître; Connaissez-vous Monique?**/Do you know Monique? **Connaissez-vous Paris?**/Do you know Paris?

L

lady **la dame, les dames;** young lady/**la demoiselle;** *in direct address,* **mesdames, mesdemoiselles**

lamp **la lampe**

language **la langue**

last **dernier, dernière**

late **tard;** later/**plus tard;** to be late/**être en retard**

to laugh **rire;** *past part.,* **ri**

lawyer **un avocat, une (femme) avocate**

leaf **la feuille**

to leap **sauter**

to learn **apprendre**

to leave **partir, quitter, laisser; elle est partie**/she left; **j'ai quitté mes amis à six heures**/I left my friends at six o'clock; **j'ai laissé mon livre à l'école**/I left my book at school; **sortir** (to go out); **elle est sortie sans argent**/she went out without any money

left (as opposed to right) **gauche; à gauche**/on (to) the left

leg **la jambe**

to lend **prêter**

less **moins; au moins**/at least

lesson **la leçon**

let's go! **allons!**

letter **la lettre**

liberty **la liberté**

library **la bibliothèque**

life **la vie**

light **la lumière;** to light/**allumer, éclairer**

to like **aimer bien;** to like better/**aimer mieux, préférer**

line **la ligne**

to listen (to) **écouter;** to listen to music/**écouter la musique**

little (small) *adj.* **petit, petite, petits, petites**

little (not much) *adv.* **peu;** a little/**un peu;** a little sugar/**un peu de sucre**

to live **demeurer, vivre**

living room **le salon**

long *adj.* **long, longue, longs, longues**

to look (at) **regarder;** I'm looking at the sky/**je regarde le ciel**

to look (for) **chercher;** I'm looking for the book/**je cherche le livre**

to lose **perdre**

to love **aimer;** love/**l'amour** *n. m.*

low *adj.* **bas, basse, bas, basses**

luck **la chance;** you're lucky/**vous avez de la chance**

lunch, luncheon **le déjeuner;** to lunch, to have lunch/**déjeuner**

M

magazine **le magazine, la revue**

magnificent *adj.* **magnifique**

mailman **le facteur**

to make **faire**

to make fun of **se moquer de**

mama **la maman**

man **un homme**

many **beaucoup (de);** I have many friends/**J'ai beaucoup d'amis**

map **la carte**

marriage **le mariage**

mathematics **les mathématiques** *n. f.*

may (can) *v.* **pouvoir;** you may come in/**vous pouvez entrer** maybe *adv.* **peut-être**

me *pron.* **me, moi** (when stressed); he knows me/**Il me connaît**; she is talking to me/**elle me parle**; give me the book/**donnez-moi le livre**

meal **le repas**

to mean **vouloir dire**; What do you mean?/**Que voulez-vous dire?**

meat **la viande**

medicine **le médicament**

to meet **rencontrer, faire connaissance, faire la connaissance de**; I met my friend at the movies/**J'ai rencontré mon ami au cinéma**; Today I met a new student/**Aujourd'hui j'ai fait la connaissance d'une nouvelle étudiante**

menu **la carte**

merchant **le marchand, la marchande**

middle **le milieu**; in the middle of/**au milieu de**

midnight **le minuit**

milk **le lait**

mirror **une glace** (hand mirror); **un miroir** (wall mirror)

mistake **une erreur, une faute**

mister **monsieur**

mom **la maman**

money **l'argent** *n. m.*

month **le mois**; in the month of/**au mois de**

moon **la lune**

more **plus**

morning **le matin**; in the morning/**le matin**; I worked all morning/**J'ai travaillé toute la matinée**; every morning/**tous les matins**

mother **la mère**

motor **le moteur**

mouth **la bouche**

movie (film) **le film**; movies (theater)/**le cinéma**

Mr. **Monsieur, M.**

Mrs. **Madame, Mme.**

much **beaucoup (de)**

museum **le musée**

mushroom **un champignon**

music **la musique**

must *v.* **devoir, falloir**; I must work now/**Je dois travailler maintenant**; One must be honest/**Il faut être honnête**; One must not lie/**Il ne faut pas mentir**

my *poss. adj.* **mon, ma, mes**; my book/**mon livre**; my room/**ma chambre**; my friends/**mes amis**

myself *pron.* **me, moi-même**; I wash myself/**Je me lave**; I did it myself/**Je l'ai fait moi-même**

N

name **le nom**

naturally *adv.* **naturellement**

near *adv.* **près (de)**

necessary *adj.* **nécessaire**; it is necessary/**il est nécessaire**

neck **le cou**

necktie **la cravate**

need **le besoin**; to need/**avoir besoin (de)**; I need a pen/**J'ai besoin d'un stylo**

neighbor **le voisin, la voisine**

neighborhood **le voisinage**

neither **ni . . . ni**; I have neither pen nor pencil/**Je n'ai ni stylo ni crayon**

nephew **le neveu**

net **le filet**

never *adv.* **jamais**

new *adj.* **nouveau, nouvel, nouvelle**; a new book/**un nouveau livre**; a new friend (boy)/**un nouvel ami**; a new friend (girl)/**une nouvelle amie**; a (brand) new suit/**un complet neuf**; a (brand) new dress/**une robe neuve**

New Orleans **la Nouvelle-Orléans**

news **la nouvelle, les nouvelles**; good news!/**bonnes nouvelles!**

newspaper **le journal**

next *adj.* **prochain, prochaine**; next time/**la prochaine fois**

next to **à côté de**

nice *adj.* **gentil, gentille**

nine *adj.* **neuf**

no *adv.* **non**

noise **le bruit**

noon **le midi**

nose **le nez, les nez**

not at all **pas du tout**; not far/**pas loin**

notebook **le cahier**

nourishment **la nourriture, l'aliment,** *m.,* **l'alimentation,** *f.*

now *adv.* **maintenant**

O

to obey **obéir (à)**; I obey my mother and father/**J'obéis à ma mère et à mon père**

of *prep.* **de**

of course **bien sûr, mais oui**; of course not!/**mais non!**

to offer **offrir**

office **le bureau**

often *adv.* **souvent**

okay **d'accord**

old *adj.* **ancien, ancienne, vieux, vieil, vieille**

on *prep.* **sur**

once **une fois**; once more/**encore une fois**

one *adj.* **un, une**; one book/**un livre**; one apple/**une pomme**

oneself *refl. pron.* **se**; One washes oneself here/**On se lave ici**

onion **un oignon**

only *adv.* **seulement, ne . . . que**; I have only two francs/**J'ai seulement deux francs; Je n'ai que deux francs**

to open **ouvrir**

opinion **un avis, une opinion**

opposite *adv.* **d'en face**

or *conj.* **ou**

343

orange **une orange**
other **autre**; the
    other/**l'autre**; another/**un
    autre, une autre**
ought to **devoir**
our *poss. adj.* **notre, nos**;
    our house/**notre maison**;
    our book/**notre livre**; our
    books/**nos livres**
outside *adv.* **dehors**
oven **un four**
over *adv.* **par-dessus**; over
    there/**là-bas**
overcoat **le pardessus**
to overcook **faire trop cuire**
to owe **devoir**

P

pain **un mal**
to paint **peindre**
paper **le papier**; sheet of
    paper/**une feuille de
    papier**; newspaper/**le
    journal**; paper airplane/**un
    avion en papier**
park **le parc**
to pass (by) **passer**
past **le passé**
pastry **la pâtisserie**; pastry
    shop/**une pâtisserie**;
    pastry cook/**un pâtissier,
    une pâtissière**
patiently *adv.* **patiemment**
to pay a visit **faire visite**
to pay attention **faire
    attention**
to pay (for) **payer**; I paid for
    the book/**J'ai payé le
    livre**
pea **le pois**; peas/**les petits
    pois**
peace **la paix**
peach **la pêche**
pear **la poire**
pen **le stylo**
pencil **le crayon**
pepper **le poivre**
perfect *adj.* **parfait, parfaite**
perhaps *adv.* **peut-être**
to permit **permettre**
person **une personne**
pharmacist **le pharmacien,
    la pharmacienne**
pharmacy **la pharmacie**
phonorecord **le disque**

picture **le tableau, une
    image**
piece **la pièce**
pin **une épingle**
pineapple **un ananas**
place **un endroit, un lieu**
to place **mettre**
plate **un plat, une assiette**
to play **jouer**; to play (a
    musical instrument)/**jouer
    de**; to play the piano/**jouer
    du piano**; to play (a
    sport)/**jouer à**; to play
    tennis/**jouer au tennis**
player **un joueur, une
    joueuse**
pleasant *adj.* **agréable**
please **s'il vous plaît** (polite
    form); **s'il te plaît** (familiar
    form)
to please **plaire (à)**
pocket **la poche**
poem **le poème**
poet **un poète, une
    poétesse**
policeman **un agent de
    police**
poor *adj.* **pauvre**
postman **le facteur**
potato **une pomme de terre**
pound **une livre**
to prefer **préférer, aimer
    mieux**
to prepare **préparer**; to
    prepare oneself/**se
    préparer**
present (gift) **un cadeau**;
    the present (time)/**le
    présent**
pretty *adj.* **joli, jolie**
priest **un prêtre**;
    priestess/**une prêtresse**
principal **un directeur, une
    directrice**
probably *adv.*
    probablement
to profit **profiter**; to take
    advantage of the
    moment/**profiter du
    moment**
promise **une promesse**; to
    promise/**promettre**
to pull (away), to pull
    (out) **arracher**
to punish **punir**
pupil **un élève, une élève**
purchase **un achat, une
    emplette**; to

purchase/**acheter**
to put **mettre**; to put
    on/**mettre**

Q

quality **la qualité**
quick *adj.* **rapide**
quickly *adv.* **vite,
    rapidement**

R

R.S.V.P. **R**épondez, **s**'il **v**ous
    plaît/Reply, please (please
    reply)
rabbit **le lapin**
rain **la pluie**; to rain/
    pleuvoir; it's raining/
    il pleut
rainbow **un arc-en-ciel**
to read **lire**
real *adj.* **vrai, vraie**
really *adv.* **vraiment**
to receive **recevoir**
record, recording **le disque**
red *adj.* **rouge**
to regret **regretter**
to relate **raconter**; to tell, to
    relate a story/**raconter
    une histoire**
religious *adj.* **religieux,
    religieuse**
to remain **rester, demeurer**
to remember **se rappeler,
    se souvenir (de)**
to remove **enlever**
to repair **réparer**; to have
    something repaired/**faire
    réparer quelque chose**
to repeat **répéter**
reply **la réponse**; to
    reply/**répondre (à)**
to request **demander, prier**
to reside **demeurer**
to respond **répondre (à)**
to return **retourner, revenir**;
    to return (home)/**rentrer**;
    to return something/
    rendre quelque chose; I
    returned the book to the
    library/**J'ai rendu le livre
    à la bibliothèque**
to reveal **révéler**

ribbon **le ruban**

riddle **une devinette**

to be right **avoir raison;** Janine is right!/**Janine a raison!**

right (*as opposed to left*) **la droite;** on (to) the right/**à droite, à la droite**

to ring **sonner**

ring (*worn on finger*) **une bague**

river **un fleuve**

roast beef **le rosbif**

room **la chambre, la pièce**

to ruin **abîmer**

ruler **une règle**

to run **courir**

S

sad *adj.* **triste, malheureux, malheureuse**

salt **le sel**

same *adj.* **même;** all the same, just the same/**tout de même**

Santa Claus **le Père Noël**

to satisfy **satisfaire**

to say **dire**

school **une école**

season **la saison**

seat **la place;** seated/**assis, assise**

second **une seconde;** Wait a second, please/ **Attendez une seconde, s'il vous plaît;** *adj.,* **deuxième, second(e);** February is the second month of the year/**Février est le deuxième mois de l'année;** the Second Empire/**le Second Empire**

to see **voir;** to see again/**revoir;** see you in a little while!/**à tout à l'heure!** see you soon/**à bientôt**

to seize **saisir**

to send **envoyer**

sentence **la phrase**

serious *adj.* **sérieux, sérieuse, sérieux, sérieuses;** seriously/**sérieusement**

several *adj.* **plusieurs**

shame **la honte**

shark **un requin**

she *per. pron. f.* **elle**

to shine **briller**

shirt **la chemise**

shoe **la chaussure, le soulier**

shoo! shoo! **Ch! Ch!**

shop (small) **une boutique**

short *adj.* **court, courte**

shoulder **une épaule**

to shout **crier**

to show **montrer**

shower **une douche;** to take a shower/**prendre une douche**

sick *adj.* **malade, souffrant, souffrante**

sidewalk **le trottoir**

since **depuis**

to sing **chanter**

singer **un chanteur, une chanteuse**

sister **une soeur**

to sit down **s'asseoir;** sit down!/**assieds-toi!** *or* **asseyez-vous!** (polite form)

sixty *adj.* **soixante**

skin **la peau**

skirt **la jupe**

sky **le ciel**

to sleep **dormir**

sleeve **une manche**

slow *adj.* **lent, lente;** slowly/**lentement**

small *adj.* **petit, petite**

to smell **sentir**

smoke **la fumée;** to smoke/**fumer**

snack bar **un bar rapide**

snow **la neige;** to snow/**neiger;** it is snowing!/**Il neige!**

snowman **un bonhomme de neige**

so *adv.* **alors;** so as to/**de façon à**

soccer (in the U.S.A.) **le football**

socks **les chaussettes,** *n.f.*

soft *adj.* **doux, douce, doux, douces**

soiled *adj.* **sale**

some (partitive) **de l', de la, du, des;** I drink some water/**Je bois de l'eau;** I

eat some meat/**Je mange de la viande;** I drink some milk/**Je bois du lait;** I eat some potatoes/**Je mange des pommes de terre;** some (of it, of them) **en;** I am eating some/**J'en mange;** *see also* pp. 49–50

something *indef. pron.* **quelque chose**

sometimes *adv.* **quelquefois**

son **le fils** (pronounce as *feess*)

soon *adv.* **bientôt**

to be sorry **regretter**

soup **la soupe, le potage**

Spain **l'Espagne,** *n. f.*

Spanish (language) **l'espagnol** *n. m.*

to speak **parler**

speed **la vitesse;** at full speed, quickly/**à toute vitesse**

to spend (time) **passer;** I am spending one week in Paris/**Je passe une semaine à Paris**

spirit **l'esprit,** *n. m.*

to spoil **abîmer**

spoon **une cuiller, une cuillère**

spring (season of the year) **le printemps**

standing *adv.* **debout**

station (bus, train, *etc.*) **une gare**

to stay **demeurer, rester**

to steal **voler**

still *adv.* **toujours, encore**

stocking **le bas**

stomach **l'estomac,** *n. m.*

to stop **arrêter;** to stop (oneself) **s'arrêter;** I am stopping the bus/**J'arrête l'autobus;** I'm stopping to take the bus/**Je m'arrête pour prendre l'autobus**

store **le magasin;** department store/**le grand magasin**

storm **un orage**

story **un conte, une histoire**

strawberry **la fraise**

street **la rue**

strong *adj.* **fort, forte;** the

stongest/**le plus fort, la plus forte**; your strongest quality/**votre qualité la plus forte**

student **un étudiant, une étudiante, un élève, une élève**

to study **étudier**

subway **le métro** (short for **métropolitain**)

to succeed **réussir (à)**

suit **le complet, le costume**

suitcase **la valise**

summer **l'été**, *n. m.*

sun **le soleil**

supermarket **le supermarché**

sure *adj.* **sûr, sûre, certain, certaine**

sweet *adj.* **doux, douce**

to swim **nager**

swim suit **un maillot de bain**

to' swing, to sway **se balancer**; a swing/**une balançoire**

Switzerland **la Suisse**

T

table **la table**

tablecloth **la nappe**

to take **prendre**; to take a walk/**faire une promenade, se promener**; to take advantage of/**profiter (de)**; to take along; to take away/**emporter**; to take off, to remove/**enlever**

to talk **parler**

taste **le goût**; to taste/**goûter**; taste some!/**goûtez-en!**

to teach **enseigner**

teacher **un maître, une maîtresse, un professeur, un professeur-dame, une femme professeur**

team **une équipe**

to tear **déchirer**

television **la télévision, la télé, la TV, la T.V.**; on

television/**à la télévision**; television set/**le téléviseur**

to tell **dire**

ten *adj.* **dix**

tense (verb) **le temps**; present indicative/**le présent à l'indicatif**

to terminate **terminer, finir**

terrific *adj.* **formidable**

than *conj.* **que**; She is taller than her sister/**Elle est plus grande que sa soeur**

to thank **remercier**; thank you/**Je vous remercie** *or* **merci**

that   I know *that* you are right/**Je sais que vous avez raison**; The book *that* is on the table is mine/**Le livre** *qui* **est sur la table est à moi**; that book/**ce livre-là**; that tree/**cet arbre-là**; that lady/**cette dame-là**; *That* is not important/*Cela* **n'est pas important**

that's right! **c'est ça!**

the *def. art.* **l', le, la, les**; the tree/**l'arbre**; the man/**l'homme**; the boy/**le garçon**; the girl/**la jeune fille**; the children/**les enfants**

theater **le théâtre**

their *poss. adj.* **leur, leurs**; their house/**leur maison**; their houses/**leurs maisons**

them *dir. obj. pron.* **les**; I like them/**Je les aime**; *as obj. of a prep.*, for them/**pour elles** (*fem.*), for them/**pour eux** (*masc.*)

themselves *refl. pron.* **se**; They wash themselves every morning/**Ils se lavent tous les matins**

then *adv.* **puis, alors**

there *adv. of place; advl. pron.* **y**; Janine va à l'école/Janine is going to school; She is going there/**Elle y va**; Où est Janine?/Where is Janine? She's there/**Elle est là**; there is, there are/**il y a**; There is a fly in the soup/**Il**

y a une mouche dans la soupe; There are many flowers in the garden/**Il y a beaucoup de fleurs dans le jardin**; there isn't, there aren't/**il n'y a pas**; There's Paul!/**Voilà Paul!**

these *dem. adj.* **ces**; these boys/**ces garçons**; these girls/**ces jeunes filles**

they *per. pron.* **ils, elles**

thick *adj.* **épais, épaisse**

thing **une chose**

third *adj.* **troisième**

thirst **la soif**; to be thirsty/**avoir soif**; I'm thirsty/**J'ai soif**

this *dem. adj.* **ce, cet, cette**; this boy/**ce garçon**; this tree/**cet arbre**; this girl/**cette jeune fille**; *dem. pron.*, **ceci**; this is true/**ceci est vrai**

those *dem. adj.* **ces**; those boys/**ces garçons-là**; those girls/**ces jeunes filles-là**

three *adj.* **trois**

through *prep.* **par, à travers**

to throw **jeter, lancer**

ticket **le billet**

time (hour, time of day) **l'heure**, *n. f.*; What time is it?/**Quelle heure est-il?**

time (duration) **le temps**; Paul spent a lot of time in France/**Paul a passé beaucoup de temps en France**

time (different instances) **la fois**; one time, once/**une fois**; two times, twice/**deux fois**; many times/**beaucoup de fois**; next time/**la prochaine fois**

tired *adj.* **fatigué, fatiguée**

to *prep.* **à**

toast **le pain grillé**

today *adv.* **aujourd'hui**

together *adv.* **ensemble**

tomato **la tomate**

tomorrow *adv.* **demain**

tongue **la langue**

tonight **ce soir**

too **aussi, trop (de)**; Rober is coming too/**Robert vient aussi**; Janine works too much/**Janine travaille trop**; There is too much noise here/**Il y a trop de bruit ici**; There are too many people here/**Il y a trop de personnes ici**

tooth **la dent**

town **la ville**

toy **le jouet**

traffic light **le feu**; red traffic light/**le feu rouge**; green traffic light/**le feu vert**

tree **un arbre**

trip **un voyage**; to take a trip/**faire un voyage**

truck **le camion**; truck driver/**le camionneur**

true *adj.* **vrai, vraie**

truly *adv.* **vraiment**

to try **essayer (de)**

to turn on (light) **allumer**

twentieth *adj.* **vingtième**

twenty *adj.* **vingt**

two *adj.* **deux**

U

umbrella **le parapluie**

unbelievable *adj.* **incroyable**

uncle **un oncle**

under *prep.* **sous**; underneath/**dessous, par-dessous, en dessous**

to understand **comprendre**

undoubtedly *adv.* **sans doute**

unhappy *adj.* **malheureux, malheureuse, triste**

United States **les États-Unis**; to the United States/**aux États-Unis**

until *prep.* **jusque**; until spring/**jusqu'au printemps**

unusual *adj.* **extraordinaire**

upset *adj.* **inquiet, inquiète**

us *per. pron.* **nous**; for us/**pour nous**

to use **employer**

useful *adj.* **utile**

useless *adj.* **inutile**

V

vase **un vase**

vegetable **un légume**

very *adv.* **très**

vest **un gilet**

to visit **faire visite, visiter**; to visit someone/**rendre visite à quelqu'un**

voice **une voix**; in a loud voice/**à haute voix**; in a low voice, softly/**à voix basse**

W

to wait (for) **attendre**

waiter **un garçon (de café, de restaurant)**; (Nowadays, a customer addresses a waiter as *Monsieur*, not *garçon*)

to walk **marcher, aller à pied**

wall **un mur**

to want **vouloir**

to wash **laver**; I washed the car/**J'ai lavé la voiture**; to wash oneself/**se laver**; I washed myself/**Je me suis lavé(e)**

to wash and get dressed **faire la toilette**

to watch **regarder**; to watch television/**regarder la télévision**

water **l'eau**, *n. f.*

way **la façon**; I like your way of talking/**J'aime votre façon de parler**

we *per. pron.* **nous**; We like French/**Nous aimons le français**

weak *adj.* **faible**

to wear **porter**

weather **le temps**; What's the weather like today?/**Quel temps fait-il aujourd'hui?**

week **la semaine**

to weep **pleurer**

well *adv.* **bien**; She works well with her sister/**Elle travaille bien avec sa soeur**

what *What* are you saying?/*Que*

dites-vous? *What* am I?/*Que* **suis-je?** or *Qu'est-ce que je suis?* *What* you are saying is right/*Ce que* **vous dites est juste**; *What* is on the table is mine/*Ce qui* **est sur la table est à moi**; *what* book?/*quel* **livre?** *what* books?/*quels* **livres?** *what* house?/*quelle* **maison?** *what* houses?/*quelles* **maisons?** *What* time is it?/*Quelle* **heure est-il?** *What?!*/**Quoi?!** *What is it?*/*Qu'est est-ce que* **c'est?** What's new?/**Quoi de neuf?** ·*What* is the date today?/*Quelle* **est la date aujourd'hui?** *What* day is it today?/*Quel* **jour est-ce aujourd'hui?** *What* color is your house?/*De quelle* **couleur est votre maison?**

wheel **la roue**

when *adv.* **quand**

where *adv.* **où**

which *pron.* The book *which* is on the table is mine/*Le* **livre** *qui* **est sur la table est à moi**; *as an adj.*, **quel, quelle, quels, quelles**; which boy?/**quel garçon?** which books?/**quels livres?** which girl?/**quelle jeune fille?** which colors?/**quelles couleurs?**

while *conj.* **pendant que**

white *adj.* **blanc, blanche**

who *pron.* **qui**; Who are you?/**Qui êtes-vous?**

whom *pron.* **qui, que**; Whom do you see?/**Qui voyez-vous?** with whom/**avec qui** The boy whom you see over there is my brother/**Le garçon que vous voyez là-bas est mon frère**

why **pourquoi**; why not?/**pourquoi pas?**

wife **une femme, une épouse**

to win **gagner**

wind **le vent**; It is windy/**Il fait du vent**

window **une fenêtre**
wine **le vin**
wing **une aile**
winter **l'hiver,** *n. m.;* in winter/**en hiver**
with *prep.* **avec**
without *prep.* **sans**
woman **la femme**
wonderful *adj.* **magnifique, merveilleux, merveilleuse**
woods **le bois, les bois**
word **le mot; la parole** (the spoken word)
work **le travail, l'oeuvre,** *n. f.;* a work of art/**une oeuvre d'art**
to work **travailler**
world **le monde**
to worry **s'inquiéter;** Don't worry!/**Ne vous inquiétez pas!** *or* **Ne t'inquiète pas!**
to write **écrire**
writer **un écrivain, une femme écrivain**
wrong **un tort;** to be wrong/**avoir tort;** You are wrong/**Vous avez tort**

Y

year **un an, une année**
yellow *adj.* **jaune**
yes *adv.* **oui**
yesterday *adv.* **hier**
you *pron.* Where are you going?/**Où vas-tu? Où allez-vous?** with you/**avec toi, avec vous;** I am giving this book to you/**Je te donne ce livre, Je vous donne ce livre**
young *adj.* **jeune**
your *poss. adj.* **ton, ta, tes, votre, vos;** your book/**ton livre, votre livre;** your mother/**ta mère, votre mère;** your books/**tes livres, vos livres**
you're welcome **de rien, il n'y a pas de quoi**
yourself *refl. pron.* **te, vous;** You wash yourself every morning, don't you?/**Tu te laves tous les matins, n'est-ce pas? Vous vous lavez tous les matins, n'est-ce pas?**

Z

zodiac **le zodiaque**

Answer Key

Leçons Préliminaires

I. La famille Paquet: Présentation (The Paquet family: Presentation)

Exercises, p. 2
I. 1. le père, une bonne épouse. 2. suis, mère, ai, bon. 3. suis, une soeur. 4. la fille, bon. 5. suis le. J'ai, famille.
II. 3, 4, 1, 5, 2. **III.** 3, 5, 2, 1, 4.

Exercises, p. 3
IV. 3, 4, 5, 1, 2. **V.** 1. Janine. 2. Claire Paquet. 3. François Paquet. 4. Coco. 5. Pierre. **VI.** 1. la fille. 2. le frère. 3. la mère. 4. le chien. 5. le père.

II. Choses (Things)

Exercises, p. 4
I. 1. grand. 2. rond. 3. bonne. 4. petite. **II.** 1. petite. 2. bonne. 3. rond. 4. grand. **III.** 4, 3, 1, 2.

Exercises, p. 5
I. 1. joli. 2. belle. 3. long. 4. jolie. **II.** 3, 1, 4, 2. **III.** 1. joli. 2. belle. 3. long. 4. jolie.

Exercises, p. 6
I. 1. grand. 2. délicieux. 3. beau. 4. intéressant. **II.** 1. grand. 2. délicieux. 3. beau. 4. intéressant. **III.** 1. c'est un garage. est 2. n'est pas. un. 3. c'est. beau. 4. c'est. est.

Exercises, p. 7
I. 1. confortable. 2. splendide. 3. charmante. 4. blanc. **II.** 4, 3, 1, 2.

Exercises, p. 8
I. 1. ouvert. 2. magnifique. 3. mignonne. 4. délicieux. **II.** 1. un parapluie, est. 2. n'est pas, est. 3. ce n'est pas, une. 4. un, délicieux.

Exercises, p. 9
I. 1. long. 2. noir. 3. beau. **II.** 4, 5, 1, 6, 2, 3.

III. Personnes (People)

Exercises, p. 10
I. 1. boit, lait. 2. danse. 3. un livre. 4. courent. **II.** 1. le garçon boit du lait. 2. La jeune fille danse. 3. Le garçon lit un livre (possibly: Un garçon lit le livre). 4. La jeune fille et le garçon courent (possibly: Le garçon et la jeune fille courent).

Exercises, p. 11
I. 1. chante. 2. écrit. 3. arrête, autos. **II.** 1. (b). 2. (a). 3. (c).

IV. L'École: la salle de classe (The School: the classroom)

Exercises, p. 12
I. Column B: 1. Madame Duval est derrière le bureau. 2. Il est une heure. 3. Il y a une carte de France sur le mur. 4. Le garçon lit un livre. 5. La jeune fille écrit une composition. 6. Le garçon est debout. 7. La jeune fille lève la main.

Exercises p. 13
II. 1. Non, madame (mademoiselle, monsieur), ce n'est pas le stylo. C'est le crayon. 2. Non, madame (mademoiselle, monsieur), ce n'est pas la feuille de papier. C'est le livre. 3. Non, madame (mademoiselle, monsieur), ce n'est pas le globe. C'est l'horloge. 4. Non, madame (mademoiselle, monsieur), ce n'est pas un élève. C'est une élève. 5. Non, madame (mademoiselle, monsieur), ce n'est pas la chaise. C'est le banc. 6. Non, madame (mademoiselle, monsieur), ce n'est pas une élève. C'est un élève.

V. La Maison: la salle à manger (The House: the dining room)

Exercises, pp. 14–15
I. 1. C'est une fleur. 2. C'est une assiette. 3. C'est une tasse. 4. C'est une cuiller (or: cuillère). 5. C'est un verre. 6. C'est un couteau. **II.** 1. UNE CHAISE. 2. UNE ASSIETTE. 3. UN TAPIS. 4. UNE FOURCHETTE. 5. UN COUTEAU. 6. UNE NAPPE. 7. UN VERRE. 8. UNE TASSE. 9. UNE CUILLER. 10. UNE FLEUR.

VI. La Ville: dans la rue (The City: in the street)

Exercises, pp. 16–17
I. 1. C'est une dame. 2. C'est un homme. 3. C'est une petite fille. 4. C'est un garçon. 5. C'est un agent de police. 6. C'est une voiture. 7. C'est un immeuble. 8. C'est un autobus. **II.** 1. UNE VALISE. 2. UN PETIT CHIEN. 3. LE TROTTOIR. 4. LE MÉTRO.

STRUCTURES AND VERBS

Work Unit 1

Exercises, pp. 22–23
I. 1. (c). 2. (d). 3. (d). 4. (b). 5. (d). **II.** 1. Janine cherche dans la commode. 2. Madame Paquet cherche dans l'armoire. 3. Monsieur Paquet cherche sous la chaise. **III.** 1. Madame Paquet est la mère. 2. Janine est la fille (possibly: la soeur). 3. Pierre est le fils (possibly: le frère). 4. Coco est le chien (possibly: le petit chien).

IV. Un acrostiche

Exercises, p. 25
I. 1. le. 2. la. 3. le. 4. la. 5. l'. 6. l'. 7. le. 8. le. 9. l'. 10. la. 11. le. 12. l' 13. le. 14. la. 15. l'.

II. Word Hunt

1. the woman	
2. the man	
3. the boy	
4. the girl	
5. the sister	
6. the tree	
7. the child	
8. the brother	
9. the book	
10. the mother	

Exercises, p. 26

III. A. 1. le père est là-bas. 2. La mère est là-bas. 3. Le garçon est là-bas. 4. La jeune fille est là-bas. 5. L'ami est là-bas. **B.** 1. La femme parle beaucoup. 2. L'homme parle beaucoup. 3. Le frère parle beaucoup. 4. La soeur parle beaucoup. 5. La famille parle beaucoup.

Exercises, p. 27

C. 1. La table est ici. 2. Le chapeau est ici. 3. La maison est ici. 4. L'arbre est ici. 5. Le café est ici. **IV.** 1. Le chapeau est dans la cuisine. 2. Le chapeau est dans l'armoire. 3. Le chapeau est dans la maison. 4. Le chapeau est dans la commode. 5. Le chapeau est dans le garage.

Exercises, p. 28

I. 1. un. 2. une. 3. un. 4. un. 5. une. 6. un. 7. un café. 8. un chat. 9. une chatte. 10. un nom. 11. un arbre. 12. une. 13. une. 14. une. 15. un.

II. Word Hunt

Exercises, pp. 29–31

III. A. 1. Un homme cherche dans l'armoire. 2. Un garçon cherche dans l'armoire. 3. Un fils cherche dans l'armoire. 4. Une mère cherche dans l'armoire. 5. Un père cherche dans l'armoire. **B.** 1. Une femme mange dans la cuisine. 2. Une jeune fille mange dans la cuisine. 3. Un ami mange dans la cuisine. 4. Un chien mange dans la cuisine. 5. Une fille mange dans la cuisine. **C.** 1. Un homme quitte la chambre. 2. Une mère quitte la chambre. 3. Un père quitte la chambre. 4. Un garçon quitte la chambre. 5. Une jeune fille quitte la chambre. **IV.** 1. Monsieur Paquet cherche son chapeau. 2. Le chien est sous la commode. 3. Nous cherchons partout. 4. Je vais en ville acheter un nouveau chapeau. 5. Coco mange le chapeau. **V.** 1. le. 2. la. 3. la. 4. l'. 5. la. 6. le. 7. le. 8. le. 9. un. 10. une. **VI.** Je cherche mon livre. Je cherche partout—sous le lit, sous la chaise, et sur la table. Où est-il? Cherchons dans le salon.

Work Unit 2

Exercises, pp. 34–35

I. 1. (d). 2. (c). 3. (a). 4. (d). 5. (a). **II.** 1. oui. 2. non. 3. oui. 4. oui. 5. oui.

III. Mots croisés

IV. Un acrostiche, p.36

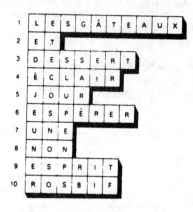

Exercises, p. 38

I. 1. les garçons. 2. les fils. 3. les chapeaux. 4. les journaux. 5. les cieux. 6. les yeux. 7. les pères. 8. les voix. 9. les mères. 10. les chats. **II.** 1. la table. 2. le nez. 3. le genou. 4. la voix. 5. l'oeil. 6. le monsieur. 7. l'homme. 8. la jeune fille. 9. l'enfant. 10. l'arbre. **III.** 1. le père. 2. l'homme. 3. les eaux. 4. les fils. 5. les tables. 6. le journal. 7. les chevaux. 8. les oiseaux. 9. l'élève. 10. les pays.

Exercises, p. 41

I. 7, 8, 5, 3, 6, 2, 1, 4. **II.** 1. au. 2. à la. 3. aux. 4. à l'. **III.** 1. du. 2. de l'. 3. de la. 4. des.

Exercises, p. 42–43

I. 4, 6, 7, 2, 10, 9, 8, 3, 5, 1. **II.** 1. des. 2. de la. 3. de. 4. du. 5. de l'. 6. de l'. 7. de. 8. du. 9. de l'. 10. de la. **III. A.** Je voudrais avoir le jambon et le poulet. J'aime aussi le veau et la saucisse. Aussi, j'adore le gâteau et la glace. Voulez-vous apporter la viande ou les desserts? **B.** Pour moi, c'est bon pour la santé. Je n'aime pas le café. J'aime mieux l'eau minérale.

Work Unit 3

Exercises, p. 46

I. 1. (d). 2. (d). 3. (c). **II.** 1. oui 2. non. 3. oui.

III. Word Hunt

D	U	C	A	F	É	D	E	S
U	M	O	N	S	I	E	U	R
P	D	U	O	D	E	L	A	O
O	C	A	U	J	A	I	M	E
I	D	C	S	P	O	I	D	U
S	E	L	A	V	O	S	N	E
S	L	A	V	I	A	N	D	E
O	E	D	O	E	L	A	E	A
N	A	E	N	A	U	E	A	E
D	U	L	S	O	M	O	N	S

Exercises, pp. 48–50

I. 1. Oui, j'ai du pain. 2. Oui, j'ai de la viande. 3. Oui, j'ai de l'eau. 4. Oui, j'ai des bonbons. 5. Oui, j'ai du beurre. **II.** 1. Non, je n'ai pas de café. 2. Non, je n'ai pas de viande. 3. Non, je n'ai pas d'eau. 4. Non, je n'ai pas de bonbons. 5. Non, je n'ai pas de beurre. **III.** 1. Oui, j'ai du bon café. 2. Oui, j'ai de jolis chapeaux. 3. Oui, j'ai de jolies jupes. 4. Oui, j'ai du bon vin. 5. Oui, j'ai de jolies cravates. **IV.** 1. Non, je n'ai pas de bon café. 2. Non, je n'ai pas de jolis chapeaux. 3. Non, je n'ai pas de jolies jupes. 4. Non, je n'ai pas de bon vin. 5. Non, je n'ai pas de jolies cravates.

Exercises, pp. 50–51

I. 1. Oui, j'ai les mains sales. 2. Oui, j'ai le visage sale. 3. Oui, j'ai les pieds grands. 4. Oui, j'ai les yeux bruns. 5. Oui, j'ai les cheveux noirs. **II.** 1. Non, je n'ai pas les pieds grands. 2. Non, je n'ai pas le visage sale. 3. Non, je n'ai pas les mains sales. 4. Non, je n'ai pas le chapeau sur la tête. 5. Non, je n'ai pas les cheveux noirs.

Exercises, p. 52

I. 1. Oui, je vais à l'école les matins. 2. Oui, je vais à la bibliothèque les après-midi (Note: The French Academy writes *après-midi* with no *s* in the plural; but with *s* is acceptable.) 3. Oui, je vais au restaurant les soirs. 4. Oui, je vais au parc les après-midi. 5. Oui, je vais au café les soirs. **II.** 1. Non, je ne vais pas au cinéma les soirs. 2. Non, je ne vais pas à l'école les matins. 3. Non, je ne vais pas à la bibliothèque les soirs.

Exercises, pp. 53–55

I. 1. Il parle français. Il prononce bien le français. 2. Elle parle espagnol. Elle prononce bien l'espagnol. 3. Elle parle italien. Elle prononce bien l'italien. 4. Il parle anglais. Il prononce bien l'anglais. 5. Elle parle allemand. Elle prononce bien l'allemand. **II.** 1. Oui, j'ai cent dollars. 2. Oui, j'ai mille francs. 3. Oui, j'ai cent livres. 4. Oui, j'ai mille amis. **III.** 1. —. 2. l'. 3. —. 4. —. 5. la. 6. le. 7. les. 8. les. **IV.** 1. J'ai les sandwichs. 2. J'ai les éclairs. 3. J'ai la saucisse. 4. J'ai des dollars. 5. J'ai une jupe. 6. J'ai les chapeaux. 7. J'ai le dessert. 8. J'ai un gâteau.

V. Jeu de mots

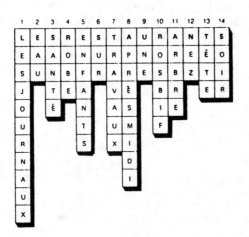

VI. A. Je voudrais du poisson. Je voudrais, aussi, de la viande. Comme dessert, je voudrais du gâteau et de la glace. **B.** C'est l'anniversaire de mon ami. Avez-vous un beau gâteau? Je desire un grand gâteau pour tous nos amis.

Work Unit 4

Exercises, p. 58

I. 1. Janine et Pierre allument le téléviseur. 2. La mère et le père entrent dans le salon. 3. Pierre et Janine regardent dans les journaux. **II.** 1. oui. 2. non. 3. oui. 4. non. 5. oui. **III.** 1. (b). 2. (c). 3. (b). **IV.** allument, marche, entrent, exclament, marche, regardez, demandent, mère, père.

Exercises, pp. 64–67

I. (a) 5, 3, 1, 2, 4. (b) 4, 5, 1, 2, 3. **II.** 1. Elle. 2. Il. 3. Elles. 4. Ils. 5. Ils. **III.** 1. Tu danses beaucoup. 2. Il danse beaucoup. 3. Elle danse beaucoup. 4. Vous dansez beaucoup. 5. Ils dansent beaucoup. 6. Elles dansent beaucoup. **IV.** 1. Je ne danse pas. 2. Tu ne danses pas. 3. Il ne danse pas. 4. Vous ne dansez pas. 5. Ils ne dansent pas. 6. Elles ne dansent pas. **V.** 1. Oui, je danse les matins; il danse aussi. 2. Oui, il cherche le chapeau; elle cherche le chapeau aussi. 3. Oui, elle étudie la leçon; j'étudie la leçon aussi. **VI.** 1. Non, je ne danse pas; il ne danse pas non plus. 2. Non, il n'étudie pas; elle n'étudie pas non plus. 3. Non, il ne cherche pas la balle; ils ne cherchent pas la balle non plus. 4. Non, elle n'écoute pas la musique; je n'écoute pas la musique non plus. 5. Non, je ne ferme pas la fenêtre; vous ne fermez pas la fenêtre non plus (possibly: nous ne fermons pas la fenêtre non plus). **VII.** 1. Je ferme. 2. Tu apportes. 3. Il étudie. 4. Elle parle. 5. Nous marchons. 6. Vous donnez. 7. Ils jouent. 8. Elles chantent. 9. Vous cherchez. 10. J'aime.

VIII. Word Search

IX. 1. Je ne parle pas. 2. Tu ne chantes pas. 3. Il n'écoute pas. 4. Elle n'oublie pas. 5. Nous ne jouons pas. 6. Vous ne désirez pas. **X. A.** Nous préférons regarder Le Tour de France à la télé. C'est notre programme favori. Nous aimons regarder les cyclistes. Papa aime tous les sports. **B.** Je préfère aller danser. J'aime beaucoup danser. J'aime la musique. Mais je n'aime pas aller au concert.

Work Unit 5

Exercises, pp. 70–71

I. 1. (c) 2. (d). 3. (c). **II.** 1. non. 2. oui. 3. oui. 4. non. 5. oui. 6. oui. **III.** 1. choisit. 2. rougit. 3. finit. 4. finissent. 5. retentit.

Exercises, pp. 72–76

I. (a) 4, 1, 2, 3. (b) 3, 4, 2, 1. **II.** 1. Il. . . 2. Elle. . . 3. Elle. . . 4. Ils. 6. Elles. . . **III.** 1. Ils finissent la leçon. 2. Tu finis la leçon. 3. Il finit la leçon. 4. Elle finit la leçon. 5. Vous finissez la leçon. 6. Elles finissent la leçon. **IV.** 1. Vous ne finissez pas le dîner. 2. Il ne finit pas le dîner. 3. Tu ne finis pas le dîner. 4. Elles ne finissent pas le dîner. 5. Ils ne finissent pas le dîner. 6. Nous ne finissons pas le dîner. **V.** 1. Oui, il finit le livre; je finis le livre aussi. 2. Oui, ils punissent les mauvais élèves; il punit les mauvais élèves aussi. 3. Oui, il choisit une nouvelle automobile; ils choisissent une nouvelle automobile aussi. 4. Oui, il obéit au garçon; ils obéissent au garçon aussi. 5. Oui, je finis la leçon aujourd'hui; elle finit la leçon aujourd'hui aussi. **VI.** 1. Non, il ne désobéit pas; je ne désobéis pas non plus (possibly: nous ne désobéissons pas non plus). 2. Non, je ne finis pas la leçon; il ne finit pas la leçon non plus. 3. Non, il ne choisit pas une auto; elle ne choisit pas une auto non plus. 4. Non, nous ne bâtissons pas une maison; ils ne bâtissent pas une maison non plus. 5. Non, je ne rougis pas (possibly: Non, nous ne rougissons pas); elles ne rougissent pas non plus. **VII.** 1. Je finis la leçon. 2. Tu saisis la balle. 3. Il accomplit les devoirs. 4. Elle bâtit une maison. 5. Nous choisissons un dessert. 6. Vous punissez le chien. 7. Ils rougissent facilement. 8. Elles désobéissent à leurs parents. 9. Je remplis le vase. 10. Vous finissez les devoirs.

VIII. Word Search

IX. A. Je ne finis pas le devoir parce que l'exercice est très difficile. La leçon est difficile aussi. Je ne comprends rien. **B.** Monsieur Berty nous donne les leçons difficiles. Il veut punir les élèves parce qu'ils parlent trop en classe. Les exercices ne sont pas faciles!

Review Test: Work Units 1-5

Exercises, pp. 77–79
I. 1. la. 2. le. 3. l'. 4. les. 5. l' 6. les. **II.** 1. une. 2. un. 3. une. 4. une. 5. un. 6. une. **III.** 1. les mères. 2. les journaux. 3. les voix. 4. les messieurs. 5. les yeux. 6. les fils. **IV.** 1. la table. 2. les eaux. 3. le nez. 4. les genoux. 5. le journal. 6. les pays. **V.** 1. au. 2. à l'. 3. à la. 4. aux. 5. à l'. 6. à la. **VI.** 4, 1, 5, 3, 2. **VII.** 1. J'ai du café. 2. J'ai de la viande. 3. Je n'ai pas de café. 4. Je n'ai pas de bonbons. **VIII.** 1. E, S, C, L, E, I, S. 2. I, E, N, E. 3. O, S, R, A, N, I. **IX.** 1. Est-ce que vous parlez français?. 2. Est-ce que Jacqueline regarde la télévision? 3. Est-ce qu'ils étudient la leçon? **X.** 1. Odette et Yvette chantent-elles bien? 2. Robert et Pierre jouent-ils à la balle? 3. Regardez-vous trop de télévision? **XI.** 1. J'aime la glace au chocolat. 2. Vous donnez des fleurs à la dame. 3. Je ferme la porte. 4. Michelle choisit une jolie robe. 5. Vous finissez les devoirs. 6. Nous bâtissons une maison.

Work Unit 6

Exercises, pp. 82–83
I. 1. oui. 2. non. 3. oui. 4. oui. 5. oui. **II.** 1. vendez. 2. vends, dix. 3. vraiment. 4. joli. **III.** 1. Je vends ce vase pour di x francs. 2. La marchande vend beaucoup de vases. 3. Après un moment, la femme ajoute.

Exercises, pp. 85–89
I. 1. Il défend sa patrie. 2. Elle vend des vases. 3. Ils entendent la musique. 4. Ils vendent leur maison. 5. Il rompt la petite barrière. **II.** 1. Elle vend des livres. 2. Tu vends des livres. 3. Vous et moi (nous) vendons des livres. 3. Ils vendent des livres. 5. Vous vendez des livres. 6. Elles vendent des livres. **III.** 1. Nous ne vendons pas la voiture. 2. Je ne vends pas la voiture. 3. Tu ne vends pas la voiture. 4. Il ne vend pas la voiture. 5. Elles ne vendent pas la voiture. 6. Ils ne vendent pas la voiture. **IV.** 1. Oui, il répond à la lettre; je réponds à la lettre aussi (possibly: nous répondons à la lettre aussi). 2. Oui, il vend la maison; il vend la maison aussi. 3. Oui, il défend la patrie; je défends la patrie aussi (possibly: nous défendons la patrie aussi). 4. Oui, il est joli; il est joli aussi. 5. Oui, elle est au marché aux puces; elle est au marché aux puces aussi. **V.** 1. Janine étudie-t-elle dans la bibliothèque? 2. Cherche-t-elle le chapeau? 3. Finit-il la leçon? 4. Choisit-elle une jolie robe? 5. Répondons-nous à la lettre? 6. Vendent-ils la maison? **VI.** Elles attendent. 2. Nous vendons. 3. Je danse. 4. Ils écoutent. 5. Vous finissez. 6. Il répond. **VII.** 1. Est-ce qu'elle finit le livre? 2. Est-ce que Monsieur Berty vend la voiture? 3. Est-ce qu'elle choisit un joli chapeau? 4. Est-ce qu'il défend la patrie? 5. Est-ce qu'Hélène ouvre la boîte?

VIII.

IX. 1. J'aime. . . 2. Vous chantez. . . 3. Janine étudie. . . 4. Je choisis. . . 5. Ils attendent. . . 6. Je vends. . . 7. Vous choisissez. . . 8. Nous finissons. . . **X.** 1. I dance, I do dance, I am dancing. 2. You finish, you do finish, you are finishing. 3. We sell, we do sell, we are selling.

XI. Word Search

N	N	O	I	L	V	E	N	D	O	U	I	N
I	L	S	P	E	R	D	E	N	T	I	C	I
E	L	L	E	S	I	M	P	O	R	T	A	N
L	U	I	E	L	L	E	A	T	T	E	N	D
E	L	L	E	S	P	E	R	D	E	N	T	O
E	J	E	R	E	N	D	S	A	L	O	R	S
V	O	S	S	E	T	M	O	I	S	O	N	T
N	O	U	S	R	É	P	O	N	D	O	N	S
U	E	A	I	P	N	A	C	E	G	L	I	L
A	E	I	T	U	D	É	F	E	N	D	S	T
V	O	U	S	R	É	P	O	N	D	E	Z	U

XII. J'aimerais aller à la foire. Mon amie Jacqueline va à la foire avec ses parents. Elle dit qu'on vend beaucoup de choses. Je voudrais acheter des cadeaux.

Work Unit 7

Exercises, pp. 92–93

I. 1. Le sport favori de Pierre est le football (possibly: Son sport favori est le football). 2. Il veut être toujours en forme parce qu'il est gardien de but dans son équipe à l'école. 3. Il mange seulement des aliments qui sont bons pour la santé. 4. Il se lève tôt (possibly: Il se lève avec le soleil). 5. Oui, Janine va jouer dans le match aussi. **II.** (Note: These are personal questions and you may answer in any number of ways.) **III.** 1. non. 2. oui. 3. oui. 4. non. 5. oui.

IV. Un acrostiche

1. L E N T E M E N T
2. E V I T E R
3. S E C O U C H E R
4. S E L E V E R
5. P O U R
6. O U
7. R É P O N D R E
8. T A R D
9. S E L A V E R

Exercises, pp. 98–103

I. 1. me. 2. me. 3. t'. 4. se 5. s'. 6. nous. 7. vous. 8. s'. 9. se. 10. se. **II.** 8, 4, 9, 6, 2, 7, 1, 3, 5, 10.

III. Word Search

D	E	I	P	T	E	C	H	E	J
J	E	L	A	U	L	A	V	R	E
D	I	S	D	T	E	J	A	U	M
I	L	S	U	E	L	O	I	N	E
A	S	A	I	L	M	A	N	G	R
J	E	M	H	A	B	I	L	L	E
I	D	U	O	V	E	E	O	A	P
I	É	S	S	E	M	E'	T	S	O
O	P	E	I	S	S	E	L	V	S
J	È	N	A	P	P	E	L	E	E
U	C	T	I	L	S	E	M	E	L
A	H	J	E	I	U	O	I	L	T
J	E	M	E	R	E	G	A	R	E

IV. 1. Je. 2. Tu. 3. Vous. 4. Ils, elles. 5. Il, elle. 6. Nous. 7. Vous. 8. Il, elle. 9. Ils, elles. 10. Je. **V.** 1. Oui, je m'amuse. 2. Oui, je me couche. 3. Oui, je me repose. 4. Oui, je m'habille. 5. Oui, je m'assieds. **VI.** 1. Non, je ne m'amuse pas ici. 2. Non, je ne me couche pas de bonne heure tous les soirs. 3. Non, je ne m'habille pas vite les matins. 4. Non, je ne m'appelle pas Jean-Jacques. 5. Non, je ne m'assieds pas ici. **VII.** 1. Se dépêche-t-il tous les soirs? 2. Je m'endors sur cette chaise. 3. Nous nous levons de bonne heure. 4. Il se lave vite. 5. Je m'amuse tous les jours. **VIII.** 1. Je m'habille dans ma chambre. 2. Ils s'amusent au théâtre les samedis (possibly: Les samedis soirs, ils s'amusent au théâtre). 3. Tu te reposes après le dîner (possibly: Après le dîner, tu te reposes). 4. Je me couche de bonne heure. 5. Nous nous dépêchons pour aller à l'école. 6. Je me lave tous les matins (possibly: Tous les matins, je me lave). **IX.** 1. Est-ce que Robert s'amuse? 2. Est-ce que vous vous endormez vite? 3. Est-ce qu'ils se couchent tard? 4. Est-ce qu'Henri est absent aujourd'hui? 5. Est-ce qu'Alice se dépêche pour aller à l'école? **X.** 1. Se repose-t-elle après le dîner? 2. Vous levez-vous très tard le matin? 3. S'assied-elle devant la porte? 4. Nous dépêchons-nous? 5. Se couchent-ils tard? **XI.** 1. Pierre ne se couche-t-il pas de bonne heure? or: Est-ce que Pierre ne se couche pas de bonne heure? 2. Ne se lave-t-il pas soigneusement? or: Est-ce qu'il ne se lave pas soigneusement? 3. Ne s'habille-t-il pas vite? or: Est-ce qu'il ne s'habille pas vite? 4. Ne se dépêche-t-il pas? or: Est-ce qu'il ne se dépêche pas? 5. Ne se prépare-t-il pas pour jouer au football? or: Est-ce qu'il ne se prépare pas pour jouer au football? **XII.** 1. Je me lave. 2. Vous vous amusez. 3. Il s'endort. 4. Elle s'habille. 5. Nous nous couchons. 6. Tu t'amuses. 7. Ils se servent. 8. Elles s'endorment. 9. Je m'amuse. 10. Madame Paquet se dépêche. **XIII.** 1. Non. C'est ma première visite. 2. Oui. Le voyage est très agréable. Excellent. 3. Pour visiter le pays. 4. Non. Je ne suis pas seul. Je voyage avec mon frère. 5. Le service est parfait. Et les repas dans l'avion sont excellents.

Work Unit 8

Exercises, pp. 106–107
I. 1. Madame Paquet aime beaucoup les ventes aux enchères. 2. Monsieur et Madame Paquet entrent dans la salle des ventes. 3. Elle lève la main pour chasser les mouches de son nez. 4. Madame Paquet offre cent francs pour le fauteuil (sans le savoir, sans le vouloir, *or any acceptable answer*), quand elle lève la main pour chasser les mouches de son nez. 5. Tout le monde regarde Madame Paquet. **II.** (Note: These are personal questions and you may answer in any number of ways; they are "oui" or "non" questions to be answered in complete sentences in French.) **III.** 1. Monsieur Paquet parle à sa femme à voix basse. 2. Madame Paquet lève la main pour chasser les mouches de son nez. 3. J'ai cent francs. **IV.** 1. Ils entrent dans la salle des ventes. 2. Je n'aime pas ce fauteuil monstrueux. 3. Tout est si élégant dans cette salle. 4. Je veux une jolie petite table ronde.

Exercises, pp. 114–117
A. Cardinal numbers. I. 1. quatre. 2. sept. 3. douze. 4. dix. 5. dix-sept. 6. douze. **II.** 1. deux. 2. quatre. 3. six. 4. huit. 5. dix. 6. vingt. 7. vingt et un. 8. vingt-deux. 9. trente. 10. trente-sept. 11. soixante et un. 12. soixante-neuf. 13. soixante-dix. 14. quatre-vingts. 15. cent. **III.** (First column) 2, 4, 5, 3, 1; (Second column) 8, 9, 6, 10, 7. **IV.** 1. (c). 2. (a). 3. (c). 4. (d). 5. (c). **B. Ordinal numbers. I.** (First column) 3, 4, 1, 5, 2; (Second column) 7. 10, 6, 8, 9. **II.** 1. première. 2. premier. 3. second. 4. seconde. 5. deuxième. 6. quatrième. 7. cinquième. 8. neuvième. 9. dixième. 10. troisième. **III.** 3, 5, 4, 2, 1. **C. Cardinals, fractions, approximate amounts, ordinals, simple arithmetical expressions. I.** 1. deux. 2. soixante. 3. vingt-cinq. 4. deux cents. 5. huit cents.

II. Word Search

III. 7, 6, 8, 1, 10, 3, 5, 4, 9, 2. **IV.** 1. trois fois neuf font vingt-sept. 2. huit moins six font deux. 3. vingt divisés par cinq font quatre. 4. sept fois cent font sept cents. 5. quatre-vingts et dix font quatre-vingt-dix. **V.** 1. $3 \times 5 = 15$. 2. $12 - 10 = 2$. 3. $10 \div 2 = 5$. 4. $2 + 2 = 4$. 5. $9 \times 10 = 90$. **VI.** 4, 5, 7, 6, 2, 8, 3, 1, 10, 9. **VII.** Je veux partir parce que je n'aime pas les meubles ici. Les fauteuils sont laids. Les tables sont laides. Tout est monstrueux. Mille francs pour la lampe?! Deux cents francs pour la petite table?! Et il y a douze mouches dans cette salle!

Work Unit 9

Exercises, pp. 121–122

I. 1. (c). 2. (d). 3. (c). 4. (d). 5. (d). II. 1. oui. 2. oui. 3. non. 4. non. 5. oui. III. 1. J'ai quinze ans. 2. Quelle heure est-il? 3. Quelle est la date aujourd'hui? 4. Il est huit heures. 5. Avez-vous un revolver? IV. (Note: These are personal questions and you may answer in any number of ways.)

Exercises, pp. 126–129

I. 3, 4, 2, 1, 5, 6. II. 1. Il est trois heures et demie. 2. Il est dix heures moins dix. 3. Il est trois heures moins un quart. 4. Il est une heure et quart. III. 1. C'est aujourd'hui le premier octobre. 2. C'est aujourd'hui le dix novembre. IV. 1. Je me lève à six heures et demie du matin. 2. Je vais à l'école à huit heures du matin. 3. Je regarde la télévision à quatre heures de l'après-midi. 4. Je dîne à six heures du soir. 5. Je me couche à dix heures et demie du soir. V. 1. Les mois de l'année sont janvier, février, mars, avril, mai, juin, juillet, août, septembre, octobre, novembre, décembre. 2. Les jours de la semaine sont dimanche, lundi, mardi, mercredi, jeudi, vendredi, samedi. 3. Les saisons de l'année sont le printemps, l'été, l'automne, l'hiver. VI. 1. Non, ce n'est pas lundi; c'est aujourd'hui dimanche. 2. Non, ce n'est pas mardi; c'est aujourd'hui lundi. 3. Non, ce n'est pas mercredi; c'est aujourd'hui mardi. 4. Non, ce n'est pas vendredi; c'est aujourd'hui jeudi. 5. Non, ce n'est pas jeudi; c'est aujourd'hui mercredi. 6. Non, ce n'est pas samedi; c'est aujourd'hui vendredi. 7. Non, ce n'est pas dimanche; c'est aujourd'hui samedi. VII. 1. Quel âge a-t-il? 2. Quelle heure est-il? 3. Quel âge a-t-elle? 4. Quelle est la date aujourd'hui? 5. Quelle heure est-il? 6. Quelle est la date aujourd'hui? 7. Quel âge ont-elles? 8. Quelle heure est-il? 9. Quel âge avez-vous? 10. Quel jour est-ce aujourd'hui? VIII. Salut! C'est moi. J'aimerais faire un voyage cet été. Veux-tu venir avec moi? J'aime voyager en avion. Et toi? Nous allons visiter La Martinique. Nous allons voir les monuments, faire des promenades au bord de la mer jour et nuit. Si tu n'as pas assez d'argent, je vais payer pour toi. Tu acceptes? À bientôt!

Work Unit 10

Exercises, pp. 132–133

I. 1. C'est aujourd'hui vendredi. 2. Dans le concours de talents, Pierre va jouer le magicien. 3. Janine est l'assistante de Pierre. 4. Non, ils n'ont pas le chapeau haut de forme, le bâton, la cape, et le lapin. 5. Coco arrive (en courant) dans la grande salle avec le chapeau, le bâton, la cape et le lapin. 6. Coco gagne le grand prix de talent. II. (Note: These are personal questions and you may answer in any number of ways.) III. C'est aujourd'hui vendredi. 2. C'est le grand jour du concours de talents. 3. Apporte-moi mon bâton; apporte-moi le lapin. 4. Je n'ai pas ta cape. 5. Et qui gagne le grand prix? Coco, naturellement! Parce qu'il a beaucoup de talent!

Exercises, pp. 135–136

I. A. -ER verbs. 1. donne, donnez, donnons. 2. apporte, apportez, apportons. 3. cherche, cherchez, cherchons. 4. aide, aidez, aidons. 5. chante, chantez, chantons. B. -IR verbs. 1. finis, finissez, finissons. 2. choisis, choisissez, choisissons. 3. bâtis, bâtissez, bâtissons. 4. punis, punissez, punissons. 5. obéis, obéissez, obéissons. C. -RE verbs. 1. vends, vendez, vendons. 2. attends, attendez, attendons. 3. descends, descendez, descendons. 4. réponds, répondez, répondons. 5. rends, rendez, rendons. II. 1. Ne chantez pas, Janine! 2. Ne finissons pas le travail maintenant! 3. Ne vendez pas la maison, Monsieur Paquet! 4. N'écoute pas la musique, Pierre! 5. N'attendez pas l'autobus!

Exercises, pp. 137–138

I. 1. Lavez-vous. 2. Assieds-toi 3. Levez-vous. 4. Asseyez-vous. 5. Lavons-nous. 6. Lève-toi. 7. Ne te lave pas. 8. Ne nous levons pas. II. 1. Ne nous lavons pas! 2. Ne vous asseyez pas! 3. Ne te lave pas! 4. Ne t'assieds pas! 5. Ne vous lavez pas! 6. Ne te lève pas! III. 2, 4, 5, 1, 3. IV. 1. Z. 2. EZ .3. EZ. 4. ISS. 5. EZ. 6. ONS. 7. DEZ. 8. PO, DE. 9. EN, EZ. 10. SS, EZ. 11. EZ. 12. A, Z. V. 1. Je voudrais acheter une plante. 2. C'est pour une amie. 3. Oui. C'est son anniversaire. 4. Oui. Je l'aime beaucoup. C'est combien? 5. Je l'achète. Voici l'argent. Merci beaucoup. Au revoir.

Review Test: Work Units 6–10

Exercises, pp. 139–141

I. Janine est au marché aux puces avec son amie Monique. OR: Monique est au marché aux puces avec son amie Janine. II. 1. Monsieur et Madame Durant vendent leur maison. 2. Le petit chien rompt la grande barrière. 3. Le professeur interrompt l'étudiant. 4. Janine rend le livre à la bibliothèque. 5. Nous entendons la musique. III. 1. ons 2. e. 3. it 4. s 5. es 6. issent. IV. 1. me. 2. te. 3. se. 4. me. 5. nous. V. 1. sept. 2. douze. 3. quatre. 4. vingt-cinq. VI. A. Il est cinq heures dix. B. Il est une heure. C. Il est six heures moins le quart (moins un quart). D. Il est sept heures et demie. E. Il est onze heures et quart. F. Il est quatre heures et quart. VII. 1. C. 2. B. 3. C. 4. D. 5. A. VIII. 1. Wash yourself! 2. Let's sit down! 3. Get up! IX. 1. S, S, E, Z. 2. E, Z. 3. I, S, S, E, Z. X. 1. Quel âge a Monsieur Durand? 2. Quel âge as-tu? 3. Quelle heure est-il? 4. Quel jour est-ce aujourd'hui? 5. Quelle est la date aujourd'hui?

Exercises, pp. 144–145
I. 1. (b). 2. (b). 3. (d). 4. (c). 5. (d). **II.** (Note: These are personal questions and you may answer in different ways.)

III. Un acrostiche

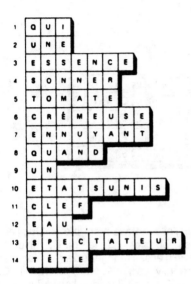

Exercises, pp. 147–150
I. 1. Oui, je lis beaucoup; elle lit beaucoup aussi. 2. Oui, j'apprends le français; elle apprend le français aussi. 3. Oui, j'ai de la glace; il a de la glace aussi. 4. Oui, je bois du jus d'orange; il boit du jus d'orange aussi. 5. Oui, je comprends la leçon; elle comprend la leçon aussi. 6. Oui, ils courent à l'école; nous courons à l'école aussi. 7. Oui, elles doivent écrire des compositions; je dois écrire des compositions aussi (possibly: nous devons écrire des compositions aussi). 8. Oui, il dit la vérité; elles disent la vérité aussi. 9. Oui, elle écrit une lettre; elles écrivent une lettre aussi. 10. Oui, je suis dans le concours de talents à l'école; ils sont dans le concours de talents à l'école aussi. **II.** 1. Non, il ne lit pas beaucoup; je ne lis pas beaucoup non plus (possibly: nous ne lisons pas beaucoup non plus). 2. Non, elle ne met pas le vase sur la table; il ne met pas le vase sur la table non plus. 3. Non, je n'ouvre pas la porte; il n'ouvre pas la porte non plus. 4. Non, elle ne part pas à huit heures; il ne part pas à huit heures non plus. 5. Non, je ne peux (or: puis) pas aller au cinéma ce soir; ils ne peuvent pas aller au cinéma ce soir non plus. 6. Non, je ne prends pas le petit déjeuner à sept heures; elle ne prend pas le petit déjeuner à sept heures non plus. 7. Non, je ne sais pas quelle heure il est; il ne sait pas quelle heure il est non plus. 8. Non, ils ne sortent pas ce soir; elle ne sort pas ce soir non plus. 9. Non, je ne viens pas ici tous les jours; il ne vient pas ici tous les jours non plus. 10. Non, je ne vois pas l'avion dans le ciel; elle ne voit pas l'avion dans le ciel non plus. **III.** 1. Ouvre-t-il la porte? 2. Est-ce qu'elle lit la lettre? 3. Prenez-vous du café? 4. Il ne fait pas la leçon. 5. Ecrivez-vous la date? **IV.** 1. Henri et Robert comprennent la réponse. 2. J'ai beaucoup de devoirs à faire. 3. Hélène et Marie sont-elles présentes aujourd'hui? 4. Michel et Jacques font-ils leurs leçons? 5. Je ne vois pas un taxi. **V.** 1. Nous voyons. 2. Je sais. 3. Ils font. 4. Ils partent. 5. Tu bois. 6. Janine devient. **VI.** 1 . Ils comprennent bien aussi. 2. Elles écrivent bien aussi. 3. Ils vont bien aussi. 4. Elles lisent bien aussi. 5. Ils voient bien aussi.

Exercises, pp. 152–155
I. 1. Buvez! 2. Viens! 3. Dites! 4. Ecrivez! 5. Lisez! 6. Ouvre! 7. Sortons! 8. Soyons! 9. Buvons! 10. Revenez! **II.** 1 . Dites la phrase. 2. Bois le lait. 3. Partez tout de suite. 4. Ferme la fenêtre. 5. Prends la valise là-bas. 6. Ecrivons la lettre. 7. Lisez le poème. 8. Sortons maintenant. 9. Revenez à l'heure. 10. Faisons la leçon. **III.** 7, 4, 6, 8, 3, 9, 1, 10, 5, 2. **IV. A.** 1. Bon! Alors, partez maintenant. 2. Bon! Alors, ouvrez la fenêtre. 3. Bon! Alors, faites la leçon. 4. Bon! Alors, écrivez une lettre. 5. Bon! Alors, lisez le journal. **IV. B.** 1. Bon! Alors, sortez maintenant. 2. Bon! Alors, soyez ici à dix heures. 3. Bon! Alors, faites le travail ce soir. 4. Bon! Alors, apprenez l'anglais. 5. Bon! Alors, parlez français. **V.** 1. C'est un objet d'habillement. C'est pour une femme. Qu'est-ce que c'est? (C'est une robe.) 2. C'est une partie du corps humain. Elle a cinq doigts. Qu'est-ce que c'est? (C'est une main.) 3. C'est un meuble. Vous dormez sur ce meuble. Qu'est-ce que c'est? (C'est un lit.) 4. C'est un fruit. Il a la couleur jaune. Qu'est-ce que c'est? (C'est une banane.)

Work Unit 12

Exercises, pp. 160–161

I. 1. Ils ont quitté la maison à sept heures et demie pour aller à l'opéra. 2. Ils sont arrivés à l'opéra à huit heures. 3. Ils ont pris leurs places à huit heures et quart. 4. La représentation a commencé à huit heures et demie. **II.** 1. oui. 2. non. 3. oui. 4. non. 5. non. **III.** 1. allée. 2. vu. 3. quitté. 4. arrivés. 5. entrés. 6. pris. 7. allée. 8. allé. 9. allé. 10 allée.

IV. Word Search

```
A L L É T F U M É L
P A R L É A L A B U
P R I S O I T N T O
R Q U I T T É U R I
U R É P O N D U F T
```

Exercises, pp. 164–168

I. A. 1. Oui, j'ai vendu la voiture. 2. Oui, j'ai acheté la propriété. 3. Oui, j'ai fini les leçons. 4. Oui, j'ai réussi la vente de la propriété. 5. Oui, j'ai fermé les portes et les fenêtres. **B.** 1. Non elle n'a pas chanté hier soir. 2. Non, il n'a pas choisi une jolie cravate. 3. Non, je n'ai pas mangé l'éclair. 4. Non, ils n'ont pas étudié les leçons. 5. Non, nous n'avons pas fini le travail (possibly: non, vous n'avez pas fini le travail). **C.** 1. Pierre a-t-il vu Madame Richy? 2. Hélène a-t-elle choisi une jolie robe? 3. Coco a-t-il mangé l'éclair? 4. Suzanne et Georges ont-ils étudié les devoirs? 5. Marie et Betty ont-elles voyagé en France? **D.** 1. Est-ce que Madame Paquet a acheté un beau chapeau? 2. Est-ce que Pierre a perdu sa montre? 3. Est-ce que Monsieur Paquet a fumé une cigarette? 4. Est-ce que Paul a mangé du chocolat? 5. Est-ce que Janine a bu un jus d'orange? **E.** 1. Madame Richy n'a-t-elle pas acheté une automobile? 2. Monsieur Richy n'a-t-il pas voyagé aux Etats-Unis? 3. Madame et Monsieur Armstrong n'ont-ils pas aimé le dessert? 4. Mathilde n'a-t-elle pas entendu la musique? 5. Joseph n'a-t-il pas choisi une jolie cravate? **F.** 1. Est-ce que Robert n'a pas dansé hier soir? 2. Est-ce que Joséphine n'a pas chanté ce matin? 3. Est-ce que Guy et Michel n'ont pas fini leurs leçons? 4. Est-ce que Françoise et Simone n'ont pas entendu la musique? 5. Est-ce que Charles n'a pas perdu son ami? **II.** 7, 10, 8, 9, 6, 3, 5, 2, 1, 4. **III.** 1. aimé. 2. quitté. 3. pris. 4. commencé. 5. parlé. 6. fumé. 7. mangé. 8. bu 9. vu. 10. dit. **IV.** 1. I danced, I have danced. I did dance. 2. You finished, you have finished, you did finish. 3. We sold, we have sold, we did sell. **V.** 1. J'ai joué. 2. Tu as pleuré. 3. Il a fini. 4. Elle a choisi. 5. Janine a chanté. 6. Nous avons dansé. 7. Vous avez perdu. 8. Ils ont répondu. 9. J'ai étudié. 10. Il a parlé. 11. Robert a travaillé. 12. Marie et Bob ont dîné.

Exercises, pp. 171–179

I. A. 1. Oui, Janine est allée au cinéma. 2. Oui, Monique est allée à l'école. 3. Oui, Robert est allé au théâtre. 4. Oui, Pierre et Raymond sont allés à l'opéra. 5. Oui, Anne et Béatrice sont allées au Canada. 6. Oui, Jacques et Jeanne sont allés à l'aéroport. 7. Oui, Monsieur et Madame Beaupuy sont allés aux Etats-Unis. 8. Oui, la mère est allée dans le garage. 9. Oui, le père est allé dans la cuisine. 10. Oui, la jeune fille est allée à la pharmacie. **B.** 1. Non, elle n'est pas arrivée à l'opéra à huit heures et demie. 2. Non, ils ne sont pas entrés dans le théâtre à huit heures. 3. Non, ils ne sont pas partis de bonne heure. 4. Non, il n'est pas resté à la maison. 5. Non, elle n'est pas sortie ce soir. **C.** 1. Yolande est-elle venue ce soir? 2. François est-il retourné à midi? 3. Les garçons sont-ils restés dans l'école? 4. Les jeunes filles sont-elles descendues vite? 5. Monsieur et Madame Paquet sont-ils rentrés à minuit? **D.** 1. Est-ce que John James Audubon est né aux Cayes à Haïti? 2. Est-ce que Napoléon Bonaparte est mort à Sainte-Hélène? 3. Est-ce que Marie-Antoinette est née à Vienne? 4. Est-ce que Valéry Giscard d'Estang est devenu Président de la République française en 1974? 5. Est-ce que Joséphine est née à la Martinique? 6. Est-ce que Marie-Antoinette est morte à Paris? 7. Est-ce que Joséphine est devenue impératrice en 1804? **E.** 1. N'es-tu pas resté à la maison? 2. N'est-elle pas tombée dans le jardin? 3. N'est-il pas parti ce matin? 4. N'êtes-vous pas arrivé à dix heures? 5. Ne sont-elles pas allées à l'école aujourd'hui? **II.** 4, 1, 2, 3, 10, 5, 6, 9, 7, 8. **III.** 1. I went . . ., I have gone. . ., I did go. . . 2. She left, she has left, she did leave. 3. We arrived, we have arrived, we did arrive. **IV.** 1. Je suis allé. 2. Tu es venu. 3. Il est arrivé. 4. Elle est partie. 5. Jean est sorti. 6. Nous sommes entrés. 7. Vous êtes tombé. 8. Ils sont montés. 9. Elles sont allées. 10. Je suis descendu. 11. Michel est rentré. 12. Elle est morte.

V. Un acrostiche

1	L	U			
2	E	U			
3	P	R	I	S	
4	A	R	R	I	V	É
5	R	I			
6	T	E	N	U	
7	I				
8	C	R	U		
9	I				
10	P	R	O	M	I	S
11	E	C	R	I	T
12	P	U			
13	A	L	L	É	
14	S	U			
15	S	O	R	T	I
16	É	T	É		

VI. 1. Suzanne a parlé. 2. Il est monté. 3. Elle est sortie. 4. Elle a compris. 5. Nous sommes arrivés. 6. Vous avez dit. 7. Elles ont lu. 8. Tu as fait. 9. Robert est resté. 10. Ils ont ri. 11. Je suis allé. 12. Madame Paquet a bu. **VII.** 1. apprendre. 2. devenir. 3. avoir. 4. couvrir. 5. croire. 6. comprendre. 7. permettre. 8. recevoir. 9. promettre. 10. vouloir. 11. devoir. 12. voir. 13. dire. 14. venir. 15. écrire. 16. être. 17. boire. 18. faire. 19. tenir. 20. lire. 21. ouvrir. 22. mettre. 23. savoir. 24. mourir. 25. rire. 26. naître. 27. revenir. 28. paraître. 29. pouvoir. 30. prendre. **VIII.** 1. eu. 2. été. 3. fait. 4. fini. 5. su. 6. lu. 7. appris. 8. défendu. 9. choisi. 10. allé. 11. sorti. 12. saisi. 13. aidé. 14. bâti. 15. joué. 16. vu. 17. dansé. 18. vendu. **IX.** 1. être. 2. avoir. 3. avoir. 4. avoir. 5. être. 6. être. 7. avoir. 8. avoir. 9. être. 10. avoir. 11. avoir. 12. être. 13. être. 14. avoir. 15. être. 16. avoir. 17. être. 18. avoir. 19. avoir. 20. avoir. 21. être. **X.** 1. Il lit un bon livre. 2. Je vends la voiture. 3. Elle va à l'opéra. 4. Nous écrivons des lettres. 5. Vous arrivez de bonne heure. **XI.** 1. Madame Paquet a eu un beau chapeau rouge. 2. Janine a bu un jus d'orange. 3. Pierre a mangé du chocolat. 4. Monique est allée au cinéma. 5. Jeanne et Joséphine sont entrées dans le théâtre. **XII.** 1. e. 2. —. 3. e. 4. e. 5. s. 6. s. 7. —. **XIII.** 1. allée. 2. arrivés. 3. entrés. 4. allée. 5. allé. 6. allé. 7. allée. 8. retournée. 9. retourné. 10. retournée. **XIV.** J'ai l'air fâché? Certainement! Je n'ai pas aimé la comédie. Je n'ai pas ri. J'ai vendu ma bicyclette pour avoir de l'argent pour payer mon billet. J'ai perdu mon argent et j'ai perdu mon temps. Pendant l'entracte, j'ai bu une tasse de café mauvais et maintenant je suis malade. Je n'ai pas fini mes devoirs pour venir ici. Voilà mes raisons!

Work Unit 13

Exercises, pp. 183–184

I. 1. Pierre a servi le dîner ce soir. 2. Il a servi le dîner pour la famille et les voisins. 3. Pierre commence à goûter le ragoût. 4. Monsieur Richy aime le ragoût. 5. Le ragoût est bien cuit (possibly: Il aime le ragoût bien cuit; or, il aime le ragoût parce qu'il est bien cuit). 6. Madame Paquet a fait le ragoût. **II.** (Note: These are personal questions and you may answer in different ways.) **III.** 1. Et comment! Il sent très bon. (Moi), j'ai grand faim (j'ai très faim). 2. Janine a raison. Il est brûlé. Je ne l'aime pas. Goûtez-en! 3. Je vais le goûter. 4. Madame Paquet rentre dans la salle à manger avec le dessert. 5. Est-ce que tout le monde aime mon ragoût? J'ai un dessert que j'ai fait aussi. Qui veut en goûter?

Exercises, pp. 190–197

I. 1. Pierre la lit. 2. Janine l'écrit. 3. Michel l'apprend. 4. Christophe les fait. 5. Alexandre l'écoute. 6. Yolande le prononce. 7. Théodore le voit. 8. Monique la dit. 9. Joséphine l'attend. 10. Anne les mange. **II.** 1. Oui, elle la dit. 2. Oui, elle l'attend. 3. Oui, il la lit. 4. Oui, il les mange. 5. Oui, elle l'écoute. **III.** 1. Non, il ne la mange pas. 2. Non, elle ne le prononce pas. 3. Non, il ne l'aime pas. 4. Non, il ne la lit pas. 5. Non, elle ne les apporte pas. **IV.** 1. Oui, je la comprends aujourd'hui. 2. Oui, je la dis toujours. 3. Oui, je les fais maintenant. 4. Oui, je le lis tous les jours. 5. Oui, je l'écris en ce moment. **V.** 1. Oui, elle la connaît. 2. Oui, elle le connaît. 3. Oui, il les connaît. 4. Oui, elle les connaît. 5. Oui, il les connaît. **VI.** 1. Oui, elle me connaît. 2. Oui, il me voit. 3. Oui, elle nous aime. 4. Oui, ils les attendent. 5. Oui, il l'adore. **VII.** 1. Oui, je t'aime bien. 2. Oui, je l'aime bien aussi. 3. Oui, je l'aime bien aussi.

4. Oui, il m'aime bien. 5. Oui, elle m'aime bien aussi. **VIII.** 1. Oui, je t'aime. 2. Oui, il m'aime. 3. Oui, je l'aime aussi. 4. Oui, il m'aime. 5. Oui, elle m'aime. **IX.** 1. Bon! Alors, écrivez-la! 2. Bon! Alors, étudiez-les! 3. Bon! Alors, lisez-le! 4. Bon! Alors, buvez-le! 5. Bon! Alors, faites-les! **X.** 1. Bon! Alors, ne l'écrivez-pas! 2. Bon! Alors, ne les étudiez pas! 3. Bon! Alors, ne le lisez pas! 4. Bon! Alors, ne le buvez pas! 5. Bon! Alors, ne les faites pas! **XI.** 1. Pierre veut le lire. 2. Madeleine veut l'apprendre. 3. Paul ne veut pas l'écrire. 4. Philippe ne veut pas la manger. 5. Gertrude ne veut pas les apporter. **XII.** 1. Oui, j'en ai. 2. Oui, j'en bois. 3. Oui, j'en mange. 4. Oui, j'en mange. 5. Oui, j'en ai. 6. Oui, j'en ai. 7. Oui, il en vient. 8. Oui, j'en peur. 9. Oui, j'en mange. 10. Oui, j'en bois. **XIII.** 1. Non, je n'en ai pas. 2. Non, je n'en ai pas. 3. Non, je n'en ai pas. 4. Non, je n'en ai pas. 5. Non, je n'en ai pas. **XIV.** 1. Bon! Alors, buvez-en! 2. Bon! Alors, mangez-en! 3. Bon! Alors, écrivez-en! 4. Bon! Alors, buvez-en! 5. Bon! Alors, mangez-en! **XV.** 1. Bon! Alors, n'en buvez pas! 2. Bon! Alors, n'en mangez pas! 3. Bon! Alors, n'en écrivez pas! **XVI.** 1. Madame Paquet l'a préparé. 2. Monsieur Richy l'a mangé. 3. Pierre l'a servi. 4. Janine les a préparés. 5. Monsieur Paquet les a préparées. **XVII.** 1. Oui, il l'a servi. 2. Oui, elle l'a préparé. 3. Oui, il l'a mangé. 4. Oui, elle l'a écrite. 5. Oui, il les a faits. **XVIII.** 1. Non, il ne l'a pas préparée. 2. Non, il ne l'a pas fait. 3. Non, elle ne l'a pas lu. 4. Non, elle ne l'a pas mangé. 5. Non, il ne les a pas faits. **XIX.** Je suis content que tu aimes le poulet. Je vais te donner la recette. J'ai cuit le poulet avec les oignons. Ne mets pas trop de sel sur le poulet. Aussi, ne brûle pas les oignons. J'ai servi le poulet aux oignons à tous mes amis. Tout le monde aime le manger.

Work Unit 14

Exercise, pp. 200–201

I. 1. Janine à prêté ses disques à Suzanne. 2. Elle veut les jouer pendant les fêtes de Noël (possibly: Elle veut les reprendre pour les écouter pendant les fêtes de Noël). 3. Non, elle ne les reprend pas. **II.** 1. Elle m'a dit que vous les avez maintenant. 2. C'est aujourd'hui le premier décembre. 3. Je ne les ai pas. Je lui ai donné les disques. Va la voir. 4. J'ai donné les disques à Mimi. Mimi les a donnés à Raymond. 5. Je lui ai donné les disques. Va le voir.

III.

Exercises, pp. 204–207

I. 1. Janine lui donne le journal. 2. Madeleine lui donne le livre. 3. Gloria lui donne la fleur. 4. Robert leur donne la balle. 5. Monique leur donne les stylos. **II. A.** 1. Je lui parle. 2. Je lui parle. 3. Je lui parle. 4. Je lui parle. 5. Je lui parle. **II. B.** 1. Je leur donne les gâteaux. 2. Je leur donne les livres. 3. Je leur donne le ragoût brûlé. 4. Je leur donne les lettres. 5. Je leur donne le jus. **III.** 1. Oui, je vous parle. 2. Oui, je lui parle. 3. Oui, je vous parle. **IV.** 1. Bon! Alors, donnez-lui le gâteau! 2. Bon! Alors, donnez-lui le parapluie! 3. Bon! Alors, donnez-lui le bonbon. 4. Bon! Alors, donnez-lui le jus de fruit. 5. Bon! Alors, donnez-lui le ragoût brûlé. **V.** 1. Bon! Alors, ne leur donnez pas le chocolat! 2. Bon! Alors, ne lui donnez pas les devoirs! 3. Bon! Alors, ne lui donnez pas le billet! **VI.** 1. Bon! Alors, parlez-moi! 2. Bon! Alors, parlez-lui! 3. Bon! Alors, parlez-leur! **VII.** 1. Bon! Alors, ne me parlez pas! 2. Bon! Alors ne lui parlez pas! 3. Bon alors, ne leur parlez pas! **VIII.** 4, 5, 2, 6, 3, 1. **IX.** 1. Oui, j'y vais. 2. Oui, j'y vais. 3. Oui, j'y vais. **X.** 1. Bon! Alors, parlez-lui! 2. Janine veut leur parler. **XI.** Tes cassettes? Ah, oui! Je les ai données à Robert. Va le voir. Va lui demander. Je les lui ai prêtées. Je pense qu'il les a prêtées à Suzanne. Je ne les ai pas. Je le regrette.

Work Unit 15

Exercises, pp.210–211

I. 1. UN CHAMPIGNON. 2. UN FAUTEUIL. 3. UN RÉVEIL. 4. UNE GIRAFE. 5. UN KANGOUROU. **II.** 1. porte. 2. yeux, n'ai pas. 3. suis. 4. n'ai pas. 5. long, peux.

III.

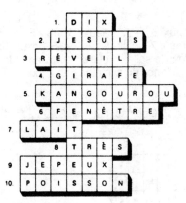

The crossword grid contains:
1. DIX
2. JE SUIS
3. RÉVEIL
4. GIRAFE
5. KANGOUROU
6. FENÊTRE
7. LAIT
8. TRÈS
9. JE PEUX
10. POISSON

Exercises, p. 213–214
I. 6, 3, 5, 1, 4, 2. **II.** 1. Qui. 2. Qui. 3. qui. 4. qui. 5. Que. 6. Qu'est-ce que. 7. Que (possibly: Qui—if the student means "whom"; *e.g.*, someone has just said something about someone and you respond with: "Whom do you say?"—I suggest not to raise this possibility at this point in class until the students know very well the difference between *qui* and *que*). 8. Qu'est-ce que. 9. Qui. 10. Que. **III.** 1. Qui mange une pomme? 2. Que buvez-vous? 3. A qui parle Monique? (possibly: Qui parle à Roger?). 4. Qu'est-ce que vous dites? 5. Qu'est-ce que Janine écrit? 6. Qui a lancé la balle? 7. Que lit-elle? 8. Qu'est-ce que vous mangez? 9. Qu'est-ce que Pierre a servi? 10. Qui a fait le ragout? **IV.** 1. Il y a beaucoup de livres et de disques dans ce paquet, monsieur. 2. J'ai oublié. Excusez-moi. 3. Oui, par avion. Il faut que ce paquet arrive vite aux Etats-Unis. 4. C'est très cher! Je n'ai pas assez d'argent! 5. Je vais aller chercher de l'argent chez moi. Merci. Au revoir, monsieur.

Review Test: Work Units 11-15

Exercises, pp. 215–217
I. 1. ma 2. mais 3. si 4. on 5. mis 6. mon 7. nom 8. ai **II.** Aimons! (Let's love!)

III.

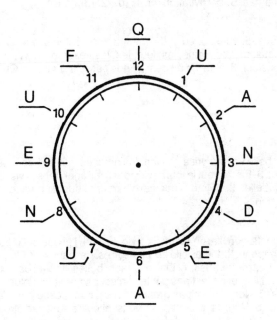

IV. 1. c. 2. b. 3. a. **V.** 1. b. 2. a. 3. c. 4. b. 5. a. **VI.** 1. c. 2. b. 3. a. 4. b. 5. d. **VII.** 1. avoir. 2. être. 3. faire. 4. dire. 5. lire. 6. savoir. 7. comprendre. 8. mettre. 9. rire. **VIII.** 1. sont. 2. ai. 3. suis. 4. a. 5. est. 6. a. 7. a. 8. est. **IX.** 1. a. 2. c. 3. a. 4. c. 5. d. **X.** 1. a. 2. a. 3. a. 4. b. 5. a. **XI.** 1. Qui. 2. Qui. 3. qui. 4. qui. 5. Que. 6. Que.

Work Unit 16

Exercises, pp. 221–222

I. 1. vrai. 2. vrai. 3. vrai. 4. faux. 5. faux. 6. faux. 7. faux. 8. vrai. **II.** 1. professeur, géographie. 2. Paris. 3. port. 4. fleuve. 5. dans, classe. 6. au, bureau. 7. continuer, leçon. 8. poser. **III.** 1. Elle est professeur de géographie. 2. La Directrice (de l'école) entre dans la salle de classe. 3. Quand Madame Ravel quitte la salle, elle va dans le bureau de la directrice. 4. Robert a lancé un avion en papier contre l'horloge. 5. La leçon finit à trois heures.

Exercises, p. 223

I. 5, 4, 2, 1, 3. **II.** Oui, cela est faux. 2. Oui, ceci est vrai. 3. Oui, c'est ça.

III. Word Hunt

IV. Paris est un port sur la Méditerranée. Cela est vrai? Faux? (Faux) La Tour Eiffel est à Paris. Cela est vrai? Faux? (Vrai) Le quatre juillet est la fête nationale de la France. Cela est vrai? Faux? (Faux) Marseille est une ville dans les Alpes. Cela est vrai? Faux? (Faux)

Work Unit 17

Exercises, pp. 226–227

I. MONSIEUR PAQUET: Moi, je ne veux pas y aller (possibly: Je ne veux pas accepter leur invitation; Non, nous n'acceptons pas leur invitation—or any acceptable response) . . . MONSIEUR PAQUET: Ils m'ennuient beaucoup. Je ne les aime pas. MONSIEUR PAQUET: (Note: In this last réplique of Monsieur Paquet, you may write any response which is acceptable from the dialogue on pp. 225–226.) **II.** 1. entre eux et nous. 2. vous voir. 3. chez eux. 4. je ne les aime pas. 5. à l'invitation. **III.** 1. (d). 2. (d). 3. (a)

Exercises, pp. 228–230

I. 1. moi. 2. lui. 3. elle. 4. nous. 5. vous. 6. eux. **II.** 1. lui. 2. moi. 3. lui. 4. elle. 5. nous. 6. vous. 7. toi. 8. eux. 9. elles. 10. lui et moi. **III** . nous, moi, toi, vous, les, leur, les, les, les, moi, y. **IV.** 1. Je cherche la rue de Rivoli. 2. Je ne comprends pas, monsieur. 3. Non. Je ne comprends pas le français. 4. Oui. Je suis américain. 5. Merci, merci.

Work Unit 18

Exercises, pp. 234–235

I. 1. La famille Paquet a une belle voiture grise. 2. Non, les grosses voitures neuves ne sont pas meilleures que la voiture de Monsieur Paquet. 3. Pierre veut le tournevis pour l'engager dans la vis. Il veut enlever la vis et l'écrou. 4. Pierre les met dans la poubelle. **II.** (Note: These are personal questions and you may respond in different ways.) **III.** 1. oui. 2. oui. 3. non. 4. oui.

Exercises, pp. 237–239

I. 1. Non, j'ai une maison grise. 2. Non, j'ai un mauvais stylo. 3. Non, j'ai une belle pomme. 4. Non, j'ai une pêche douce. 5. Non, j'ai un vieux chapeau. **II.** 1. Oui, elle est petite; il est petit aussi. 2. Oui, il est furieux; elle est furieuse aussi. 3. Oui, elle est gentille; il est gentil aussi. 4. Oui, elles sont belles; ils sont beaux aussi. 5. Oui, elle est neuve; elles sont neuves aussi. **III.** 1. Non, elle n'est pas petite; il n'est pas petit non plus. 2. Non, il n'est pas mauvais; il n'est pas mauvais non plus. 3. Non, il n'est pas gros; elle n'est pas grosse non plus. 4. Non, il n'est pas muet; elle n'est pas muette non plus. 5. Non, ils ne sont pas étroits; elles ne sont pas étroites non plus. **IV.** 1. (d) 2. (c). 3. (c). 4. (b). 5. (b).

Exercises, pp. 241–243

I. 1. Oui, j'aime ma petite voiture neuve. 2. Oui, j'aime votre parapluie rouge. 3. Oui, j'aime votre maison blanche. 4. Oui, j'aime ton amie Monique. 5. Oui, j'aime ses grosses pommes. 6. Oui, j'aime ta jolie soeur. 7. Oui, j'aime vos jaquettes. 8. Oui, j'aime tes robes. 9. Oui, j'aime leurs gâteaux. 10. Oui, j'aime mon livre. **II.** 1. Oui, c'est ma voiture. 2. Oui, c'est mon chapeau. 3. Oui, c'est son livre à lui. 4. Oui, c'est ma maîtresse de français. 5. Oui, c'est leur maison. **III.** 1. Oui, ce sont mes stylos. 2. Oui, ce sont leurs crayons. 3. Oui, ce sont mes gâteaux. 4. Oui, ce sont vos (or: tes) pommes. 5. Oui, ce sont nos (or: vos) pêches. **IV.** votre, ma, votre, votre, vos, sa, son, nos, leurs. **V.** 1. Je mange ma pêche. 2. Il mange son sandwich. 3. Ils mangent leur chocolat. 4. Elles mangent leur soupe. 5. Je mange mes petits fours. **VI.** 1. Oui. Je veux y aller avec toi. Qu'est-ce que c'est? 2. Merveilleux! Je n'ai jamais vu un film français. 3. Okay. Je vais leur téléphoner tout de suite. 4. Je vais être là. 5. Nous allons à un café-restaurant pour avoir de la glace et de la pâtisserie.

Work Unit 19

Exercises, pp. 247–248
I. 1. lit, de l'horoscope, lui. 2. le meilleur. 3. plus forte. 4. le plus. 5. du moment, semaine, nouvelles. **II.** 1. faux. 2. vrai. 3. vrai. 4. faux. 5. vrai. **III.** 1. Pierre lit son horoscope. 2. Demain va être un jour parfait. 3. Une personne vous aime beaucoup. 4. Il y a un requin dans l'eau. 5. Le téléphone sonne.

Exercises, pp. 250–251
I. 1. Quel est votre (or: ton) nom? (possibly: Comment vous appelez-vous? or: Comment t'appelles-tu? or: Comment est-ce que vous vous appelez? or: Comment est-ce que tu t'appelles?). 2. Quelle est votre (or: ton) adresse? (Note: Please see p. 249 in book for the expected "Quelle est votre adresse?" and "Quel est votre nom?".) 3. Quel âge avez-vous? (or: Quel âge as-tu? or: Quel est votre âge? or: Quel est ton âge?). **II.** (Note: These are personal questions, and you may answer in different ways.) **III.** 1. Quel. 2. Quelles. 3. Quels. 4. Quelle. **IV.** 5, 3, 1, 4, 2.

V. Word Hunt

Exercises, pp. 252–253
I. A. 1. Je mange cette pêche. 2. Je mange ce gâteau. 3. Je mange ces petits fours. 4. Je mange cet ananas. 5. Je mange cette tomate. **I. B.** 1. Etudiez-vous cette leçon? 2. Etudiez-vous ce livre? 3. Etudiez-vous ces pages? 4. Etudiez-vous ces phrases? 5. Etudiez-vous ce poème? **I. C.** 1. Nous allons au cinéma avec ces jeunes filles. 2. Nous allons au cinéma avec cet ami. 3. Nous allons au cinéma avec cette amie. 4. Nous allons au cinéma avec ce jeune homme. 5. Nous allons au cinéma avec ces étudiants. **II.** 1. Bien! Je vous donne ce journal! 2. Bien! Je lui donne cette pomme! 3. Bien! Je leur donne ces pommes frites! **III.** 1. Je vais manger cet ananas et ces tomates. 2. Je vais écrire cette leçon et ces phrases. 3. Je vais boire ces vins et ces bières. 4. Je vais envoyer cette lettre. 5. Je vais acheter ce livre.

Exercises, pp. 256–259
I. 1. Non, il est moins grand que sa mère. 2. Non, elle est moins grande que son père. 3. Non, elle est moins intelligente que Janine. **II.** 1. Madame Paquet est plus grande que Janine. 2. Janine est moins grande que Pierre. 3. Mathilde est plus petite que Monique. 4. Suzanne est moins petite que Joseph. 5. Monsieur Richy est aussi grand que Monsieur Paquet. 6. Madame Paquet est aussi petite que Madame Banluc. **III.** 1. Non, ce n'est pas vrai. Janine est la plus intelligente du cours de mathématiques. 2. Non, ce n'est pas vrai. Suzanne est la plus grande du cours de français. 3. Non, ce n'est pas vrai. Simone est la moins grande de la famille. 4. Non, ce n'est pas vrai. Charles est le plus beau du groupe. 5. Non, ce n'est pas vrai. Hélène est la plus petite. **IV.** 1. Oui, cette phrase est moins facile que les autres; ces questions sont plus faciles que les autres aussi. 2. Oui, ce poème est plus difficile que les autres; cette leçon est plus difficile que les autres aussi. 3. Oui, cette voiture est plus belle que les autres; ces maisons sont plus belles que les autres aussi. 4. Oui, ce garçon est plus beau que les autres; ces jeunes filles sont plus belles que les autres aussi. 5. Oui, cette banane est plus délicieuse que les autres; ces gâteaux sont plus délicieux que les autres aussi. **V.** 1. plus. 2. grand. 3. aussi. 4. plus jolie. 5. le moins.

VI. Le Mot Mystère

The mystery word is VOITURE; the scrambled letters that remain are, starting with the first line across: R, V, O, E, I, T, U.

VII. Bonjour! Vous désirez? Une chemise? Une cravate? Nous avons beaucoup de belles chemises. Voulez-vous regarder ces chaussettes? Elles sont vraiment jolies et elles ne coûtent pas beaucoup. C'est pour vous? Ou c'est pour une autre personne? C'est pour une soirée? Regardez! Vous avez choisi? C'est un grand plaisir de vous aider.

Work Unit 20

Exercises, pp. 263–264

I. 1. oui. 2. oui. 3. non. 4. non. 5. non. **II.** 1. (d). 2. (a). 3. (c). 4. (b). 5. (c). **III.** 1. te coucher. 2. jeté. 3. toute. 4. meilleure. 5. plus. 6. moins.

Exercises, pp. 266–268

I. 1. distinctement. 2. seulement. 3. courageusement. 4. constamment. 5. patiemment. 6. fièrement. **II.** 1. Monsieur Richy aime beaucoup le ragoût brûlé. 2. Le professeur a bien parlé. 3. Janine a parlé constamment. 4. Elle est déjà partie. 5. Pierre a beaucoup mangé. **III.** 1. bien. 2. plus. 3. aussi . . . que. 4. plus . . . que. 5. moins. 6. le moins.

IV. Le Mot Mystère

The mystery word is FRANCE; the scrambled letters that remain are, starting with the third line across: F, C, A, R, N, E.

V. Silence! Robert, quel âge as-tu? Et toi, Debbie, quel âge as-tu? Vous savez, tous les deux, que vous n'êtes pas sages! Robert, tu es capricieux. Et toi, Debbie, tu es capricieuse. Vous avez abîmé tout! Cela suffit! (That's enough!). Pas de programme de télé ce soir! Robert, va te coucher. Debbie, va te coucher aussi! Maintenant! Vite!

Exercises, pp. 269–273

I.

II.

III.

IV. 1. première. 2. grande. 3. bonne. 4. tout. 5. mauvaises. 6. toutes. 7. excellente. 8. studieuse. 9. jolie. 10. blanche. **V.** 1. gentiment. 2. franchement. 3. affreusement. 4. amèrement. **VI.** 1. bien. 2. mal. 3. vite. 4. combien. 5. comm ent. 6. pourquoi. 7. où. 8. quand. 9. beaucoup. 10. assez. **VII.** 1. bien. 2. rapidement. 3. toujours. 4. aussi. 5. déjà.

Work Unit 21

Exercises, pp. 277–278

I. 1. Madame Paquet est malade. 2. Elle a mangé quelque chose qui lui a donné mal à l'estomac. 3. Elle est malade depuis hier. 4. Le docteur lui donne du médicament. 5. Il doit partir parce qu'il va dîner (or: il doit partir pour aller dîner) au Coq d'or. **II.** 1. Madame Paquet est malade depuis hier. 2. Absolument rien! 3. Pas même un oeuf à la coque! 4. Dis-moi ce que tu manges et je te dirai ce que tu es! (or: Dites-moi ce que vous mangez et je vous dirai ce que vous êtes!). 5. Prenez ce médicament et ne mangez rien. **III.** 1. Le docteur n'est pas arrivé. 2. Madame Paquet est malade depuis hier, n'est-ce pas? 3. Il est dans la chambre depuis quinze minutes.

IV. Mots-croisés

Exercises, pp. 281–285

I. 1. Non, je ne danse pas bien. 2. Non, mon père ne chante pas souvent. 3. Non, ma mère ne lit pas beaucoup. 4. Non, mes amis n'écrivent pas bien. 5. Non, je ne fume pas. **II.** 1. Non, je ne parle jamais beaucoup. 2. Non, mon père ne boit jamais beaucoup de lait. 3. Non, ma soeur ne travaille jamais beaucoup. 4. Non, mon ami n'étudie jamais beaucoup. 5. Non, je ne bois jamais beaucoup d'eau. **III.** 1. Non, Lucille ne mange rien. 2. Non, Guy n'écrit rien. 3. Non, je ne lis rien. 4. Non, Madame Paquet ne fait rien. 5. Non, je n'étudie rien. **IV. (A).** 1. Non, je n'ai rien dit. 2. Non, elle n'a rien bu. 3. Non, mes amis n'ont rien étudié. 4. Non, je n'ai rien lu. 5. Non, je n'ai rien écrit. 6. Non, je n'ai rien bu. 7. Non, elles n'ont rien mangé. **IV. (B).** 1. Non, je n'ai jamais voyagé en Angleterre. 2. Non, je ne suis jamais allé au Canada. 3. Non, je n'ai jamais vu un film français. 4. Non, elle n'est jamais allée à l'opéra. 5. Non, il n'a jamais lu un journal français. 6. Non, ils ne sont jamais allés en Espagne. 7. Non elles n'ont jamais mangé un éclair. **V.** 1. Je sais que vous êtes malade. 2. Madame Paquet est dans son lit parce qu'elle est malade, n'est-ce pas? 3. Je mange quand j'ai faim (or possibly: Quand j'ai faim, je mange). 4. Le docteur va venir dans quelques minutes. 5. En une heure, le docteur est venu. **VI.** 1. être. 2. avoir. 3. aller. 4. attendre. 5. dire. 6. prendre. **VII.** 1. Il est absent depuis lundi. 2. Elle attend le docteur (or: Elle l'attend) depuis vingt minutes. 3. J'attends l'autobus (or: Je l'attends) depuis dix minutes. 4. Je travaille ici depuis le premier avril. 5. Je lis ce livre (or: Je le lis) depuis une heure. 6. Je lis ce livre (or: Je le lis) depuis ce matin. **VIII.** 1. Oui, il faut boire pour vivre. 2. Oui, il faut étudier pour apprendre. 3. Oui, il faut parler français dans la classe de français. 4. Oui, il faut parler espagnol dans la classe d'espagnol. 5. Oui, il faut faire les devoirs pour apprendre. **IX.** 1. J'ai déjà trouvé du travail pour l'été prochain. 2. Je vais vendre des téléviseurs dans un grand magasin. 3. Tu peux travailler avec moi. 4. Il faut parler avec Monsieur Dubois dans le grand magasin. 5. C'est une très bonne idée. Bonne chance!

Work Unit 22

Exercises, pp. 289–290

I. 1. vrai. 2. faux. 3. vrai. **II.** (Note: This is free composition and you may write statements in French in different ways.) **III.** 1. Joseph et Joséphine sont allés (or: vont) au cinéma samedi. 2. Ils sont entrés (or: entrent) chez la chiromancienne. 3. Ils n'ont rien appris (or: n'apprennent rien) chez la chiromancienne. 4. François Paquet lui a payé (or: lui paye) dix francs pour les révélations.

Exercises, pp. 290–294

I. 1. Nous la changeons aussi. 2. Nous le corrigeons aussi. 3. Nous les appelons aussi. 4. Nous l'employons aussi. 5. Nous les achetons aussi. **II.** 1. Nous la lançons aussi. 2. Nous les avançons aussi. 3. Nous les levons aussi. 4. Nous la payons aussi. **III.** 1. Janine et Monique sont allées au cinéma. 2. Nous avons voyagé aux Etats-Unis. 3. Madame Sétou a regardé fixement la main de Madame Paquet. 4. Madame Sétou a révélé les secrets de votre main. 5. Claire et François Paquet ont acheté des souvenirs. **IV.** 1. Nous arrangeons les fleurs. 2. Il achète une cravate. 3. Ils appellent la police. 4. Tu emploies le dictionnaire. 5. Nous prononçons le mot.

Exercises, pp.296–297

I. 1. Oui, je vais faire un voyage au Canada. 2. Oui, elle va écrire une lettre. 3. Oui, il va jouer dans le parc. 4. Oui, ils vont voyager en Angleterre. 5. Oui, nous allons répondre à la question. **II.** 1. Non, je ne veux pas acheter une nouvelle voiture. 2. Non, il ne veut pas corriger les devoirs. 3. Non, il ne veut pas prononcer le mot. 4. Non, elle ne veut pas employer le dictionnaire. 5. Non, il ne veut pas fumer une cigarette. **III.** 4, 1, 3, 5, 2. **IV.** 1. Il n'y a pas un grand parc dans cette ville. 2. Il n'y a pas un arrêt d'autobus ici. 3. Il n'y a pas dix garçons dans la classe. **V.** 1. Oui, j'ai lu *Le livre de mon ami* d'Anatole France il y a trois mois. 2. Oui, il a vu Pierre il y a dix minutes. 3. Oui, je suis allé(e) en Californie il y a un an. 4. Oui, elles sont arrivées il y a une demi-heure. 5. Oui, elle est partie il y a une heure. **VI.** Il y a vingt membres dans le club à présent. Nous commençons l'année à l'école avec une surprise-partie. Nous mangeons de la cuisine française. Nous arrangeons des programmes à l'école. Pendant l'été, nous voyageons ensemble, par exemple, au Canada. Nous corrigeons les devoirs des étudiants qui ont besoin d'assistance. Nous effaçons le tableau pour notre professeur de français, Madame Coty, et nous plaçons des fleurs dans un vase sur son bureau.

Work Unit 23

Exercises, p. 300

I. 1. Il est allé acheter une radio stéréophonique. 2. Janine a préparé un grand déjeuner. 3. Madame Paquet est allée chez le coiffeur. 4. Pierre a acheté une boîte de chocolats. 5. La radio stéréo ne marche pas d'abord parce que Monsieur Paquet n'a pas branché la radio sur la prise de courant. **II.** 1. non. 2. oui. 3. oui. 4. non. 5. oui. **III.** 1. Monsieur Paquet a acheté (or: achète) une radio stéréo. 2. Janine a préparé (or: prépare) le déjeuner. 3. Pierre est allé (or: va) chez un confiseur pour acheter une boîte de chocolats.

Exercises, pp. 304 – 306

I. 1. de. 2. à. 3. —. 4. de. 5. à. 6. —. 7. —. 8. à. 9. de. 10. de **II.** 1. Oui, j'ai envie d'aller au cinéma; ils ont envie d'aller au cinéma aussi. 2. Oui, elle a besoin d'aller au supermarché; elles ont besoin d'aller au supermarché aussi. 3. Oui, je suis sorti(e) sans dire un mot; elle est sortie sans dire un mot aussi. 4. Oui, j'apprends à lire le français; il apprend à lire le français aussi. 5. Oui, j'ai horreur de manger dans un restaurant sale; ils ont horreur de manger dans un restaurant sale aussi. **III.** 1. (c). 2. (d). 3. (d). **IV.** 3, 5, 1, 2, 4. **V.** 1 (d). 2. (c). 3. (c). **VI.** 1. Oui. J'aime beaucoup le basket-ball. 2. Oui. C'est la meilleure équipe. 3. Oui. Il est superbe! 4. Nous allons gagner. 5. Bien sûr! Je vais venir.

Review Test: Work Units 21–23

Exercises, p. 307

I. 1. Je ne fume pas. 2. Madame Paquet n'est pas grande. 3. Nous n'allons pas au cinéma. **II.** 1. quand. 2. parce qu'. 3. que. **III.** 1. elle. 2. depuis. 3. temps. 4. attend. **IV.** 1. b. 2. a. **V.** 1. J'ai besoin d'aller chez le dentiste. 2. Vous avez raison et j'ai tort. OR: Tu as raison et, moi, j'ai tort. 3. Nous n'avons pas peur de traverser la rue. 4. J'ai envie de dormir. 5. Il est intéressant d'aller à un musée. **VI.** 5, 4, 1, 3, 2.